Scientific and Technical Libraries

Scientific and Technical Libraries

Their Organization and Administration

SECOND EDITION

Lucille J. Strauss

CHEMISTRY AND PHYSICS LIBRARIAN
THE PENNSYLVANIA STATE UNIVERSITY

Irene M. Shreve

FORMERLY CHIEF LIBRARIAN
ELI LILLY AND COMPANY
LIBRARY AND EDITORIAL CONSULTANT

Alberta L. Brown

FORMERLY HEAD LIBRARIAN
THE UPJOHN COMPANY
LIBRARY CONSULTANT

A WILEY-BECKER-HAYES PUBLICATION

BECKER AND HAYES, INC.
a subsidiary of John Wiley & Sons, Inc.
New York · London · Sydney · Toronto · Bethesda

Library of Congress Catalog Card Number: 71-173679

ISBN 0-471-83312-6

Printed in the United States of America.

10 9 8 7 6 5 4 3 2 1

Foreword

This book is our third effort to prepare a manual of library practice in the specific areas of the life and physical sciences, including their applications, or technology. The first resulted in the book *Technical Libraries: Their Organization and Management,* which was published in 1951 by the Special Libraries Association. It was actually the result of a prolonged project of the SLA's Science-Technology Division. A revision was published in 1964 by Interscience-Wiley as *Scientific and Technical Libraries: Their Organization and Administration* of which the present book is a second edition.

In view of the continuing developments in the scientific literature, a reflection of what is happening in the sciences, it was necessary to update this guide to library operation. We hope that it will continue to be as useful as both previous editions in their respective periods in the history of librarianship.

LUCILLE J. STRAUSS
IRENE M. SHREVE
ALBERTA L. BROWN

August 1971

Preface

The intent of this second edition remains the same as in the first: to provide an introduction to the organizational procedures and essential functions of a special library or information service in the sciences and their related technologies. It is primarily a guide to practices evolving from past experience and recent developments. Emphasis is on the fundamental traditional aspects; newer techniques such as mechanization are referred to where pertinent but detailed explications are left to publications specializing in these areas.

Although most of the relevant literature has been surveyed, in fact representing a continuous process on the part of the authors, there is no attempt to provide a complete review in this purposefully brief text. Cited references are suggestive rather than exhaustive.

The book is designed to serve multiple purposes. First the needs of practicing librarians, particularly those who are just beginning their careers, and require a general guide and source of operational and bibliographic information, have been given special consideration. A second purpose is to provide a textbook for library school and other advanced students whose interests are oriented toward the literature of the life and physical sciences. The book could also help persons in management positions of organizations in which the establishment of a library is contemplated, presenting, if only from a review of the contents, the scope of such a department. Finally it should be a good resource for library consultants engaged in assisting management to make the right decisions. The requirements of all of these audiences have been assessed and endeavor made to meet their somewhat varied requirements.

It is recognized that many evolutionary changes are in progress in the broad area of the communication of scientific information, some of which will unquestionably influence practices now being followed. However, it is still necessary to improve methods employed in existing libraries as well as to outline procedures for the development of new information centers. Specifically, this includes the selection and acquisition of appropriate publications, the necessary technical processing so that they can be consulted easily, and the provision of information from them in response to requests. It is within this framework that the various chapters are organized. The overall plan comprises twelve chapters, each of which treats a broad aspect of library administration, and these are supplemented by an Appendix consisting of two main parts: a listing of basic reference publications and a series of bibliographies relating to narrow subject fields.

We thank our many colleagues who have been generous in providing supporting facts, suggestions, and inspiration both from published works and from willing discussion of personal experiences. Particular appreciation is due those who permitted the use of the illustrative materials that appear in this book.

LUCILLE J. STRAUSS
IRENE M. SHREVE
ALBERTA L. BROWN

August 1971

Contents

Scientific and Technical Libraries

1

Scientific and Technical Libraries

What and Where They Are

Any organization in which activities are centered around the physical or life sciences and their related technologies must be cognizant of the great body of published information that comprises the scientific literature. This vast recording of the continuous investigation of scientific problems constitutes a store of already determined facts, which, if its existence is recognized, can be a resource of inestimable importance. To take full advantage of this available storehouse it is imperative that a unit in the organizational structure be responsible for locating and supplying "whatever knowledge and experience that may advance its activities," according to Morley's original and, although phrased some years ago, still valid definition (1) of what this member should do in support of the parent body. This unit has usually been designated as a "special" library because of its unique functions.

In recent years there has been increased recognition of the potentiality dormant in the scientific literature which has resulted in more attention to attendant problems and a consequent emergence of professional groups whose interests are related to, but not the same as, those of librarians. The term first used to designate this pertinent area was "documentation," which has subsequently evolved into "information science," whose practitioners operate in domains that certainly approach, asymptotically at least, the established functions of special librarians. This development is reflected in the several separate professional organizations whose programs are so closely parallel that it is necessary for those

1

who wish to be aware of advancements relating to the use and management of the scientific literature to be members of two or even three of these societies.

One way of detecting the real differences between the library and information science groups is to examine the stated purposes of two organizations based in the United States. The Special Libraries Association has published a detailed statement of its objectives and standards (2) with the following as introduction:

1: Objectives—The special library is a major source of information in the organization it serves.

The special library staff is responsible for providing the library materials and services designed to meet the information requirements of the library's clientele in fields pertinent to the purposes and work of the organization.

Following this are outlines of what is required to support the objectives, specifically staff, services, collection, physical facilities, and budget. Under services it is pertinent to note that "Reference Services include literature searching, compiling bibliographies, abstracting, and indexing."

The American Society for Information Science (ASIS) changed its name in 1968 from American Documentation Institute, thereby indicating that some kind of evolution must have been in progress. A real problem is implicit in defining "information science" as is apparent in the attempt made by Borko (3) who states that:

It is concerned with that body of knowledge relating to the origination, collection, organization, storage, retrieval, interpretation, transmission, transformation, and utilization of information. This includes the investigation of information representations in both natural and artificial systems, the use of codes for efficient message transmission, and the study of information processing devices and techniques such as computers and their programming systems. . . .

It is evident that ASIS has tried to write a definition with no loopholes. However, study of proclaimed intentions of both SLA and ASIS reveals that they have much in common. SLA is perhaps more broadly inclusive, while the emphasis of ASIS is on the philosophy of subject analysis rather than on the administration of a library service. Both are concerned with the development of systems and methods for making the content of the literature accessible.

Not only are professional organizations whose members are directly involved with the scientific literature concerned about problems, but also on a national level the United States Government is alerted to the importance of information as a resource. Several nationally constituted bodies are working as investigative and advisory agents to help the whole scientific community. One important step was taken with the establishment of the Office of Science and Technology, which is counseled by the President's Science Advisory Committee, representing nongovernment scientists, and by the Federal Council for Science and Technology, representing government scientists. The Federal Council has established a very active Committee on Scientific and Technical Information (COSATI). One of COSATI's contributions is the publication, *Recommendations for National Document Handling Systems in Science and Technology* (4). It is expected that a permanent National Commission on Libraries and Information Science will be established.* Other government agencies have been concerned with science information for many years, for example, the National Academy of Sciences-National Research Council with its program of working committees in eight broad scientific divisions. The National Academy of Sciences with the National Academy of Engineering has produced an extensive elaboration of the problems as expressed by a large group of experts in a report published in 1969 titled, *Scientific and Technical Communication: A Pressing National Problem and Recommendations for Its Solution.* This is actually a COSATI Report.

Although some of these expressions of concern might suggest that the containment of the scientific literature is completely out of hand, this is not exactly the case. There are in existence about 11,000 special libraries and information centers in the United States and Canada according to the *Directory* edited by Kruzas (5) with a representative number in other countries. This total includes all subject fields, but a large number of the services listed are devoted to scientific or technical subjects, actively providing the facts needed to increase understanding of natural laws and to promote the general welfare.

The library services with which this book is concerned may be included in any of the subject areas suggested in Figure 1, which was designed by Ellingham in 1948 and is reproduced here by permission of the Royal Society. In the years since this delineation was prepared additional areas have been developed or evolved from the original fundamental ones; for example, the several aspects of nuclear science in relation to chemistry, physics and engineering, or more recently, environmental control and oceanography. The details of such evolvements are recorded in the literature of the sciences, and it is with this kind of information that these particular library services are concerned. Their main purpose is to secure, assemble, and make available all information that relates in any way to a specific subject, locating it not only in the normal standard

---

* It was named and announced in mid 1971.

publications but also in the less obvious and sometimes ephemeral presentations such as reports emanating from government sponsored research. Thus unique files are cumulated for the specific benefit of the organizations they are designed to serve.

In order to execute this function effectively the members of the library staff must have knowledge of the multidisciplinary sciences involved as well as competence in the practices and techniques of library science. They must also be aware of new procedures that can be used as they are developed in relevant disciplines. Henkle (6) once observed that an identifying feature of a special library service is that "it involves participation by the librarian in the seeking and organizing of information for special purposes." Of equal importance is the ability to communicate effectively whatever may be needed from the assembled files.

From what has been stated thus far, it is apparent that there is a major difference between the general library and the special one. The distinction has been no better expressed than by Kyle (7) who pointed out that the chief dissimilarity lies in the fundamental unit comprising them. In the general library the unit is the book, pamphlet, or other gross item, whereas in the special situation it is the particular bit of information contained in the book or other publication. The general library is designed to serve the public whose members usually must locate the information for themselves. The special library is prepared to provide specific information on request from its clientele. Dr. Kyle further avowed the special library's obligation to produce information which may not even be in published form but which can be detected only by knowing how and where to direct discreet inquiry. In the most effective services even future requirements are anticipated by alert observation of development in the organization so that information is ready when it is needed.

The information service for an organization dealing with the sciences customarily maintains a regular and systematic alerting operation that consists essentially of the acquisition of a well selected collection of books, periodicals, pamphlets, governments publications, including patents and reports, and any other unique items, all issuing from a multitude of publishing bodies. Additionally, intramural records such as research reports, technical correspondence, and market surveys must also be brought together and made available for immediate consultation by being adequately classified or indexed, then filed according to an appropriate system.

Procedures for organizing information are usually derived from standard methods developed for nonspecialized libraries, and these methods are modified if necessary to suit the requirements of a particular situa-

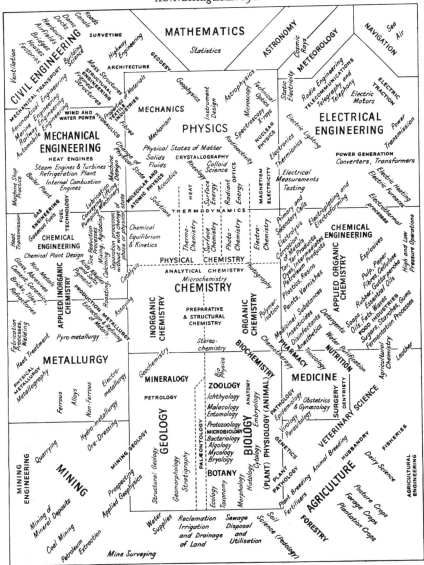

A CHART ILLUSTRATING SOME OF
THE RELATIONS BETWEEN THE BRANCHES OF NATURAL SCIENCE AND TECHNOLOGY
H.J.T. Ellingham. 1948.

First published in a paper submitted to the Royal Society Scientific Information Conference, 1948.
Reproduced, with minor modification, by permission of the Royal Society.

Figure 1. Some of the relations between the branches of natural science and technology. From H. J. T. *Ellingham*, 1948.

5

tion. The classification scheme used for books can be expanded for more explicit identification. The contents of important books can be analyzed, sometimes chapter by chapter. Individual articles in periodicals should be indexed if the published abstracting or indexing services do not serve interests adequately. Other materials such as drawings, maps, and even photographs that require special treatment may have to be handled differently. As the carefully selected collection grows, it becomes an ever more valuable asset.

In recent years, initially as a result of the expanding technologies of the war years, the scientific literature has increased in volume at such a rate that improvements over conventional methods of coping with this quantity have been sought. Traditional methods of filing and indexing are too slow to be satisfactory when large numbers of items must be handled, and answers to these problems have been in a ferment of development for more than a decade. New systems employing automation or mechanical devices of various kinds are now past the testing stage and are in use for several library-related purposes. Some procedures are executed efficiently by electronic accounting machines that can sort and select accurately and rapidly. Still others can be programmed for computers if the volume and intricacy warrant this expense. However, these are only more sophisticated methods for doing the same things that can be done on a lesser scale by means of the compiling and indexing methods generally used in any scientific-technical library.

DESIGNATION OF SCIENTIFIC-TECHNICAL LIBRARIES

The special libraries or information services in the subject areas under consideration are individually designated in the organizations where they are located by any one of a variety of names. In some instances the name reflects placement of the unit in the organization plan; in others it indicates a specific domain of activity. The word "library" is not always used because it is thought that the connotation is not sufficiently broad. Some of the designations known to be in use are the following:

Scientific Library
Technical Library
Technical Information Service
Technical Information Division
Information Center

Information Service (or Services)
Research Library
Research Laboratories Library
Research Center Library
Technical Literature Research Department
Research and Development Library
Science Information Service
Central Information Service
Engineering Library
Biological Sciences Library
Physical Sciences Library

The name does not always accurately reflect the activities encompassed by the service. In some cases a library only is indicated; in others a library may be included as one of several distinctive units in a multidivisional operation in alignment with other units in which the pursuits are related but each of such magnitude as to warrant separation. For example, a Technical Information Division might be comprised of the following:

1. Library
2. Report and Technical Writing Group
3. Reports Indexing Group
4. Technical Correspondence Group

Obviously, such an elaboration is necessary only when the scale of operations is large; in a smaller enterprise all functions would be handled by one staff.

The term "library" is used in this book to designate the scientific and technical information services under consideration, and emphasis is on those functions that are ordinarily included as pertinent to a library program. Each chapter is devoted to one of the comprehensive areas of performance.

The point of view taken here is that the word "library" is broad enough to encompass all that is implicit in the various terminologies relating to the collection and dissemination of information, while recognizing that the vocabulary changes continuously with the advent of relevant professional activities. A special library service of the kind delineated in this book is a far more dynamic operation than is implied in Webster's (8) definition of a library, "a collection of books, manuscripts, etc., kept for study or reading," although this covers the basic concept accurately. Promotion and active participation in the program of the organization are just as important as is the development of a good collection of materials.

LOCATIONS OF SCIENTIFIC AND TECHNICAL LIBRARIES

Libraries in which the subject focus is on the sciences and technologies are located in a variety of situations. In the United States and Canada most function as units of industrial companies. Others are in governmental agencies, universities or technical colleges, research institutes, professional associations, trade associations, public libraries, and institutions such as hospitals or clinics. Many of the larger academic communities provide branch libraries for their individual schools or colleges in which the sciences are taught and research pursued. Public libraries have departments devoted to scientific subjects and services that qualify them as fitting the special category. Then there are a few large, independent science libraries that are maintained for use by anyone needing to consult their resources. The subject fields represented in these many and varied locations embrace the whole range of the sciences, theoretical and applied. Some cover a specific, well-defined subject field; others must be multidisciplinary.

The most comprehensive listing of specialized libraries in all fields in the United States and Canada is the Directory which was compiled by Kruzas, the second edition published in 1968 and already referred to earlier in this chapter (5). It includes about 11,000 individual services in alphabetical order by name, followed by principal staff members and brief descriptions of the collections. This is a very significant compilation for which supplementary volumes either are already available or are in prospect. The *Geographical-Personnel Index* was published in 1969, and a listing of new special libraries is to be issued at 6-month intervals.

The several types of locations of scientific-technical libraries are shown in the following outline. Each broad category is then discussed in detail:

A. Industrial organization
   1. As a department at the company's central plant
      a. Serving a centralized unit only
      b. Serving both headquarters and all other divisions
   2. As a department at each division or plant either in one geographic area or in widely separated locales (includes conglomerate companies if separate libraries are not maintained)
   3. As a unit of a main research and development department
      a. Serving research and development department only
      b. Serving research and development plus other units

    4. As a unit of an information division in line with others such as technical writing, patent, or technical correspondence
B. Academic institution
    1. As a branch of a central library to serve individual school or college
    2. As adjunct to a single department
    3. As one centralized library serving the whole institution, such as, a technological institute
C. Public library
    1. As a science-technology division
    2. As an independent library
D. Professional association—As a division in headquarters offices to serve members of the societies represented
E. Trade association—As a division in headquarters offices to serve staff members, particularly if research laboratories are maintained, as well as needs of member companies
F. Research organization—As a division serving all projects
G. Government bureau or other unit
    1. As a department serving the unit
    2. As a centralized service for several units
H. Institution
    1. As a department to serve staff members
    2. As a service to others than staff, that is, patients in a hospital

Each of the situations in the foregoing outline is discussed in further detail.

Industrial Organizations

The outline of locations for library services shows several options for placing a library in an industrial organization. There is in fact considerable variance in the ways that information units are placed in organizational frameworks, as Bedsole (9) revealed in an extensive survey called *Library Systems in Large Industrial Organizations* in 1961. This exhaustive review of 117 corporations disclosed that there were several organizational patterns extant with respect to the manner in which information services are provided. According to Bedsole's findings they fall into four broad categories: (1) one library service for the whole corporation; (2) several libraries operating independently in various plant locations; (3) one central library with branches administered under its control; and (4) various combinations of the first three. A clear conclusion from this study was that there is no one system that can be recommended as universally effective or desirable for all industrial organizations.

In actual working relationships with clientele, individual library service often cuts across department lines although the physical placement of the library is determined by the parent organization. This is evident from a study of corporate organization charts designed to show supervisory relationships among all segments of an enterprise. A survey made by Strieby (10) as early as 1952, *Organizational Relationships of Special Libraries,* preceding Bedsole's similar study, shows also that there is no indication that uniform placement of the library is advisable. Some years later, in 1957, in a further study of the same subject, Strieby (11) concludes that this situation "is but a reflection of the fact that there is no mutually exclusive field for the operation of an industrial library."

Another study of the operations of scientific library services, somewhat similar to that performed by Bedsole but narrower in scope, was undertaken by the Division of Chemical Literature of the American Chemical Society in 1958 (12), and their report entitled, *Administration of Technical Information Groups,* gives the findings of the investigation of 300 companies in the chemical or closely related industries. Here there was a common pattern of organization inasmuch as 80% of the information services were integral parts of research and development divisions.

Strieby (13) has provided cogent advice in the matter of determining where to place a library in an organization scheme as expressed in the following statement:

An important fact to keep in mind in fitting the library into the organizational scheme is that if the library is established for the benefit of one department, such as personnel, market research, or engineering, it naturally becomes an integral part of that particular department. It will then be difficult to provide a company-wide information program, since other segments of the company may not feel free to make full use of the service. Therefore it is essential for the library to occupy a strategic spot in the organization—one where it can function effectively for all parts of the business.

Graham (14) supports this idea and expands upon it with some good general principles:

The following principles will help to locate the library on the organization chart: (a) The library should serve all departments with equal effectiveness. (b) The librarian should have personal access to heads and personnel in all departments. He should represent the library at interdepartmental meetings, and should be in a position to know the operation and functions of all departments and their personnel. (c) Personnel should have direct access to library services and facilities. Use of the library and requests for library services should not ordinarily have to follow administrative channels.

In fortifying itself against competition, no profit-seeking organization can afford to take refuge in a state of complacency. Progressive industries show their viability by modifying organizational structures to suit changing conditions. In these developmental changes the information services are inevitably involved, moved from one area to another, centralized or decentralized, and placed wherever they best benefit the enterprise.

An example of an evolving library system in a major company is the one belonging to the Eli Lilly and Company. In 1954 Maurice and co-workers (15) described a service that operated as three distinct units: (1) Scientific Information Service; (2) Business Information Service; and (3) Library Extension Service. Shortly thereafter, as reported by Davidson (16) in an article outlining the history of this information system, a fourth unit (4) Library Agricultural Service was added.

Although these libraries operated independently insofar as reference service and circulation were concerned, such functions as cataloging, purchasing, binding, and processing interlibrary loans continued to be centralized in the Main Library under the supervision of the Chief Librarian who functioned as a department head in the Lilly organization. However, reflecting the company trend, library organizational decentralization began with the establishment of the Library Agricultural Service in 1958. Then in 1962, the Business Information Service became the Business Library on separating from the Scientific Research component to join the Market Research Division, and even later, the Personnel Planning Division. Decentralization of library operations gained impetus from this separation, the Scientific Library then handling purchasing and binding for Indianapolis libraries and interlibrary loans for the Agricultural Service at Greenfield. In 1968, the Legal Divisions Law Library was organized officially. These details have been supplied by Lage (17) in 1969. But these are not all of the information services that this company found necessary. The record of activity in archival items is so important that a separate Lilly Archives Collection has been functioning since 1956.

Is there a relationship between the success of a business and its attention to the scientific-technical literature? Investigation of those in the forefront of developmental activity would show that where there is expanding growth, full advantage is taken of all sources of information by having good information services.

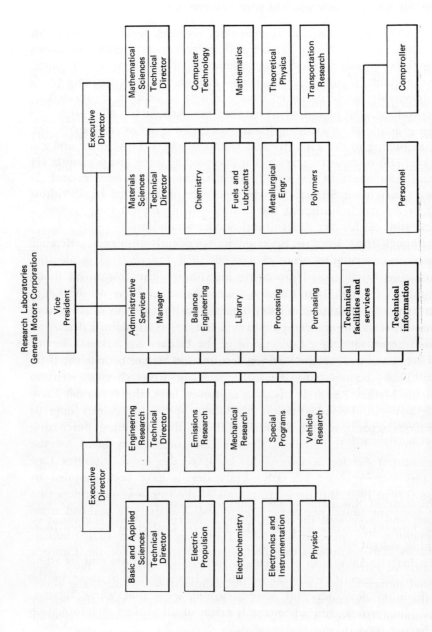

Figure 2. Organizational chart of the Research Laboratories of the General Motors Corporation.

Research Laboratories
General Motors Corporation

Vice President

Executive Director

Executive Director

Basic and Applied Sciences — Technical Director
- Electric Propulsion
- Electrochemistry
- Electronics and Instrumentation
- Physics

Engineering Research — Technical Director
- Emissions Research
- Mechanical Research
- Special Programs
- Vehicle Research

Administrative Services — Manager
- Balance Engineering
- Library
- Processing
- Purchasing

Technical facilities and services

Technical information

Materials Sciences — Technical Director
- Chemistry
- Fuels and Lubricants
- Metallurgical Engr.
- Polymers

Mathematical Sciences — Technical Director
- Computer Technology
- Mathematics
- Theoretical Physics
- Transportation Research

Personnel

Comptroller

Figures 2 to 9 illustrate some typical industrial situations where library services are shown in the organization chart.

Academic Institutions

In the academic situation the chief contention is whether teaching and research are better served by one completely centralized library or by branches serving individual colleges or schools. The opposing points of view have been argued much and often, with those who use publications in limited subject areas wanting them as close to their laboratory or office as possible, while some library administrators prefer the alleged economies of central services. Scientists measure one way, libraries another.

Among those expressing opposing points of view were Wells (18), a physicist who argued for the departmental library. He was answered by Shera (19) who was equally certain that the scientist would be better served by the consolidated science library. Cooper (20) subsequently made an extensive study called *Organizational Patterns of Academic Science Libraries,* concluding that there must be a compromise between the needs of users and practicalities. The recommendation was that there should at least be a modification of full centralization by agreeing to no smaller subdivisions than engineering, physical sciences, and biological sciences in a large university.

There can be no recommendation as to what system is best for an institution. Each must work out for itself what is acceptable to its users and what can be afforded. As an example of one of the happiest university communities, Figure 10 shows the Purdue University Libraries Organization Chart. It is apparent that where a subunit collection has been needed, it has been supplied.

Public Libraries

In some of the major public libraries the science divisions are very strong and serve well the interests of industries in their communities, augmenting the necessarily limited resources of individual company libraries. An example is the Technology Department of the Carnegie Library of Pittsburgh that has been so effective that it has been given special monetary support by industry administered through the efforts of the local section of American Chemical Society. Also, the Science Division of the New York Public Library has been a mainstay to industry, particularly through its efficient photoduplication service.

A somewhat different public library devoted to scientific interests is

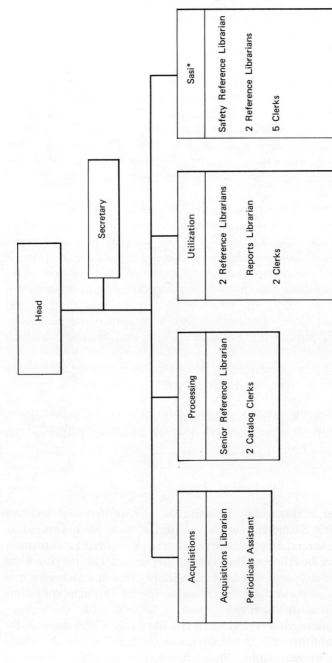

Figure. 2a Functional organization of Technical Information Divisions' professional staff, GMC **Research Laboratories**

Head

Secretary

Acquisitions

Acquisitions Librarian

Periodicals Assistant

Processing

Senior Reference Librarian

2 Catalog Clerks

Utilization

2 Reference Librarians

Reports Librarian

2 Clerks

Sasi*

Safety Reference Librarian

2 Reference Librarians

5 Clerks

*System on automotive
safety information center

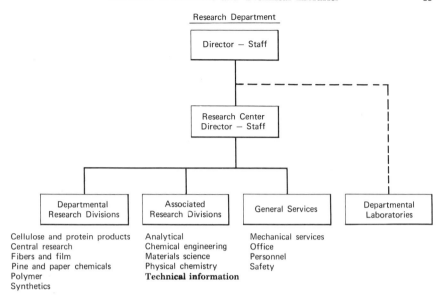

Figure 3. Organizational chart for Hercules Research Center, Hercules Inc.

the unique John Crerar Library in Chicago, Ill. It operates as a single self-contained unit, not as a branch. Its collection includes only the sciences, technologies, and medicine. An extensive literature searching and current awareness service is conducted in a close working relationship with industry. Similar to Crerar is the Linda Hall Library in Kansas City, Mo., its collection somewhat smaller since it does not include medicine. It is available to the public and is an excellent interlibrary loan source.

Professional Associations

An example of a library service maintained by professional societies is the Engineering Societies Library located in New York City. It is sponsored by the several engineering groups that have their headquarters offices in the same building as the library, the United Engineering Center. Although the primary purpose of the library is to provide information to members of the societies, others may use its excellent collection of publications in all fields of engineering.

Another outstanding library is one in the Chemists' Club, also in New York. It was established for and is supported by members of the Club, but nonmembers whose purposes are serious may use it.

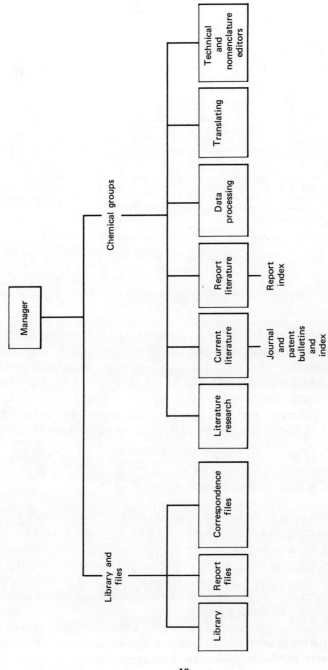

Figure 3a. Technical Information Division. Hercules Research Center, Hercules Inc.

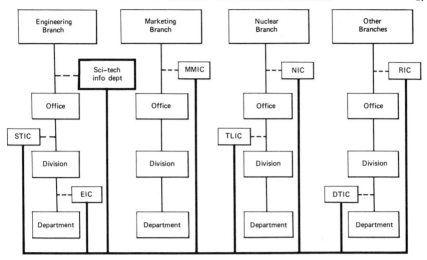

Figure 4. Organizational chart reflecting the scientific and Technical Information Department within the Lockheed-Georgia Company.

Trade Associations

Industries operating in a common area sometimes form trade associations to provide centralized services. An information center is usually considered to be an essential department. The Institute of Gas Technology, for example, maintains a technical library in its headquarters in Chicago, Ill. Also, an excellent library supports the testing program of the Union Technique Interfédérale du Batiment et des Travaux Publics in its work with construction materials in Paris.

Research Organizations

It is imperative that a research organization in which the projects range over diverse subject areas in a continuously changing pattern have an information source commensurate with its needs. Two examples of this kind of situation are Mellon Institute of Industrial Research in Pittsburgh, Pa., and Battelle Memorial Institute in Columbus, Ohio, plus its additional locations in Europe. In this same category is Arthur D. Little Company of Boston, Mass., a private consulting firm. As would be expected, all of them have excellent libraries.

Government Agencies

Units of national or state government agencies working in scientific areas may have need for their own literature services. Although there

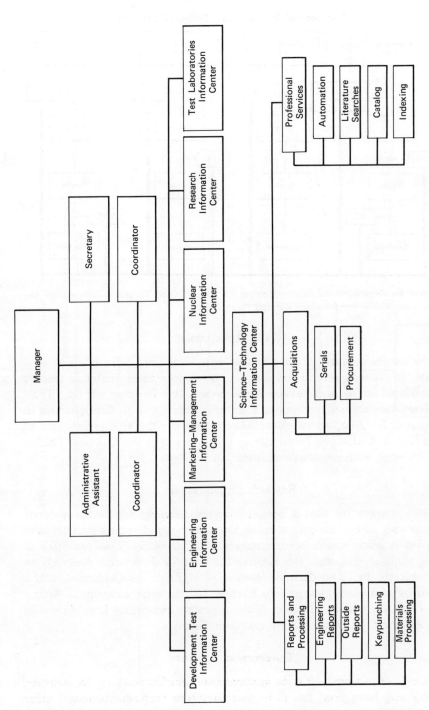

Figure 4a. Scientific and Technical Information Department. Lockheed-Georgia Co.

18

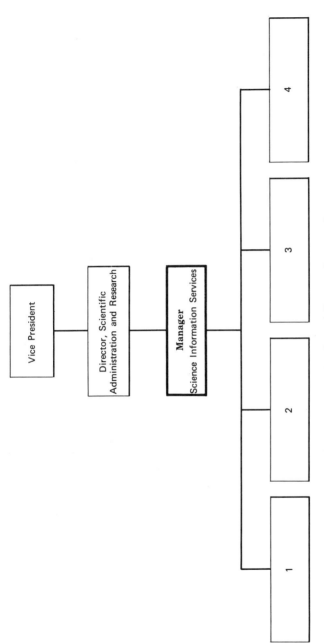

Vice President

Director, Scientific
Administration and Research

Manager
Science Information Services

1   2   3   4

1. Science library services [central library and processes]
2. Documentation services [abstracting literature searches]
3. Patent information services [patent abstracts searching]
4. Business information services [business library with separate
    budget from administrative division]

Figure 5. Organizational chart of Abbott Laboratories.

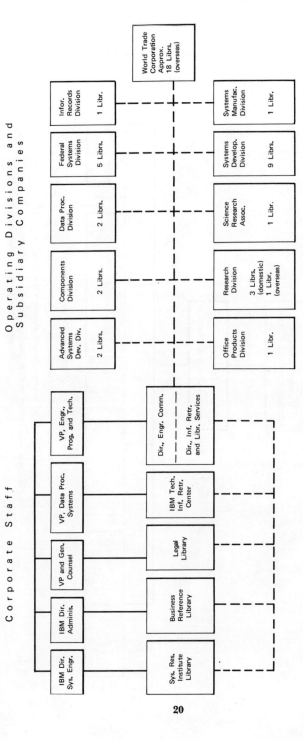

Figure 6. International Business Machines Corporation Libraries.

(Decentralized, with staff responsibility and guidance provided by Director of Information Retrieval and Library Services.)

20

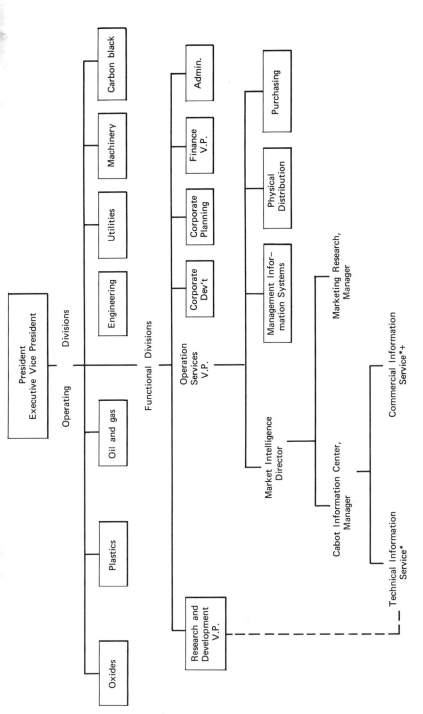

Figure 7. Organizational chart of Cabot Corporation

* Based on technical library at R & D Center.
† Based on business library at corporate headquarters.

21

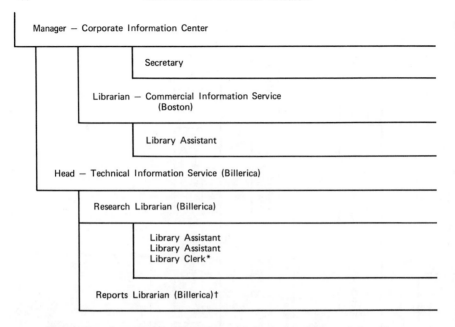

Figure 7a. Organization of Corporate Information Center, Cabot Corp.
* Part-time high school student (10 hours/week).
† Part-time professional librarian (20 hours/week).

are few in state government departments, there are many operating under some kind of sponsorship of the federal government. In Washington, D. C. there are numerous science libraries—such as those in the U.S. Patent Office, the National Bureau of Standards, the U.S. Geological Survey, the Bureau of Ships, the Department of Agriculture, the National Library of Medicine, and the U.S. Bureau of Mines. Some of these have subunits such as the regional Department of Agriculture Libraries in Philadelphia, Pa., and New Orleans, La., the Cryogenic Center in Boulder, Colo., a branch of the National Bureau of Standards. The *U.S. Government Organization Manual,* which is revised annually, includes organization charts for government agencies and departments that always indicate the position of the library in the overall organization.

Institutions

An example of an institution requiring a library service is a hospital or clinic. Here it is necessary to have a collection of books, periodicals, and reports needed by members of the health professions connected with

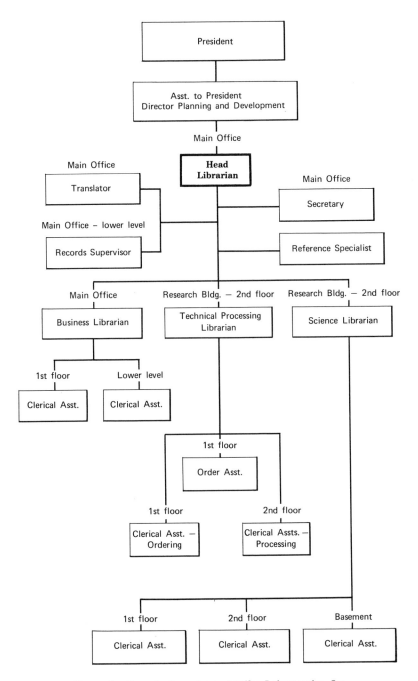

Figure 8. Organization chart of Miles Laboratories, Inc.

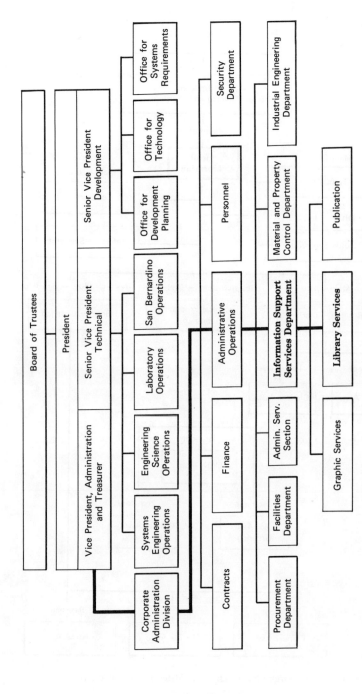

Figure 9. Organizational chart of Aero Space Corporation.

24

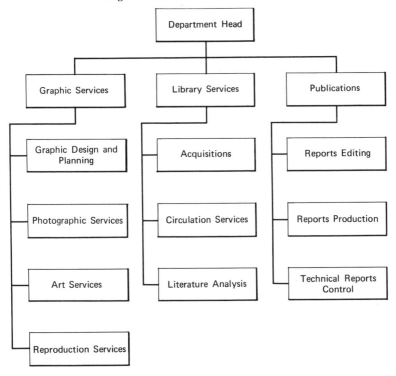

Figure 9a. Information support services. Aero Space Corporation

the hospital. There may also be a service for patients as part of general therapy as well as recreation.

These then are the usual locales for scientific libraries. There may well be other situations, however, where such collections are in existence but they would not come under any such broad categories as are outlined here.

ORIGINS OF SCIENTIFIC-TECHNICAL LIBRARIES

Libraries in the areas under consideration originate because of specific localized needs for organized information services to support research, to aid technical development, or to act as a very necessary adjunct to education. Ideally, a library is planned as an integral department in the plans for the organization as a whole. This does happen in rare instances. Far more often the need is recognized only after the books and periodicals accumulate haphazardly in offices and laboratories. Eventually,

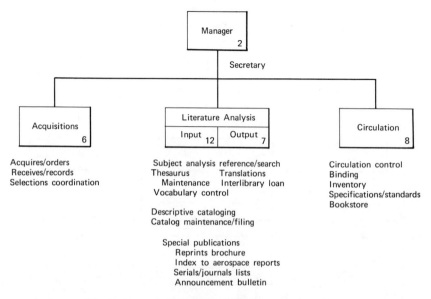

Figure 9b. Library services, Aerospace Corporation

as expanding activities develop, there comes the realization that these publications must be brought together and a competent staff put in charge. In the more favored situation plans for the library are formulated at the same time as are the components it will serve.

PLANNING FOR A SCIENTIFIC-TECHNICAL LIBRARY

The first step in planning for a library is to analyze all aspects of the environment in which it will be located. What subject coverage will be required? Will business interests have to be considered in addition to purely scientific concerns? Who will comprise the clientele—research scientists only, or will other not-quite-relevant parts of the organizational community be expecting some attention that may rightly be due them? Research in the sciences will need one kind of material, the solving of technical problems another.

It would be beneficial at this point to consult either of two checklists as aids to library planning. First there is Fisher's pamphlet entitled *A Checklist for the Organization, Operation and Evaluation of a Company Library,* the second edition of which was published in 1966 (21). Then Stevenson's (22) article, entitled *Checklist for Review and Evaluation of Technical Libraries,* outlines the chief strong points to be sought in an effective library service, ranging from physical facilities to reference

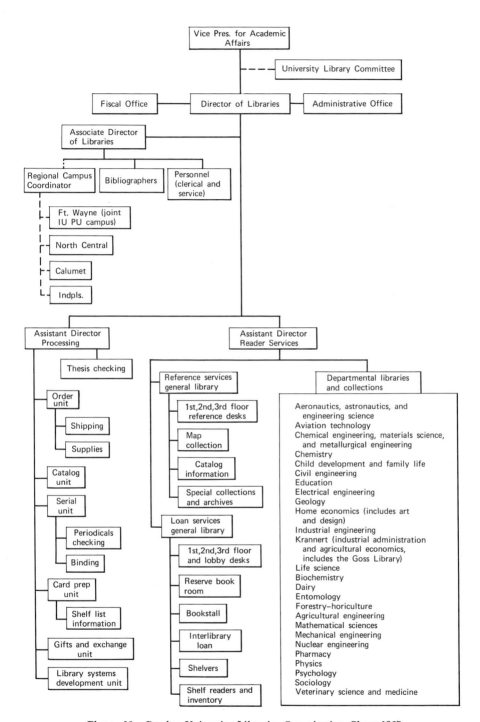

Figure 10. Purdue University Libraries Organization Chart 1967.

resources. As extensive a survey as possible at this time may be profitable, discussing tentative conclusions with executive officers and any other persons whose opinions could be helpful, before plans are definite.

Advice may be sought also from persons outside the organization, particularly from those who are administering library services in situations similar to the one being planned. Visits to such libraries are certain to be fruitful because advantage can be taken of both the successful and unsuccessful experiences of others who have faced the same kind of task. The cooperative spirit is very strong in this profession.

There is also the possibility of seeking help from consultants, either individuals whose experience qualifies them to charge a daily fee plus expenses, or companies whose business it is to operate in various ways in the information field. Advertisements in professional journals sometimes tell who and where these services are, and societies maintain rosters of qualified consultants, as does the Special Libraries Association, for example, at its headquarters and at local chapters. In 1969 R. R. Bowker published the first comprehensive compilation of library consultants (23).

At some point in the planning stage the head of the projected service will have been employed. Once this appointment has been made the character of the information service begins to take shape, though the individual should not impress his own personality on the service too strongly. It is vital that this administrator be able to comprehend exactly what is needed for the particular situation. He must then be given strong support to accomplish the envisioned purpose.

MAIN FUNCTIONS OF A SCIENTIFIC-TECHNICAL LIBRARY

In the book, *Research in Industry,* edited by Furnas (24) it is stated that the primary function of an industrial library is "to pass on to the users important information necessary to their work." This is a sound generalization that is applicable to a scientific-technical information service in any location. As an extension of this initial advice Royer (25) observes that the head of such a service "could expand his job to cover many parts of the great area of communication," thereby challenging those who practice the profession seriously to exercise imagination to envision what relevant responsibilities might reasonably be undertaken. When the resources at hand are adequate and administrative procedures efficient, the process of passing on information to those who need it can be accomplished in various ways.

It is pertinent here to outline the broad functions of a library of the type under discussion. The most important are the following:

1. Development of the collection of books, periodicals, and other items.
2. Maintenance of indexed files of selected subject references.
3. Dissemination of currently published information by means of personal notifications, preparation and distribution of library bulletins or by using centralized services.
4. Circulation of books and routing of periodicals.
5. Filing and indexing of internal reports and technical correspondence.
6. Maintenance of reference service to supply instant answers.
7. Compilation of bibliographies.
8. Editorial assistance with internal publications.
9. Translation of foreign language publications.
10. Personalized service of various types.

These broad activities are the chief ones administered in the majority of scientific-technical information services or libraries. There are others that are unique to particular situations where the staff is alert to recognize specific ways of manipulating resources to assure that the clientele does not miss anything that might be of use. Royer, in the aforementioned article (25), indicates that management is likely to appreciate an enterprising approach. See also Chapter 12.

Study of the total situation for which a library is being planned will lead to a decision as to what will be the best plan for the organization to be served. Can all of the needed functions be administered from one central unit or should there be divisions with specified assignments? Decentralization will be advisable if the locations of various operations are dispersed or if there are divisional separations.

The most economic and generally satisfactory arrangement is to establish a central library service with subordinate units in other needed locations. The costs should be less if such operations as book and periodical ordering and cataloging are done at a central point, than if they are done individually at each branch. Moreover, it is easier to develop a purchasing policy that avoids unnecessary duplication.

A library can be effective only if its role and functions are definitely delegated and recognized. It should be a distinctive unit in the organization it serves and should operate at the same administrative level as other departments with comparable responsibilities. The head of the service should be directly subordinate to an administrative officer high enough in the echelon of management for easy communication with those who determine policies. Strieby (10) found that in several industrial organizations these officers were the Secretary, the Vice President of Industrial

Relations, or the Vice President in Charge of Research. In one instance it was the Office Manager, a situation not likely to induce the most efficacious library operation. In research laboratories the reporting officer is likely to be the Director of Research.

In some situations a library committee, consisting of appointed members from departments or divisions for which the service is designed, can be helpful. Such a diverse advisory group will have opinions concerning policies and can develop into an important liaison between the information service and its clientele. Its usefulness in this respect is discussed further in Chapter 12. There must be free communication and mutual understanding, a condition admittedly difficult to attain, if a satisfactory working climate is to be achieved. There are, however, opposing opinions on the desirability of library committees; Greer (26) and Birdwell (27) report good experiences with them, whereas White (28) found them more hindrance than help. The potential positive results are so worthwhile, nevertheless, the idea is certainly one to be considered.

PROFESSIONAL SOCIETIES

The role of the specialized information service is by no means static. Developments of the ways in which its functions are executed are as continuous as are the ever-changing sciences and technologies comprising the field of operations. Means exist for keeping abreast of these advances. Several professional societies provide regular meetings and conferences. They sponsor publications that enable those practitioners who are enterprising and capable, to contribute to the growth of their mutual profession. Others can benefit from their ideas and shared experience.

There are several types of associations in the areas of library and information sciences to which membership is open. Some do have specific requirements for full membership. The societies whose activities are most directly concerned with the aims and purposes of this book are the following:

Special Libraries Association, 235 Park Avenue South, New York, 10003
American Society for Information Science, 2011 Eye Street, N.W., Washington, D. C. 20006
Division of Chemical Literature of the American Chemical Society, 1155 Sixteenth Street, N. W., Washington, D. C.
Medical Library Association, 1025 Walnut Street, Philadelphia, Pa.
Aslib, 3 Belgrave Square, London S W 1, England
Association de Documentalistes et Bibliothécaires Spécialisées, 21 Rue du Docteur Blanche, Paris 16, France

Additionally, other organizations, both national and international, promote activities that relate to the purposes of special information services. In the United States there is the American Library Association that now has a Division of Information Science and Automation. In Great Britain, the Library Association is somewhat concerned with the special situation. UNESCO has a Division of Libraries, Documentation, and Archives, which publishes a bulletin reviewing world-wide developments. The International Federation for Documentation (FID) has supported many information projects since its inception in 1895. All of the major library organizations cooperate through the International Federation of Library Associations (IFLA).

In the United States a growing awareness of the significance of information has led to the establishment of the Committee on Scientific and Technical Information (COSATI), an advisory body to the Executive Branch of the government. Its chief purpose is to investigate the possibility of establishing a vast national network through which any location in the country could place requests for items that would be stored for searching by computer and delivered either as instant copy or projection on a screen.

Another major effort is the intensive study of the literature relating to the field of physics by the American Institute of Physics, through grants from the National Science Foundation. Every aspect of this literature is being investigated, from the ways in which physicists use it to the development of classification schemes appropriate to the newer expansions of the field. Information may be almost everybody's business.

There are few other books similar in scope and purpose to this book, but the following supplement and complement its coverage and could help in solving problem situations or in providing an additional perspective.

Special Libraries: A Guide for Management, E. G. Strable, Ed., Special Libraries Association, New York, 1966. A brief, explicit guide.

Handbook of Special Librarianship and Information Work, W. Ashworth, Ed., 3rd ed., revised and enlarged, Aslib, London, 1967. Fourteen chapters written by individual authorities, extensive treatment.

Handbook of Medical Library Practice, G. Annan and J. Felter, Eds., 3rd ed., Medical Library Association, Chicago, 1970. Entirely rewritten. Supplemented by Separate volume entitled *Medical Reference Works, 1679–1966,* scheduled to be kept up to date. Although the intention is to serve medical libraries specifically, there is much that is pertinent to other types of scientific libraries.

The Information Center; Management's Hidden Asset, Morton F. Meltzer, American Management Association, New York, 1967.

Relevant also although from different points of view are these:

How to Manage Your Information, B. E. Holm, Reinhold, New York, 1968.

Industrial Libraries Throughout the World, K. G. B. Bakewell, Pergamon, Oxford, 1969.
Scientific and Technological Communication, S. Passman, Pergamon, Oxford, 1969.

CONCLUSION

It is an accepted fact that any scientific enterprise must keep in touch with developments as they happen and must be prepared to review what has been done in the past. In order to do these things effectively a library, either as an information service in itself or as an adjunct to such a unit, is vitally necessary. The importance of preceding laboratory research by adequate literature research should be obvious. If the results of investigative work have been published, they can almost certainly be found much more quickly through the indexing and abstracting services than by risking repetition in the laboratory. Despite the growing volume and complexity of the scientific literature, diligent effort in approaching it can be rewarding if the facts needed have been published, though, of course some fields are less well serviced than are others. For the broad situation Phelps (29) has expressed a reassuring opinion in an article entitled, "Engineering Information—All is Not Lost."

Finally, Loeb's observation concerning the role of the library in promoting the advance of science has yet to be better expressed (30):

Real discoveries are actually made in the library and subsequently tested out in the laboratory. A new discovery is a new combination of old ideas and those combinations are most likely to occur in the mind of the scientist, not when he is handling material things, but when he is brooding over the thoughts of other men and rethinking them himself. In those hours of profound reflection, the new combination may occur to him, and then he goes to the laboratory to verify or disprove. The library remains the great essential to discovery.

REFERENCES

1. L. H. Morley, *Contributions Toward a Special Library Glossary*, 2nd ed., Special Libraries Association, New York, 1950.

2. Special Libraries Association Professional Standards Committee, "Objectives and Standards for Special Libraries," *Spec. Libr.* **55**, 672–680 (1964).

3. H. Borko, "Information Science: What is It?" *Amer. Doc.* **19**, 3–5 (1968).

4. Committee on Scientific and Technical Information (COSATI), *Recommendation for National Document Handling Systems in Science and Technology*, Vol. I–II, and Appendix A, PB 168 267, AD 624 560, Clearinghouse for Federal Scientific and Technical Information, Springfield, Va., 1965.

5. A. Kruzas, *Directory of Special Libraries and Information Centers,* 2nd ed., Gale Research Company, Detroit, 1968.

6. H. W. Henkle, "Introduction: What is Special?" *Libr. Trends* **1,** 169–172 (1952).

7. B. Kyle, "Administration," in *Handbook of Special Librarianship and Information Work,* W. Ashworth, Ed., 3rd ed., Aslib, London, 1967, p. 14, Chap. II.

8. *Webster's New Collegiate Dictionary,* G. & C. Merriam Co., Springfield, Mass., 1956.

9. D. T. Bedsole, "Library Services in Large Industrial Corporations," Ph.D. Dissertation, University of Michigan, 1961.

10. I. M. Strieby, "The Place of the Library in the Organization," in *Proc. Executive Conf. Organizing and Managing Information,* sponsored by University College, The University of Chicago et al., February 1, 1957.

11. I. M. Strieby, "Organizational Relations of Special Libraries," *Libr. Trends* **I,** 173–187 (1952).

12. "I/EC Special Feature—Administration of Technical Information Groups," *Ind. Eng. Chem.* **51,** 48A–61A (March 1959).

13. Irene M. Strieby, "Looking Around: The Company Library," *Harvard Bus. Rev.* **38,** no. 3, 36 (May-June 1959).

14. Earl C. Graham, "Administrative Policies for the Special Library; An Inventory," *Spec. Libr.* **45,** no. 9, 368 (November 1954).

15. J. Maurice, H. E. Loftus, and I. M. Strieby, "Company-Wide Library Service," *Spec. Libr.* **45,** 53–63 (1954).

16. H. I. Davidson, "The Lilly Library—76 Years," *Spec. Libr.* **57,** 391–394 (1966).

17. L. Lage, Personal communication.

18. D. A. Wells, "Individual Department Libraries versus Consolidated Science Library," *Phys. Today* **14,** 40–41 (1961).

19. J. Shera, "How Much is the Physicist's Inertia Worth?" *Phys. Today* **14,** 42–43 (1961).

20. M. Cooper, "Organizational Patterns of Academic Science Libraries," *Coll. Res. Libr.* **29,** 357–363 (1968).

21. E. L. Fisher, *A Checklist for the Organization, Operation and Evaluation of Company Library,* 2nd ed., Special Libraries Association, New York, 1966.

22. C. G. Stevenson, *Checklist for Review and Evaluation of Technical Libraries, Spec. Libr.* **58,** 101–111 (1967).

23. J. N. Berry, Ed., *Directory of Library Consultants,* R. R. Bowker, New York, 1969.

24. C. C. Furnas, Ed., *Research in Industry; Its Organization and Management,* Van Nostrand-Reinhold, Princeton, N. J., 1948.

25. G. L. Royer, "Management's Expectations from the Services of a Special Library," *Spec. Libr.* **51,** 191–192 (1960).

26. Y. E. Greer, "Operating a Library with a Library Committee," *Spec. Libr.* **50,** 237–239 (1959).

27. E. N. Birdwell, "Managing a Library with a Library Committee," *Spec. Libr.* **50,** 235–237 (1950).

28. H. S. White, "Operating a Library without a Library Committee," *Spec. Libr.* **50,** 241–243 (1959).

29. R. H. Phelps, "Engineering Information—All is Not Lost," *Science* **129**, 25–27 (January 2, 1959).

30. J. Loeb, "Library's Place in Research," *Ex Libris* **1**, 74 (September 1923); *Abstr. Spec. Libr.* **14**, 179 (1923).

BIBLIOGRAPHY

Anthony, L. J. and M. Gosset, "Harwell Atomic Energy Research Establishment Library," *Libr. Assoc. Rec.* **63**, No. 2, 42–44 (February 1960).

Astali, R., *Special Libraries and Information Bureaux*, Bingley, London, 1966.

Bakewell, K. G. B., *Industrial Libraries Throughout the World*, Pergamon, Oxford, 1969.

Ball, D., "Technical Libraries for Industries," *N. Carolina Libr.* **25**, 28029 (Winter 1969).

Boaz, M. T., "Evaluation of Special Library Services for Upper Management," *Spec. Libr.* **59**, 789–791 (1968).

Conrad, C. C., "Coordination and Integration of Technical Information Services," *J. Chem. Doc.* **7**, 111–114 (1967).

Elias, A. W., Ed., "Technical Information Center Administration," *TICA Conf. Proc.*, Drexel Institute of Technology, June 1964, and 1965, Spartan, Washington, D.C.

Gonzolez, E. W. and F. E. McKenna, "Creative Organization: The Librarian as Manager, a Symposium," *Spec. Libr.* **55**, 548–558 (1964).

Graham, R. A., A. E. Lee, and R. L. Meyer, "The Creation of a New Technical Information Center for a Diversified Chemical Company," *J. Chem. Doc.* **8**, 60–68 (1968).

Harper, S. F., Ed., *Proc. Executive Conf. Organizing and Managing Information*, University College, University of Chicago, 1958.

Hayes, R. M. and J. Becker, *Handbook of Data Processing for Libraries*, Becker and Hayes, Inc., 1970.

Hilker, E. W., "The Franklin Institute Library," *PLA Bull.* **23**, 98–104 (November, 1967).

Jackson, E. B., "Portrait of a Special Library System," *Lib. J.* **87**, 3962–3965 (1962).

Johns, A. W., *Special Libraries: Development of the Concept, Their Organization and Services*, Scarecrow, New York, 1968.

Kent, A. and J. Canter, *Specialized Information Centers*, Spartan, Washington, D.C., 1965.

Kleser, P. E., "Special Libraries: Their Organization, Administration and Services," M.L.S. Thesis, University of Toledo, 1964.

Knox, L. T., "How Much Information Service?" *J. Chem. Doc.* **2**, 27 (1962).

Kyle, B., Ed., *Focus on Information and Communication*, Aslib, London, 1965.

Lefebre, L., "The Special Library: What It Is and What It Can Do for Business and Industry," *Spec. Libr.* **48**, 53–57 (1958).

Library Association, *Standards for Hospital Libraries*, The Association, London, 1965.

Lowry, W. K., "Some New Concepts in Library Service," *Bell. Lab. Rec.* **42**, 207 (1964).

Madden, M. E., "Streamlined Special Library," *Libr. J.* **84**, 2557–2560 (1959).

Marvin, J. C., "Public Library as a Special Library," *ASLP Bull.* **10**, 26–33 (1964).

Meckly, E. P., "The Technical Information Facility of Koppers Research Center," *J. Chem. Doc.* **8**, 66–69 (1968).

Morozova, E. N., "Technical Libraries and the Scientific and Technical Information System in the USSR," *IATUL Proc.* **1**, No. 1, 13–23 (March, 1966).

Redmond, D. A., "Optimum Size: The Special Library Viewpoint," *SLA Sci-Tech News* **20**, 40–42 (Summer 1966).

Rees, A. M., "Mecial Libraries and the Assessment of User Needs," *Bull. Med. Libr. Assoc.* **54**, 99–103 (1966).

Schutze, G., *Documentation Source Book*, Scarecrow, New York, 1965.

Simon, B. V., "The Need for Administrative Know-How in Libraries," *Bull. Med. Libr. Assoc.* **57**, 160–170 (1969).

Slater, M. and P. Fisher, *Use Made of Technical Libraries*, Aslib, London, 1969.

Waldron, H. J., *"The Business of Running a Special Library,"* *Spec. Libr.* **62**, 63–70 (1971).

Walsh, R. R., "Branch Library Planning in Universities," *Libr. Trends*, **18**, 216–222 (1969).

Wasserman, P., "The Special Library: A Management Resource," *Libr. J.* **89**, 4288–4294 (1964).

2

Staff for a Scientific Technical Library

Responsibilities and Qualifications

Those who administer the services in a scientific-technical library must be well suited to the work both in temperament and in training, because the degree of success is directly dependent upon staff abilities and attitudes. Good service should be efficient and flexible, rendered in a dignified and pleasant manner. It might be thought unnecessary to state these apparently obvious injunctions, but in any situation where work must sometimes be done under stress, personalities should not be in conflict. Efficiency loses effect if procedures cannot be modified or if requests are not accepted amiably. Therefore, the importance of having staff members who are well-adjusted and whose intellectual capacities are of high caliber cannot be overemphasized.

The administrator of the service is the most influential member in determining the character of the library, but all assistants share the responsibility. In this chapter the qualifications for library work devoted to the physical or life sciences and their related technologies are reviewed. Requisite education and training are outlined.

SIZE OF STAFF

One of the first decisions to be made is the number of staff members required for the level of service wanted. The situation under consideration may be either the staffing of a new library or an assessment of an already established one to increase its effectiveness. Some of the other chapters of this book should be consulted at this point to determine the scope of the service.

There are some circumstances where, if the volume of work to be done is not too great, perhaps because a library is in an initial stage, the unit can be staffed by one professionally trained person aided by a clerical assistant. If the full potential of a good information service is to be realized, however, this would not be adequate for a long period of time. As the use made of publications grows and the size of the collection of materials expands, one person cannot be expected to do everything adequately. Consequently, other staff members, both clerical and professional, must be employed to take over certain activities.

There are several ways of approaching the answer to the question of how many staff members are needed for an efficient library service. One is to study the results of surveys of organizations similar to the one contemplated. Several such investigations have provided some pertinent facts.

An examination of the practices in effect in certain types of libraries, principally in industrial corporations, was undertaken as a research project by Bedsole (1) who published his findings as a Ph.D. dissertation to which reference has been made in Chapter 1. He investigated the libraries of 117 large corporations representing a total of 350 libraries, and reported the numbers of staff members employed in all of them. Another study by Gibson (2), using 27 corporations as a sample, produced results that anticipated those of Bedsole. Sharp's survey (3) was of 25 libraries of companies operating in the field of electronics. The findings with respect to the sizes of library staffs of these three investigators are summarized in Table 1. Some figures reported by Nicholson (4) are included for historical comparison.

It is evident that most of the figures cited in this table essentially agree, except for the column giving ratios of library staff to engineer/scientists served. Bedsole's findings indicate a very high number of patrons for each library staff member in contrast to the earlier report by Nicholson which showed a remarkably small number. No doubt this reflects the sharp increase in research staffs and the fact that library expansion has not kept pace insofar as can readily be detected.

A British publication titled *Education and Training for Scientific and Technological Library and Information Work,* issued in 1968 (5) reports that in Great Britain there are five information scientists for every hundred scientists working in research and development compared with two per hundred in 1958, an encouraging increase. A detailed account is presented of the situations in which information workers and special li-

Table 1

Investigator	Date	No. of libraries	No. on library staff	Average No. on library staff	Ratio library staff to engineer/ scientists
Bedsole	1961	350	From 1 to 67	5.1	1 : 122
Gibson	1956	27	From 1 to 13	5	1 : 52
Sharp	1958	25	From 1 to 22	5	1 : 48
Nicholson	1940	Not given	From 1 to 13	Not given	1 : 30 and 1 : 20

brarians are employed, the types of functions performed, and the several ways open for acquiring professional competence. As in the United States, there is strong awareness of the need to encourage persons with a scientific bent to be apprised of opportunities for work with the literature, ranging from activities involving library administration to the analysis of data.

SYSTEMS ANALYSIS

If while drafting the plans for the library service an effective analysis of the whole system and its component parts has been performed, a procedure suggested in Chapter 1, data will be available from which to deduce the number of essential staff members. It may be necessary to develop each function in greater detail, including the steps required to perform them. Bolles (6) illustrated concisely a method of using flow charts to analyze library operations, showing how this approach should be applied to repetitive tasks. Moore (6) also has excellent advice on how to accomplish a systems analysis, by first collecting information as to how duties are performed, then reducing this to chart form, and finally analyzing the charts to detect how efficiency might be increased. A noteworthy point made by Moore is the advisability of maintaining a continuous analysis program. In the initial stages this critical planning should be a primary responsibility of a library staff member. The project as a whole can be helped by the dispassionate viewpoint of a professional analyst, one who may be on the staff of the organization or who comes in as a consultant.

A case study of a situation where procedural analysis was applied is reported in a monograph by Herner and Heatwole (8) with this pertinent title, *The Establishment of Staff Requirements in a Small Research Library*. These authors use as illustration an organization in which a scientific staff of 400 was to be provided with a suitable library service. After systematic investigation the recommendation was that an adequate staff should consist of 3.2 professional members and 3 clerical assistants. This would be an ideal circumstance, one rarely realized.

The growing necessity for better use of the burgeoning literature, particularly in research organizations, indicates that library staffs in general should be larger than those reported in Bedsole's fundamental study (1). There has not been significant improvement in subsequent years judging from the results of a survey, primarily of salaries, reported by Special Libraries Association in 1967 (9). Of a total of 3821 libraries (all subject fields represented) 971 had staffs of only 1 to 2 members.

Certain specific factors in every situation always influence the size of the staff required. Some responsibilities may be assigned that involve a significant amount of clerical attention, such as the handling of technical correspondence which may sometimes be allotted to the library. It is important that the proportion of professional staff members and clerical assistants be in proper relation so that the special qualifications of both are best utilized.

POSITION EVALUATION

Before discussing the individual staff positions, certain general matters concerning the staff as a whole should be considered. If the previously discussed procedure of analyzing the responsibilities assigned to each position has not been done in sufficient detail, it must be performed before anything further can be done about procuring staff members. This evaluation will determine salary rates, a primary necessity before positions can be offered. Salaries should be on a par with those in other departments of the organization where educational requirements and expected accomplishments are comparable. Suggested figures are cited in Chapter 3.

Since the majority of the libraries with which this book is concerned are operating units in larger organizations, the personnel policies necessarily follow those already in effect. An example of a still valid scheme of classification of personnel in an industrial research framework is illustrated in the book, *Research in Industry* (10). The position of head of the library service is shown in relation to other positions on the research staff; the rating is professional and the status that of department head. More recently the title of "Manager" is often used to conform with modern usage. In developing the detailed classification of positions for the whole staff of the library, appropriate subordinate ranks equivalent to positions in other departments should be assigned.

Examples of staff organization charts are shown in some of the illustrated Figures 2 to 9 in Chapter 1.

As stated in Chapter 1, in the discussion of the placement of the library in overall organization plans, this service may be fitted into a scheme in several ways. This means that the administrative head will report to different officers in various organizations. In an academic situation the head of a branch library may report directly either to the director of libraries or to an assistant director. In industry it may be to a vice president of a company of moderate size or to an assistant to a vice president of a major corporation. The title of this officer makes no real difference as long as it be one high enough to be able to give strong support. More important is belief and confidence in the potential role of the literature service. Strieby (11) discusses this matter fully in a paper on "The Place of the Library in the Organization."

In the process of evaluating each position on the library staff, the duties should be defined and applicable titles determined. Suggestions for appropriate titles are given in the sections of this chapter where the various positions are described in detail.

STAFF MANUAL

The facts gathered in the course of developing descriptions for staff positions ought to be preserved in a form readily accessible for future consultation. One recommendation is that they provide the framework for a staff manual in which the functions of the library are described in terms of the duties of each staff member. Such a record is invaluable, although it requires disciplined effort to produce. Wesner (11) reports an attempt to locate examples of staff manuals as guides in the preparation of one. It may be surprising that few libraries were found to possess them. It was generally agreed, Wesner was reassured, that the idea is excellent, but there were not many administrative heads of libraries who had been able to produce one. Wesner, however, did undertake to organize a manual and concluded that "the preparation of such a manual consumes hours of time—and [I] hasten to add that it will be worth every minute of it." The potential significance of the staff manual is discussed in another context in Chapter 12.

A manual may be prepared as a typed copy with several carbons if only three or four are needed, or it can be duplicated to provide a greater number. It is advisable to design it so that it can be kept in loose-leaf notebooks for convenience in adding material as well as quickly deleting portions as they are superseded.

One of the most important sections in a manual covers personnel policies affecting all staff members. Working hours, vacation allowances, sick leave, and any other pertinent matters should be stated explicitly. Even such seemingly small matters as the coffee break policy should be specified to avoid misunderstanding.

The duties of each staff member should be outlined in enough detail to permit a qualified person to perform what is required. Such specifications make certain that everyone understands who is responsible for every category of service and also assure uniform observance of methods once they are instituted. An alternate procedure that may be preferred in libraries where there is only one professional staff member and one or two clerical assistants is to provide a detailed outline of procedures and not to specify who is to perform each function.

A manual serves other purposes in addition to providing a guide to the execution of duties. It can be an excellent introduction to the library for new staff members, giving them an immediate perspective of its broad functions so that they can quickly appreciate the role of their individual assignments with respect to the whole program. Boots (13), moreover, makes a strong point in observing that a manual provides administrative officers with concrete evidence of the vital function of the library. It can be unquestionable proof of a well-administered operation.

STAFF POSITIONS

Librarian

Title

The administrative head of a scientific-technical library may be given any one of several titles. The title can be appropriately "Librarian." Frequently a more definitive designation is preferred. It may be derived from the name chosen for the library, examples of which are cited in Chapter 1. If the heads of comparable departments are called "Manager" or "Supervisor" it will be advantageous in considering personnel policy to use such a title. Some of the commonly used titles are the following:

Technical Librarian
Research Librarian
Technical Research Librarian
Chief Librarian
Supervisor of Library
Director of Library (or Libraries)
Manager of Technical Information Service
Library Administrator
Head

In this book "Librarian" is used for convenience to refer to the person in charge of the library service no matter what it may be called. Of course, other librarians on the staff have distinctive titles.

Responsibilities

So varied are the activities of a library in the fields of science and technology, usually encompassing segments of both, that the administrative head must be capable of carrying on and supervising diversified operations. Where the size of staff is minimal, the librarian executes many operations. He must plan, organize, and direct all of the main functions of the service, interpreting needs as they develop and anticipating them. He must keep in mind the policies of the organization and comprehend its problems if he is to fulfill its information requirements effectively. Specifically, the broad operations for which the librarian is responsible are these:

Planning the physical arrangement of allotted space and selecting furniture and equipment
Preparing budget
Selecting personnel and assignment of duties—staff organization
Selecting and purchasing procedures for books, periodicals, and other publications
Supervising classification and cataloging of books and indexing of other materials
Supervising readers' services
Supervising reference requests
Executing literature searches
Reviewing and abstracting from current publications and preparing a library bulletin or other current awareness service
Translating from other languages
Contributing to, and rendering editorial assistance with, organizational publications

Supervising files of special materials—laboratory notebooks, research reports, and organization archives

Attending organization meetings, research conferences, and seminars

Preparing annual reports to management outlining activities and future plans

Maintaining professional relations

Some of these duties can be performed by other staff members if they are available and qualified. Other tasks that should certainly be delegated are the following:

Circulating procedures, including statistics
Filing cards, pamphlets, loose-leaf services
Recording and filing periodicals
Binding procedures
Requisitioning of supplies
Inventorying collection
Processing interlibrary loans

These main responsibilities will be required in almost every library situation. Others may be considered appropriate by some organizations, and these should be worked into the flexible framework of this uniquely designed service.

Qualifications and Training

Certain qualifications of an administrator in a scientific-technical library can be stated, but existing libraries so vary the emphasis of their activities that requirements cannot be stipulated as mandatory for success. Those who are the most effective in these positions do not fit a pattern, and therefore do not provide data from which to draw conclusions. Since the requirements of few situations are the same, the experience and training of a prospective applicant for a position may be viewed differently. A successful librarian must first be a well-educated person with an appreciation for scholarship and its needs. Brown (14) stresses the importance of the personal attitude, stating that the science librarian should have a natural liking for his work and should find personal satisfaction in knowing the literature of his field. He should be confident that what he does as a library research worker is highly significant to the success of the program of the organization. In the opinion of Hunt (15) the competent science librarian should possess a "high degree of intelligence, intellectual curiosity, and an excellent memory." Knowledge of publications in the field and how to use them is essential, as is reasonable acquaintance with the particular sciences involved.

If the duties of the librarian are primarily administrative, that is, consist largely in supervising readers' services and technical processes, then training in library science is of chief importance. However, in situations where he works more closely with the literature, performing literature searches and compiling bibliographic reports, knowledge of the scientific subjects is paramount. He must have administrative ability to some degree if a staff of any size is to be supervised; in fact it can be a challenge to achieve the best working relationships with a staff of any size. Thus a person who is to head the service must have a combination of skill in library science, in subject knowledge, and in administrative ability, each in proportion to suit the particular position. There is increasing need to be also aware of the emergent information science developments.

In addition to the more readily measured qualifications there is the elusive one of personality which is equally significant in determining the potential success of the individual as a librarian. Ideally the individual should be personable, well-adjusted, poised in manner, and able to deal pleasantly with people. Not only is it necessary to establish a dignified relationship with the library clientele and to maintain good staff cooperation, but also it is expedient to develop cordial dealings with professional associates. The person who possesses an attractive personality has an incalculable asset to achieve success.

Lively discussions of the formal education necessary for librarians serving in science and technology have occurred intermittently since the 1930s. With the meteoric increase in need for scientific and technical information created by World War II and the insufficient numbers of qualified persons to enter the profession, opinions as to how to recruit subject specialists, with or without library degrees, were frequently aired in the professional journals. There was some concern that the profession would be weakened by filling positions too hurriedly with those whose qualifications might not meet these standards that could not be easily defined. Actually it is very difficult to discern the consequences of this emergency. Certainly some individuals came into this field who otherwise might not have considered it.

The question of the kind of program for training librarians to administer scientific-technical librarians has not yet been resolved, despite the continuous attention of committees of the professional associations. A Joint Committee on Library Education sponsored by the Council of National Library Associations met in 1949 (16) and as a consequence of its work Voigt (17) published in 1954 a proposed curriculum for scientific and technical librarianship. The following statement indicates the difficulty of reaching firm agreement:

. . . Another basic consideration is that of whether specialized library-school education, or even any library school training at all is essential for the technical librarian. The answer is the same in this field as in most others. The subject specialist with some natural inclination and ability in librarianship can become, if he wishes, an effective science and technology librarian in his own field. . . . The value of library-school training lies largely in the methods and procedures which are learned and perhaps even more in the resultant acquaintance with the organization of large libraries and methods of extracting information from them . . . .

More recently Special Libraries Association has held three forums on Education for Special Librarianship. The principal papers given at the second one held in Minneapolis in 1966 are published in the January 1967 issue of *Special Libraries* and cover a broad range of aspects of the subject, from reviews of what library schools are teaching to ideas of what should be taught.

Formal education in library science in the United States consists of an intensive one year program leading to a master's degree. A prerequisite is the bachelor's degree. In most library schools the curriculum is broadly based as preparation for work in general libraries. However, there has been a slow growing trend toward recognizing the needs of special libraries for which specific courses have been instituted. Owens (18) surveyed the situation in 1960 and found that of 31 library schools, 26 had courses in special librarianship. In 1966 Bromberg (19) again surveyed the situation and found that all but one of the schools responding stated that they did indeed offer courses, but it was very difficult to detect exactly what was being taught. Emphasis appeared to be on special materials, library planning, personnel, budget, and public relations. In recognition of the specific requirements of the field of information science, some library schools have provided an option for training in this direction, the distinction being chiefly in more attention to automation. Among the initiators of such programs have been the School of Library Science of Case Western Reserve University, the Graduate School of Library Science of Drexel Institute of Technology, the Graduate School of Library and Information Science of the University of Pittsburgh, and the Graduate School of Library Service at the University of California at Los Angeles.

For persons with serious professional intentions there are excellent opportunities at certain library schools to attain a doctoral degree. Well-paying scholarships are available to individuals whose aptitudes indicate that they are likely to achieve a higher level of success if this extra training is undertaken early enough in their careers.

Regularly scheduled library school courses are supplemented and augmented by short institutes and conferences that are sponsored by library schools, professional associations, and government agencies. Brief, intensive courses are sometimes offered during the few days immediately preceding the annual conventions of such organizations as the Special Libraries Association and the American Society for Information Science to provide an opportunity for those already practicing in the profession to keep abreast of developments. Also, the American Management Association includes library-oriented programs in its efforts to help its members keep up with modern methods in all areas, and as a real service sometimes offers the same course in both East and West Coast cities. Such opportunities are usually well advertised in professional journals and through direct notifications to members of societies.

As libraries become more complex operations it is likely that a library science degree will be a general requirement for most administrative positions because it provides one sure measure of competence. Working experience may also be adequate training for an upward step, especially for an individual who has been active professionally and taken advantage of continuing education opportunities.

It may be pertinent to mention here that requirements for membership in professional associations vary. Some insist upon a bachelor's degree and may even specify an accredited institution; others accept experience or employment in a relevant field. Still others consider that interest is enough to warrant acceptance in the society.

Assistant Librarian

Responsibilities

The assistant librarian is responsible for those functions of the library that are delegated to him, usually in those areas in which he has special competence. Additionally, he must be equal to taking charge of the whole operation in the absence of the head.

Qualifications and Training

Qualifications are determined by the particular requirements of the situation. In general, they should not fall far short of those indicated for the head position. An academic degree with a major in the appropriate science is almost mandatory; library-school training ensures the best preparation. One of these qualifications may be lacking in some measure but this can be remedied by guided working experience or courses while employed. In developing a staff it is possible, and certainly desirable, to select individuals whose qualifications complement one another rather than duplicate too closely. If the librarian is a subject specialist, for example, it may be beneficial to have an assistant whose aptitudes are in developing library routines.

PROFESSIONAL LIBRARY ASSISTANTS

On a staff that requires more than two professionally trained members, the additional ones are employed to perform specific functions. The more common professional positions are outlined in the following sections.

Reference Librarian

Responsibilities

Where activity is on a large enough scale a reference librarian is needed full time to answer reference questions. He does some searching of the literature to answer almost any type of query and combines his primary duty with the performance of some literature searches.

Qualifications and Training

The reference librarian must be familiar with the literature of the fields in which he does his work. To achieve this, a bachelor's degree with major courses in the sciences is a necessary background, and an advanced degree is highly desirable experience for using the literature. Library schools have courses that provide introduction to the scientific literature, and some offer them in the summer term or as part of their continuing education program for those already employed.

Acquisitions Librarian

Responsibilities

An acquisitions librarian is in charge of placing orders for all publications. This includes books, periodicals, pamphlets, patents, reports, and anything else that is wanted. Equipment and supplies may come under his jurisdiction.

Qualifications and Training

To discharge his duties effectively, the acquisitions librarian must know how to locate and deal with vendors and agencies to be certain that they supply needed publications quickly and accurately. If he has not had prior experience he must learn how to develop requisite procedures. The best preparation includes a bachelor's and a library science degree; the latter curriculum will have included a course in acquisitions processes.

Literature Searcher or Abstracter

Responsibilities

A literature searcher systematically investigates the pertinent publications to locate specific information or to compile bibliographies on assigned subjects. He may also abstract the references if required. The searcher may work primarily either with the book and periodical literature, with patents, or sometimes with both. Searching assignments that involve reviews of the literature of a particular subject require expertise in the use of reference sources and knowledge of the subject. He must possess a special mental flexibility to cope with various approaches to indexing, especially if he is to use computerized sources effectively.

The person performing literature searches must be capable of organizing his results in the most comprehensible form for users. He may be required to evaluate and summarize information in a formal report.

Qualifications and Training

The first requirements for a literature searcher are knowledge of the subjects involved and the ways of the literature in which they are recorded. A bachelor's degree is required as a minimum, with major courses in science. Graduate study, of course, increases potential capabilities. Reading knowledge of other languages may be a necessity. Strieby (20) outlines these essential background needs for chemists for non-laboratory research positions in technical fields, a patent library, or a technical library.

This work with the literature demands a unique ability to visualize research problems, patience with detail, and, to be truly effective, intellectual aggressiveness. The only way to acquire proficiency in literature searching is by experience, especially by working with others who can offer guidance. An expedient approach to the literature can be devious, and much can be learned from in-service training. The ability to write in a clear, direct style is imperative.

It may not be recognized, without being brought to attention, that once a literature searcher has been trained he can do this work other than at the home library. It will, of course, be necessary at times to visit a major library to use materials found only there, but it is also worth considering, for example, what the Miles Laboratories Library has done in continuing to use a former staff member who moved to Chicago. There she receives assignments for searches to be done at the John Crerar Library, an arrangement that is particularly fitting because the Miles company is one of the industrial supporters of the library.

Translator

Responsibilities

A staff translator is required to translate from other languages into acceptable idiomatic English or whatever language is required. Articles from periodicals, patents, correspondence, or even books may be assigned for translation.

Qualifications and Training

Knowledge of other languages as well as a superior command of English (or whatever the official language) is essential. A translator must be familiar with the terminology of the sciences with which he works and know the importance of exactly equivalent terms. It is not satisfactory, for example, for the term "electron gun" to be rendered as "electric pistol." He should develop some sense of the reliability of sources and authors of the publications whose languages he handles.

An academic degree with emphasis on courses in science or engineering is an obvious requirement along with as much formal study of languages as possible. There must be a natural propensity for learning language since acquiring others may be necessary if they are useful professionally.

Cataloger and Indexer

Responsibilities

A cataloger is responsible for the complete process of preparing books for filing location and for making the card catalog an effective guide to the information these books contain. This requires, in a scientific-technical library, the adaptation of standard cataloging procedures and classification schedules to the necessities of the specific situation. A system for preparing and filing catalog cards must be established.

The indexing of articles in periodicals, patents, and pamphlet material may be done by a cataloger or, where large numbers of documents must be handled, by staff members employed for this specific duty. It is advisable to have all indexing done under the direction of, or in consultation with, the cataloging staff to achieve a uniform point of view. As machines or other nonconventional methods of indexing for information retrieval are increasingly applied, the coding required should be a part of this area of operation. Filing of special materials such as complicated loose-leaf services may be also assigned.

Qualifications and Training

Knowledge of cataloging procedures and their underlying philosophy is essential for a cataloger. He should appreciate and have some knowledge of the subjects involved and an awareness of continuing developments in the realm of science. A bachelor's degree, for which some courses in science have been included, and a master's degree in library science are necessary. The cataloger should have a specific aptitude for the work, be particularly patient with details, and have a high regard for accuracy.

A person who does indexing should have mental qualities similar to those of a cataloger, and his education should include a bachelor's degree as a minimum. Library science training is not as necessary, although the courses dealing with the special coding and indexing procedures for computer applications, usually indicated as information science, would be very helpful.

Systems Analyst

Responsibilities

Only in a very large operation or one in which activities must be organized and controlled in several locations would there be need for this highly specialized professional. His duties would include a major role in analyzing all procedures, introducing coordination where appropriate, and determining how to increase overall efficiency. This staff member knows how to utilize automation. Probably he would work only part time for the library, particularly after he has solved its problems.

Qualification and Training

Ideally, a systems analyst who would be most effective in working with library and scientific literature problems would have training in both areas—mathematics and logic relating to systems theory and as much library science as might be needed for comprehension of library-oriented functions that could be made more efficient through systematic analysis. A bachelor's degree with major courses in mathematics, logic, and computer science supplemented by certain courses in library or information science are suggested.

Subprofessional Assistants

Responsibilities

The subprofessional assistant or library technician performs assigned duties such as book circulation routines, preparation of periodicals for binding, keeping of systematic records, and anything in fact that does not require the background of the fully trained professional. His work will have to be surpervised because of the exceptions that occur in scientific publications. No routine is safe.

Qualifications and Training

There has been much debate concerning the employment of subprofessional assistants in libraries, but because of the shortage of fully qualified personnel and the fact that there are many duties that do not require the full attention of a person with a master in library science degree, persons with some lesser training should be employed, as indeed they are, in almost any library. Shores (21) calls the potential role of the library technician "a professional opportunity" and supports the contention that one way of helping the librarian to realize his full capabilities is to free him of the routine tasks that are not beyond the grasp of a clerical worker. Steele (22) summarizes the controversy and defends a program for the training of library technicians. There are perhaps as many as 100 individual courses of such training in the United States and Canada, most of them in vocational-technical schools or junior colleges.

Typist-Clerk

Duties

The duties of a typist-clerk depend largely upon the number of other staff members. On a small staff the assignments are more varied and may include such tasks as card filing which is done by library assistants or subprofessional assistants in larger operations. All typing, shelving of books, checking in of periodicals, and any miscellaneous jobs such as these may be assigned to this person.

Qualifications and Training

A high school education with special training in office skills should be adequate for the work required. Higher than average intelligence is necessary because of the complicated details of the materials involved.

Secretary

Duties

A secretary works closely with the librarian, transcribing letters, filing correspondence, and keeping a record of the many details that accompany a busy executive position. Where the scope of activity is not large, the secretary may also perform some of the duties of a typist-clerk or even of a library assistant.

Qualifications and Training

Ordinarily, a high school education followed by a business school course is adequate for this position. The ideal type of person is one who possesses a strong willingness to be helpful, and who is alert to aid the librarian in all possible ways.

It may be desirable to employ a college graduate in this position if special responsibilities are to be delegated.

PROCUREMENT OF STAFF MEMBERS

Professional

Professional personnel may be sought in several ways. Advertisements of openings can be inserted in such periodicals as *Special Libraries, American Documentation, Chemical and Engineering News,* or *College and Research Libraries.* Persons available for employment place their notices in these periodicals also.

Another approach is through schools of library science. They keep records of their graduates and can supply full information about them. It is good policy to keep in touch with certain schools if new staff members are needed from time to time. Some schools maintain work-study programs, and this can be a means of enlisting a good staff member, already trained in the procedures of the library, if it is feasible to risk some time in taking such a student.

A third channel for finding professional staff members is the employment service operated by certain scientific and library-oriented societies. Among these are: The American Chemical Society, Special Libraries Association, and American Society for Information Science. They operate from national headquarters and provide special opportunities for employers to meet prospective employees at annual or semiannual meetings. There is also some activity within local chapters.

Large organizations have personnel departments that are experienced in locating qualified persons to fill different positions. They can be helpful in screening potential candidates. When they send representatives to interview graduates at colleges and universities, these interviewers can watch for good candidates for the library staff.

There is also a National Registry for Librarians, a service of the Illinois State Employment Service, 208 South LaSalle St., Chicago, Ill. 60604. This does function as an effective centralized clearinghouse and operates a placement bureau at ALA conferences.

Clerical

For clerical positions, local high schools and business schools or state employment offices can be approached. Also, a central personnel office may be able to suggest persons who have had some experience in other units of the organization, particularly for up-grading opportunities. It is wise to be as selective as possible because any position in the library requires a high order of intelligence and attention to detail.

CONCLUSION

Whatever the size and composition of the staff, its members must be able to and willing to work harmoniously as a steadfast unit in strong support of the objectives of the enterprise of which it is a part. It behooves the administrative head to create an atmosphere that inspires all co-workers to be active, willing contributors to the effective operation of the library. The importance of this rapport is further stressed in Chapter 12.

REFERENCES

1. D. T. Bedsole, "Library Systems in Large Industrial Corporations," Dissertation, University of Michigan, 1961.
2. E. B. Gibson, "What Can Be Learned from a Library Survey?" *Spec. Libr.* **48**, 133–138 (1957).
3. H. S. Sharp, "A Survey of Electronics Libraries," *Spec. Libr.* **49**, 157–160 (1958).
4. A. L. Nicholson, private communication.
5. H. Schur and W. L. Saunders, *Education and Training for Scientific and Technological Library and Information Work,* Her Majesty's Stationery Office, London, 1968.
6. S. W. Bolles, "The Use of Flow Charts in the Analysis of Library Operations," *Spec. Libr.* **58**, 87–90 (1967).

7. E. Moore, "Systems Analysis: An Overview," *Spec. Libr.* **58**, 87–90 (1967).

8. S. Herner and M. K. Heatwole, *The Establishment of Staff Requirements in a Small Research Library*, ACRL Monograph 3, Association of College and Research Libraries, Chicago, 1952.

9. "A Study of 1967 Annual Salaries of Members of the Special Libraries Association," *Spec. Libr.* **58**, 217–254 (1967).

10. C. C. Furnas, Ed., *Research in Industry*, Van Nostrand-Reinhold, Princeton, N. J., 1948.

11. I. M. Strieby, "The Place of the Library in the Organization," *Proc. Executive Conf. Organization and Management*, University College, University of Chicago, Chicago, Ill., 1957.

12. J. Wesner, "Training of Nonprofessional Staff," *Spec. Libr.* **46**, 434–440 (1955).

13. R. Boots, "Suggestions for the Preparation of a Staff Manual," *Spec. Libr.* **34**, 292–294 (1943).

14. D. F. Brown, private communication.

15. J. W. Hunt, "Science Librarianship," *Science* **104**, 171–173 (1946).

16. A. H. Lancour, Ed., *Issues in Library Education. Report of the Conference on Library Education*, Council of National Library Associations (1949), Princeton, N. J., December 11–12, 1948.

17. M. J. Voigt, *et al.*, "Education for Special Librarianship," *Libr. Quart.* **24**, 1–20 (January 1954).

18. E. W. Owens, "A Survey of Special Library Education," *Spec. Libr.* **51**, 288–293 (1960).

19. E. Bromberg, "Quick Look at Courses on Special Libraries," *Spec. Libr.* **58**, 22–23 (1967).

20. I. M. Strieby, "The Problem of Literature Chemists in Industry," in *Training of Literature Chemists*, Advances in Chemistry Series 17, American Chemical Society, Washington, D.C., 1956.

21. L. Shores, "Library Technician; A Professional Opportunity," *Spec. Libr.* **59**, 240–245 (1968).

22. C. I. Steele, "Library Technicians—The Big Controversy," *Spec. Libr.* **60**, 45–49 (1969).

BIBLIOGRAPHY

Anon, "Training Program for Science Librarians at the University of Tennessee," *Med. Libr. Assoc. Bull.* **58**, 78–79 (1970).

Bracken, M. C. and C. W. Shilling, "Survey of Practical Training in Information Science," *Amer. Doc.* **28**, 113–119 (1968).

Brown, A. L., "The Measurement of Performance and Its Relation to Special Library Service," *Spec. Libr.* **50**, 379–394 (1959).

Callendar, T. E., "Training of Special Library Staff," *Aslib Proc.* **18**, 16–19 (1966).

Darling, L., "Personal Views of Personnel Administration," *Bull. Med. Libr. Assoc.* **58**, 346–349 (1970).

Dawson, J. M., "Not Too Academic," *Coll. Res. Libr.* **27**, 37–39 (1966).

Haslam, D. D., "Staffing of Industrial Libraries," *Libr. Assoc. Rec.* **68**, 213–219 (1966).

Heilprin, L. B., *et al.*, Eds., *Proc. Symp. Education for Information Science*, Warrenton, Va., September 7–10, 1965, Spartan, Washington, D. C., 1965.

Kozumplik, W. N., "Time and Motion Study of Library Operations," *Spec. Libr.* **58**, 585–588 (1967).

Meyer, R. S., "Library Technicians Training Programs and Special Libraries," *Spec. Libr.* **59**, 453–456 (1968).

Petru, W. C. and M. W. West, Eds., *The Library: An Introduction for the Library Assistant*, Special Library Association, New York, 1967.

Shera, J. H., "An Education Program for Special Librarians," *Educ. Libr.* **1**, 121–128 (Winter 1961).

Simms, D. W., "What Is a Systems Analyst?" *Spec. Libr.* **59**, 718–721 (1968).

Sloane, M. N., "SLA Chapters and Continuing Education," *Spec. Libr.* **58**, 24–26 (1967).

Stebbins, K. B., *Personnel Administration in Libraries*, 2nd ed., revised and largely rewritten by F. E. Mohrhardt, Scarecrow, New York, 1966.

Taylor, R. S., *Curriculum for the Information Sciences*, Report 12, final report, recommended courses and curricula, Center for the Information Sciences, Lehigh University, Bethlehem, Pa., September 1967.

3

Budget

Costs of Operation

GENERAL CONSIDERATIONS

When the establishment of a library service is contemplated, it is essential that the financial requirements be investigated. After it is decided what types of service are wanted, it is possible to anticipate the cost with fair accuracy, and this should be estimated as part of the preliminary planning process. In fact, costs may influence to some extent what can be undertaken at the outset.

It is recommended that a definite budget be developed within which the information activity is to operate. That this has long been recognized as proper practice was shown in surveys reported some years ago by Gibson (1) and Sharp (2) who investigated representative groups of libraries in engineering and electronics companies and found that monetary control was thus exercised. In this period also, the late 1950s, Knox (3) reported the results of a study of 85 library services in chemical companies, half of which supplied actual budget figures. These examples show that budgeting is a usual procedure.

Another citation of budgets is included in the detailed *Profiles of Special Libraries* that have been compiled as prototypes by Leonard (4). Although figures are not suggested, the ratios of amounts that might be spent for the several essential budgetary items offer good guide lines. Of the six profiles of typical special libraries, four are scientific/technical situations.

In its statement of *Objective and Standards for Special Libraries* published in 1964 (5) the Special Libraries Association treats the subject of budget only briefly, suggesting that the Library Administrator be responsible for proposed expenditures and that the greater proportion of the total be allotted to staff salaries. Although agreeing, in general, with this idea, Randall (6) warns that without a strong literature collection a highly paid staff cannot function effectively.

The way in which the library budget is administered is determined by the system followed by the organization to which it is connected. In some instances the budget is a distinctly separate unit. In others where it is a subgroup of a larger division, a detailed budget may not be considered necessary, so that only the total expenditures would be known with any certainty. Though this practice may be satisfactory in some instances, it is not recommended. It is desirable from several standpoints to have a breakdown of figures showing exactly how much is being spent for salaries and books and periodicals, as well as for the unique services that are provided by the library. An occasion could arise that would call for facts and figures to justify the operation as an economic asset.

In considering the costs of the library service generally, and in view of the fact that a large number of scientific and technical libraries are located in industrial research organizations, usually as a part of a research and development activity, the amounts spent for library and related functions are closely related to total research budgets. From an historical perspective a survey of research expenditures made by the National Association of Manufacturers (7) in 1948 to determine the relationship between total sales and funds spent for research is still of some significance. At that time it was found that about 2% of an active industrial organization's sales income was allotted for research. By 1955 this figure had increased to 2.8% (8). In 1958 the percentage of research budgets allotted to information services was known to range from as low as 1.5% to as high as 10%. These figures were provided in a survey by Knox (3) of a group of chemical companies. There is general evidence that the proportion of research budgets spent for information services still lies within this range of from 2 to 10%.

The proportion of the budget allotted to the information service is influenced by attitude of the management of the enterprise it serves as well as by the nature of its functions. A highly competitive business is more likely to be aware of a necessity to keep abreast of all pertinent publications. Monetary resources will, of course, have some bearing, especially in a business that is not yet firmly established, although it is at this stage that the support of a good library is greatly needed. In all

of the other noncompetitive situations where science libraries are located adequate funding is equally important.

It is admitted that libraries are expensive, and few economies can be
recommended. One temptation is to have a good clerical staff member in
charge in the belief that as long as publications are kept in order scientists and engineers can use them. Theoretically this might be defended,
but actually most scientists and engineers receive so little introduction to
the literature of their fields as part of their educations that they need the
assistance that can be given only by an information specialist.

An excellent review of financial requirements is outlined by Randall
(9) in his article "Budgeting for a Company Library." Because his article
is based on broad experience in an IBM library, his approach to the
development of a library budget is meaningful, as it follows the steps proposed in the SLA Library Profiles (4) and many figures are cited. The
total for the hypothetical library discussed in detail came to $171,050
annually for an organization of 1200 employees, 800 of whom are active
library users. This is a maximum figure for the most extensive of possible services.

The several essential areas for which costs must be planned are discussed in detail in the subsequent sections of this chapter. Figures are
quoted as examples, but they must always be regarded as tentative and
subject to modifications, such as salary differentials according to geographical location. As with every other kind of activity in the 1960s and
early 1970s, the trend is upward.

BUDGET ITEMS

For a contemplated service a projected budget consists of two parts,
the first an initial amount to start operations, of which a portion is
included in the second part, the annual appropriation. Initial costs will
vary widely, depending upon the needs and the scope of the service
envisioned. If every item of equipment from a desk for the librarian to
multilevel book stacks, and from a handbook to a complete file of the
major abstracting publication must be purchased before the first query
can be accepted, this sum will obviously have to be much larger than it
would be if there were already some equipment on hand.

Salaries

Because staff salaries constitute the largest of the several divisions
of the total budget, they are considered first. In Leonard's profiles (4) for

special libraries the suggested range is 67 to 72% of the total. As an initial step, compensation for the administrative head is a primary decision. It is influenced by several factors in addition to going rates, because good candidates are usually in short supply. If extensive experience is required in addition to subject knowledge, the salary must be higher than for a person of lesser qualifications. For example, in a library located in a metropolitan area where major public or semiprivate collections are accessible, it is advisable to pay well for an experienced individual who can take full advantage of these resources. In an isolated situation, it may be better to spend a larger proportion of the available funds for the purchase of as extensive a collection as possible. However, recognition of the importance and potential contribution of this chief of staff to the effectiveness of the information program will dictate compensation on a par with administrators of other departments of comparable educational preparation and requirements.

After the salary range for the head of the service is determined, those for the assistants are decided. Responsibilities involved and stipulated requirements are influencing factors, as are salaries paid in other departments for comparable positions. Many organizations have salary schedules with ranges in each category for both professional and clerical positions.

In Table 1 salaries are suggested for two types of staffs; in the first instance there are from two to four members serving a potential clientele of no more than 1000; in the second there are from five to thirty serving more than 1000 scientists or engineers. The figures are admittedly tentative because many factors must be taken into consideration. Salaries are

Table 1   Staff Salaries

Position	Staff of 2 to 4 Serving up to 1000 ($)	Staff of 5 to 30 Serving 1000+ ($)
Librarian (or Administrative Head)	10,000–13,000	12,500–20,000
Assistant Librarian (Professional)	9,000–11,000	10,000–14,000
Reference Assistant		8,500–12,000
Cataloger or Indexer	8,500–10,000	9,000–12,000
Literature Searcher		8,500–12,000
Translator		9,000–11,000
Abstracter or Editor		8,000–11,000
Systems Analyst		11,000–14,000
Subprofessional Assistant	6,000– 7,000	6,500– 7,500
Secretary	4,000– 5,000	4,500– 5,500
Typist-Clerk	3,500– 4,500	4,000– 5,000

influenced by geographical location and type of industry or situation, such as research institute, academic institution, public library, or government agency, each of which has its own compensating peculiarities. Trends change also. Although at one time salaries in the academic realm were not as high as in industry, by 1967 university salaries were competitive.

Periodically the Special Libraries Association surveys its members' annual salaries. Such an appraisal was made in 1969, and an elaborate analysis of the results is reported in the July/August 1970 issue of *Special Libraries* (10). All possible relationships are shown between factors such as type of employer, size of staff, work responsibilities, education, job experience, and age. The mean annual salary for a total of 3594 special libraries, noting that these are in all subject areas, was $11,800 (an increase from $9620 in 1967) a figure that was undoubtedly invalid before it was published, having already moved up in accord with all other professional salaries. The mean for subject specialists in college and university libraries was $11,900.

In order for this presentation to provide guide lines to those who are needing budget information, suggested figures for salaries for essential staff positions are hazarded in Table 1.

Budget Items Other Than Salaries

Although budget figures may vary appreciably, it is possible to cite figures for standard items to give some idea of the order of magnitude

Table 2   Suggested Budget

Items	Initial Amount ($)	Annual Amount ($)
Furniture and equipment	5,000–10,000	500
Books	3,000– 5,000	500–1,000
Subscriptions to periodicals and reference services	3,000– 6,000	3,000–6,000
Periodicals, backfiles	4,000– 5,000	1,000–2,000
Binding	400	400
Photocopies	200– 400	200– 400
Supplies	300– 400	300– 400
Special equipment, data processing, computer	500– 1,000	500–1,000
Computer tape services	500– 3,000+	500–3,000+
Travel	300– 500	300– 500
Insurance	150	150

of the total funds required. Minimum expenditures for a small library covering a restricted subject field and serving no more than 1000 potential users are suggested in Table 2. General overhead costs are not considered. Each item is discussed in some detail subsequently.

Furniture and Equipment

The essential furniture and other general equipment are specified in Chapter 4. Only costs are considered here. Though the chairs, tables, and desks designed for library use may appear to be expensive, their excellence and durability warrant purchasing. Library furniture can be used indefinitely with complete satisfaction so that it is better to make a modest beginning with a plan to add what is necessary annually. However, if large stack areas are required, a better price is possible if ordered all at once.

In 1970 some examples of prices were the following: for steel shelving $60 for an initial unit and $40 for additional ones; for a table seating four $150; for a straight chair $30; for an index table 10 feet long, 5 feet wide, with double shelf in the middle $750. It is obvious that the minimum amount mentioned in the suggested budget, namely $5000, would not provide much furniture of this type, but it could allow a start.

Books

When a library service is started, an initial sum should be designated for immediate purchase of the books known to be standard works in the fields represented. The basic reference works, handbooks, treatises, scientific dictionaries, encyclopedic sets, and monographs written by recognized authorities should be acquired first. The initial amount suggested, $3000, would not buy many volumes when the average price of scientific books is $20 and some sets such as the Beilstein *Handbuch der organische Chemie* almost $4000, but it is wise to move slowly and to make careful selection to realize maximum value from money spent. However, when these prices are compared with those of laboratory equipment, where one item can cost as much as $15,000, with the chance that a book costing $20 could provide the same information that might be determined in the laboratory, too much caution in the acquisition of books is poor economy.

Periodicals

A significant proportion of the annual budget should be spent for subscriptions to periodicals. They are of such vital importance that, should the necessity arise for a cut in the budget, other items should be sacrificed in their favor. It can be difficult ever to replace issues of certain journals in restricted subject fields because the original number printed is not more than the subscription list. Subscription prices for scientific periodicals are high, few being as little as $20, and many more than $100. The price of *Chemical Abstracts* was $1500 in 1969, $1950 in 1971.

Treating serials separately from periodicals is a matter for individual decision. These are usually issued as bound volumes, often annually, or less regularly, but they similarly are in series that are issued for an unspecified period of time. They may be grouped with periodicals or books, or may be considered as a separate category.

If the subscription list is well selected, it should not vary significantly from year to year unless it must reflect major changes in organizational interests. Allowance must be made, however, for newly published titles, and for increases in prices.

Periodicals—Back Files

Files of periodicals constitute what may be the most important area of the library's resources, and immediate efforts should be made to acquire back files of those titles that will be needed without question. A few thousand dollars can be spent very quickly, particularly for long runs of the major journals. Moreover back runs are not always readily available when wanted so that it may take several years to assemble all that are needed. Money should be set aside for this purpose or special arrangements made with a dealer who will be helpful in locating what is needed.

A major decision to be made is whether to acquire journal files in microform. An increasing number of titles are available on microfilm, and microfiche is now widely used. Storage space is saved for volumes not consulted frequently, and the improved reading devices make microforms a good solution for new libraries or for established ones in which space is diminishing.

Binding

The costs for binding depend upon the rate at which back files of periodicals in as-published form are acquired in addition to the volumes to be bound annually from current subscriptions. Sometimes back files are already bound when purchased but more frequently they are not and they should be preserved and made ready for use by prompt binding. In 1969 the price for binding a single volume 12 inches in height, 3 inches thick, in plain buckram was at least $4.25. Binding of the volumes of *Chemical Abstracts* for one year, 14 volumes, comes to about $70.

Photocopies

Two kinds of photocopy services must be provided, first, duplicating materials in hand, and second, purchasing copies of items from outside sources. Improvements in copying machines and their low cost of operation make it possible for any library to have at least one for use by staff and clientele. Such equipment is available either by renting or purchasing. The low rental charges, as little as $20 a month plus a small charge for each copy made, make this an attractive arrangement. If many articles must be ordered from other libraries, the costs can mount to a considerable figure as some charges are as high as 50¢ a page for service expenses. However, there is a trend on the part of some major libraries that do a large business in supplying photocopies to provide microform copies because this can be done at much lower prices. Phelps (11) explains why the charges for such a service as the one maintained by Engineering Societies Library must be high enough to cover the costs of the many relevant operations involved.

A publication such as a bulletin or other current awareness service provided by the library may be a budget item of several thousand dollars a year, particularly if printed covers at least are included. A centralized photoduplication service in the organization will be the most economic method for providing a bulletin.

Supplies

The particular functions administered by the library determine whether the amount required for supplies is significant. All stationery, cards, printed forms, mending materials, pamphlet boxes, and miscellaneous office supplies are included. If one or more major library bulletins are issued, the cost of mats and paper for this one purpose can come to a few hundred dollars a year.

Special Equipment

In this category come such major items as microfilm or microfiche readers or reader-printers, and any of the several types of equipment for the automation of any procedures. A reader for microforms costs as little as $300, and it may come free with a large enough order for publications in microform. A reader-printer is about $1200, although less expensive models are being designed.

Data processing equipment is usually rented, and the fees range from $275 for a terminal to $1000 a month for shared use of the central data storage facility. However, the simpler operations of IBM card punching and sorting for the preparation of special lists are much less costly.

Computer Tape Services

Computer tape services might be included with subscriptions to periodicals and reference services and are considered here as a separate item chiefly because of their high costs. Some are provided in conjunction with abstracting journals such as *Chemical Abstracts, Biological Abstracts,* and *Nuclear Science Abstracts.* Others offer selected material from the periodical literature, as for example, does the Institute for Scientific Information. Costs will range from a few hundred to more than a thousand dollars a year.

Insurance

Because the collection of publications constituting the library represents an investment that is continuously appreciating, it should be insured adequately against whatever hazards may threaten. It should be realized that fire is only one of the possible damaging agents that can do harm in a library. Water from leaking roofs or internal building failure can ruin books. Help in approaching the question of library insurance is available in several published articles. Mixer (12) outlined a procedure followed in evaluating a university collection, and though the actual values are not realistic in view of increased costs, these are readily updated. In addition to books there may be other unique items such as archival material that merit special insurance. A wise precaution is to microfilm the card catalog because it is certainly a vulnerable and irreplaceable part of the library, though with the increasing popularity of book catalogs this is not always such a great problem.

A policy for special libraries has been developed by Hartford Fire Insurance Company in 1965 (13) incorporating the features of the American Library Association approved model policy developed for the Library Testing Program.

Travel

It is good policy to provide a definite amount in the budget to enable the head of the library service to attend meetings of professional and scientific societies or even take special short courses. Other staff members also should be encouraged to be active professionally in this way because such participation enlivens personal interest in the development of the best possible information program which should involve the whole staff. Awareness of what is being done by others certainly benefits the organization that recognizes the value of providing for this kind of continuous education.

Another reason for travel may be the necessity of visiting large bibliographic centers when the resources at hand are not adequate for exhaustive literature searches. It is important also to visit other libraries occasionally to observe similar situations and discuss new developments with fellow professional associates. These travel requirements are especially important when the library is in a remote location that does not afford the kind of easy communication possible in a metropolitan area.

CONCLUSION

Final decision as to what is to be spent to make it possible for an organization to take full advantage of all published and otherwise available information should be reached after submission of a suggested budget by the head of the service to the official to whom he is directly responsible. The spending of funds should be strictly accountable.

REFERENCES

1. E. B. Gibson, "What May Be Learned from a Library Survey," *Spec. Libr.* **48**, 133–138 (1957).

2. H. S. Sharp, "A Survey of Electronics Libraries," *Spec. Libr.* **48**, 1570160 (1958).

3. W. T. Knox *et al.*, "Administration of Technical Information Groups," *Ind. Eng. Chem.* **51**, 48A–61A (1959).

4. R. S. Leonard, *Profiles of Special Libraries*, Special Libraries Association, New York, 1966, and *Spec. Libr.* **57**, 179–184, 227–231, 327–331 (1966).

5. Special Libraries Association, "Objectives and Standards for Special Libraries," *Spec. Libr.* **55**, 672–680 (1964).

6. G. E. Randall, "Special Library Standards, Statistics, and Performance Evaluation," *Spec. Libr.* **56**, 379–386 (1965).

7. *Trends in Industrial Research and Patent Practices*, National Association of Manufacturers of the United States of America, Patents and Research Committee, New York, 1948.

8. Anon, "Research: How Many $$ in 1955?" *Chem. Eng. News* **33**, 1175 (1958).

9. G. E. Randall, "Budgeting for a Company Library," *Spec. Libr.* **58**, 166–172 (1967).

10. Special Libraries Association Personnel Committee, "SLA Salary Survey 1970," *Spec. Libr.* **61**, 333–348 (1970).

11. R. H. Phelps, "Factors Affecting the Costs of Library Photocopying," *Spec. Libr.* **58**, 113 (1967).

12. C. W. Mixer, "Insurance Evaluation of a University Library's Collection," *Coll. Res. Libr.* **13**, 18–23, 29 (1952).

13. Announcement in *Spec. Libr.* **56**, 322 (1965).

BIBLIOGRAPHY

Bach, H., "Why Allocate?" *Libr. Res. Tech. Serv.* **8**, 161–165 (Spring 1964); Rebuttal, F. W. Hanes, with rejoinder, *Ibid.* **8**, 408–416 (Fall 1964).

Fazar, W., "Program Planning and Budgeting Theory: Improved Library Effectiveness by Use of the Planning-Programming-Budgeting System," *Spec. Libr.* **60**, 423–433 (1969).

Humphrey, J. A., "Survey of Library Administration, Budget and Finance," in *Library Surveys*, M. F. Tauber and I. R. Stephens, Eds., Columbia University Press, 1967, pp. 109–122.

4

Space Planning and Equipment

Planning for the most efficient use of whatever space may be allotted for library purposes should be approached as a most important task. No matter what the size, shape, or location, developing the best possible layout for the functioning units in relation to each other is very much like solving a puzzle and requires acute judgment. In addition to the advice and suggestions offered in this chapter, a similar introduction, "Library Planning," by L. J. Anthony as chapter 8 in the third edition of the Aslib *Handbook of Special Librarianship* (1) provides an excellent review of what is involved.

ASSESSMENT OF SPACE REQUIREMENTS

Before any active planning of the physical layout of the library is begun, it is advisable to study broadly the overall intention of the contemplated service. At this point the process of systems analysis can be utilized to advantage as Moore (2) advises. This method of detailed outlining of all of the steps necessary for the execution of the several operating functions is an outgrowth of the "time and motion" studies initiated in the beginning of the century to improve industrial efficiency, and refined more recently to meet the rigorous requirements of computers. Moore, in applying this discipline to the library situation states that "systems implies the total picture—from the library's objectives, its reason for being, the demands made upon it, its users' needs and requirements; the raw materials, sources of data, and kinds of information handled; the processing methods, acquisitions and indexing; and its files which serve as a link between indexing input and output. It includes the equipment and the personnel." Starting with these comprehensive ideas and developing each phase in logical outline, the space planning project can be pursued.

The decisions reached in the first round of space planning may be tentative, but they provide a starting point from which to develop the most efficient use of assigned space in an existing building or to specify what is needed in consultation with an architect who may be working on building plans. Fundamental requirements can be anticipated with fair accuracy and should reflect the basic character of the intended service. Compromises must be reached to fit limits imposed by such unalterable obstacles as dimensions or budgets. In any library service the broad requisites are (1) areas for housing the collection, (2) areas for clientele to make use of the collection, and (3) areas for administration and operations by staff members. Each of these is discussed in the subsequent parts of this chapter.

There are few libraries of the types considered here that are large enough to occupy a whole building. The majority, as services designed for a parent organization, are assigned space in a building that is adjacent to offices and laboratories, usually on one floor, or divided between two or more. The shape may be square, rectangular, L-shaped or almost any possible geometrical modification as a consequence of unavoidable architectural features. It may be in one large room or be partitioned. Whatever the space, it is strongly recommended that it be centrally located with respect to the community of potential clientele. An inconvenient location can present an insuperable drawback to a fully effective operation.

An intelligent approach to the planning problem is to take advantage of the experience of others. Visits to libraries as nearly similar to the one in prospect as possible should certainly be made if feasible. Additionally much potentially helpful information is found in many publications dealing with library planning. Even those concerned with public and university libraries can provide information useful to the smaller special situation. For example, Metcalf's book (3) on academic and research library buildings is replete with fully documented facts on much equipment and many arrangements relating to the convenient use of books and their best housing, specifications for lighting, and the many requirements of good layout. Also, Lyle's (4) *The Administration of the College Library,* as well as Wheeler and Githens's (5) *The American Pub-*

lic Library Building: Its Planning and Design, with Special Reference to Its Administration are excellent sources for ideas. Most relevant of all, however, is the publication edited by Lewis (6) entitled *Special Libraries; How to Plan and Equip Them,* which includes many photographs and illustrations, including floor plans.* The series of articles reporting the planning of new libraries published in the periodical *Special Libraries* in the 1950s and 1960s is also recommended. These sources in addition to the first-cited discussion of planning by Anthony (1) can provide a good background from which to start a project.

Additional cogent advice is to be found in the papers comprising the *Symposium on Technical Information Facilities Planning and Modification* which was sponsored by the Chemical Literature Division of the American Chemical Society in 1968. Several of the papers are in the *Journal of Chemical Documentation* for May 1968. The accounts of individual experiences in studying needs and reaching decisions could be invaluable if read at the right moment. The paper by Skolnik (7), "Designing a Technical Information Center—In Retrospect" is a good, brief delineation of the development of a major information service over a period of several years with adequate illustrations of the layout of space.

Some general advice on space planning includes the admonition to keep the ultimate layout as flexible as possible. One should avoid interior walls and use equipment to divide areas. Enough electrical outlets must be provided and the need for extra voltages for some kinds of equipment such as Xerox or other copiers anticipated. Installation of a blank conduit, especially in a new building, is advised.

It is most important at the outset to try to obtain the largest possible area for the library. It is bad economy to begin too modestly, because it is very costly to have to move books and equipment within a couple of years. It must be recognized that the volume of scientific and technical publications has been increasing steadily with no prospect of any decrease in the immediate future. The time to present strong argument for the largest space in a preferred location is before layout planning is begun; once the area is fixed the best way of utilizing it to purvey information must be achieved.

Whether to seek outside assistance from a professional consultant is a question for each individual situation. Sometimes an individual skilled in the design of libraries can be worth the fees charged if those who will administer the service are inexperienced or have not yet been em-

* Updated by *Planning the Special Library* E. Mount, ed., Special Libraries Association, New York, 1972.

ployed. The suppliers of furniture and equipment are prepared to offer some assistance though not on the same basis as a consultant. In 1969 R. R. Bowker Company published a *Directory of Library Consultants* which includes advice as to how to select and make use of such assistance in several areas of library operation including space planning. Opinions of librarians who have used consultants can be illuminating, since reports range from pro to con.

SPACE ALLOCATIONS

In the opening paragraphs of this chapter three main areas of operation were indicated as essential for a scientific information service. These are discussed in the following sections. The requirements for the principal activities are considered as units which are subsequently fitted into the available space.

Area for Housing the Collection

The overall perspective in broad planning will have provided some figures to foretell the number of volumes that are anticipated for a 5 to 10 year period at least. Book stacks to hold these volumes will be a first necessity. Standard library shelves are 3 feet wide but there are several choices of depth, from a shallow 6 inches to 12 inches to hold large periodical volumes. In figuring the number of shelves that will be needed the estimate can be based on an average of four books or three bound periodical volumes to 1 linear foot. The maximum number of shelves to a section is seven. For periodicals the average is likely to be six.

Book stacks stand as single-faced 3-foot sections against wall space, or as free-standing double-faced sections in open areas with a minimum of 3 feet of aisle between units, each of which is itself 2 feet wide so that at least 5 feet are needed for each range of stacks which can consist of from one to six sections. More than six is not recommended, although more can be used if it is considered desirable. Calculations should be as generous as possible to avoid crowded conditions for as long as possible. When shelves are too tightly filled, continuous shifting is necessary, and this is a waste of manpower.

In planning the stack areas consideration should be given to the possibility of a multilevel installation. If there is a floor-to-ceiling height of at least 15 feet, a two-level stack can be managed. Because this permits the most efficient use of square footage, it should be used if at all feasible.

Randall's (8) report on the planning of library space includes an unusually interesting example of different ways of placing book stacks in an area 61 feet by 54 feet. One arrangement allowed only 200 shelf sections, whereas a tighter but still acceptable rearrangement increased the capacity to 223 sections. The descriptions in this article of the several types of standard library shelving would be helpful to anyone who must solve a similar problem. Shelving is discussed also in a later section of this chapter.

In addition to standard stack-height shelving, some units in counter height topped with a solid working surface are likely to be useful. This is good for housing reference publications needed for brief consultation and used on the spot. Such shelving serves to divide areas or to channel traffic if this is desirable.

Another necessity is for some type of equipment to display current issues of periodicals. One economical practice is to use book shelving with as many as ten shelves hung on one section. Journals can then be stacked, three or four titles to a shelf, or shelving known as the divider-type is sometimes preferred for this purpose. Such shelves have closely spaced notches into which upright dividers can be slipped to make a neat space to fit each publication. A special type of equipment for the display of unbound periodicals provides a sloping shelf to hold single issues. This shelf may be rigid or hinged so that it can be raised to reveal storage space for the accumulated unbound issues. A unique design of equipment called Oblique Filing for this purpose features flexible hammocks hung on rods; this permits a very economical use of space. These several types are named and details given in the section of this chapter on equipment.

Filing cases are needed for pamphlet materials and correspondence. Large numbers of soft-bound items such as technical reports can be placed on divider-type shelving using as many vertical dividers as are necessary to keep things orderly. For papers, traditional drawer-type filing equipment is satisfactory or the newer side-opening style may be preferred. Any type can serve a double purpose as space dividers.

Consideration should be given to the possible necessity for a vault to secure classified materials that must be handled in conjunction with certain government-sponsored research. Strict regulations are specified for controlled access, and these involve closely guarded locking devices. Also, in many research laboratories note-book records and research reports relating to work done in the organization are kept in an area that is locked and circulated only under certain conditions. The nature and volume of these materials must not be overlooked.

There may be some other types of materials in addition to regular publication forms for which provision must be made. Among these might be the several kinds of microforms, microfilm on reels or cassettes, or in short strips; microcards, microfiches; or aperture cards. Computer tapes may be required. Also pictures, drawings, or slides are sometimes in some collections. The storing of any of these items could be either a major or a minor matter.

After preliminary investigation of the requirements for housing the various components of the collection is begun, the next step is to consider how the collection will be used.

Area for Clientele to Use the Collection

The second important area is that required for readers. It is difficult to predict with any degree of certainty how many places for library users will be in demand at one time. Influencing factors are the total number of potential readers and the locations of their laboratories or offices. If the library is in a good central location with inviting facilities, the clientele may develop the habit of consulting the materials they need right there rather than borrowing. A general guideline from which to calculate might be to provide seating for a maximum of 10% of the total clientele. This area is not to be thought of as only whatever open space there is available for tables and chairs but should include all provision for seating; a few small tables or carrels in stack areas, carrels in other areas if these are thought to be desirable, and seats at index tables or reading machines—anywhere in fact that a reader might use materials.

Tables in various sizes and shapes should be selected for different places. A medium size, about 4 by 6 feet will be the most useful. Smaller ones, the single-reader size particularly, are usually too small to accommodate more than one bound periodical volume when open. Large tables are not likely to be popular because most persons like to have a table to themselves when engaged in serious study.

In placing tables a minimum of $3\frac{1}{2}$ feet should be left between a table and a wall and 5 feet between tables. It is sometimes desirable to place tables end to end, leaving no free space between them or only a few inches. If the right types of furniture are selected, rearrangements can be made to meet readers' preferences after the service is in operation.

Whether to provide carrels of the kind designed for individual use with enclosing panels for privacy is a matter to be considered cautiously. These are not always appreciated, not even in academic situations where it might be supposed that students would like them. In libraries where research workers at times spend extended periods in the library, small enclosures to accommodate a desk are likely to be preferable. Here personal papers and a number of books can be used without disturbance until a project is completed.

Some spot in the library might be designed to be a comfortable place to spend a few minutes, perhaps browsing in current periodicals or even reading a newspaper. A few growing plants, too, add to the general atmosphere. Ways of creating an inviting setting are discussed more in Chapter 12.

Somewhere in a building where research is in active progress seminar rooms are needed for small meetings. This provision might be made in the library, possibly by installing folding doors of one type or another that can be used to partition the end of a room for short periods.

Areas for Administration

For effective administration the members of the library staff must have good places in which to do their work. In any situation there must be a general service desk. This is the information center to which all queries are directed either in person or by telephone. If books are also charged from here it can be a busy spot, depending upon the size of the total operation. In one of limited scope, other duties such as some record keeping can be done here, but in others it may be necessary to have more than one person on duty in peak periods.

If at all possible, the head of the library should have an office, or at least a desk, where some degree of privacy is afforded. Administrative duties require conferences, interviews, and telephone conversations that should not be disturbing to others. Moreover this administrator has work to do that demands concentrated effort.

Each additional staff member should have a desk situated in his own working domain. At least 40 square feet of space is desirable for each desk.

Provision should be made for a general work room in which to handle mail, prepare periodicals for binding, and any such tasks that should be performed out of sight and sound of readers. There should be running water in this room. Supply cabinets and coat racks for staff may be in this area, unless there can be a separate staff room.

Special equipment such as duplicating machines and microform readers that may be used by both staff members and clientele should be placed where they are accessible to everyone. A separate room is highly desirable with adequate control of lighting and ventilation.

It is increasingly necessary to make special provision for whatever automation equipment is used for library purposes, either initially or in the foreseeable future. Not only do the various units, from the simple card punching and collating devices to data storage systems require space, but also they are major producers of heat and noise and should therefore be placed as far away from other operations as possible.

Layout Planning

After the approximate size of the fundamental areas of activity have been estimated, rough sketches of possible layouts can be made to visualize how to best use the space available or assist an architect in designing plans for a new structure. By trying various arrangements of the basic areas, the best one will ultimately be determined. An excellent suggestion made by Joannes (9) was that at this stage one chart outlining the salient features of the overall library operation and another showing work flow or functional relationships can be very illuminating. This is in accord with Moore's (2) advice concerning the application of systems analysis.

Some general principles to be kept in mind are first that the service area where circulation and reference activities are conducted should be immediately evident to anyone entering the room. Consideration should be given to the desirability of multiple entrances because in some situations there are reasons for controlling access. In others it is highly desirable to have more than one means of entry for the convenience of patrons. Book stacks should be positioned with the thought in mind that both staff members and readers will want to get to them as easily as possible. The card catalog and indexing publications must also be accessible to everyone. Aesthetics may have to give way to expedience.

Furniture and equipment should be used for partitioning areas where possible. Where these cannot serve, demountable metal units that are simple to install and change will enclose whatever areas are required. The eventual necessity to shift and change in response to the growth of the collection and size of staff should be anticipated. Movable walls are much easier to cope with than are permanent ones.

In studying the several major areas of operation various arrangements suggest themselves until the right one is achieved, and it is likely that it will incorporate a number of unwanted compromises. It is useful during this process to make cut-outs to scale of the furniture and equipment because these can be changed more readily than drawings. For large scale planning it is worthwhile to procure the miniature models available from M & M Industries, South Milwaukee, Wis., P.O. Box 91. These are actual scale models of such items as book stacks, tables, desks, and chairs. The functions of the library must be fully comprehended by those who execute the specifications, and it is an important responsibility for the librarian to be able to communicate effectively with architects or building supervisors.

Layouts of some well-planned libraries are shown in Figures 1 to 3. Photographs of some libraries in action are illustrated in Figures 4 and 5.

Placing of Books and Periodicals

A very important feature of space planning is the relative placement of the various types of publications. Reference volumes used most often should be within easy reach of the main desk and telephone. In fact, some of these, such as certain handbooks and dictionaries, may be kept at this desk. Other reference publications ought to be in this vicinity too, unless the operation is large enough to have a separate reference section with a staff member usually present.

As has been indicated previously, the files of indexing and abstracting publications are used with greatest convenience if they are grouped together in one area. If wall space is available the "abstract bar" arrange-

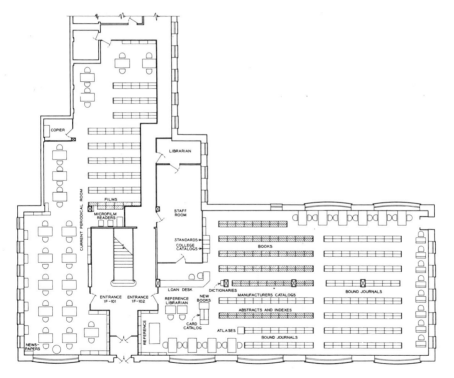

Figure 1. Technical Information Library, Bell Telephone, Murray Hill, N.J.

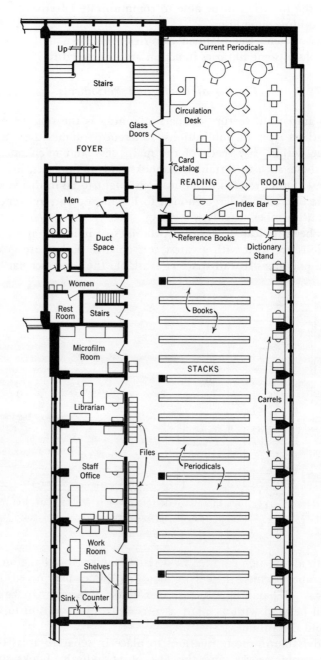

Figure 2. Ford Motor Company Engineering Staff Library.

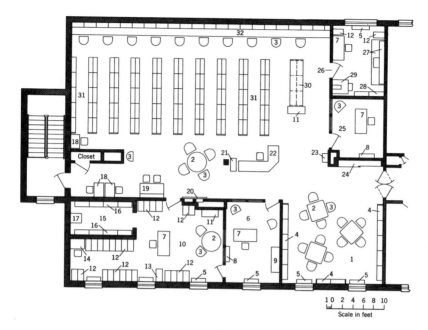

KEY TO FLOOR PLAN

1. Current periodical area
2. Reading tables
3. Arm chairs
4. Periodical display rocks
5. Air conditioning units
6. Librarian's office
7. Library staff desk
8. Counter-high book shelves
9. Credenza
10. Documents room
11. Card catalogs
12. Filing cases
13. Correspondence tray and stand
14. Microfilm reader
15. Fireproof vault
16. Shelving for vertical filing
17. Microfilm cabinet
18. Carrel desks
19. Encyclopedia table
20. Bulletin board and periodical list
21. Book truck
22. Charging desk
23. Dictionary stand
24. Dord Hunter display case
25. Assistant Librarian's office
26. Workroom
27. Cupboards for supplies— sink
28. Book stacks
29. Kordex cabinet and table
30. Counter-high shelving for vertical filing
31. Book and bound periodicals stack area
32. Abstract bar

Figure 3. Mead Corporation Library. The total area is 3360 square feet. Seating capacity is 35, exclusive of the library staff.

ment, with a desk-high counter, or desk-size shelves that hang on shelving supports, above which shelves for bound volumes are placed, is an excellent way of handling files of indexes or abstracts. Or large index tables can be used with as many as two shelves in addition to the table top to hold the volumes.

It is advisable in most situations to place in separate areas the books or monographic works, and the files of periodicals. Books should, of

Figure 4. Charles C. Lauritsen Library, Aero Space Corporation. (interior, upper level).

course, be on the shelves in order of classification number. Periodicals may be classified and shelved according to number, but this is not as necessary. These volumes can be shelved alphabetically by title or grouped in any other way if an index to locations is provided. Periodicals should be as near as possible to the indexing and abstracting guides to their contents.

The question of how to deal with unbound issues of periodicals is handled in different ways, according to the preference of those who administer the particular situation. If there is room to keep them with the current issues, they may be stored there until they are bound. If not, readers prefer them put with the bound files rather than in a less accessible storage spot. However, the possibility of losses must be considered because it is not always easy to replace single issues.

In some libraries the cumulative indexes to those periodicals that publish them are kept in the vicinity of the abstracting-indexing publications rather than with the individual titles to which they relate. This

Figure 5. Library, Federal Aviation Administration, Southern Region, Atlanta, Ga.

makes it more likely that they will be noticed and used at those times when they might be helpful.

Another increasingly significant category of publications that may merit a section of its own in the library is the review serial—the "Advances in . . . ," "Progress in . . . ," "Annual Review of . . . ," and their like. Their potential usefulness may be increased if they are brought to attention by being placed in one area. The individual chapters in these valuable publications comprise critical summaries of specific topics that provide quick introductions to subjects about which there is such a large amount of information in the recent literature that it would be difficult to assess without lengthy searching.

All factors must be considered judiciously in developing the plan for placement of these natural divisions of the collection. Their most effective use may depend in large measure upon the artfulness of their arrangement.

Provision for Pamphlets and Other Individual Items

Filing cabinets and divider-type shelving have already been mentioned for housing materials such as pamphlets and correspondence. Special boxes designed to hold small, soft cover items are very convenient. Unusual materials in the form of photographs, slides, and maps will be best preserved and used if they are kept in suitable files. These will not be in any one area, but should be easy to reach for staff, clientele, or both.

LIGHTING

In developing the plan for the areas of activity the important factor of proper illumination must be kept in mind. Windows will have some influence on the placement of some equipment, but it is not necessary to consider them as a source of light because of the availability of a variety of equipment for artificial lighting. Book stacks can always be relegated to areas that must be lighted artificially at all times. The general type of lighting will be determined quite possibly by the kind used in the building where the library space is located. However, the units should be positioned so that the illumination is effectively directed. Shadows on the bottom shelves of book stacks can be very annoying, especially if they might have been easily avoided.

Opinions vary as to the best type of artificial light. The fluorescent variety has found increasing acceptance, particularly since the tone has been modified to make it more like natural light. There are some individuals, however, who are sensitive to it and who must not be exposed to it for prolonged periods. After some study of this problem at the Graduate School of Business of Harvard University Holway and Jameson (10) suggested that fluorescent tubes should be shielded to deflect the ultraviolet rays since these appeared to be the only tangible source of physical annoyance.

In the book on library planning Metcalf (3) discusses the matter of lighting in detail, telling the advantages and disadvantages of the two principal types, fluorescent and incandescent. Cost is one of the main advantages of the former; the tubes use little current and are long lived. In some situations a combination of the two types provides a pleasing effect. In addition to ceiling fixtures a few table lamps add to the attractiveness of a reading area.

Because lighting is so critical for the comfortable use of printed materials, thorough study of requirements for a particular library is imperative. Kraenbuehl (11) has made excellent suggestions as to the quality and quantity of illumination needed for various types of library-related activities. The Committee on Library Lighting of the Illuminating Engineering Society published recommendations in 1950, among which was a minimum of 30 foot candles for reading areas and was reported to be working on a revision of its standards in 1967 (12). Metcalf (3) commented upon the steady increase in the number of foot-candles advised by experts, citing that whereas 70 foot candles were proposed in 1959, this has since been increased to over 100, an amount that could well cause discomfort to some persons. One important overall objective is to achieve as glare-free a condition as possible.

AIR-CONDITIONING

It is now recognized that the atmosphere in which books—and people —are housed should be controlled. For the sake of their physical preservation books should not be exposed to extreme conditions of temperature and humidity. Gates (13) recommends that books be kept where temperatures vary no more than from 65 to 75°F, and the humidity from 30 to 50%. Also, it is highly desirable to filter dirt from the air before it sifts onto receptive volumes. Precleaning of the atmosphere precludes the eventual necessity of dusting books and other surfaces.

FLOORING

The question of what kind of floor covering to install is a more important feature than might be recognized at first thought. Factors to consider are the well-being of those staff members who must walk miles in the course of their work, the problem of noise on hard surfaces, aesthetic appearance, and the no small matter of cleaning. If there is the possibility of choice, consideration should be given to carpeting, at least for those areas where there is much traffic. The care of carpet may actually be less difficult than is the keeping in proper condition of other types of floor covering. However, linoleum, rubber tile, vinyl tile, and similar materials can be entirely satisfactory. Whatever is used, the color should add to the decor as much as possible. The whole matter of flooring has been fully investigated and reported in extensive detail as a *Library Technology Project Publication* (14). Expert advice on maintenance procedures for all materials is included.

FURNITURE AND EQUIPMENT

Suggestions are made here for the various kinds of furniture and equipment that are primary requirements. Although manufacturers are mentioned, this does not necessarily imply unqualified recommendation.

Nothing is cited, however, unless it is thought to have some merit. The individual purchaser must make his own discriminating investigation before committing his orders.

For sources of information concerning such items the aforementioned comprehensive work by Metcalf (3) can be very helpful for its authoritative descriptions of standard types of equipment. The *Library Journal* reports continuously on things newly marketed and publishes also a *Buyers' Guide*. The *Bowker Annual* is another good compilation. Excellent surveys of special items such as microform readers and copying machines appear from time to time in the magazine *Administrative Management*. When planning to equip a library it is advisable to locate the nearest dealer who handles major furnishings either by writing to headquarters offices of manufacturers or consulting telephone directories. The *Thomas Register of Manufacturers* is the most inclusive listing of the makers of all kinds of manufactured articles. Advertisers in library journals also supply good leads.

A very significant service devoted to the examination of library equipment has been in existence long enough to have issued a collection of authoritative reports on various broad categories. This is known as the Library Technology Program that is sponsored by the American Library Association, 50 East Huron Street, Chicago, Ill. 60611. Its broad purpose is to test and compare all kinds of processes, materials, and devices that are in large-scale use in libraries. It is here, for example, that it is possible to learn what kind of book truck will roll easily over carpet. A list of publications issuing from the program is available. They cover such topics as photocopiers, binding methods, book stacks, and circulation systems.

The broad categories of furniture and equipment required for efficient operation of a library service are outlined and discussed in the following sections of this chapter.

Furniture

The essential items of furniture include the following:

1. Tables and chairs for clientele.   The number and size of the tables will be determined by the space allotted for readers as well as by individual preferences. The most generally useful size is about 4×6 feet rather than either the very small or large sizes. Some individual seating either as carrels or small tables should be worked into the arrangement near book stacks, or in otherwise unless corners where they are likely to be wanted. Some tables of special design for a specific purpose such as for indexes are tables with double-faced shelving in the middle, one or

even two shelves high. These can provide an effective area for using indexes and abstracts. If there is good wall space a so-called abstract bar can be built using standard book stack shelving with a table-high counter for consultation of the volumes placed above it on the shelves.

Chairs can be tested for comfort by obtaining samples and having a number of persons try them. As a rule, a straight, armless chair is best suited for use at tables, though a newer one having short arms is finding increasing favor. Some lounge chairs, particularly in the area where current periodicals are shelved, will entice readers. A few stools in some places, perhaps near the card catalog, or a bench with padded top as a convenient seat or partial traffic divider are sometimes worth consideration.

2. Desks and chairs for staff members. Every staff member with special tasks to perform should have his own desk and chair of a type to suit his duties. The head of the service may require a large, executive style desk to accommodate the major projects pertinent to his position. Some desks should accommodate typewriters. An extra work table may be needed in some offices.

Chairs should be carefully selected to suit the individual and the desk at which it is to be used to encourage good working performance with minimum fatigue. The only real test for a chair is to try it.

3. Central control desk. The main service desk must be designed so that all functions centering in its area can be executed. A multiplicity of activities may have to be conducted here, particularly in a one- or two-man operation. Records of book loans, answers to telephoned queries, assistance to persons coming in for help, are the kinds of things that will be done at this central desk. If the volume of such work is not great, ordinary office desks may serve, but it is likely that several units of the type made for large libraries may be more efficient. These are usually of counter height, and it may be desirable to use several of these in conjunction with a desk-high unit because this is preferable for consultations. Provision must be made here for whatever type of special book charging equipment is used, up to the inclusion of terminals for an automated system. On such a scale, other activities such as reference service will certainly be given at another location. It is most important that this central service unit be developed by the head of the library service or other principal staff member, and not by an unaided architect.

4. Card catalog. A primary necessity in most libraries is a unit of card-filing drawers designed specifically to meet library specifications for 7.5 by 12.5 centimeter cards and equipped with holding-rods. This may be of either the traditional wood or the newer plastic which is finding increasing acceptance. The units come in a range of sizes, from four drawers

up to as many as sixty. A start can be made with a fifteen drawer catalog on a base at counter height and eventually add another on top of it. Or only counter height might be acquired because of the convenience of being able to use the tops for consulting the drawers. Before determining how many drawers are wanted it may be wise to consider all of the possible files that might be accommodated in this way. Such things as special indexes that accumulate gradually may be assigned space in this catalog if foresighted planning allows.

5. Special furniture items. (*a*) A stand for an unabridged dictionary with space below for a few other reference books is a worthwhile convenience. (*b*) A rack for the display of newly acquired books that can be placed in an eye-catching spot is worth consideration. A book truck, especially one with a sloping top shelf can also be used for this purpose. (*c*) An exhibit case for display of a possibly wide range of items, from some of purely historical significance to a collection of reprints of articles published by members of the organization is highly desirable if there is space and money for something not strictly utilitarian.

Some Manufacturers of Library Furniture

The Buckstaff Company, 1127 S. Main St., Oshkosh, Wisc. 54901.
Gaylord Brothers, Inc., P.O. Box 61, Syracuse, N. Y. 13201. Also in Stockton, Calif.
W. H. Gunlocke Chair Company, Wayland, N. Y.; Whittier, Calif., Dallas, Tex.
Knoll Associates, 320 Park Ave., New York, N. Y. 10022.
Library Bureau, Remington Rand Office Systems, 801 Park Ave., Herkimer, N. Y. 13350.
Myrtle Desk Company, High Point, N. Carolina 27261.
Harry Probber, Inc., 979 4th Ave., New York, N. Y. 10016.
Jens Risom, Inc., 444 Madison Ave., New York, N. Y. 10022; Fall River, Mass.
Sjostrom USA, Library Furniture, 1717 North Tenth St., Philadelphia, Pa. 19122.
Steelcase, Inc., 1120 36th St., S. E., Grand Rapids, Mich. 49508.
The Worden Company, Holland, Mich. 49423.

Shelving

Shelving that is specifically designed to hold books is strongly recommended. It may be of either wood or steel although steel has a greater capacity and is easier to maintain and manipulate. In order to achieve a more gracious appearance some units of incidental shelving such as counter-height sections for special reference works might be of wood.

All types of book shelving should be investigated before the selection is final. The greater portion will be the standard ordinary shelf type, with attention given to having an adequate number of shelves 10 or 12 inches deep to hold large volumes of periodicals, but there is likely to be need for some special kinds such as the divider type. This has closely spaced notches into which upright dividers can be slipped to hold up pamphlet material or current issues of periodicals. Manufacturers' catalogs are freely available and should be studied to learn about both the standard and innovative types of shelving for books and other library materials.

Although it does not exactly fit the category of shelving, its purpose is so similar that a unique idea for holding unbound, pamphlet-type items is mentioned here. Its chief feature is an open-ended hammock to which metal rings are attached to be hung on rods that attach to uprights similar to those from which book shelves are hung. These holders come in a variety of sizes up to one large enough to hold newspapers. They provide a sure means for keeping limp papers neatly vertical. The name of this system is Oblique Filing, available from Robert P. Gillotte & Co., Inc., P.O. Box 5735, 2230 Commerce Drive, Columbia, S. Carolina 29205.

In planning a total layout for a library, consideration should be given to the desirability of providing more than one means for housing books. Most collections include a significant number of volumes that are used rarely but which are important enough that they should be within reach. If they are not to be replaced by microforms, they can be kept more economically on a type of shelving called compact or storage shelving. Its purpose is to make possible the storing of almost twice as many volumes in a given space by such means as fastening two sections of shelving to fit together so that one swings open when something is wanted. In large installations stacks can be placed on rails and thus run tightly in a solid block with access dependent upon a motor drive. Simpler storage shelving can be worth consideration in any situation. Even ordinary shelves, in particular, those 12 inches deep, can be used as a kind of compaction device by shelving small volumes two deep, thus doubling capacity.

Some Manufacturers of Library Shelving

W. R. Ames Company, Shelving Division, 1001 Dempsey Road, Milpitas, Calif. 95035; representatives in principal cities.

Art Metal, Inc., Jamestown, N. Y. 14701.

Bro-Dart Industries, P.O. Box 923, Williamsport, Pa. 17704, and 56 Earl St., Newark, N. J. 07114.

Demco, Box 1488, Madison, Wisc. 53701.

Estey Corporation, Wayside & Shafto Roads, North Shrewsbury, N. J. 07725.

Globe-Wernicke Company, 12 Worth St., New York, N. Y. 10013; 1505 Jefferson Ave., Toledo, Ohio 43364.

Hamilton Manufacturing Company, 1935 Evan St., Two Rivers, Wisc. ("Compo," a storage type).

Library Bureau, Remington Rand Office Systems, 122 East 42nd St., New York, N. Y.
    10017; 801 Park Ave., Herkiner, N. Y. 13350, also in principal cities.
Republic Steel Corporation, Manufacturing Division, Youngstown, Ohio 44505.
Stackson (Formerly C. S. Brown & Co.), 7535 Hillcrest Drive, Wawatosa, Wis.
Virginia Metal Products, Division of Gray Manufacturing Co., Orange, Va. 22960.

Filing Equipment

Filing provision must be made for many kinds of materials, from ordinary correspondence to microform copies of various formats, and for all of these, numerous types of systems and equipment have been designed. Some of the types available are suggested here.

In any situation there is need for standard office filing cabinets, either the pull-out drawer type or the newer styles that open from the side are somewhat easier to use. These side-filing cabinets can be stacked to take full advantage of floor space and also act as a needed partition. Suppliers of office equipment can provide full details, or in a large organization, the central purchasing office has such information. Consera-filer, supplied by Supreme Equipment and Systems Corp., 170 53rd St., Brooklyn, N. Y. 11232, is one good lateral filing type.

For the filing of cards, the basic card catalog has already been mentioned, but there may quite possibly be other kinds of cards for which special provision must be made. Small rotary files with cards, perhaps 2 by 3 inches, that snap in place easily are useful to indicate locations of special collections of reference materials or of periodicals. There are many makers of such devices, among them Roll-dex, and they are sold in office equipment establishments. For accommodation of large numbers of cards there are motorized units such as the Kard-veyer sold by the Library Bureau of Remington Rand.

It has already been suggested that pamphlet materials might be kept on divider-type shelving or in the Oblique hammocks. However, for smaller collections, pamphlet boxes of various kinds are almost certainly needed. Designs differ slightly. Some are open top and front; others have one side only open; some have a slanted opening. Some are more rigid than others, hence more expensive. The least costly are in two pieces that come folded flat to be assembled as needed. Some of the satisfactory ones are supplied by the following firms:

Bro-Dart, P.O. Box 923, Williamsport, Pa. 17704; designed according to ALA Technology Project specifications, three sizes.
Demco Library Supplies, Box 1488, Madison, Wisc.; Box 4231, Hamden, Conn. 06514; Box 1586, Fresno, Calif.; economy pamphlet storage boxes, shipped flat.
The Gaylord Company, Syracuse, N. Y. The Gaylord Princeton File, also steel cabinets for slides, microforms, and tapes.

The Magafile Company, P.O. Box 3121, St. Louis, Mo. 63103; two parts to be creased and fitted, thirteen heights, three widths.
The National Metal Edge Box Company, 344 North 12th St., Philadelphia, Pa.

Microforms of the several types now in use require equipment or cabinets designed especially for each kind. It was once thought that film required carefully controlled temperature and moisture conditions, but as long as the ordinary situation does not range to extremes there is little deterioration. Two companies that supply storage cabinets for film are the Recordak Corporation, subsidiary of Eastman Kodak Company, and Microcard Editions, Publishing Division of Microcard Corporation, subsidiary of National Cash Register Company, 901 26th St., N.W. Washington, D.C. 20037.

Short strips of microfilm may be put into pockets and filed in drawers. Some specially designed devices are cited later in this chapter under indexing equipment.

Microfiche in large quantity can be filed in cabinets, but for a small number a method such as is offered by Boorum & Pease Company, 84 Hudson Ave., Brooklyn, N. Y. 100201, is convenient. The idea is based on an easel-type three-ring binder with sheets of heavy paper so designed that units of microfiche, tab cards, aperture cards, or microfilm images slip in in such a way that they can be readily selected. Top edges are visible. Microfiche should always be in protective covers or envelopes.

Slides or transparencies require special filing cases if they are part of a collection. Uniquely designed equipment is available from the Technicon Company, 215 East 149th St., New York, N. Y. 10051. Portable slide boxes are useful for lending a selection of slides. For small numbers they can be used for storing. Cabinets of special design for filing, storing, and editing transparencies and negatives is sold by Elden Enterprises, P.O. Box 4201, Charleston, West Virginia 25332.

Record-Keeping Equipment for Periodicals

There are several systems for keeping records of periodicals—current issues as they are received and back files of bound or otherwise preserved volumes. Choice depends upon the number of titles to be accommodated, on whether the record is to be consulted by staff only or by staff and clientele, and ultimately the personal preference of the person deciding how this should be done. For a collection of more than 1000 titles, consideration might be given to a computer system for handling the complete record, from notation of receipt of single issues to the binding of complete volumes. The most popular manual system is based on a unit card, one for each title and on them a complete record is noted. The cards are filed in special holders so that they overlap, leaving only the titles visible. Any kind of card file can be utilized, either rotary, arc type, or even simple index cards for a very small number of titles. The record for each title must be complete and include the exact title, space for noting receipt of issues, indication of location if necessary, note of complete holdings, and record of when volumes are sent to the bindery. It may be desirable also to have here subscription records—where ordered, when paid for, and when renewals are due.

Some types of equipment and their suppliers are the following:

Acme Visible Records, Acme Visible Records, Inc., General Offices. Crozet, Va.; printed forms are filed in book-type holders or trays in such manner that a quarter of an inch, enough upon which to type a title, is left visible. There are other types such as the Flexoline, adaptable for library purposes. Rotary ones are either manual or equipped with a motor.

Demco Visible File. Demco Supplies. 110 S. Caroll St., Madison, Wisc. 53701, or 83 Wallace St., New Haven, Conn.; printed card forms, fitting into overlapping holders, filed in trays leaving edges visible; interchangeable with Kardex and other systems.

Kardex, Library Bureau of Remington Rand Systems (Division of Sperry Rand Corp.), 122 East 42nd St., New York, N. Y. 10017; printed record cards similar to Demco for use in book-type covers or steel units holding trays. They market also Victor Sectional equipment in which the same cards and holders fit. One major advantage is that a start can be made with only one tray plus top and bottom sections to which additional trays can be added as needed. One tray holds fifty cards.

Wheeldex, Wheeldex & Simpla Products, Inc., 425 Fourth Ave., Corner 29th St., New York, N. Y. 10016; this is a ferris-wheel type of device, to the hub of which cards attach by shallow notches. The wheel turns for easy consultation and permits filing of large numbers of cards in a minimum of space. A range of sizes available.

Card-o-Guides, Diebold, Inc., 828 Mulberry Road S. E., Canton, Ohio; offers several types of equipment; among them a device in the shape of an arc to which notched cards attach securely yet are readily removed. Some models equipped with motors.

The aforementioned examples suggest some of the methods that can be adopted for the keeping of records of periodicals or any other kinds of materials that must be added to frequently and easy to consult.

Microform Readers and Reader-Printers

Many satisfactory microform reading machines are on the market, with new and improved features being developed steadily. In ordinary library use, however, a machine lasts a long time and rarely needs to be replaced because of obsolescence. Circumstances, of course, may require the most up-to-date capabilities, and it is then advisable to provide the most efficient model.

When there is intention to purchase a reading device all potential requirements should be surveyed. Will a machine that can be used only for reading suffice or will it be preferable to have one that can be used both for reading and making of legible copies of selected pages? Perhaps both will be needed. For sound background information, *Guide to Microreproduction Equipment,* 4th edition (with Supplement, 1970) by H. W. Ballou, published by the National Microfilm Association in 1969, is an excellent source. A compilation of all readers and printers on the market in 1969 with names of makers and models is provided by the magazine *Administrative Management* in its April 1969 issue.

Some reading machines are small enough to be readily portable and can be used at a desk in moderately subdued light. The large models may be equipped with motors for quick transport of film, a highly desirable feature when long films must be read or searched. Some systems permit the preselection of a frame at which the transporting mechanism will stop. Consideration should be given to the need for using a reader for more than one size of film, usually 16 or 35 millimeter, or whether other forms such as aperture cards should be accommodated. All of these aspects should be investigated before purchasing decisions are reached. Prices range from about $200 to $1500 or more.

In addition to the making of copies the same size as the original there may be good reason to produce reduced-size copies in one microform or another. Microfilm is the oldest type and has long been used for library purposes, for such applications as the recording of laboratory notebooks but its potentialities for other possibilities are endless. For example, Devlin (15) reports that the filming of all incoming correspondence is proving to be a superior method for its control at Esso Production Research Company. It is also readily feasible to develop microfiche systems, or even to prepare microfiche from microfilm according to a system developed, for instance, by Business Systems Markets Division of Eastman Kodak Company. Equipment to do such tasks may be either rented or purchased outright, depending upon various factors such as relative costs and whether needs are continuous or sporadic.

Duplicating Equipment

In any library it is necessary to provide some kind of equipment for making copies of materials easily and inexpensively. In view of the continuous developments and improvements of methods for reproducing printed pages this is now readily possible. There is likely to be need for duplicating both typed and printed copy in quantities from as few as one or two to as many as several hundred. Specific examples include catalog cards and index file cards, pages for a library bulletin, and special forms such as routing slips and personal notification slips. A major copying activity is the supplying of articles from periodicals for the convenience of readers. It is likely to be desirable to have a copying machine available for clientele to use themselves as well as another one for library staff.

Many large organizations have a central duplicating service. This can be called upon for doing copying jobs of such complexity or scale that they should not be undertaken by the less skilled library staff. For example, if several hundred copies of the library bulletin are required and there are more than a few pages to be assembled, this service should be used.

When duplicating equipment is to be purchased for the library all of the potential requirements should be considered. Some machines can reproduce only from specially prepared mats thus limiting their application to typed materials only. Others will handle either typed or printed items, but will produce only one copy from a matrix. Certain equipment can take single sheets only, thus precluding its use for periodicals, whereas other types can be used for both purposes. If the volume of work to be done is great enough, two machines with different capabilities may be desirable.

In recent years there have been many developments resulting in new processes for providing rapid copying of graphic materials as well as improvements in older processes. In fact, new models of long available equipment are being introduced continuously. Evidence of the activity in this area is attested by the extensive bibliographies relating to new happenings compiled and published from time to time by Kiersky (16) and usually published in the journal *Special Libraries*. Hawken (17) has provided good descriptions of the techniques involved in the several chief types of copying devices, and the evaluations of the performances of the machines on the market in 1961 are a good guide to what to watch for in deciding which machine to purchase for a library purpose.

Now so many copying machines are available that it is not practical to attempt in so brief a presentation to make specific recommendations. Of electrostatic devices alone there were almost 100 models being offered in 1969. Two comprehensive surveys of all types including offset, spirit, stencil, electrostatic, diazo, diffusion, and thermographic appear in *Administrative Management* for January and December 1968. There are tabulations that give the names of makers and models with indications of the performance possibilities. The next step is to locate a dealer in such equipment, locally if possible.

Costs of copying equipment range from as little as $30.00 for the most simple type to more than $1000 for a sturdy, efficient machine to produce many copies quickly. Some are available on a rental basis which can be an economic arrangement, particularly because the responsibility for keeping a machine in good operating order rests with its owner.

Equipment for Nonconventional Indexing and Filing

Application of one of the newer nonconventional filing and indexing systems requires the use of special kinds of cards, in most instances, that may be handled either manually or mechanically. Investigation of such methods is necessary when the scale of operations is so large that traditional methods do not suffice. Attention is directed to Chapter 8 where the broad subject of indexing and filing is treated in some detail. Here some of the various types of equipment are cited. Inquiries should be made to those companies that have developed methods that might suit the situation in hand. Help and advice will be given to achieve satisfaction in the installation of a system. Some operate under a license agreement only and payment is in rental fees. For a detailed discussion with illustrations of equipment, see Chapter 8 of *Methods of Information Handling* by Bourne, Wiley (1963).

Indexing Equipment

Manual Systems

EDGE-NOTCHED CARDS—NEEDLE SORTING

E-Z sort: E-Z Sort Systems, Ltd., 351 Bryant St., San Francisco, Calif. 94107.

Findex: W. K. Walthers, Inc., 1245 N. Water St., Milwaukee, Wisc.

Zatocard: Zator Co., 140½ Mt. Auburn St., Cambridge, Mass.

Flexisort system: Superior Business Machines, Inc., 285 Madison Ave., New York, N. Y. 10017.

Keysort: Royal McBee Corp., Port Chester, N. Y.; also in other cities.

Needlesort: Arizona Tool and Die Co., 31 East Rillito St., Tucson, Ariz.

FIELD-PUNCHED CARDS—NEEDLE OR OPTICAL SORTING

Termatrex; Jonker Business Machines, Inc., P. O. Box 265, 404 N. Frederick Ave., Gaithersburg, Md.

Omnidex: Howard Benson, P. O. Box 825, Pomona, Calif.

Keydex: Royal McBee Corp., 850 Third Ave., New York, N. Y. 10022.

Uniterm cards: Documentation, Inc., 4833 Rugby Ave., Bethesda, Md. 20014, and American Institute of Chemical Engineers.

Combination Indexing and Filing Systems

FOR FILM COPIES

Aperture cards (for single frames or short strips).

Filmsort, Inc., 50 South Pearl St., Pearl River, N. Y. 10965; edge-notched or IBM-type card.

Royal McBee Corp., Port Chester, N. Y.; edge-notched or IBM type cards.

Remington Rand Corp., 315 Fourth Ave., N. Y.

International Business Machines Co., 590 Madison Ave., New York, N. Y. 10022; IBM cards.

2. Microfiche files.

Documentation Incorporated, 4833 Rugby Ave., Bethesda, Md. 20014.

Microdocumentation Division, Docuform system.

Recordak Division, Eastman Kodak Company, Rochester, N.Y. 14680.

3. Jacket cards (for short strips).

Filmsort, Inc., 50 South Pearl St., Pearl River, N. Y. 10965.

Ohio Envelope Company, 341 Calhoun St., Cincinnati, Ohio, Vis-a-jac.

N.B. Jackets Corp., 31–35 31st St., Long Island City, N. Y. 11106.

4. Positive prints, made from microfilm for applying on cards.

Microstrip: Hall and McChesney, 1233 Oswego Blvd., Syracuse, N. Y.

Microtape: The Microcard Corp., 365 South Oak St., West Salem, Wisc.

5. Reels of microfilm.

Rapid Selector: U. S. National Bureau of Standards, Documents on 35-mm microfilm with identifying code in dots beside frame for selection by electronic scanner; prototype model only.

Filmorex: 74 Rue des Saints-Peres, Paris, France; system similar to rapid selector.

Miracode: material copied on microfilm stored in cassettes for instantaneous retrieval of any needed item; Recordak Corp., Business Systems Markets Division, subsidiary of Eastman Kodak Company.

6. Minicard.

A unique system developed by Recordak Corp., subsidiary of Eastman Kodak that features tiny chips of film upon which are recorded complete documents; these are filed on rods from which individual items can be selected.

SYSTEMS STORING DOCUMENT IMAGES—INDEXES SEPARATE

1. CRIS: Command Retrieval Information System, Information Retrieval Corporation, 1000 Connecticut Ave., Washington, D. C.

2. VERAC: Avco Corporation, Electronics and Ordnance Division, Cincinnati, Ohio.

Machine Systems

Machine systems comprise the complex array of components relating to or deriving from a computer base. Developments in the application to information handling or other library operations of such magnitude that they cannot be coped with by manual methods are being handled by computers. So much, however, is happening in this area that the *Annual Review of Information Science and Technology* can scarcely keep pace. It is not likely that a library will have enough activity to warrant the installation of a complete computer facility for its own use, but its business may be welcomed at the organization's central installation. However, certain units such as card punchers and sorters are economic in some situations.

Among the companies supplying data processing equipment adaptable for retrieval of the kind of information that is published in the scientific-technical literature are the following:

Behnson-Lehner, Santa Monica, Calif.
Burroughs Corporation, Research Center, Paoli, Pa.
General Electric, GE Information Systems Section 290-38, 1 River Road, Schenectady, N. Y. 12305.
Honeywell, Computer Control Division, Framingham, Mass. 01701.
IBM, International Business Machines, Corporation, 590 Madison Ave., New York, N. Y. 10022.
RCA Computers, Cherry Hill, N. J. 08034.
Remington Rand, Inc., Division of Sperry Rand Corporation, Univac Division, 315 Fourth Ave., New York, N. Y. 10010.

MISCELLANEOUS SUPPLIES AND EQUIPMENT

Catalogs issued by library supply houses should be obtained and studied for suggestions of items that could make the operation of the library more efficient. The most active of these companies are the following:

Bro-Dart Industries, 56 Earl St., Newark, N. J.; 520 King St. West, Toronto, Canada.
Educational Corp., Dept. E-4, Library Supply Division, Box 1488, Madison, Wisc. 53701.
Demco Library Supplies, P.O. Box 1772, New Haven, Conn.
Gaylord Brothers, Inc., Syracuse, N. Y. 13201, and Stockton, Calif. 95201.
Library Bureau of Remington Rand, Inc., 315 Fourth Ave., New York, N. Y. 10010, offices in other cities also.
Library Efficiency Corp., 36–38 West 20th St., New York, N. Y. 10011.

Some of the more obviously necessary miscellaneous items are these:

1. Bulletin board.
2. Dictionary stand with top for large reference volume and shelves below for some smaller ones. Several revolving stands to be placed on tables or counter-height shelving units can be useful.
3. Book trucks. Care should be taken to select trucks that are well constructed and suitable to the terrain over which they must travel, such as carpeted floors. Perhaps one with a book trough for display of a selected groups of books; for instance, recent acquisitions, or some to be used for a special project, is worth considering.
4. Storage cabinet. A metal one for office supplies is convenient. Built-in cabinets in the work room, even the kind designed for kitchens, are very useful.
5. Stool or ladder for reaching high shelves, as many as may be required.

6. A few materials for mending torn paper and preserving bindings before they deteriorate too badly. An excellent product for mending torn paper or covering worn pages is Perma-film that bonds to a paper surface with slight pressure. Available from Henry G. Lissauer, 79 Fifth Ave., New York, N. Y. 10003.

There are other similar products, but the ordinary pressure tapes, cellulose acetate, should be avoided because they are not designed to last permanently. Another necessity is the cloth-like adhesive mending tape that comes in several widths. The wider ones are economic because they can be cut to desired sizes. Among the trade names are Mystik Cloth Tape, sold by Gaylord Brothers, Fastape from Demco Library Supplies, and Book-Aid from Bro-Dart Industries. The liquid plastic adhesive is another excellent mending aid because it dries to leave a clear film. It is useful for tipping-in loose pages, mending bindings, and such things as fastening several issues of periodicals together if this is desirable. Some of the trade names are Book-Saver, Magic Mend, Bind Art, Elmer's Glue.

Any library is likely to be faced with the task of caring for a heterogeneous collection of materials in forms other than the traditional book, some of which may present real problems in locating the proper storage equipment. One such situation may be the keeping of classified documents that must be kept in locked cabinets, and for these the Mosler Safe Company, 1401 Wilson Blvd., Arlington, Va., 22209, is prepared to provide a variety of safe-type cabinets.

CONCLUSION

The effective allocation of space is one of the most important of the initial tasks to be performed in planning a library service. In fact it is likely to be a continuous activity as changes must be made to accommodate the growth of the collection and development of various functions. Every possible source of assistance should be exploited in designing even the most modest of libraries. Among these are publications dealing with the subject, manufacturers' literature, and most rewarding of all, functioning libraries. Those who have had experience in planning will usually be ready to share what they have learned. Time and effort spent at this stage will at least minimize the chance of avoidable errors.

REFERENCES

1. L. J. Anthony, "Library Planning," in *Handbook of Special Librarianship and Information Work*, W. Ashworth, Ed., 3rd ed. Aslib, London, 1967.

2. E. Moore, "Systems Analysis: An Overview," *Spec. Libr.* **58**, 87–90 (1967).

3. K. D. Metcalf, *Planning Academic and Research Library Buildings*, McGraw-Hill, New York, 1965.

4. G. R. Lyle, *The Administration of the College Library*, 3rd ed., H. W. Wilson, New York, 1961.

5. J. L. Wheeler and A. M. Githens, *The American Public Library Building: Its Planning and Design*, Scribner, New York, 1941.

6. C. M. Lewis, *Special Libraries; How to Plan and Equip Them*, Special Libraries Association, New York, Monograph 2, 1963.

7. H. Skolnik, "Designing a Technical Information Center—In Retrospect," *J. Chem. Doc.* **8**, 70–73 (1968).

8. G. E. Randall, "Library Space and Steel Shelving," *Spec. Libr.* **53**, 96–102 (1962).

9. E. Joannes, "Planning the Special Library"; presented before the Pharmaceutical Section, Science-Technology Group, Special Libraries Association, Los Angeles, Calif., June 1949.

10. A. H. Holway and D. A. Jameson, *Good Lighting for People at Work in Reading Rooms and Offices*, Harvard University Division of Research, Cambridge, Mass., 1947.

11. J. G. Kraenbuehl, "Modern Library Illumination," in *Library Buildings for Library Service*, H. Fussler, Ed., American Library Association, Chicago, Ill., 1947.

12. Committee on Library Lighting, Illuminating Engineering Society, "Recommended Practice of Library Lighting," *Illum. Eng.* **45**, 185–197 (1950). Note announcing revision, *Spec. Libr.* **58**, 364 (1967).

13. R. H. Gates, "Modern Air Treatment," in *Library Buildings for Library Service*, H. Fussler, Ed., American Library Association, Chicago, Ill., 1947.

14. *Floors: Selection and Maintenance*, Library Technology Project, Publication 13, American Library Association, Chicago, Ill., 1967.

15. T. J. Devlin, "Use of Microfilm in Internal-Mail Control," *J. Chem. Doc.* **10**, 22–25 (1970).

16. L. J. Kiersky, "Bibliography on Reproduction of Documentary Information, 1966," *Spec. Libr.* **58**, 335–347 (1967); **59**, 261–265 (1968); **60**, 434–436, 497–498 (1969).

17. W. R. Hawken, "Full-Size Photocopying," in State of the Library Art, Vol. 5, R. Shaw, Ed., Rutgers University Press, New Brunswick, N. J., 1961 and photocopying from bound volumes; *A Study of Machines, Methods, and Materials*, Library Technology Project Publication 4, American Library Association, Chicago, Ill., 1962; supplements, 1963, 1964.

BIBLIOGRAPHY

General

Anthony, L. J., "Library Planning," in *Handbook of Special Librarianship and Information Work*, 3rd ed., W. Ashworth, Ed., Aslib, London, 1967.

Fry, A., "Library Planning, Furniture and Equipment," in *Handbook of Medical Library Practice*, 3rd ed., G. L. Annan and J. W. Felter, Eds., Medical Library Association, Chicago, Ill., 1970.

Lewis, C. M., Ed., *Special Libraries: How to Plan and Equip Them*, Special Libraries Association, New York, SLA Monograph 2, 1963.

Metcalf, K. D., *Planning Academic and Research Library Buildings*, McGraw-Hill, New York, 1965.

Library Buildings and Equipment Institutes

University of Maryland, 1959, *Guidelines for Library Planners*, ALA, Chicago, 1960.

Kent State University, 1961, *Planning Library Buildings for Service*, ALA, Chicago, 1964.

Chicago, 1963, *Problems in Planning Library Facilities: Consultants, Architects, Plans, and Critiques*, ALA, Chicago, 1964.

St. Louis, 1964, *The Library Environment, Aspects of Interior Planning*, ALA, Chicago, 1965.

Library Journal, R. R. Bowker, New York; monthly feature: "Buyers' Guide"; December issues devoted to library architecture.

Specific Features

Avedon, D. M., *NMA Glossary of Terms for Microphotography and Reproduction Made from Microimage*, 5th ed., National Microfilm Association, P. O. Box 386, Annapolis, Md. 21404, 1970.

Berkeley, B., *Floors: Selection and Maintenance*, Library Technology Project Report 13, ALA, Chicago, 1968.

Brenner, L. "A Design for the Display and Storage of Current Periodicals," *Bull. Med. Libr. Assoc.*, **57**, 281–282 (1969).

Condit, C. W., "The Building Arts in the Service of Librarianship," *Bull. Med. Libr. Assoc.* **50**, 167–176 (1962).

Cunha, G. D. M., *Conservation of Library Materials: A Manual and Bibliography on the Care, Repair, and Restoration of Library Materials*, Scarecrow, Metuchen, N. J., 1967.

Friedlander, M. O., "Planning the New Library: Grumman Aircraft Engineering Library," *Spec. Libr.* **55**, 96–100 (1964).

Gage-Babcock and Associates, *Protecting the Library and Its Resources: A Guide to Physical Protection and Insurance, Report on a Study*, Library Technology Project Publication 7, ALA, Chicago, 1963.

Gawrecki, D., *Compact Library Shelving*, Library Technology Project Publication 14, ALA, Chicago, 1968.

Hawken, W. R., *Copying Methods Manual*, Library Technology Project Publication 11, ALA, Chicago, 1967.

Hewitt, H. and A. S. Vause, *Lamps and Lighting*, American Elsevier, New York, 1967.

Horton, C., *Cleaning and Preserving Bindings and Related Materials*, 2nd ed., Library Technology Project Publication 16, ALA, Chicago, 1969.

Jordan, R. T., "Lighting in University Libraries," *UNESCO Bull. Libr.* **17**, 326–336 (1963).

Kennedy, C. and T. E. Keys, "Mayo Clinic Library: An Experience in Remodeling and Expansion," *Bull. Med. Libr. Assoc.* **46**, 249–269 (1958).

Kiersky, L. J., "Bibliography on Reproduction of Documentary Information," *Spec. Libr.* **58**, 335–347 (1967).

Kiersky, L. J., "New Developments in Photoreproduction," *Spec. Libr.* **60**, 434–436 (1969).

Kurth, W. H., *Moving a Library, Scarecrow*, Metuchen, N. J., 1966.

Metcalf, K. D., *Library Lighting*, Association of Research Libraries, Washington, D. C., 1970.

Spyers-Duran, P., *Moving Library Materials*, revised ed., Library Technology Project Publication, ALA, Chicago, 1965.

Stevens, G. W. W., *Microphotography*, 2nd ed., Wiley, New York, 1968.

5

Books and Other Publications

Selection and Acquisition

When a new library is started or one already in existence evaluated, the task of determining what books and other supporting publications should be in the collection is a challenging one. It is a real responsibility to see that funds are spent wisely to provide what is needed to promote the progress of the organization served. The results of these decisions will stand on the shelves as evidence either of painstaking selection or of haphazard gathering. In view of the increasing number of books published and the many publishers of scientific books, it is not always easy to decide which titles to acquire. Also the more limited the budget, the more difficult the task.

Before starting selection procedures, it is necessary to make some basic decisions concerning the character of the collection contemplated. How many volumes should be purchased initially, and how many might be added annually? These numbers are governed to some extent by the limits of budget and space provisions. With a tentative number fixed upon, the selection process can be started.

BOOK SELECTION

One approach to selecting titles for a specific collection is to survey the types of publications that comprise the scientific-technical literature, exclusive of periodicals for present intentions, as these are treated in Chapter 6. Emphasis here is on the traditional book or monograph with due recognition of the existing changes as completely new kinds of formats appear. In addition to books, however, there are other categories of unique publications that are equally important for the information they provide. Books are considered first here, then advice is given on to how to locate and procure such things as government publications, trade literature, directories, specifications, equipment catalogs, and academic dissertations.

Books constitute the largest segment of the part of the collection under consideration, but even they are not all of one character and may be grouped as follows:

1. Monographs and texts. Titles published usually in single volumes devoted to one subject or basic subdivision of a broad field.

2. Treatises. A work so exhaustive in its detailed coverage of a subject area that it must be issued in from two to as many as twenty or more volumes.

3. Proceedings. and symposia. Single or multiple volumes issued either from single professional meetings or from a series of meetings held more or less regularly. The papers presented are published together as a permanent record.

4. Dictionaries. An alphabetical listing of terms relating to a field of science with brief definitions provided. Also, foreign language lexicons.

5. Encyclopedic works. An alphabetical arrangement of topics, all relating to an area of science, for which extensive information is supplied.

6. Handbooks. Compilations consisting principally of physical data, providing compressed presentations of fundamental information relating to a branch of science, for example, chemistry, physics, or biophysics.

7. Serials such as annual reviews. Titled variously as "Annual Review of . . . ," "Advances in . . . ," "Progress in . . . ," usually published annually, but sometimes not as regularly. Individual chapters consist of scholarly reviews of recent developments in a narrow range of subject.

8. Special compilations of information. These range from brief pamphlets presenting data for a very limited field to many-volumed works covering a broad range of subjects.

These eight categories encompass every kind of book to be considered for this part of the collection. They are issued chiefly by independent publishers whose main business is to publish books in science and technology. These companies are located in all countries where scientific investigation is conducted, and books are in respective languages. Others are the products of professional societies. Methods for selecting and purchasing books are outlined herewith.

PROCEDURES FOR BOOK SELECTION

A primary necessity in determining what books to acquire for a collection is to know what has been published in the subject fields to be covered; then one must judge their relative merits on the basis of such factors as authors' reputations and standards of publishers. As guides to what is in print, lists of titles from any available sources such as catalogues issued by known publishers, bibliographies, and compilations from certain helpful book dealers can be assembled and studied. It should be apparent that the persons choosing these books must have some knowledge of the sciences involved. Standard works will already be familiar, and these constitute the nucleus with which to begin. As initial selections are made, complete bibliographic data should be noted systematically even though not all titles will be ordered.

No possible source of assistance should be ignored in this process of search and selection. If the subject areas coincide with any that are represented in the Appendix of this book, a good start is conveniently provided. Advice should be sought, too, from those who will use the library, particularly from members of a library committee, one of the functions of which might be continuous counsel concerning acquisitions.

Some examples of good, wide-ranging lists of scientific and technical books are shown here.

Some Source Lists of Scientific and Technical Books

General Scientific

Les Sources du travail bibliographiques, Tome III, Bibliographies spécialisées—sciences exactes et techniques, L. N. Malclés, Librairies E. Dorz, Geneva; Librairies Minard, Paris, 1958. Though now more than a decade old, this is still important as an exhaustive and critically selective listing of major publications, without prejudice as to language, of all scientific subject areas.

Scientific, Medical, and Technical Books Published in the United States of America, 1930–1956, R. R. Hawkins, Ed., 2nd ed. A selected list of titles in print with annotations. Books published to December 1956. National Academy of Science-National Research Council, Washington, D.C., 1958.

American Scientific Books, 1960–1962, 1963–1964, 1964–1965, P. B. Steckler, Ed., R. R. Bowker, New York, 1963, 1964, 1965. Cumulated from American Book Publishing Record.

Aslib Select List of Standard British Scientific and Technical Books, E. A. Baker, Ed., 6th ed., Aslib, London, 1966.

Catalogue of Lewis's Medical, Scientific and Technical Lending Library, 2nd ed., H. K. Lewis & Co., Ltd., London, 1965, 2 vol.

Science Reference Sources, 5th ed., F. B. Jenkins, M.I.T. Press, Cambridge, Mass., 1969. Extensive coverage of subjects.

McGraw-Hill Basic Bibliography of Science and Technology: Recent Titles on More than 7000 Subjects, McGraw-Hill, New York, 1966. Comprehensive, running to 738 pages.

Guide to Reference Material, Vol. 1, *Science and Tehnology,* A. J. Walford, Ed., 2nd ed., The Library Association, London, 1966. Comprehensive and universal.

Catalogue collectif des livres français de science et technique, 1950–1960, Introduction by Piganiol, Cercle de Librairie, Paris, 1962; supplements, 1960–1962, 1964; 1963–1964, 1965; 1965–1966, 1967.

Guide to Russian Reference Books, Vol. 5, *Science, technology, medicine.* K. Maichel, Ed., The Hoover Institution, Stanford, Calif., 1967.

Irregular Serials and Annuals; An International Directory, 2nd ed. E. Koltay, Ed., R. R. Bowker, New York, 1971. A classified guide to current foreign and domestic serials, excepting periodicals issued more frequently than once a year.

The Directory of Published Proceedings, Interdok Corporation, White Plains, N. Y. Issued monthly and cumulated in annual volumes.

International Compendium of Numerical Data Projects, Committee on Data for Science and Technology, Springer-Verlag, New York, 1969. Best source for compilations of data.

Science and Technology: A Purchase Guide for Branch and Small Public Libraries, M. Bennett, Compiler, Carnegie Library of Pittsburgh, Pittsburgh, Pa., 1963. Updated annually.

Lists of publications of the relevant professional scientific and technical societies.

Specific Subject Fields

MATHEMATICS, PHYSICS, ENGINEERING

Guide to the Literature of Engineering, Mathematics, and Physics, S. Goldman, AD608053, National Technical Information Service, Springfield, Va., 1965.

Selected Books and Journals in Science and Technology, I. Johnson, M.I.T. Press, Cambridge, Mass., 1959. Brief, well-selected list of standard titles.

Guide to the Literature of Mathematics and Physics, Including Related Works on Engineering Science, N. G. Parke, III, 2nd ed., Dover, New York, 1958. Includes an extensive list of books on physics, mathematics, chemistry, research, and science in general with comments on outstanding works.

Physics Literature; A Reference Manual, J. K. Whitford, 2nd ed., Scarecrow, Metuchen, N. J., 1968.

Handlist of basic reference material for librarians and information officers in electrical and electronic engineering, E. M. Codlin and R. S. Lawrie, Compilers, Aslib, London, Electronics Group, 1969.

Chemical Engineering Library Book List, 5th ed., American Institute of Chemical Engineers, New York, 1966.

CHEMISTRY

Journal of Chemical Education, Annual September issue includes comprehensive list of books of major publishers that are exhibited at the Fall Meeting of the American Chemical Society. Available also as separate.

A Guide to the Literature of Chemistry, E. J. Crane, *et al.,* 2nd ed., Wiley, New York, 1957.

Chemical Publications, M. G. Mellon, 4th ed., McGraw-Hill, New York, 1965.

Literature of Chemical Technology, 2nd ed., Advances in Chemistry Series, No. 78. The American Chemical Society, Washington, D.C., 1968. Includes extensive bibliographies on a number of subjects of chemical technology.

BIOLOGY, AGRICULTURE, MEDICINE

Biological and Biomedical Resources Literature, A. E. Kerker and H. T. Murphy, U.S. Department of Health, Education & Welfare, Washington, D.C., 1967.

Literature of Agricultural Research, J. R. Blanchard and H. Ostvold, University of California Press, Berkeley and Los Angeles, Calif., 1958. Includes most important books in the several areas of agriculture and related sciences.

Physician's Book Compendium, Plus Quarterly Supplements, M. Celnik, Ed., Marcel Dekker, New York, 1970. Ten thousand titles, annual revision.

MINING AND METALLURGY

Mining, Minerals, and Geosciences, S. R. Kaplan, Interscience-Wiley, New York, 1965.

Guide to Metallurgical Information, E. B. Gibson and E. W. Tapia, 2nd ed., Special Libraries Association, SLA Bibliography No. 3, New York, 1965.

SPACE SCIENCE

Space Science and Technology, B. M. Fry and F. E. Mohrhardt, Interscience-Wiley, New York, 1963.

Catalogs of Scientific Libraries

Another type of selective listing is the card catalog of a major scientific library, particularly as these have been made available in reduced size format by G. K. Hall and Company, 70 Lincoln St., Boston, Mass. 02111. For example, the catalogs of the Engineering Societies Library in New York, and the John Crerar Library in Chicago have been duplicated in this way. These two are especially good sources for consultation because of their classified subject arrangement.

Comprehensive List that Includes Science

Guide to Reference Books, C. M. Winchell, 8th ed., American Library Association, Chicago, Ill., 1967, Section E, *Pure and Applied Sciences*; *first supplement*, 1965–1966, E. P. Sheehey, 1968; second supplement, 1967–1968, E. P. Sheehey, 1970.

National Bibliographies

The United States Catalog, 4th ed., H. W. Wilson Co., New York, 1928. This is a listing by author and title of all books published in the United States and England that were in print on January 1, 1928, and brought up to date by the supplementary publication, *Cumulative Book Index*, which is issued monthly and accumulated periodically. A directory of publishers is included. Available in all large libraries.

A Catalog of Books Represented by Library of Congress Printed Cards Issued to July 31, 1942, Committee of Research Libraries, 1942–1946, reprint, Pageant Books, New York, 1958. Cards issued August 1, 1942–December 31, 1948. 167 volumes plus

42 supplementary volumes, Library of Congress, Washington, D.C. 1948; Author catalog 1948–1952, 24 volumes, Library of Congress, Washington, D.C. 1953.

The National Union Catalog, 28 volumes, Card Division, Library of Congress, Washington, D.C., 1953–1957, 1958: Subject catalog, 1950–1954, 20 volumes, 1955–1959, 22 volumes, Rowman and Littlefield, New York, 1960–1964, 25 volumes, Edwards Brothers, Ann Arbor, Mich., 1965 to date, Washington, D.C., Library of Congress Card Division (N.B. All LCC and NUC on microfiche from Microcard Editions, 901 Twenty-sixth St., N.W., Washington, D.C. 20037.)

Library of Congress and National Union Catalog Author Lists, 1942–1962: A Master Cumulation, Gale Research Company, Detroit, Mich., 1971.

British National Bibliography, The British Museum, London. A classified listing of books published in Great Britain. Issued weekly since January 1950, cumulated annually.

Biblio. Bulletin Bibliographique des Ouvragas parus en langage française dans le monde entiér, Librairie Hachette, Paris.

Deutsche Bibliographie, 1947— Frankfurt.

Deutsche Nationalbibliographie und Bibliographie des im Ausland erscheinen deutschsprachigen Schrifftums, 1931—. Leipzig.

Books in Print, R. R. Bowker, New York. Annual listing by author and title of available books published in the United States.

Subject Guide to Books in Print, R. R. Bowker, New York.

The Reference Catalog of Current Literature 1957, J. Whitaker and Sons, Ltd., London, or R. R. Bowker, New York, 1957, 2 vols. Records all books in print and on sale in the United Kingdom at the end of the year 1957.

Though many of the cumulative listings cited here are generally inclusive of important works irrespective of language or place of publication, it is admitted that the emphasis may be on books most easily accessible in the United States. However, in the process of selecting titles for acquisition it must be recognized that results of scientific investigation are being published in many countries and consequently in languages other than English. Detection of those contributions that are most significant is not as easy as it is to discern those that are familiar, but they cannot be ignored in situations where coverage must be complete. Some clues can be found from frequently cited titles appearing in bibliographies. Also opinions can be sought from scientists working in relevant fields.

After studying source lists and making tentative selections, it can be rewarding to visit a library that covers the same fields of interest and examine its holdings. It is inevitable that good titles that might otherwise be missed will be found, and even cursory examination of a large number of books will reveal some that are not as advertised.

Another means of preliminary review of doubtful or uncertain titles is to ask publishers to submit them on approval. This is a time-consuming procedure and a privilege that should not be abused, but it is sometimes the only way of both getting wanted books promptly and not wasting funds on some that may not be suitable. It is usually true that reputable publishers are careful to guard against issuing books of poor quality, though there may be other reasons for a title to be rejected. Furthermore it may take awhile to become confident of the products from a relatively new publisher.

Published reviews of books can sometimes help in reaching a decision of whether to purchase. A source for locating reviews of books that were published in past years is the journal *Technical Book Review Index* (TBRI), which includes a reprinting of these explicit judgments, quoted in entirety or in part. This TBRI has been issued since 1935 by Special Libraries Association, and because there has always been selectivity in choosing titles to be included, it is surprisingly easy to locate specific reviews of significant titles.

RECORD OF TITLES SELECTED

In the process of accumulating titles of books for possible purchase, it is necessary to keep a systematic record. This is most efficiently done by noting them individually on a card or slip of standard size, preferably the 7.5×12.5 cm catalog card dimensions, always including full data. Or if an automated system is in operation, an IBM punch card might be employed. Perhaps the eventual order form with carbon copies could be used to obviate typing over. Whatever is used, as many of the following items as possible should be included:

> Author's name (or names), surname with first name plus initial, or
>   corporate author
> Title, complete and accurate
> Edition
> Price
> Number of copies
> Place of publication
> Date
> Name of publisher
> Source of announcement

As decisions are made to acquire, it can be worthwhile to retain the rejections in a file with notes of the reasons for refusing. There may be some that might be reconsidered upon reexamination or marked for purchase when more money becomes available.

SELECTION OF CURRENTLY PUBLISHED BOOKS

Thus far the discussion has related particularly to books already published, but inasmuch as they are forthcoming continuously there must also be sources for what is being published so that those of interest can be purchased promptly. Since there is no one source to be relied upon for book announcements in all fields of science, those that are found to be most fruitful must be discovered and then scanned consistently. Announcements of newly published books may be found in the following media:

1. Announcements directly from publishers. They maintain mailing lists and send advertising periodically to libraries.
2. Publishers' advertisements in periodicals.
3. Reviews in periodicals. Also listings without reviews.
4. Special notices and booklets announcing new titles such as those supplied by certain book dealers.
5. General listings that include scientific books.

Every individual responsible for the selection of books will develop his own way of spotting new titles in his area of interest and will learn which sources are most rewarding. The process of selection becomes even more of a challenge with the increasing interdisciplinary relationships of the sciences which require special omniscience to recognize how these are developing.

One method for acquiring books as they are published that has been promoted by publishers and book dealers in recent years is to establish an agreement whereby all books in specific subject categories are sent automatically. As long as there is the privilege of return of those titles that may not be wanted, this arrangment is satisfactory, particularly if funds are not limited and there is space to accommodate more books than would be acquired if selection were by individual title. Some of these plans are described later in this chapter under "Publishers' Services."

Even if standing order plans are used, there is always need to learn what is being published. As has been indicated, there are certain listings that announce the new books regularly. Among the best of these are the following:

Publishers Weekly. This periodical includes a list of all books and important pamphlets published each week in the United States, with some annotations. Publishers' advertisements, and occasional issues featuring scientific and technical books make this essential for every library. In addition to the weekly, the publisher, R. R. Bowker Co., provides the following three excellent services.

American Book Publishing Record. A monthly cumulation of titles announced in *Publishers Weekly* arranged by Dewey classification number. Published since 1960.

Forthcoming Books. Published bimonthly, lists books to be issued in the coming 5-month period. *Subject Guide to Forthcoming Books,* a separate publication.

Library Journal. Includes quarterly lists of scientific, technical, and medical books announced for publication by publishers.

Science. A weekly periodical issued by the American Association for the Advancement of Science publishes reviews of a few important titles, lists a significant number of others.

Nature. This British weekly journal devoted to the sciences has excellent reviews of some books, remarkably current, and announcements and advertisements of others. Once a month includes a comprehensive listing, *Supplement: Recent Scientific and Technical Books.*

Quarterly Review of Biology. Includes extensive coverage of new books in the biological areas.

Science News. This weekly published by Science News Service lists some of the books of the week.

Science Progress. A Quarterly review. Publishes excellent essay reviews and lists books received. Almost 200 titles in one issue.

Applied Mechanics Reviews. A critical review of the world literature in applied mechanics and related engineering science. Monthly. Includes reviews of books.

Physics Today. Monthly periodical includes excellent reviews of books in the field of physics and lists many others newly published.

Analytical Chemistry. Well-written reviews of a few important books in each issue, additional ones listed.

Choice. Some science books included in this selective listing.

Science Books. High school level chiefly, but good coverage.

Chemical Abstracts. At the end of each subject section in individual issues new titles are noted with no attempt at abstracting. International coverage.

Dealers' publications such as *Stechert-Hafner Book News,* 31 East 10th St., New York, N. Y. 10013; *Scientific Books,* James Thin, 53–57 South Bridge, Edinburgh, Scotland; *Blackwell's Catalogs,* Blackwell's Broad Street, Oxford, England.

Aslib Book List. Monthly from the British Association of Special Libraries and Information Bureaux, always known as Aslib. Titles with annotations.

Publishers announcements. All publishers are willing to send notices to libraries that are likely purchasers.

Professional societies' announcements.

Library Accession Lists

New Technical Books. A Selective list with descriptive annotations. Monthly from The New York Public Library, The Research Libraries, 5th Ave. & 42nd St., New York, N. Y. 10018.

BOOK PUBLISHERS

A selection of the major publishers of the greater number of scientific books is provided here. These are the most active in the several countries where such publication is a productive business. For comprehensive listings the compilations *Books in Print (U.S.)*, *British Scientific and Technical Books*, and *Publishers' International Yearbook; World Directory of Book Publishers*, 4th edition 1966–1967, may be consulted.

Some Publishers of Scientific and Technical Books: A Selected List

United States

Academic Press, 111 Fifth Ave., New York, N. Y. 10003
Addison-Wesley Publishing Co., Inc., Reading, Mass. 01867
Allyn & Bacon, Inc., 470 Atlantic Ave., Boston, Mass. 02210
Ann Arbor-Humphrey Science Publishers, Drawer No. 1425, Ann Arbor, Mich. 48106
American Elsevier Publishing Co., Inc., 52 Vanderbilt Ave., New York, N. Y. 10017
Becker & Hayes, Inc., 6400 Goldsboro Road, Bethesda, Md. 20034 (a subsidiary of John Wiley & Sons, Inc.)
W. A. Benjamin, Inc., 1 Park Ave., New York, N. Y. 10036
Blaisdell Publishing Co., 275 Wyman St., Waltham, Mass. 02154
R. R. Bowker Co., 1180 Avenue of the Americas, New York, N. Y. 10036
Butterworth Inc., distributed by Plenum Publishing Corp., 227 West 17th St., New York, N. Y. 10011
Chemical Publishing Co., 200 Park Avenue South, New York, N. Y. 10003
Chemical Rubber Co., 18901 Cranwood Parkway, Cleveland, Ohio 44128
Chilton Book Co., 401 Walnut St., Philadelphia, Pa. 19106
Marcel Dekker, 195 Madison Ave., New York, N. Y. 10016
Dover Publications, Inc., 180 Varick St., New York, N. Y. 10014
Dowden, Hutchinson & Ross, Inc., 10 North 7th St., Stroudsburg, Pa. 18360
Franklin Publishing Co., Palisade, N. J. 07024
Gordon & Breach, Science Publishers, Inc., 150 Fifth Ave., New York, N. Y. 10011
Hafner Publishing Co., Inc., 260 Heights Road, Darien, Conn. 06820
Hayden Book Companies, Inc., 116 West 14th St., New York, N. Y. 10011
Holden-Day, Inc., 500 Sansome St., San Francisco, Calif. 94111
Holt, Rinehart and Winston, Inc., 383 Madison Ave., New York, N. Y. 10017
Lea and Febiger, 600 S. Washington Sq., Philadelphia, Pa. 19106.
J. B. Lippincott Co., E. Washington Sq., Philadelphia, Pa. 19105
The Macmillan Co., 866 Third Ave., New York, N. Y. 10022
McGraw-Hill Book Co., 330 W. 42nd St., New York, N. Y. For orders: P. O. Box 400, Hightstown, N. J. 08520
The M.I.T. Press, 50 Ames St., Cambridge, Mass. 02142
The C. V. Mosby Company, 3207 Washington Blvd., St. Louis, Mo. 63103

Pergamon Press, Inc., Maxwell House, Fairview Park, Elmsford, N. Y. 10523
Pitman Publishing Corporation, 20 East 46th St., New York, N. Y. 10017
Plenum Publishing Corporation, 227 West 17th St., New York, N. Y. 10011
Prentice-Hall, Inc., Box 500, Englewood Cliffs, N. J. 07632
John F. Rider, Publisher, Inc., distributed by Hayden Book Companies Inc.
Rowman & Littlefield, Inc., 84 Fifth Ave., New York, N. Y. 10011
Howard F. Sams and Co., Inc., Publishers, 4300 West 62nd St., Indianapolis, Ind., 46206
W. B. Saunders Company, 218 West Washington Square, Philadelphia, Pa. 19105
Spartan Books, Inc., 432 Park Avenue South, New York, N. Y. 10016
Springer-Verlag New York, Inc., 175 Fifth Ave., New York, N. Y. 10010
Charles C Thomas, Publisher, 301–27 East Lawrence Ave., Springfield, Ill. 62703
University Park Press, 115 Chamber of Commerce Bldg., Baltimore, Md.
Van Nostrand Reinhold Company, 450 West 33rd St., New York, N. Y. 10001
John Wiley & Sons, Inc., 605 Third Ave., New York, N. Y. 10016
Wiley-Interscience—A division of John Wiley & Sons, Inc., 605 Third Ave., New York, N. Y. 10016
The Williams and Wilkins Company, 428 East Preston St., Baltimore, Md. 21202

Great Britain

George Allen and Unwin, Ltd., Ruskin House, 40 Museum St., London, W.C. 1
Edward Arnold and Company, 41 Maddox St., London, S.W. 1
Benn Brothers, Ltd., 154 Fleet St., London E.C. 4
Bell and Sons, Ltd., York House, 6 Portugal St., London W.C. 2
Butterworth and Co., Ltd., 88 Kingsway, London W.C. 2
Cambridge University Press, The Pitt Bldg., Trumpington St., Cambridge
Chapman and Hall, Ltd., 11 New Fetter Lane, London E.C. 1
Evans Technical Books, Montague House, Russell Square, London W.C. 1
Grafton and Co., 105 Great Russell St., London W.C. 1
Hutchison and Co., Ltd., 178–202 Great Portland St., London W. 1N 6AQ
Longman Group—Burnt Mill, Harlow, Essex, England
Methuen and Co., Ltd., 11 New Fetter Lane, London E.C. 1
Oliver and Boyd, Ltd., Tweedsdale Court, 14 High Street, Edinburgh, Scotland
Oxford University Press, Ely House, 37 Dover Street, London W. 1
Taylor and Francis Ltd., 18 Red Lion Court, Fleet St., London E.C. 4
Thomas Nelson and Son, 36 Park St., London W. 1

Germany

Akademie-Verlag GMBH, Leipziger Strasse 3–4, 108 Berlin, E. Germany
Akademische Verlagsgesellschaft Geest and Portig KG, Sternwarten Strasse 8, 701 Leipzig, E. Germany
Johann Ambrosius Barth, Ohm Strasse 6, 8 Munich 23
J. F. Bergmann, 8 Munich 27, Trogerstrabe 56, W. Germany
Ferdinand Enke Verlag, Hasenbergsteige 3, 7 Stuttgart 1, W. Germany
Walter De Gruyter and Co., Genthiner Strasse 13, 1 Berlin 30, W. Germany
Carl Hanser Verlag, Kolberger Strasse 22, 8 Munich 80, W. Germany
Springer Verlag, Neuenheimer Landstrasse 28–30, 69 Heidelberg, Heidelberger Platz 3, 1 Berlin 33, W. Germany
R. Oldenbourg Verlag KG, Rosenheimer Strasse 145, Postfach 80 13 60, D-8000, Munich 80

E. Schewizerbart'sche Verlagsbuchandlung, Johannes Strasse 3A, 7 Stuttgart W

J. F. Steinkopf Verlag, Marien Strasse 11–13, Postfach 1116, 7 Stuttgart M

France

Dunod, 92 Rue Bonaparte, Paris VI

Gauthiere-Villars Editeur, 55 Quaides Grands-Augustins 75, Paris VI

Hermann et Cie, 6 Rue de la Sorbonne, Paris V

Masson et Cie, 120 Boulevard Saint-Germain, Paris VI

Holland

North-Holland Publishing Co., 308–311 Keizergracht, Amsterdam

Elsevier Publishing Co., Jan van Galenstraat 335, P.O. Box 211, Amsterdam

Wolters-Noordhoff N.V., Oude Boteringestraat 22, P.O. Box, Groningen

Italy

Riccardo Patron, Via Zamboni 26, Bologna

Ulrico Hoepli, Corso Matteotti 12, Milan

Nicola Zanichelli, Via Irnerio 34, 40126 Bologna

Casa Editrice Sansoni, Via Mazzini 46, 50132 Florence

Liberia Scientifica C. Manfredi, s.r.l. Viala Papiano 47, Milan

Denmark

Munksgaard, International Bookseller & Publishers, Inc., Prags Blvd. 47, DK 2300,
Copenhagen S

Spain

Espasa Calpe, S.A., Rios Rasas 26, Apartado 547, Madrid 3

Canada

Renouf Publishing Co., Ltd., 2182 Catherine St., W. Toronto 25

DIRECT PUBLISHERS' SERVICES

Certain publishers of scientific books encourage the establishment of direct standing order arrangements with them. In general, the purpose is to circumvent the delays in having to wait for announcements of titles and then placing the orders with a dealer. Whether the automatic method of receipt is advantageous is a matter to be determined according to individual circumstances. The separate procedures involved can be more troublesome than the possibility of getting the books more quickly justifies. Standing orders for books from certain publishers can be also placed through a dealer.

Details of standing order procedures vary from one publisher to another. Usually a subject outline prepared by the publisher is marked to show the categories of books wanted and acceptance of specific requirements. There is usually the privilege of return of any titles not needed. Some discount is likely to be allowed. Though this may not be found to be an ideal solution for the acquisition of all books, it is worth serious consideration for titles published as series because these should be acquired as quickly as possible and require no decisions as to whether they should be kept. For large scale application to all books, standing order agreements with the major publishers may be advantageous only if funds are plentiful and space unlimited.

Some examples of publishers' standing order plans are the following:

Pergamon Press, Inc. A Charter Subscription Plan is administered either directly with a library or through a book dealer. The purchaser is allowed a 10% discount if books are handled by the vender. There are three categories of direct purchasers; (a) those who agree to buy 1000 volumes a year and get a discount of 40%; (b) those who buy 500 volumes a year get a discount of 30%; and (c) those who buy 250 volumes a year get a discount of 20%.

John Wiley & Sons, Inc. The standing order plan can be handled either directly or through a book dealer. Academic Libraries receive a discount of 10%. Shipping is from Somerset, N. J. or Salt Lake City, Utah for the 19 Western states. Acceptance of all books would require a budgetary commitment of about $5000 a year, in 1970, for about 400 titles. Subject categories may be selected.

Van Nostrand Reinhold Company. The standing order plan is particularly directed toward public school and college libraries. Books in certain categories can be specified. The discount permitted is 40% on trade titles; 20% on professional reference and college books.

PROCEDURES FOR ORDERING BOOKS

Before any orders for books are placed, the most efficient routines must be determined. If, as is usually the case, the library is a unit within a larger organization, conference with the chief purchasing officer will be necessary. When policy requires, requisitions can be handled through a central purchasing department provided that the staff member of the library responsible for such matters is permitted to specify where orders should be directed. The preferable procedure is for permission to be granted for the library to send orders directly to the one or more book dealers who will handle the major part of this business. Book buying is a highly specialized activity, the details of which are certainly more familiar to a librarian than to a general purchasing office. Of course, in certain situations such as government-related operations, it is obligatory to comply with the broadly specified rules. In a university with branch libraries, actual purchasing is usually done centrally.

The best general procedure is to place the orders for the majority of books with a capable dealer. Some effort should be spent in locating such an agent who will be willing and able to develop a good working relationship, be painstaking in procuring the difficult-to-find items, and ready to respond to emergency needs. This deputy undertakes the responsibility of getting books from all publishers, thereby eliminating many detailed routine transactions with the purchaser. Certain dealers handle both new and old books, a combined service that is especially helpful when out-of-print titles are needed—a likely situation when a major collection is started.

Some of the book dealers who are known to be dependable in procuring scientific and technical books are listed in this chapter. Some attempt has been made to include as wide a scope of geographical location as possible, but it is by no means comprehensive. Only by experience can the right vender be determined. It is recommended that local possibilities be investigated and used because of the advantage of easy communication; however, often the small dealer cannot work effectively with the sources of supplies. Telephone directories will provide the name of any dealer in the vicinity, and then he should be approached.

Whether it will be necessary to use more than one dealer, experience alone may determine. Some can procure publications readily no matter what their origins; others do not have the skills and special knowledge required to get materials from other countries. It may therefore be desirable to find an agent who specializes in world wide operations or one in each of the countries from which books will be needed with some frequency. In an organization that has branches or affiliates in other countries, a cooperative arrangement should be established for mutual benefits.

Some dealers, and publishers also, allow a discount to libraries on the list prices of books, usually about 10% on scientific titles. However, good service is a much more important factor in selecting an agent than the possibility of this small saving. Moreover, where the total volume of business placed annually is not large, discounts should not be expected.

A service offered by some dealers is to provide catalog cards unmarked or with call numbers (Library of Congress usually) with each book if these are available. The problem is, however, that this centralized cataloging service, potentially so helpful, is often as much as 2 years behind with the scientific books and libraries cannot wait for them. If some titles in other fields are purchased it is definitely worthwhile to take advantage of whatever help is available to get them on the shelves quickly. Some agents offer full treatment, from catalog cards to labels. A list of representative book dealers follows:

Dealers in Scientific Books—A Selected List

Alabama

Smith & Hardwick, Inc., 405 North 20th St., Birmingham, Ala. 35203
Book Shop, 22 Dunnavent's Mall, Huntsville, Ala. 35801

Arizona

Intermountain Book Co., 1814 North 25th Drive, Phoenix, Ariz. 85009

California

Richard Abel & Co., Inc., 1506 Gardena St., Glendale, Calif. 91204
Richard Abel & Co., Inc., Industrial Center Bldg., Gate 5, Road Marinship, Sausalito, Calif. 94965
Stacey's of Palo Alto, 405 California Avenue, Palo Alto, Calif. 94306
San Diego Technical Book Co., 816 Broadway, San Diego, Calif. 98101
J. W. Stacey, Inc., 15255 E. Don Julian Road, City of Industry, Calif. 91747
Technical Book Co., 253 Spring St., Los Angeles, Calif. 90012
Westwood Technical Book Co., 2056 Westwood Blvd., Los Angeles, Calif. 90025
Zeitlin & Ver Brugge, 815 N. La Cienega Blvd., Los Angeles, Calif. 90069
Stacey's of San Francisco, 581 Market St., San Francisco, Calif. 94105

Colorado

Richard Abel & Co., Inc., 2101 S. Marion, Denver, Colo. 80210
R. R. Technical Bookfinder's, P.O. Box 1038, Littleton, Colo. 80120
Stacey's Books of Denver, 725 18th St., Denver, Colo. 80202

Connecticut

Key Book Service, 425 Asylum Street, Bridgeport, Conn. 06610
Research Books, Inc., Haddam, Conn. 06438

Delaware

Greenwood Bookshop, 110 W. 9th Street, Wilmington, Del. 19801

District of Columbia

Sidney Kramer Books, 1722 "H" St. N.W., Washington, D.C. 20006
Students Book Co., 2120 Pennsylvania Ave., Washington, D.C. 20037

Florida

Technical Guide Publications, 3040 N. 29th Avenue, Hollywood, Fla. 33020
W. E. Falk Books, P.O. Box 937, North Miami, Fla. 33135

Georgia

Richard Abel & Co., Inc., 1784 N. Dacatur Road, Atlanta, Ga. 30307
J. A. Majors Co., 139 Forrest Ave., N.E., Atlanta, Ga. 30303

Illinois

Richard Abel & Co., Inc., 1312 27th St., Zion, Ill. 60099
Baker & Taylor, Inc., Gladiola Avenue, Momence, Ill. 60954
Kroch's & Brentano's Inc., 29th S. Wabash Ave., Chicago, Ill. 60603
Login Brothers, 1445 W. Jackson Blvd., Chicago, Ill. 60607

Indiana

James L. Theilman Books, 1237 Wabash Avenue, Terre Haute, Ind. 47801

Louisiana

Majors Scientific Books, Inc., 147 S. Liberty St., New Orleans, La. 70112
Siler's Inc., 130 Carondolet St., New Orleans, La. 70112

Maine

Eastern Book Co., 131 Middle St., Portland, Me. 04112

Maryland

Cucumber Book Shop, 5611 Kraft Drive, Rockville, Md. 20852
Gordons Book Center, 118 E. Baltimore St., Baltimore, Md. 21202

Massachusetts

Richard Abel & Co., Inc., 47 Athletic Field Road, Waltham, Mass. 02154
Book Clearing House, 423 Boylston St., Boston, Mass. 02116
The Book Place, 22 South Shore Industrial Park, Hingham, Mass. 02043
Brown & Connolly, Inc., 779 Boylston St., Boston, Mass. 02117
Campbell & Hall, Inc., 989 Commonwealth Ave., Boston, Mass. 02140

Michigan

Emery-Pratt Co., 1966 W. Main St., Owosso, Mich. 48867
Xerox University Microfilms, 300 N. Zeeb Road, Ann Arbor, Mich. 48106

Minnesota

Monarch Book Co., 900 E. 80th St., Minneapolis, Minn. 55420
Quality Book Shoppe, 2053 Ford Parkway, St. Paul, Minn. 55116

Missouri

Matthews Book Co., 3140 Park Ave., St. Louis, Mo. 63104
Midwest Library Service, 11400 Dorset Road, Maryland Heights, Mo. 63042

Nevada

Baker & Taylor Co., Inc., 380 Edison Way, Reno, Nev. 89502

New Jersey

Richard Abel & Co., Inc., 1003 Fries Mill Road, Blackwood, N. J. 08012
Baker & Taylor Co., 50 Kirby Avenue, Somerville, N. J. 08876
Carol Cox Book Co., P. O. Box 389, Paramus, N. J. 07652
Educational Reading Services, 320 Route 17, Mahwah, N.J. 07430
Grayson Book Services, 390 Cliff St., Fairview, N. J. 07022
Makely's, 39 W. Scott Ave., Rahway, N. J. 07065
A.H. Roemer Co., Inc., 1166 W. Chestnut St., Union, N. J. 08873
Wellington Book Co., Inc., 33–49 Whelan Road, East Rutherford, N. J. 07073

New Mexico

Holman's, 401 Wyoming Blvd., N.E., Albuquerque, N. Mex. 87112

New York

Ancorp, Inc., 131 Varick St., New York 10013
Ballen Booksellers International, Inc., 115 E. 23rd St., New York 10010
Bookazine Co., 303 W. 10th St., New York 10014
Circa Publications, Inc., 415 5th Ave., Pelham, N. Y. 10803
C.W. Clark Book Co., 564 Smith St., Farmingdale, N. Y. 11735
Coutt's Library Services, Inc., 907 Ontario Ave., Niagara Falls, N. Y. 14305
Dimondstein Book Co., Inc., 38 Portiman Road, New Rochelle, N. Y. 10801
E.B.S. Inc., Book Service, 290 Broadway, Lynbrook, N. Y. 11563
L. H. Gleichenhaus & Co. Empire State Bldg., Rm. 1416-A, New York 10001
George Eliot Medical Books, 35–53 24th St., Long Island City, N. Y. 11106
International University Booksellers, Inc., 101 5th Ave., New York 10003
McGraw-Hill Bookstore, 330 W. 42nd St., New York 10036
Sci-Tech Book Service, 252 W. 30th St., New York 10001
Servitium Book Co., 37 Riverdale Ave., Yonkers, N. Y. 10701
Specialized Book Service, 35 Audrey Ave., Oyster Bay, N. Y. 11771
Taylor-Carlisle Book Corp., 115 E. 23rd St., New York 10010
Van Riemsdyck Book Services, Inc., 89–25 130th St., Richmond Hill, N. Y. 11418
Walter J. Johnson, Inc., 111 5th Avenue, New York 10030

Ohio

Richard Abel & Co., Inc., 1672 Upper Sandusky Rd., Marion, Ohio 43302

Oklahoma

Interstate Library Service, Subsidiary of Baker & Taylor, Inc., 4600 N. Cooper, Oklahoma City, Okla. 73118

Oregon

Richard Abel & Co., Inc., P.O. Box 4245, Portland, Ore. 97208

Pennsylvania

Bro-Dart Books, Inc., P.O. Box 923, Williamsport, Pa. 17701
Franklin Book Co., 441 Johnson St., Jenkintown, Pa. 19406

Philadelphia Book Co., 22 N. 9th St., Philadelphia, Pa. 19107
Rittenhouse Book Store, Inc., 1706 Rittenhouse Square, Philadelphia, Pa. 19145
RSC, Inc., 20–28 N. Pennsylvania Ave., Morrisville, Pa. 19067
United States Book Co., 1701 Murray Ave., Pittsburgh, Pa. 15217

Texas

J. A. Majors Company, 8911 Directors Row, Dallas, Tex. 75247
J. A. Majors Company, 1806 Southgate Blvd., Houston, Tex. 77025

Vermont

New England Book Service, Charlotte, Vt. 05445

Virginia

Artech Corp., 2816 Fallfax Drive, Falls Church, Va. 22042

Washington

Library System Service, 12535 Lake City Way, N.E., Seattle, Wash. 98125

West Virginia

Major's Bookstore, Inc., 221 Hale St., Charleston, W. Va. 25301

Dealers in Other Countries

Canada

American News Company, Ltd., 474 Wellington St., West, Toronto, Ontario, Canada
Diffusion Dunod, Inc., Suite 806, 3637 Est. bd Metropolitain, Dep. Grossiste, Montreal,
    Quebec, Canada
Dussault, 1315 Lafontaine, Montreal 24, Canada
Librairie Ducharmelt, 995 St. Lawrence St., Montreal, Quebec, Canada
McAinsh and Co., Ltd., 863 Bay Street, Toronto 5, Ontario
W. H. Smith and Son (Canada) Ltd., 224 Yonge St., Toronto, Ontario, Canada
University book stores in the university towns.

Great Britain

Blackwell's, 5 Alfred Street, Oxford, England
Bowes and Bowes Ltd., 9 Bow St., London W.C. 2, England
Wm. Dawson and Sons, Cannon House, Macklin Street, London W.C. 2, England
W. and G. Foyle, 119–125 Charing Cross Rd. 5 London W.C. 2, England
Claude Gill Books Ltd., 481 Oxford St., London, England
Haigh and Hochland, Ltd., 365 Oxford Road, Manchester 13, England
W. Heffer and Sons, Ltd., 3–4 Petty Cury, Cambridge, England
H. K. Lewis and Co., Ltd., P.O. Box 66, 136–8 Gower St., London W.C. 1, England
Library Service and Supply Co., Universal House, 4 Footscray Road, Eltham, London
    S.E. 9, England
Scientific Circulations, Ltd., 111 Eastbournce Mews, London W. 2, England
W. H. Smith and Son, Technical Book Service, Scruttan St., London E.C. 2, England

B. F. Stevens and Brown, Ltd., Ardon House, Mill Lane, Godalming, Surrey, England
Hubert Wilson, Ltd., 161 Borough High St., London S.E. 1, England

France

Victor Attinger, 4 Rue Goff, Paris 5, Fr.
Brentano's, 37 Rue de l'Opera, Paris, Fr.
Desforges, Librairie des Sciences Pratiques, 29 Quai des G rand Augustin, Paris 6, Fr.
Librairie B. Arthaud, 23 Grand Rue, Grenoble-Isere, Fr.
Librairie Hachette, 79 Boulevard Saint-Germain, Paris 6, Fr.
Librairie Lavoisier, Technique & Documentation, 11 Rue Lavoisier, Paris 8e, Fr.
Librairie Scientifique Hermann, 6 Rue de la Sorbonne, Paris, Fr.

Denmark

Jul. Gjellerup Boghandel, Soelvgade 87, 1307 Copenhagen K. Denmark
Ejner Munksgaard Ltd., Norregade 6, 1165 Copenhagen K., Denmark
Polyteknisk Boghandel, Oester Voldgade 10, 1350 Copenhagen K., Denmark

Germany

Buchhandlung Harri Deutsch, Graefstrasse 47, 6 Frankfurt/Main 90, Germany
Otto Harrasowitz, Taunus Strasse 5, 6200 Wiesbaden, Germany
Hubert Hermanns, Ludwigsallee 57, Aachen, Germany
Lange & Springer Wissenschafrliche Buchhandlung, Heidelberger Platz 3, 1 Berlin 31
  —(Wilmersdorf), Germany
Librairie Muller, Eppelstrasse, 19 C, Stuttgart, Germany

Holland

E. J. Brill, Oude Rijin 33a, Leiden, Holland
Dekker en Nordemann, O.Z. Voorburgwal 243, Amsterdam C, Holland
Martinus Nijhoff, P.O. Box 269, The Hague, Lange Voorhaut 9–11, Holland
Noording Noord Nederlandse Boekhandel, Oosterstraat 11, Groningen, Holland
Swets & Zeitlinger, Keizersgracht 471–487, Amsterdam, Holland

Italy

Anglo-American Book Co., s.r.k. Via delle Vita 57, Rome, Italy
Hoepli Ulrica via Hoepli 5, 20121 Milan, Italy
Libreria Internazionale Rizzoli, Galleria Colonna-Largo Chigi 15, Rome, Italy
Messaggerie Italiane, Via Guilo Carcano 32, Milan, Italy

Portugal

Libraria Bertrand, Rua Garrett 73, Lisbon, Portugal

Spain

Afrodisia Aguado, S.A. Marqúes de Cubas 5, Madrid 14, Spain
Cientificao Tecnica, Sancho Davila 27 (Dep. Grossiste) Madrid, Spain
Libreria Cientifica Medinaceli del C.S.I.C. Duque de Medinaceli 4, Madrid, Spain
Libreria Tecnica Extranjera, C/Tuset 8–10 (Edificio Monitor) Barcelona, Spain

Switzerland

Librairie Payot, S.A. Editions Payot, rue Centrale, 1003 Lausanne, Switzerland
Wepf and Co., 5 Eisengasse, 4001 Basel, Switzerland

Mexico

Librairies Francaise, 12 Paseo de la Reforma (C.D.) Mexico City, Mexico
Libraria Internatiocnal S.A., Cedro No. 512, Apartado Postal 26–370 Mexico 4, D.F.
Manual Bonilla, Tiber 38 Desp. 201–202, Mexico 5, D.F.

South America

Ao Livro Tecnico, 81, avenue Rio Branco, Rio-de-Janeiro, Brazil
Fuchs y Cia, avde Roque Saenz Pena, 760, Buenos Aires, Argentina
Libreria Politecnica, Calle Villaflor, Sabana Grande, Apartado de Este 4845, Caracas,
     Venezuela
Livraria Triangulo, Rua Baro de Itapetininga, 255 Lojas 23 e 24, Caixa Postal 30317,
     Sao Paulo, Brazil

Once the book dealer has been selected, details of placing orders should be outlined. In the course of selection, complete and accurate information relating to each title must be noted. The next step is to decide in what form the orders will be organized. It is possible to list titles perhaps alphabetically by author on letterhead stationery or to use the organization's own requisition forms. This is not very satisfactory, particularly if large numbers of books are ordered, because it is almost certain that not all of the titles will be supplied at one time which means that the list must be checked and rechecked, and billing can become confused.

The recommended alternative to the listing of titles is to use individual order forms in multiple copy. These are standard catalog card size, designed to indicate all possible information required for a single title, and are available from library supply houses. They are essentially the same format as is recommended in the early part of this chapter for selection purposes, and in fact should be used for the dual function. The number of carbon copies needed can be decided after counting the possible uses:

> 1 or 2 to be sent as orders (1 to be returned with the book)
> 1 to be used to order Library of Congress catalog cards
> 1 to remain as record of order

Four carbons are certainly the minimum that should be considered. One copy should accompany the books through the whole of its technical processing with any relevant notes added as it moves along. An example

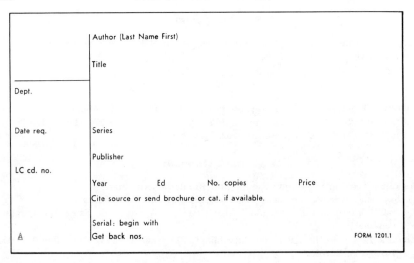

Figure 1.

of a printed order form is shown as Figure 1. Some dealers supply such forms.

AUTOMATION OF ORDER PROCESS

Many libraries have automated the book ordering process where there is access to the necessary equipment. As in other applications of automation, the details of any specific procedure must be developed through consultation with those who develop the programming for the organization. A few libraries have their own systems personnel who have good comprehension of what is involved. A helpful description of an actual situation in a scientific library is outlined by Miller, Lee, and Nilsson (1) where initially 1000 titles with a total of 1300 copies were ordered. The essential piece of equipment to begin the operation was an IBM 632 electronic typing calculator. The rationality of the automated system is shown in the orderly manner in which all data relating to a title—specifically Library of Congress classification, date of publication, price, number of copies, catalog cards, and name of person requesting—can be kept together for the fastest possible processing. Another concise presentation of automated acquisition procedures, this one for an academic organization, is given by Dunlap (2) who reports on the University of Michigan Library's procedure.

INTERNATIONAL STANDARD BOOK NUMBERING

A system for specific identification of book titles that had been in use in Great Britain for several years was adopted in the United States in 1968. This is known as International Standard Book Numbering, which is a remarkably clever yet simple device for providing every book published with a unique number, always nine digits in length. The first three digits identify the publisher, the next five a title issued by that publisher, and the ninth is a working or control unit. For example the ISBN L-0-471 93751 7 serves to indicate a book published by John Wiley & Sons entitled *An Introduction to Plant Diseases* by B. E. J. Wheeler. (N.B. The L-0 is added by the publisher for internal purposes). These ISBN's will be assigned henceforth to all books published, and it is expected that eventually all titles in print will be so tagged. R. R. Bowker Company administers the system in the United States.

It is apparent that this numbering system is potentially very helpful in an automated acquisition system particularly if it can be used by both the individual library placing orders and the dealer. Even if it is used only by the dealer it should serve to speed the delivery of books. Shaw (3) proposes a further refinement, the assignment of an identifying number to every library and also to every book dealer or even every book store. It would then be feasible to prepare punched cards with the library's number as well as that of the dealer and thus introduce a truly universal automated distribution system. The idea certainly merits consideration as a means of making the book purchasing process efficient.

GIFTS

It is not unfitting to mention the possibility of acquiring books and other publications as gifts, particularly from staff scientists of the organization who no longer want personal items. Though it might be considered a nuisance at times to be the recipient of stacks of miscellaneous materials of little apparent value, it is possible that among such discards some very desirable publications will be found. Early issues of periodicals acquired before the library started its subscriptions, classic works long out-of-print, or archival publications are some of the kinds of things that make careful sorting worthwhile. Those that are not needed can sometimes be sold if this permission is first asked of the donor.

ACCESSION RECORDS

A systematic record of acquisitions should be established and maintained. This can be done very simply, perhaps by cumulating a file of order slip copies for the year. Another method, once very popular in libraries, is to enter each title in a large ledger in which sections are assigned to the main classes of the scheme used, or titles can be entered in order of accession, assigning an accession number to the book if this is used by the library. Also there is much to be said for the use of the accession number as a unique identification to be marked in the book simultaneously. However it is kept, this information will be useful for inclusion in the annual report to provide facts to management if requested and to show the subject areas in which purchasing is done.

PUBLICATIONS OTHER THAN BOOKS

While books as monographic works provide scientific information as it reaches an advanced state of development and provide maximum knowledge in a minimum package, other unique publications are of importance in a specialized collection. Periodical literature is, of course, another segment so significant that it merits a complete chapter (see Chapter 6). The types of publications considered here vary widely and originate from many sources. Some are easily located; others must be sought through diligent scanning of journals that carry notes of such items of concern and also appropriate official listings.

Most of these publications are small in size and cannot be handled by the usual cataloging processes; they must be indexed and kept in special files. Many are in numbered series of which either all publications or only selected ones are required. Their value may be permanent or ephemeral and they may be eventually retained or discarded. Several types of important publications are discussed in the following section; advice concerning their finding and methods of acquiring is given.

The most complete and comprehensive guide to the type of publications considered here is the booklet edited by Jackson (4), *Acquisition of Special Materials*. Each of its eight chapters is devoted to one category of those items that are both difficult to locate and to acquire. Its overall bibliography includes 394 citations, an indication of its exhaustive coverage. The presentation here is necessarily condensed, but it does cover the major points as introduction to this area of the literature.

Government Documents

There is much scientific and technical information published in the voluminous literature of government documents. They flow continuously from national, state, and municipal bodies, though the greatest number of present interest are issued under the sponsorship of U.S. Government agencies. However, those of possible pertinence from other countries or from lesser bodies should not be ignored. Because of their disperse character, some of these publications can be difficult to detect so that it is advisable to become acquainted with some of the existing guides.

For background information concerning U. S. Government publications two books can be very helpful. One is the fundamental work long known as *Boyd's United States Government Publications: Sources of Information for Libraries,* which was ultimately revised by Rips in 1949. The other is *Government Publications and Their Use,* 4th ed., by Schmeckebier and Eastin whose last revision was in 1969. Since many government publications are serials the *Guide to United States Government Serials and Periodicals,* which is revised annually by J. L. Andriot and published by Documents Index, McLean, Va., is an invaluable source.

A number of national government and government-related agencies have been producing publications of high merit for many years. Others got started only since World War II. Some of the major issuing agencies are the following:

U. S. Atomic Energy Commission
U. S. Bureau of Mines
U. S. Department of Agriculture
U. S. Geological Survey
U. S. Department of Health, Education, and Welfare
U. S. National Bureau of Standards
U. S. Office of Naval Research
National Aeronautics and Space Administration
National Science Foundation
National Academy of Science—National Research Council
The Smithsonian Institution

Each of these bodies has such a large publishing program that it has its own guides or cumulative lists. The comprehensive announcement source is the *Monthly Catalog of United States Government Publications* which has been issued since 1895, but it does not cover everything produced and makes no attempt to include either minor items or the technical reports which are discussed in detail in a later section of this chapter.

Most of the regularly published items are available by purchase from the Superintendent of Documents, U. S. Government Printing Office, Washington, D.C. 20402. The office sells coupons that are convenient in ordering inexpensive items since cash or coupons must accompany orders. Where acquisition is on a large scale it is worthwhile to arrange for a deposit account, which can be done for a minimum of $25. When no charge is specified, requests are sent to the issuing agency. It can be a convenience to delegate the responsibility for procuring documents to a special subscription service such as Government Publications Service, Bernan Associates, 4701 Willard Ave., Washington, D.C. 20015. They will even handle standing orders for series publications that appear irregularly.

The discussion thus far applies only to the standard publications put out by the long established agencies, that is, their bulletins, monographs, and circulars. In more recent years, principally since World War II, another even more voluminous literature has emerged. This is known as the *Technical Report Literature.* Individual reports in great number come from private companies doing research under government contract, from university laboratories similarly sponsored, and from government laboratories. Most of these documents are available to anyone having the requisite tenacity to detect those of possible concern, but some are "classified" and may be read only by persons who can establish "a need to know," which usually means that they themselves are working under contract and have been granted "clearance." Many reports are eventually declassified. Because this burgeoning literature is so extensive it has been necessary to provide special guides and abstracting publications to deal with it.

Detailed histories of the development of the government-sponsored technical report are outlined in the book edited by Weil (5), *The Technical Report,* which covers all types of technical reports (including non-governmental). Tallman (6) provides a concise history of their origins. This all began with the Office of Research & Development (OSRD) in 1941, to be continued indefinitely. The clue to recognition of such a report is a notation consisting of a combination of capital letters and numerals, perhaps more than one such set. The letters usually indicate the place where the work was done or possibly the distribution agency. Contract numbers may be indicated. Some of the simpler of these codes could be the following: WADC-69, NP-4462, NYO-7743, PB-1792, or AD 498. A little experience makes these easy to recognize and the *Dictionary of Report Series Codes* compiled by Redman (7) is an excellent guide to the more obscure.

One way of surveying the whole category of technical reports is through the listings that are provided as guides to them. These are next described individually.

Government Reports Announcements, Vol. 1, 1946, to date, is issued twice a month, and is a guide to reports from a number of sources. It is published by the National Technical Information Service, U. S. Department of Commerce, Springfield, Va. 22151, for $30 a year, $37.50 foreign. Since 1968, all items are supplied in standardized format either as legible copy for $3, or microfiche for 90¢. Prepaid coupons are available, deposit accounts are accepted, or cash can be sent with orders. There is a special FAST announcement service that calls attention to a small number of noteworthy titles, for $5 a year. Hitherto these documents were sold by the then Office of Technical Services or the Library of Congress, both of which for this purpose have been supplanted by the NTIS which publicizes report literature.

Brief though its existence has been, *Government Reports Announcements* has had four previous titles. When it was first published, as a means of listing available captured German and Japanese documents during World War II, it was called *Bibliography of Scientific and Industrial Reports,* and then was changed to *Bibliography of Technical Reports.* In 1954 it became *U. S. Government Research Reports,* and in 1965 the word "Development" was interjected to indicate expanded coverage as this is the broadest based of the technical report announcement media. In 1971 the designation was again changed to *Government Reports Announcements.*

Technical Abstract Bulletin (TAB), Vol. 1, 1944 to date, lists documents considered to have some connection with defense interests and is available only to persons involved with such activities, particularly those who are doing work under defense related contracts. It is published by the Defense Documentation Center for Scientific and Technical Information (DDC) which was originally called Armed Services Technical Information Agency (ASTIA) prior to 1963. The reports listed in TAB are prefaced by the letters "AD" which initially served to identify them as ASTIA Documents. Both classified and unclassified reports were once included in TAB; now only classified reports are cited. The original title was *Technical Information Pilot* which was changed in 1953 to *Title Announcement Bulletin.* In 1956 it was changed to *Technical Abstract Bulletin.*

Nuclear Science Abstracts, Vol. 1, 1948 to date, is an abstracting publication issued under the auspices of the Atomic Energy Commission (AEC) by its Office of Technical Information. It provides abstracts of reports emanating from AEC sponsored research, and also of relevant articles in periodicals, duplicating in some measure coverage of *Physics Ab-*

stracts and *Chemical Abstracts.* There are good indexes, in particular the cumulative report number index. Directions for ordering copies of reports are in every issue. They are available on microcard or microfiche. Depository collections are open for consultation in a number of major libraries. Computer tape service was initiated in 1969.

Abstracts of Classified Reports, Vol. 1, 1944 to date, cites only classified reports. This is a publication of the Atomic Energy Commission's Division of Technical Information Extension. Consequently, distribution is highly restricted to persons whose security clearance is proven.

For documents relating to space research *Scientific and Technical Aerospace Reports,* Vol. 1, 1963 to date, is published by the National Aeronautics and Space Administration and commonly known as STAR. It is a guide to the reports issued in conjunction with research sponsored by NASA. In coordination with STAR another publication titled *International Aerospace Abstracts* is published to cover the book and periodical literature. NASA provides an excellent guide entitled *The NASA Scientific and Technical Information System,* NASA, Washington, D.C. 20546, 1969(?).

To promote the use of the report literature twelve regional Technical Report Centers were established in 1962 in locations well distributed over the United States. Reports from agencies such as NASA, AEC, Department of Defense (DOD), Office of Naval Research (ONR), and many others are contributed to this effort. The centers are located in the following cities:

Federal System of Regional Technical Report Centers

LOCATION OF CENTERS AND THE AREA SERVED BY EACH

Atlanta, Ga., Georgia Institute of Technology (serving Alabama, Florida, Georgia, Mississippi, South Carolina, and Tennessee).

Cambridge, Mass., Massachusetts Institute of Technology (serving Maine, Massachusetts, New Hampshire, Rhode Island, and Vermont).

Chicago, Ill., John Crerar Library (serving Illinois, Indiana, Michigan, Minnesota, and Wisconsin).

Dallas, Tex., Southern Methodist University (serving Louisiana, Oklahoma, and Texas).

Boulder, Colo., University of Colorado (serving Colorado, New Mexico, North Dakota, South Dakota, Utah, and Wyoming).

Kansas City, Mo., Linda Hall Library (serving Arkansas, Iowa, Kansas, Missouri, and Nebraska).

Los Angeles, Calif., University of California (Los Angeles campus) (serving Arizona and Southern California).

New York, N. Y., Columbia University (serving Connecticut, New Jersey, and New York).

Pittsburgh, Pa., Carnegie Library of Pittsburgh (serving Kentucky, Ohio, Pennsylvania, and West Virginia).

San Francisco, Calif., University of California (Berkeley campus) (serving Hawaii, Nevada, and northern California).

Seattle, Wash., University of Washington (serving Alaska, Idaho, Montana, Oregon, and Washington).

Washington, D. C., Library of Congress (serving Delaware, District of Columbia, Maryland, North Carolina, and Virginia).

The report literature does pose problems, although they are not insuperable once their peculiarities are understood and the helpful available guides used. One of these guides is entitled *Science Information*

Table 1   Availability of Government Technical Information

	Unclass DOD R&D Reports	Class DOD R&D Reports	Mil-Specs and Standards	NASA R&D Reports	NASA Specs and Standards	AEC R&D Reports	Federal Specs and Standards	Summary of On-Going R&D Efforts
Order documents from								
Hard copy	h	b	e	g h	No	h i	c	b j
Microfilm	b h	b	No	h	No	i	No	No
Work unit summaries (DD Form 1498)	12 b	12 b	No	12 b 12 j	No	12 j	No	b j
Index to documents	3 f 10 h	3 b	1 a	5 a f	No	7 f a	4 ª	No
Abstracts of documents	h 2 6 11	2 b	No	6 a 9 f	No	8 a	No	No
Subscription to specific subjects	h	No	1 d	g	h	g h i	4 c	No

Key

Publications

1. *Department of Defense Index of Specifications and Standards*
2. *Technical Abstract Bulletin (TAB)*
3. *TAB Index*
4. *Index of Federal Specifications and Standards*
5. *Scientific and Technical Aerospace Reports (STAR) Index*
6. *STAR Abstracts*
7. *Nuclear Science Abstracts (NSA) Index*

8. *Nuclear Science Abstracts*
9. *International Aerospace Abstracts*
10. *U. S. Government Research and Development (USGRDR) Index*
11. *Government Reports Announcements*
12. *Work Unit Summaries*

Addresses

a. U.S. Government Printing Office, Washington, D.C. 20402
b. Defense Documentation Center (DDC), Cameron Station, Alexandria, Va. 22314
c. Federal Supply Service, Naval Weapons Plant, Washington, D.C. 20407
d. Director, Naval Publications and Printing Office, Bldg 4, Section D, 700 Robbins Avenue, Philadelphia, Pa. 19111
e. Naval Supply Depot, 5801 Tabor Ave., Philadelphia, Pa. 19120
f. Selected Public or University Libraries
g. Scientific and Technical Information Division, Code ATSS, NASA, Washington, D.C. 20546
h. National Technical Information Service, 5285 Port Royal Road, Springfield, Va. 22151
i. USAEC, Division of Technical Information, P.O. Box 62, Oak Ridge, Tenn. 37830
j. Science Information Exchange (SIE), 1730 M Street NW, Washington, D.C. 22036

From the Air Force Office of Aerospace Research (8).

Available from the Atomic Energy Commission, designated as TID 4550, 11th revision April 1969, which is supplied by the Office of Technical Information Extension, P.O. Box 1001, Oak Ridge, Tenn. 37830.

An explicit chart outlining ways of procuring technical reports has been prepared by the Air Force Office of Aerospace Research (8). It is reproduced in Table 1. *Chemical Abstracts* in its first issue each year gives directions for ordering reports that are abstracted.

There are differences of opinion among scientists as to the significance of the report literature. Some contend that it wastes time to try to keep abreast of it because any information of real importance will eventually be published in periodicals. Although this may be largely true, the detailed data in some reports are not likely to be published elsewhere. However, according to Randall (9) technical reports in the field of aeronautics, had in 1959 a median life of only 1.5 years; in physics it was found to be somewhat longer—2.4 years. Two years later Burton and Green (10) substantiated this, stating that "the reports do not constitute a significant portion of the cited physics literature." While it may be necessary to acquire some reports in many libraries, it may be possible to discard them after a couple of years. A recommendation is to purchase in microfiche form, thus simplifying the storage space question.

The chief reason why these technical reports are not cited more extensively may be that they are not easily accessible. Gray and Rosenberg (11) published evidence in 1957 that only about one half of the significant data contained in government sponsored research reports were published in the formal literature within 2 to 3 years. Possibly the establishment of the twelve report file centers will bring them to the attention of a wider range of users.

Patents

Patents constitute a unique category of government documents that are so important to industrial activity that some corporations maintain separate patent libraries. In brief, a patent is the record of an agreement whereby an inventor discloses his invention in return for which he is granted exclusive rights to its monetary exploitation for a period of 17 years (this period varies in different countries). These rights are usually assigned to a company, which may be continuously redesigning its plant processes to take advantage of inventions. In many libraries, principally those in companies engaged in product development, it is as necessary to provide the patent literature as it is to have books and periodicals. Of primary concern here are those issuing in the United States, although it is likely that where interests are at all serious, patents of other countries should be watched also.

Each week the *Official Gazette* of the United States Patent Office announces the patents granted for inventions, designs, and trademarks that have been issued for that period. The *Gazette* can be scanned quickly because the convenient subject groupings (*a*) general and mechanical, (*b*) chemical, and (*c*) electrical, make it easy to select those patents of interest. Since early 1971, the *Gazette* is issued as two separate parts, the *Patent Office Gazette* and the *Trade Mark Gazette*. Where this is a regular procedure it is advisable to order a supply of coupons in denominations of 10¢ or 25¢ from U. S. Department of Commerce, Patent Office, Washington, D.C. 20231. Deposit accounts are accepted. Coupon orders for copies must be sent to Box 9, Patent Office, Washington, D.C. 20231. Individual copies of patents cost 50¢ to be paid in cash or by coupon.

When interests are well defined and on a sustained basis, it is advisable to place subscription orders for all issues in specified classes. These classes are selected from the *Manual of Patent Office Classification,* with advice from the organization's patent counsel if accessible.

Another patent subscription service is provided through the National Technical Information Service from which these documents are supposed to be distributed on 16-mm microfilm within 2 weeks after they are announced in the *Gazette*. If all categories are required, the price is $895 a year, or $600 for the General and Mechanical, $300 for Electrical, and $300 for Chemical. Microfilm copy is available for patents issued from 1966 to date.

Mail service from the Patent Office is sometimes rather dilatory, taking up to a month for orders to be filled. When time is an important factor, recourse to express service is advisable, and there are a number of such agencies operating from Washington. One is Air Mail Patent Service, Munsey Bldg., Washington, D.C. 20004. The price for the first copy is $1.50, and 75¢ for additional ones instead of the official 50¢.

For patents from other countries there are publications similar to the *U. S. Official Gazette* that can be subscribed to if this is warranted. In Great Britain it is the *Official Journal*. A very efficient international service is provided by Derwent Publications Ltd., Rochdale House, Theobalds Road, London, W.C. 1, England, from which several periodicals listing recently issued patents can be obtained on subscription. Among these are *Chemical Patents Journal, Plastics Chemicals Patents Journal, Petrochemical Patents Journal, British Patents Gazette, German Patents Gazette,* and *Commonwealth Patents Gazette*. Additionally, Derwent has other services such as FARMDOC which brings together comprehensive information concerning pharmaceutical patents, and PLASDOC, a similar compilation covering plastics. Fast service via magnetic tape is available.

If complete patent coverage is not required, such sources as *Chemical Abstracts* in which the most significant chemical patents are abstracted, or the periodical *Industrie Chimique Belge* that provides listings of Belgian chemical patents (where there is a "quick-action" patent office) may suffice. *Chemical Abstracts* lists the addresses of patent offices in all countries in its first annual issue. Copies may be ordered from these offices (prices are indicated in the list of addresses), or photocopies can be supplied by the U. S. Patent Office. Some of the large public libraries in various cities have files of patents from other countries, principally from Great Britain, France, and Germany.

State and Municipal Documents

The occasional state or municipal publication that may be needed can be noted from announcements in local media or identified from the particular department from which it issues, for example, state regulatory bodies. If it is necessary to watch for such items, the *Monthly Checklist of State Publications* should be subscribed to; this has been compiled by the Library of Congress since 1910. Knowledge of investigational work in progress or of prior publications from certain agencies will indicate sources to be watched. Some states have lists of their publications. Orders may be placed either directly or with the regular book dealer.

Documents from Countries Other than the United States

Government documents issued in other countries are announced in periodicals, and there are official lists similar to those of U.S. agencies. In Great Britain the Department of Scientific and Industrial Research provides compilations from the individual units of which it is comprised. There is also a *Government Publications Monthly List* from Her Majesty's Stationery Office, London. British Government publications can be obtained from Pendragon House, 899 Broadway Ave., Redwood City, Calif., 94063. Additional offices are maintained in Washington, D.C., Chicago, Ill., and San Francisco, Calif. For technical reports similar to those issued by the U.S. Atomic Energy Commission there is the *Guide to UKAEA Documents,* J. R. Smith, Ed., 3rd ed., published in 1963.

Canada has significant publications resulting from research and investigational work in its Department of Mines, National Research Council, and other agencies. Inquiries and requests for lists of titles should be sent to the central government offices. Archer (12) has provided advice concerning the procurement of Canadian provincial government documents.

On an international scale the United Nations has become a major source of publications; those of scientific and technical concern coming from such specialized agencies as the Food and Agriculture Organization (FAO) and the International Atomic Energy Agency (IAEA), both of which issue their own lists. The United Nations Education, Scientific, and Cultural Organization (UNESCO) has a monthly bulletin entitled *Bibliography: Documentation: Terminology,* which is an excellent source for notices of important national and international bibliographic activities. Full information is supplied for procuring the titles cited.

Dissertations and Theses

Much valuable information appears in doctoral dissertations and master's theses written by candidates for degrees in colleges and universities. Much of this is not accessible because these presentations are not covered by the indexing and abstracting publications. Some of the results of the research done for this scholarly purpose are published eventually, but usually in a condensed form and long after the work has been done. It may be worth some effort to tap these sources, particularly if it is known that investigational work in subject areas of interest is being done at certain academic institutions.

Doctoral dissertations written at universities in the United States are listed in a periodical entitled *Dissertation Abstracts International* which is expanding its scope and since 1969 is divided into Section A, "The Humanities and Social Sciences" and Section B, "The Sciences and Engineering," and published by University Microfilms from 1953 to date. From 1933 to 1957 the Association of Research Libraries issued annually *Doctoral Dissertations Accepted by American Universities* under the editorship of D. B. Gilchrist *et al. Dissertation Abstracts International* includes chiefly those dissertations from a group of universities that send these documents to University Microfilms to be microfilmed. Microfilm or xerox copies may be purchased, a service intended to supplant interlibrary lending.

Another guide to dissertations was introduced in 1970 by University Microfilms as a periodical entitled *Dissertation Digest*. This is a listing by titles in subject groupings with prices for Xerox and microfilm copies of dissertations; the abstracts of these appear later in *Dissertation Abstracts International*.

Stephens (13) provides a comprehensive list of sources for locating dissertations written in the United States and other countries. Examples of these listings are as follows:

Jahrverzeichnis der deutschen Hochschulenschriften, Deutsche Bucherei, Leipzig, annual.

Catalogue des Theses et Ecrits Academiques, Minister d'Education National, Paris, annual.

Some publications that provide information concerning dissertations in specific fields are as follows:

Directory of Graduate Research: Faculties, Publications, and Doctoral Theses in Departments or Divisions of Chemistry, Biochemistry, and Chemical Engineering at United States Universities, Committee on Professional Training, American Chemical Society, 1155 Sixteenth St., N.W., Washington, D.C. Published biennially since 1955. Includes authors and titles of "doctoral theses."

Dissertations in Physics: An Indexed Bibliography of all Doctoral Theses Accepted by American Universities, 1861–1959, M. L. Marckworth, Compiler, Stanford University Press, Stanford, Calif., 1961.

Bibliography of Theses Written for Advanced Degrees in Geology and Related Sciences at Universities and Colleges in the United States and Canada through 1957, J. Chronic, H. Chronic, and Petroleum Research Corporation, Pruett Press, Boulder, Colo., 1958.

A Bibliography of Graduate Theses on Geophysics in United States and Canadian Institutions, G. E. Tarbox, Colorado School of Mines, Golden, Colo., 1958.

It is possible to borrow copies of dissertations from some universities but others have stopped this practice. Those that cooperate in the University Microfilm Project expect that this service supplants lending. Sometimes it may be necessary to have a microfilm copy made to special order.

Master's theses are even more difficult to locate because there have been no published listings. Usually the only source is the card catalogs of the universities at which they are written. However, in 1962, University Microfilms initiated an attempt to provide a publication listing them. This is entitled *Masters Abstracts,* but initially only sixteen institutions participated.

The results of research reported by students in universities in countries other than the United States may sometimes be of interest; these are even more difficult to obtain. Some periodicals carry announcements and abstracts, such as *Angewandte Chemie,* which cites certain ones in German institutions, and *Industrie Chimique Belge,* which lists Belgian ones in the field of chemistry. In Great Britain, Aslib has published lists of dissertations accepted by universities in Great Britain and Ireland.

Reprints

It is often desirable to obtain reprints of important papers published in journals either as extra copies or, if a journal is not of sufficient interest to justify subscription, as an occasional article wanted that may be obtained from the author. This procedure in general is not as important as it was before copying devices were so prevalent. However, it is possible to write to an author to ask for a reprint, a favor he is likely to grant willingly as long as his supply lasts, but he will appreciate the courtesy of having his postage refunded and receipt acknowledged.

Company Reports

In any organization in which research is done, the results are usually written as formal reports. These are understandably closely guarded, at least until all benefits are realized. There could be some circumstances in which a report might be loaned so that polite inquiry would not be amiss, particularly if direct competition is not involved. Some reports are distributed quite freely, constituting a form of the previously discussed trade literature. A certain astuteness is requisite in detecting where and how this source of information might be tapped.

Translations

Translations of articles from periodicals principally, or of books occasionally, from other languages into English are frequently required in libraries serving fundamental scientific research and are also likely to be wanted for subjects of technical interest. That this requirement is not an easy one to satisfy is attested by Bush (14) in a report on the problems of fifty pharmaceutical and fifty chemical firms. A majority of these companies require translations; about half of them use commercial agencies and the rest use either individuals or members of their own staffs. The range of prices charged by agencies found by Bush is noteworthy, from 50¢ to $5 per hundred English words for all languages. All translations, however, need not be purchased. A large number are on file in collections from which they may be either borrowed or copies supplied for little cost.

When a translation is needed a first step might be to determine whether one is already available. In the United States the National Translations Center located at John Crerar Library, 35 West 33rd St., Chicago, Ill. 61616, houses the collection that was initiated by Special Libraries Association and by 1969 had grown to more than 140,000 items. Additions, which are contributed chiefly by industrial companies, are announced in a semimonthly bulletin, *Translations-Register Index,* published by SLA which succeeded *Technical Translations,* formerly issued by the U. S. Department of Commerce, Office of Technical Services, which superseded *Translation Monthly,* the original publication of SLA. Because the collection housed at Crerar consists of contributed translations from various sources, there is no relationship between the dates of publication of the original publications and the translations; thus the listings are completely random. However, indexes make the location of a specific item fairly simple.

Another source is the *World Index of Scientific Translations,* a quarterly published by the European Translation Center, 101 Deelenstraat, Delft, The Netherlands, since January 1967. This serves to increase significantly the coverage of the National Translations Center.

In Great Britain the chief collecting point for translations is the National Lending Library at Boston Spa. Other sources are the Department of Scientific and Industrial Research and Aslib. It is likely that the NLL will soon be recognized as the official center and an attempt made to contribute copies of all translations.

In 1970 a cooperative agreement was made among the three aforementioned translation agencies which will make the resources of all of them even more readily accessible to users.

If a translation is not already on file it may be advisable to approach one of the many organizations that prepare translations as a business. Some of these are more efficient than others, especially when subjects require comprehension of the science involved for accurate interpretation. A comprehensive guide to these services is the booklet *Translaters and Translations*, Services and Sources, 3rd ed., compiled by Kaiser and published by Special Libraries Association in 1965. Bush (14) tells of some of the things to watch for when contracting for translations.

Trade Literature—Equipment Catalogs

The various types of publications put forth by industrial companies principally for advertising purposes comprise what is in some situations a very important resource commonly known as "trade literature." These often provide accurate technical information about products or materials that are offered for sale, and a collection can be so useful that it merits a special spot in the library. Some companies issue occasional pamphlets describing certain items, or lists of products, rarely with prices, but usually with full descriptions and properties where applicable. These can be located by reading advertisements in appropriate periodicals and special sections where such items are regularly noted. Mailing lists are maintained by companies understandably eager to advertise their wares to possible purchasers. There is usually no charge for trade literature. Some libraries use simple forms for requesting free materials, acknowledging their receipt, a courtesy that builds good will.

A particularly important category of trade literature consists of product descriptions and specifications as contained in manufacturers' catalogs. Because these are so numerous they are difficult to acquire and maintain in order. The answer to the problem of many volumes of catalogs has been to reproduce them in microform. Among those with the greatest coverage are the following:

Thomas' Register of Manufacturers, Thomas Publishing Company, 461 Eighth Ave. New York 10001. This service provides the catalogs on microfiche of most of the manufacturers represented in the annual list.

Sweet's Catalogs, Sweet's Industrial Information Systems, Palo Alto, Calif. More than 600,000 pages of catalogs are available on microfilm.

Vender-Spec-Microfile, Information Handling Service, Inc., Denver, Colo. 80200. Engineering and parts catalogs from 15,000 suppliers, all on microfilm.

Transister Information Microfile, D.A.T.A., Inc., 32 Lincoln Ave. Orange, N. J. 07050. Data on transistors, diodes, rectifiers, microcircuits.

Standards and Specifications

Published standards and specifications for various procedures and materials are vitally important in many organizations where products must meet specified requirements. Both national and international groups are responsible for either writing specifications for materials or determining what these should be by organizing testing programs from which results the appropriate decisions are made. Government agencies, trade associations, and even individual companies devise standards of many sorts. In the United States the U.S. National Bureau of Standards carries out a broad program of investigation and develops national guides. The largest nongovernmental organization in this field is the American Society for Testing and Materials, 1916 Race St., Philadelphia, Pa. 19103, whose many committees produce standards for thousands of materials and procedures for their testing. These are published in about thirty volumes, which are available also on microfilm. The centralizing agency for this activity is the United States of America Standards Institute which grants ultimate approval, if its own requirements are met, and bestows the seal of "U. S. Standard" on all those that qualify.

A list of sources of published standards and specifications is included in the Appendix of this book. However, a truly exhaustive report is the book *Standards and Specification, Information Sources,* by Struglia (15). This includes every possible type of material and all of the organizations concerned with this aspect of quality maintenance.

Publications in Forms Other than Paper Print

As the process of distributing information becomes more complex because of the need to reach larger audiences with increasing volumes of material, the printed page has been supplemented by other methods of presentation. Most of these fall in the category of "audio-visual," but all of them do not. Among those finding acceptance are the following:

1. Computer tapes to be used by the purchaser with his own compatible equipment. Such things as very large compilations of data and selected references from the periodical literature are available in this form. Some of these services are cited in Chapter 10.

2. Microform appears in many guises, making it difficult to follow the constantly changing terminology and always newer methods of using this versatile basic idea. Initially, microfilm was used in continuous strips wound on reels which were threaded manually on a reading machine, but this method is being supplanted by the cassette or cartridge, a small box

in which the film is permanently stored so that when the box is inserted in the reader a device catches the film and advances it to the page wanted for viewing on a screen.

Another film form is the microfiche, a kind of film card in a now standardized size, approximately 4 by $5\frac{3}{4}$ inches. There is even the ultrafiche, an even greater reduction to accommodate more than the eighty pages of print of the fiche.

Film loops are essentially large circles of microfilm upon which a single topic is presented as an animated movie that runs in a special projector, repeating as many times as the learner requires. Laboratory techniques and other special subjects best comprehended visually are usually the kinds of materials offered.

Standard moving picture films, many with sound and in color, are being produced to present scientific subjects in detail. They take from 15 minutes to an hour to run. Even briefer presentations such as film strips provide supplementary illustrative materials.

3. A method used less but open to further exploitation are transparencies which overlay in groups to show complex processes graphically.

4. Groups of slides which project on a screen can illustrate almost any kind of subject.

Of these methods of presenting information some are fully adaptable as publication media—to present original material as a form of publication. Others such as microfilm and microfiche are more applicable as secondary publication media, a means of economically copying material originally published on paper.

Many publishers of books provide some materials in these other-than-paper-print forms, as does John Wiley & Sons in increasing volume and variety. There are also specializing organizations such as Kalmia Company, Concord, Mass., that offers, for example, technicolor film loops illustrating quantitative chemistry laboratory techniques.

Some of the professional scientific societies sponsor the making of movies on subjects of recent development. Although it might appear that these materials are designed principally for academic use, it should be apparent that their educational possibilities are unlimited and can well serve to keep scientists up to date wherever they are employed.

CONCLUSION

In developing the collection of books and related publications, every possible source and type of presentation should be considered for its potential pertinence. Vital information can be found in all kinds of publications ranging from the most seemingly insignificant pamphlet to the most authoritative scholarly treatise. The process of locating, selecting, and procuring those titles to be used by the people the library services requires wide familiarity with what is published and constant vigilance to see that nothing of value escapes notice.

REFERENCES

1. E. F. Miller, B. W. Lee, and J. D. Nilsson, "Automated Book Ordering and Receiving," *Spec. Libr.* **57**, 96–100 (1966).

2. C. R. Dunlap, "Automated Acquisitions Procedures at the University of Michigan Library," *Libr. Resour. Tech. Serv.* **11**, 192–202 (1967).

3. R. Shaw, "CATCALL," *Coll. Res. Libr.* **31**, 89–95 (1970).

4. I. H. Jackson, Ed., *Acquisition of Special Materials*, San Francisco Bay Region Chapter, Special Libraries Association, San Francisco, Calif., 1966.

5. B. H. Weil, Ed., *The Technical Report—Its Preparation, Processing, and Use in Industry and Government*, Reinhold, New York, 1954.

6. J. Tallman, "History and Importance of Technical Reports: Part I," *Sci. Tech. News* **15**, 44–46 (Summer 1961); Part II, *ibid.*, 164–172 (Winter 1962).

7. H. Redman and L. E. Godfrey, Eds., *Dictionary of Report Series Codes*, Special Libraries Association, New York, 1962; 2nd ed. in preparation, 1970.

8. *U. S. Air Force Office of Aerospace Research Newsletter*, STINFO Report.

9. G. E. Randall, "Technical Reports—Value Short Lived," *Spec. Libr.* **50**, 447–450 (1959).

10. R. E. Burton and B. A. Green, "Technical Reports in Physics Literature," *Phys. Today* **14**, 35–37 (1961).

11. D. E. Gray and S. Rosenberg, "Do Technical Reports Become Published Papers?" *Phys. Today* **10**, 18–21 (1957).

12. J. H. Archer, "Acquisition of Canadian Provincial Documents," *Libr. Resour. Tech. Serv.* **5**, 52–59 (Winter 1961).

13. I. R. Stephens, "Searching for Theses, Dissertations, and Unpublished Data," in *Searching the Chemical Literature*, Advances in Chemistry Series 30, revised, American Chemical Society, Washington, D.C., 1961.

14. D. Bush, "Problems in Translation," *Spec. Libr.* **58**, 173–178 (1967).

15. E. J. Struglia, "Standards and Specifications—Information Sources, Gale Research Company, Detroit, 1965.

BIBLIOGRAPHY

Bedsole, D. T., "Formulating a Weeding Policy for Books in a Special Library," *Spec. Libr.* **49**, 205–209 (1958).

Coppola, D., "International Bookseller Looks at Acquisitions," *Libr. Resour. Tech. Serv.* **11**, 243–246 (Spring 1967).

Stevens, R. E., Issue Ed., "Problems of Acquisitions for Research Libraries," *Libr. Trends* **18**, No. 3 (1970).

Wulfenkoetter, G., *Acquisition Work: Processes Involved in Building Library Collections*, University of Washington Press, Seattle, 1961.

6

Periodicals

Selection, Acquisition, and Recording

Periodicals constitute a most important part of a science-technology library's resources because they publish the immediate results of experimental research and technological developments. A continuous record of scientific advance is presented in these journals, although it is not an account easily read since related information is usually scattered among many papers. The more. volumes of periodicals in any one collection, particularly of long runs of basic titles, the more of this record there will be at hand to be put together, and it is for this reason that these publications, in contrast to most monographic works, appreciate in value with time. Papers accepted for publication by prestigious journals have had to be approved by authorities in the subject fields, a requirement that has kept standards high, thereby creating a body of literature of inestimable significance. The selection of which periodicals to be acquired on current subscription as well as what back files to collect merits very careful consideration.

Recognition of the potential benefits awaiting discovery and interpretation in this part of the literature is shown by the policy of many libraries in spending a greater portion of the budget for subscriptions and back files than for books. Scientific periodicals are expensive and their prices seem to be on a steady rise. However, in the event that budget cuts have to be absorbed, subscriptions to the major periodicals should never be dropped, thinking that volumes missed can be purchased in more prosperous times. It is too often impossible to locate certain issues at any price, although microform copies are being made available in increasing number, and there is an active program for reprinting titles that are in demand. The acquisition and servicing of periodicals is a serious responsibility.

DEFINITION AND CHARACTERISTICS OF PERIODICALS

Periodicals are serial publications issued in parts as continuing titles, usually at regular intervals and for an indefinite period of time. Subscriptions must be paid in advance to receive current issues. The term "periodical" is the designation most broadly applicable to this part of the literature. The word "journal" is often used interchangeably, although it is reserved by some persons for the strictly scholarly publications. "Magazine," another germane term, connotes the popular or trade types.

Periodicals issue from a variety of sources. Many of the most consequential are sponsored by the prominent professional societies; in fact, some having the longest histories are still associated with their original founding organizations. Others are independent enterprises, while some come from government agencies. The important scientific journals have distinctive characters and maintain strong editorial policies. There are those that publish only brief reports of original research; others confine their attention to exhaustive reviews of work in an active state of development. Still others are concerned with the reporting of the productive applications of ideas that have achieved fruition after lengthy experimentation in the laboratory and pilot plant. In view of the many areas of scientific and technological activity, some thousands of individual periodicals record and thereby publicize the results of investigative work performed in laboratories worldwide.

As aids to locating information in the large number of individual articles in these many periodicals, specialized indexing and abstracting publications constitute their own unique category of periodicals. As every subject field has its own periodicals, the indexing and abstracting ones cover the broad areas of chemistry, physics, biology, or engineering while others serve a specific subdivision only. However, there is increasing interdisciplinary activity in the sciences and the sharp limits between chemistry and physics or between chemistry and biology are no longer neatly drawn, a situation that is readily evident in the relevant literature.

This chapter is concerned specifically with the serial publications known as periodicals or journals. The other kinds of serials such as the annual reviews, the "Advances in . . . ," "Progress in . . . ," and so on can be treated similarly by placing standing orders for them and even recording them in check-in files if it seems advisable to do so; or they may be treated as books. If they are considered to be in the same category as periodicals it means that their recording increases the total volume of this record without real advantage.

SELECTION OF TITLES FOR SUBSCRIPTION

The selection of periodicals for current subscription and purchase of back files requires an investigative study to achieve complete understanding of the research and any other activities to be supported. The whole program should be surveyed, and as much foresight exercised as possible to detect the directions of eventual programs. It is necessary to be reasonably certain that as much information as possible that relates to subjects of concern will be immediately available. One still helpful survey is the monograph published by Brown (1) in 1956 entitled *Scientific Serials: Characteristics and Lists of Most Cited Publications in Mathematics, Physics, Chemistry, Geology, Physiology, Botany, and Entomology.* Presumably those publications to which reference is made most frequently are the most significant, and by actual counting, Brown produced lists of titles in the order of their thus proven value. In support of this concept are the data gathered by Garfield (2) as a result of careful review of references cited in the *Science Citation Index* (SCI). A group of most frequently cited titles becomes evident when large numbers of references used in the bibliographies of articles in periodicals are compiled as they are in the SCI.

The list of basic periodicals required for a library in its initial state is relatively easy to determine. Advice and suggestions should certainly be actively sought from those who will be using this literature. Research scientists actively investigating certain fields will know of some titles that should be acquired even though they are not among those most frequently cited. If a broad program of fundamental research is to be served, the publications of the relevant professional societies will certainly head the list. In addition to the strictly scholarly journals, others such as some dealing with the economics of industrial activity, the marketing of products, or any other direction of possible concern should be included. The listings of essential publications in the specific subject areas represented in the Appendix of this book should be helpful in the process of title selection. Then when the library is in operation, note should be made of the periodicals from which articles must be obtained from outside sources, and when these attain a definite frequency, subscriptions should be considered.

Abstracting and indexing periodicals that cover the subject fields in which there is interest must be procured also. The scope of the collection is increased materially by these publications because they bring to hand coverage of the less obvious and fringe-interest publications in which occasional articles of importance do appear, but not frequently enough to warrant subscriptions. In 1950 there were about 50,000 scientific and technical periodicals being published, and by 1960 the number approached 60,000, well on the way to Brown's (1) prediction of over 100,000 by 1979. It is apparent that no one library can subscribe to more than a few hundred at best and must depend upon indexing and abstracting services for the information published in all others.

After making certain that primary needs of scientific and technical subject areas will be met, it is wise to review the situation served by the library in its broadest context to determine whether some additional types of periodical publications should be added. Members of the technical sales department, for example, should perhaps have access to certain business magazines, and it is usually advisable to subscribe to at least one daily newspaper such as *The New York Times,* as well as *The Wall Street Journal.* A few magazines of quite general content, such as those reporting political and financial news, may be useful. The cost of these additional items will be small in proportion to the total amount spent for subscriptions, and they may prove to be of great worth in promoting the use of the library. It is good practice to review the whole list annually so that new titles can be added and those of lesser value removed.

A unique type of technical periodical is designated by the term "controlled circulation," that is designed specifically to reach an audience of individuals engaged in active practice in a certain industry. These publications are sent gratis to such persons, but it is sometimes difficult to get the names of libraries on the mailing lists. If there is such a problem, it is likely that the name of the librarian or other staff member will be acceptable so that the publications can be available in the library. Among such periodicals are *33, Industrial Research,* and *Chemical 26.*

There are numerous specialized compilations that list scientific and technical periodicals, some of them limited to specific fields. Consultation of one or more of these in the process of setting up a subscription list is likely to be profitable. Some of these aids are the following:

Scientific Periodicals Only

World List of Scientific Periodicals Published in the Years 1900–1960, 4th ed., P. Brown and G. B. Stratton, Eds., Butterworth, London, 1963–1965, 3 volumes, almost 60,000 titles.

Guides to Scientific Periodicals: An Annotated Bibliography, M. J. Fowler, The Library Association, London, 1966, 1048 items.

Guide to Scientific and Technical Periodicals: A Selected and Annotated List of Those Published in English, R. C. Martin and W. Jett, A. Swallow, Denver, Colo., 1963, 325 titles.

Scientific Serials, C. H. Brown, ACRL Monograph 16, Association of College & Research Libraries, American Library Association, Chicago, Ill., 1956.

Current Serials Received by the National Lending Library, H.M.S.O., London, 1965.

Current Periodicals in the Science Museum Library: A Handlist, H. D. Phippin, compiler, H.M.S.O., London, 1965.

A List of Scientific and Technical Serials Currently Received by the Library of Congress, Science, and Technology Division, U.S. Government Printing Office, Washington, D. C., 1960, approximately 13,000 titles.

Directory of Canadian Scientific and Technical Periodicals: A Classified Guide to Currently Published Titles, 4th ed., National Research Council (Canada), NRC 10889, Ottawa, Canada, 1970.

Guide to Latin American Scientific and Technical Periodicals: An Annotated List, Pan American Union, General Secretariat, Organization of American States, Washington, D. C., 1962.

Union List of Russian Scientific and Technical Periodicals Available in European Libraries, Vol. I and supplement, L. J. Van der Wolk and S. Sandstra, Netherlands University Press, Amsterdam, 1963, 1965.

Scientific and Technical Serial Publications of the Soviet Union, 1945–1960, N. T. Zikeev, Science and Technology Division, Library of Congress, Washington, D.C., 1963, 5091 titles.

Japanese Journals in Science and Technology: An Annotated Checklist, G. S. Bonn, New York Public Library, New York, 1960.

Directory of Japanese Scientific Periodicals, National Diet Library, Tokyo, 1967.

Periodicals in Specific Fields

ACCESS. Key to the Source Literature of the Chemical Sciences, Chemical Abstracts Service, Columbus, Ohio, 1969, with quarterly supplements, 12,000 titles, including conferences and congresses. Title changed to *CAS Source Index Quarterly.*

A Guide to the Literature of Chemistry, E. J. Crane, A. M. Patterson and E. B. Marr, 2nd ed., Wiley, New York, 1957; includes comprehensive lists of journals classified as to country of origin and subject areas of chemistry.

Chemical Publications, Their Nature and Use, M. G. Mellon, 4th ed., McGraw-Hill, New York, 1965; has lists of journals in chemical fields.

Biological Abstracts List of Serials, Biosciences Information Service of Biological Abstracts, Philadelphia, Pa., annual, about 5700 titles in 1970.

Literature Sources in the Biological Sciences, A. E. Kerker and E. M. Schlundt, Purdue University Libraries, Lafayette, Ind., 1961.

World List of Pharmacy Periodicals, T. Andrews, American Society of Hospital Pharmacists, Washington, D. C., 1963, 900 titles.

World Medical Periodicals, World Medical Association, 10 Columbus Circle, New York, 1957.

Periodicals Relevant to microbiology and Immunology: A World List—1968, B. Tunevall, Ed., Wiley, New York, 1969.

Periodica Geologica, Paleontologica et Mineralogica, J. Lomský, Ed., Nakladetsivicesklovenske Akademie Ved., Prague, 1950.

Guide to the Literature of the Zoological Sciences, R. C. Smith, 6th ed., Burgess, Minneapolis, Minn., 1962.

A Recommended List of Basic Periodicals in Engineering and the Engineering Sciences, W. H. Hyde, Ed., ACRL Monograph 9. Association of College and Research Libraries, American Library Association, Chicago, 1953, 533 titles.

Aeronautical and Space Serial Publications? A World List, Science and Technology Division, The Library of Congress, Washington, D. C., U. S. Govt. Printing Office, 1962.

List of Periodicals in the Field of Nuclear Energy, revised ed., International Atomic Energy Agency, IAEA, Vienna, 1963, 523 titles.

List of Translations

A Guide to Scientific and Technical Journals in Translation, C. J. Himmelsbach and G. E. Boyd, Special Libraries Association, New York, 1968, chiefly from Russian to English.

INDEXING AND ABSTRACTING PUBLICATIONS

In order to get full benefit from the periodical literature it is necessary to have the appropriate indexing and abstracting publications as access to their contents. It may be desirable to have complete files of these publications although the original journal files are acquired for a limited span only. Some lists of abstracting and indexing publications follow. Reference is directed also to the Appendix of this book.

Lists of Abstracting and Indexing Publications

A Guide to the World's Abstracting and Indexing Services in Science and Technology, United States Library of Congress Science and Technology Division, National Federation of Science Abstracting and Indexing Services, Report 102, U. S. Government Printing Office, Washington, D.C., 1963, 1855 entries.

List of Periodicals and Bulletins Containing Abstracts Published in Great Britain, Royal Society of London, The Royal Society, London, 1949, about 127 items.

Index Bibliographicus, Vol. 1, 4th ed., "Science and Technology," Westerman, The Hague, Federation Internationale de Documentation, 1959, 118 pages.

A Guide to United States Indexing and Abstracting Services in Science and Technology, National Federation of Science Abstracting and Indexing Services, 301 East Capitol Street, Washington, D.C., 1960.

Abstracting and Indexing Sources for Literature on Metals and Metal Fabrication, E. Mount, John Crerar Library, Chicago, 1953, Bibliography 2, 26 pages.

Bibliography of Engineering Abstracting Services, M. Landuyt, Special Libraries Association, New York, 1955, SLA Bibliography 1, 231 services listed.

"Abstracting and Indexing Services of Physics Interest," D. E. Gray and R. S. Bray, *Amer. J. Phys.* **18,** 274–299 (May 1950); **18,** 578–579 (December 1950), reprinted and issued by Office of Technical Services as PB 99951.

"Abstracting and Indexing Services in Electronics and Related Electrical Fields,"
J. Milek, *Amer. Doc.* **8**, 5–21 (January 1957).
*Current Indexing and Abstracting Periodicals in the Medical and Biological Sciences:
An Annotated List,* 2nd ed., World Health Organization, Geneva, 1959, 35 pages,
supplement in *Libr. News* **12**, suppl. 2.

Comprehensive Lists of Periodicals

Ayer Directory of Newspapers, Magazines, and Trade Publications, N. W. Ayer & Sons,
Inc., Philadelphia, Pa., annual. A geographically classified listing that includes
virtually all titles published in the United States, its territories, and Canada.
British Union-Catalogue of Periodicals, a record of the periodicals of the world, from
the seventeenth century to the present day, in British libraries, including the
World List of Scientific Periodicals, K. Porter, Ed., Archon-Shoe String Press, Ham-
don, Conn., 1955–1958, 1968, 4 volumes. Quarterly supplements, cumulated an-
nually.
Internationale Bibliographie der Fachzeitschriften—World Guide to Periodicals, 5th
ed., K. -O. Sauer, Jr., Verlag Dokumentation, Munche-Pullach, 1967, 2 volumes.
The Standard Periodical Directory, Oxbridge Publishing Co., Inc., New York, 1970.
Guide to all United States and Canadian periodicals.
Ulrich's Periodicals Directory, E. J. Graves, Ed., 14th ed., R. R. Bowker, New York,
1971.
Union List of Serials in the United States and Canada, E. B. Titus, ed., H. W. Wilson
Co., New York, 1965, 5 volumes. This is kept up to date by the following:
New Serial Titles, Joint Committee on the Union List of Serials, Washington, D.C.
Monthly, with quarterly and five-year cumulations. Provides titles with library
locations of newly started periodicals.
Irregular Serials and Annuals: An International Directory, E. I. Koltay, Ed., 2nd ed.,
R. R. Bowker, New York, 1971.

ACQUISITION OF PERIODICALS

There are two parts to the process of acquiring periodicals for a specific collection; first is the selection of those for which current subscriptions are to be placed; second is the determination of those for which it
will be necessary to acquire back files, with attendant judgments as to
how far back and in what form—microform or as published. Each of
these aspects is considered separately here.

Current periodicals are acquired by subscription orders for the greater
number of titles. Some few may be received through membership in
professional societies, though this should not be done for a library if
personal membership privileges are abused.

As to the actual placing of subscriptions it is possible to order each
title directly from its publisher, but it is much more efficient to put the
whole list in the hands of an agency whose sole business it is to handle

the details of the process. One order written annually or established on an "until forbid" basis eliminates numerous individual orders and bills. There are only a few publications that cannot be ordered in this way, and these must be treated according to specified procedures.

When initiating the subscription list it may be desirable to submit it to more than one agency for competitive bids, though it is not likely that for scientific periodicals there will be significant differences in the total price quoted. There can be some saving realized if orders are placed for more than one year, quite often for certain titles it is for three. Efficient service should be sought, especially in recent years when the expansion of business and increase in numbers of periodicals published has made the vender's task apparently much more difficult, although he is likely to blame his problems on conversion to automation. Some agencies take care of both domestic and foreign subscriptions. When large numbers of titles are required, it may be advisable to use dealers located in more than one country.

All subscriptions should be established so that they expire at some specified time of the year, usually with December issues because most volumes are then complete. However, there may be good reason why expiration dates should be at some other time or staggered if budget arrangements so require. For assurance of continued receipt, bills should be paid two to three months in advance of expiration dates.

It may be obligatory to process all orders through a central purchasing department, in which case procedures must be completely understood by the person responsible. Because of the many problems that can arise, it is highly preferable for the acquisitions staff member to deal directly with the subscription agent. Strieby (3) describes a situation where a transfer of responsibility for subscriptions from a central purchasing office to the library was effected. The benefits to everyone concerned were immediately recognized, and there was no thought of returning to the previous system.

The simplest way of placing orders for periodicals is to list them alphabetically by title and indicate the volume and issue number with which subscription is to begin. As a help to the agent they should be grouped according to the countries in which they are published. Individual order slips in multiple copy can also be used to handle such orders. After the agent has accepted the list he renders a bill that must be paid promptly for service to begin. This system is economical and satisfactory for a group of up to several hundred titles.

For subscriptions approaching 2000 or more, or fewer if there are attendant complications of multiple copies for different locations, an automated system is highly desirable. In the literature there are many explicit descriptions of methods for establishing computerized control of periodicals that include every possible aspect, from ordering to routing. Wilkinson (4) outlines the development of a system for 2800 titles, providing the benefit of experience with an initial attempt that was too limited and was eventually improved to the point where it produced eleven output products, from a Serials Register to a Monsanto List of Serials, using unit record equipment with computer assistance for a cost of $500 a year in 1967. Its success was so satisfactory that ultimately use of a real-time computer is anticipated. Another application is described by Jones (5) in an article entitled "Computerized Subscription and Periodicals Routing in an Aerospace Library," for a library handling 1600 subscriptions, an application initially reported by McCann (6).

Relevant to the handling of periodical records by computer is the establishment of official code designations for titles, simple four-letter combinations that identify individual journals and known as ASTM Coden because the American Society for Testing and Materials sponsors the project. Hammer (7) has reviewed this important accomplishment, pointing to its many implications, although it has not been accepted universally.

For straightforward abbreviations of titles there is the *American Standards for Periodical Titles Abbreviations* designated as Z39.5-1969 which is issued the United States of America Standards Institute, Room 906, 10 East 40th St., New York 10016. This is an officially recognized list of rules for abridging titles in an effort to avoid the real problems in identification when everyone uses his own sometimes careless judgment. Some professional societies tend to follow their own practices as does the American Chemical Society, which also publishes a list of full titles that shows their contractions.

Whatever the procedure for placing subscriptions, one or more agents have to be chosen. Some of the agencies that are known to give satisfactory service are listed here. There are doubtless others in various localities that could be equally dependable. It would be wise to investigate to be certain that anyone offering to undertake this function has adequate experience and facilities to perform effectively.

Subscription Agencies—A Selected List

United States

Clark Subscription Agency, 400 West Madison St., Chicago, Ill.

EBSCO Subscription Services, EBSCO Building, 826 South Northwest Highway, Barrington, Ill. 60010. Offices also in Minneapolis, Minn., Braintree, Mass., San Francisco, Calif., Birmingham, Ala., Red Bank, N. J., Los Angeles, Calif., Springfield, Va.

F. W. Faxon Company, Inc., 15 Southwest Park, Westwood, Mass. 02090
Four Continent Book Corporation, 156 Fifth Ave., New York, 10010. Russian titles.
Franklin Square-Mayfair, 545 Cedar Lane, Teaneck, N. J. 07666
Hanson-Bennett Magazine Agency, 180 N. Wabash Ave., Chicago, Ill.
McGregor Magazine Agency, Sandstone Bldg., Mount Morris, Ill.
The Moore-Cottrell Subscription Agencies, Inc., North Cohocton, N. Y.
Stechert-Hafner-Inc., 31 East 10th St., New York 10013
The Turner Subscription Agency, Inc., 235 Park Avenue South, New York 10003
Charles E. Tuttle Co., Rutland, Vermont. Specializes in publications from the Far
    East.

Canada

William Dawson Subscription Service, 60 Front St., Toronto, Canada
Gordon & Gotch, Ltd., 43 Victoria St., Toronto, Canada

Great Britain and the Continent

Blackwell's, Broad St., Oxford, England
Dekker & Nordemann, N.V. o.z., Voorburgwal 243, Amsterdam C, Holland
B. F. Stevens & Brown, Ltd., Ardon House, Mill Lane, Godalmey, Surrey, England
Swets Subscription Service, Keizersgracht 487, Amsterdam, Holland

The American Library Association published in 1963 a pamphlet entitled *International Subscription Agents,* a joint project of its Serials and Acquisitions Sections, and the Resources and Technical Services Division. In addition to names and addresses, full details concerning the types of materials handled, quality of service, and billing policies are provided.

RECORDS OF RECEIPT OF PERIODICALS

There are several possible systems for keeping records of the receipt of single issues as well as the cumulated holdings of periodicals, any of which are satisfactory if kept meticulously. From the placing of the order to the ultimate binding of a completed volume, the location of every issue of a journal must be known. Even the date of receipt of an issue can be important, especially where patent situations are involved. Periodical files constitute a useful resource in direct proportion to their completeness; each individual issue is a link in a continuous chain. In establishing the system for record keeping, provision should be made for noting the following items for each title:

Exact full title (As printed or manipulated according to the rule of placing name of publishing body first, that is, *American Acoustical Society, Journal of*)

Current volume number, year, indication of receipt of individual
issues with date thereof
Frequency
Note of title page and index for each volume
Record of volumes held
Binding information
Where and when ordered, period covered by order, date for renewal

This record-keeping process can be either manual or automated. The
automated application can be partial by using electronic data processing
assistance or fully computerized. This decision will be based somewhat on
the number of titles to be handled and on the accessibility of equipment.
The articles by Wilkinson (4) and Jones (5) referred to earlier in this
chapter give details of the processes involved in the development of an
automated system. In any situation this must be done with the help of a
professional programmer.

For a manual system there are well-designed forms available, cards to
be used in especially designed holders that slip into metal trays, shingled
to expose the edges of the cards upon which the titles are typed. Ex-

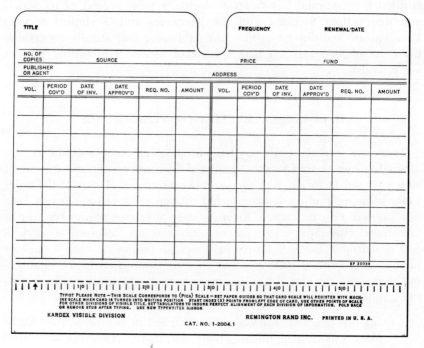

Figure 1. Order record form for periodicals (Kardex).

amples of such cards, available from library supply houses, are shown as Figures 1 and 2. Further details are given in Chapter 4.

The name of the library and any other identifying mark that may be wanted should be stamped on the cover of each issue of a periodical. This might be the copy number if more than one subscription is carried, and whether it is to be circulated. The stamp showing ownership can incorporate a rotating dater for establishing dates of receipt.

It is desirable, even a necessity, to provide a list of holdings and the locations of journals placed in a spot where it can be consulted easily. In a small operation the record file itself can serve this purpose. It is possible to compile a list of titles by making Xerox copies of titles directly from the trays of the Kardex type. A major advantage of a mechanized system is the ease with which listings can be produced and updated. Wilkins (8) describes an excellent method for coping with the record-keeping problem by using rotary wheel-type equipment. Since it is simple to remove and replace cards for updating or making any kind of needed notation, maintenance is convenient. Whatever the system adopted, both library staff and clientele must have ready access to the records.

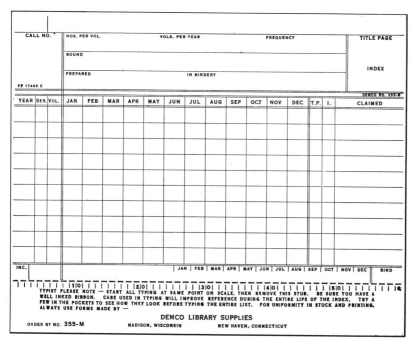

Figure 2. Monthly periodical check-in record for periodicals (Demco).

ACQUISITION OF BACK FILES OF PERIODICALS

In the process of planning the library service and establishing the subscription list for journals to be received currently, some thought has to be given to the requirements for back files. These runs should be chosen as carefully as possible because they represent a continuous expense just for shelf space. The chief basis for decision should, of course, be the amount of use they will command, but this can be difficult to anticipate until after a library has been in operation for a time. After a trial period a study can be made such as is reported by Strain (9) who found that in one library at least, the pattern of demand was not as strong for the scholarly publications as might have been expected. The recommendation resulting from the review was for highly selective retention and reliance upon agreements among a number of libraries in the area to each one preserve files of little-used titles.

Another study by Groos (10) focussed upon titles thought to be consulted infrequently but actually it was revealed that it is very important to provide as wide a range of periodicals as possible. In this statistical investigation made in 1964 it was found that 38% of the users read journals carrying only 13% of the articles requested; 15% of the clientele would not have been served at all if there had been no journals prior to 1944, and 21% would have had only part of their requirements fulfilled if the less-used volumes had not been at hand.

For a new library where the planning can be flexible or for one facing the end of possible shelf space, the solution is to consider seriously the acquisition of earlier volumes in microform copy. There is a choice of microfilm, microcard, or microfiche, though not all titles are available in all three forms. There are catalogs such as the *Guide to Microforms in Print,* published by Microcard Editions, Inc., 910 26th St. N.W., Washington, D. C. 20037, and announcements from those publishers where it can be learned what is offered. There is also the booklet, *A Union List of Publications in Opaque Microforms* by E. M. Tilton, 2nd ed., Scarecrow, New York, 1964. Some thought and preliminary investigation should be expended before deciding what type of microforms to acquire unless a multiplicity of reading machines to accommodate all forms can be purchased.

Those files of the periodicals that are preferred in the original print form can be procured from dealers who specialize in finding and putting together complete runs. It is sometimes possible to obtain them from the publishers, but it is more preferable to submit a list of wanted back files to a dealer who should be asked for price quotations. As a word of caution, the list should be left in the hands of only one agent, at least for a reasonable period of time in order to avoid simultaneous searching on the part of several dealers for titles actually for one customer.

Another procedure is to acquire a collection of dealers' catalogs that list their stocks of titles on hand. Prices are not likely to vary significantly. However, the most convenient and ultimately effective method is to locate a dependable agent who will find not only the readily available publications but also those not as easy to locate. It can take several years to put together a good collection of periodicals. Some subscription agents deal also in back files.

A helpful guide to dealers in back files is the compilation by F. J. Neverman entitled *International Directory of Back Issue Vendors; Periodicals, Newspapers, and Documents,* 2nd enlarged ed., Special Libraries Association, New York, 1968. A selected list includes the following.

Dealers in Back Files of Scientific and Technical Periodicals

United States

Abraham's Magazine Service, 56 East 13th St., New York 10013
G. H. Arrow, 218 South 4th St., Philadelphia, Pa.
Ashley-Ratcliff Corp., 27 East 21st St., New York
Robert Bentley, Inc., 993 Massachusetts Ave., Cambridge, Mass.
John W. Caler Publications Corp., 7506 Clybourn Ave., Sun Valley, Calif. 91352
The Arthur W. Clarke Co., 1214 Brand Ave., Glendale, Calif.
Cosmos Book Co., 1991 Broadway, New York, N. Y. (For Russian publications)
Four Continent Book Corp., 156 Fifth Ave., New York 10010
Dianco, Box 2121, Palos Verdes Peninsula, Calif. 90274
Paul Gottschalk, Inc., 21 Pearl St., New York 10014
James C. Howgate, Star Route, Rotterdam Junction, N. Y.
International Art and Science Book Co., 192 Broadway, New York 10007
International University Booksellers, Inc., 103 Fifth Ave., New York 10013
Alfred Jaeger, 115 East 23rd St., New York 10010
Walter J. Johnson, Inc., and Johnson Reprint Corp., 111 Fifth Ave., New York, 10013
Kraus Periodicals, Inc., 805 Mamaroneck Ave., Long Island, N. Y., and Kraus Reprint
    Corp., 16 East 46th St., New York 10017
Periodicals Supply Service, 207 West 29th St., Baltimore, Md.
Schoenhof's Foreign Books, Inc., 1280 Massachusetts Ave., Cambridge, Mass.
Kurt L. Schwarz, 450 North Beverly Drive, Beverly Hills, Calif.
Stechert-Hafner, Inc., 31 East 10th St., New York 10003
Swets and Zeitlinger, 19 Waterloo Ave., Berwyn, Pa. 19312 (U. S. Office of Dutch firm)
Henry Tripp, 92–06 Jamaica Ave., Woodhaven, N. Y. 11421
Western Periodicals Co., 13000 Raymer St., North Hollywood, Calif.
Zeitlin Periodicals Co., Inc., 817 South La Brea, Los Angeles, Calif. 90036

In Countries Other than the United States

Blackwell's, Broad Street, Oxford, England
Wm. Dawson and Sons, Ltd., Cannon House, Folkstone, Kent, England
Dekker en Nordemann N.V. e.z.-Voorburgwal 243, Amsterdam C, Holland
Otto Harrassowitz, 6200 Wiesbaden, P. O. Box 349, Germany
Library Service & Supply Company, Universal House, 4 Footscray Road, Eltham,
     London, S.E.9, England
The Scientific Book Supply Service, 5 Fetters Lane, Fleet St., London, E.C. 4, England
Swets and Zeitlinger, Keizersgracht 471, Amsterdam C, Holland

There are, of course, many other dealers able and willing to provide good service in locating files of needed journals. For ease of communication, local agents should be sought whenever possible.

Another means of finding back files is to watch the advertising columns of certain journals such as *Science* and *Chemical and Engineering News*. Individuals who want to dispose of personal files, particularly those acquired through memberships in professional societies, frequently offer sets at advantageous prices. Wants can be advertised also.

An enterprise in which any library can participate to its own advantage and also contribute to others is the United States Book Exchange, Inc., 3335 V St., N.E., Washington, D.C. 20018. This is a service sponsored by library and professional associations to serve as a clearing house for the exchange of printed materials, principally periodicals. A library participates by contributing unwanted items, thereby establishing credits against which it may place requests for publications it needs. A modest membership fee is involved.

Another aspect of the periodicals market place is that of the library itself as seller. Libraries often find themselves recipients of files of journals as gifts not needed at the moment or in the foreseeable future. If these are submitted to a dealer, it can sometimes be surprising to find that a few odd volumes are worth more in cash or credit than would have been suspected.

PRESERVATION OF PERIODICAL FILES

If periodical files are to be preserved, the individual issues must be handled as carefully as their full use allows, then brought together as complete volumes and treated according to the merit of each title in a particular situation. Some will be given sturdy commercial bindings as the best protection. Others may be worth keeping for a limited time only, perhaps five to ten years, and these may either be filed in boxes designed for the purpose or temporary methods for keeping them together in volumes can be applied, chiefly with the aid of plastic adhesive applied to the backs of the stacked issues.

Careful judgment should be exercised in determining which titles to bind commercially because the expense is significant as it recurs annually, and shelf space must be provided. An alternative procedure is to retain original copies for a certain period, then provide microform copy only. Some publishers are making microform copies of journals available simultaneously with printed copies, such, for example, as Wiley/Interscience does with the *Journal of Polymer Science* which is offered on 16-mm microfilm, and Gordon and Breach in producing microfiche editions of all of its journals. There has been some reluctance on the part of library users to accept these forms, but with the improvement of reading devices to the point of making possible the immediate provision of enlarged copies of selected pages this objection should be overcome.

Procedures for Binding

When a number of volumes of the titles selected for binding have accumulated, they must be prepared meticulously before being sent to a commercial binder. All issues must be present and placed in order, but they need not be collated page by page because this is done in the binding process. Title pages and indexes for each volume must be in evidence, perhaps marked by the placing of protruding slips. Indexes may appear in any one of several ways, apparently according to the whim of the publisher, a practice that may eventually be influenced by the activities of Committee Z39.5 of the United States of America Standards Institutes (11). Until that day, indexes must be looked for as a few loose pages slipped into an issue, possibly in the last issue or more probably in a succeeding one, or bound in as the last pages of the last issue of a volume. A title page may be part of the index pages or it may be a first page of the first issue of a volume. To further the confusion publishers have been known to vary their practices from one year to the next, thereby making this seemingly simple procedure a time consuming task. If the index is combined with the title page, it must be bound at the front of the volume. The preferred place for it is at the end. For some journals no true alphabetical index is provided. Instead, a table of contents to be bound at the front of a volume stands in its place. Individual binding slips should be prepared for each volume, noting especially any changes from the last one bound.

Ordinarily a single volume is preferably bound in one cover, though it must be divided if it approaches a thickness of more than 4 inches. The inclusive paging of each part should be indicated on the spine rather than the months because references are usually cited by volume and page numbers. Suggestions for the division of volumes are sometimes supplied by the publisher who provides several title pages appropriately designated. Special marking should draw attention to such things as the inclusion of special numbers, unique page numbering, or anything else that will aid the user in finding what he needs.

The binding responsibility should be given only to an establishment that is able to meet such standards of performance as have been formulated by The Library Binding Institute, 501 Fifth Avenue, New York 10016, from which a list of members located throughout the United States can be obtained. It is advisable to find one as close at hand as possible to minimize shipping time, although some binders do include pick-up and delivery service weekly for distances up to several hundred miles.

Scientific and technical periodicals present very special problems that must be comprehended by those who do the binding. Individual issues may be published in such a way that parts must be separated to be brought together in separate volumes. Titles change, or one title splits into an A and a B part, all of which makes it impossible to set up immutable binding instructions.

As for material to use for binding, library buckram is the most generally used. Some of the newer plastic-impregnated fabrics are proving to be satisfactory also, particularly because they can be cleaned with a damp cloth. The choice of colors is a more significant feature than it might appear because their distribution among different titles that are shelved in proximity determines the ease with which they are detected. Darker shades are usually preferable since they do not show soil readily, but it is also desirable to take advantage of this as an opportunity of making the shelves pleasantly attractive. Some colors fade more readily than others. A good effect is achieved by having some titles bound in black with gold lettering, and interspersing with colors, insofar as this can be done in view of the likelihood of adding new titles.

A regular program for binding should be established. In most situations it is wise to send a few volumes at regular intervals rather than have them all done at one time. The staff member in charge of this procedure should develop a complete program, including the instructions for each title, the lettering and spacing on the spines, and then be on watch for changes as they happen.

Temporary Binding

Journals that must be retained for a certain period but are not worth commercial binding must be handled in some way to keep issues from straying. They can be tied in bundles or filed in boxes, but the better way is to apply a temporary binding. The simplest treatment is to stack the issues comprising a volume, put a weight on top to hold them firmly, and then paint the spines with liquid plastic adhesive, using several coats if necessary. This will suffice for some purposes, or stiff cardboard covers can be attached, using broad tape for spines. Directions for accomplishing this are willingly supplied by the vendors of the adhesive materials. The method of treatment of these periodicals will depend upon the amount of use they will have to take, and the availability of staff to do the work.

CONCLUSION

Periodicals constitute the most important segment of the whole of the scientific-technical literature. Proskauer (12), in a review of their role and function, has aptly called them "selective information filters." As such, these periodicals, or access to their contents, must be made available promptly to any community of scientists where investigative work is being done.

REFERENCES

1. C. H. Brown, *Scientific Serials*, ACRL Monograph 16, Association of College & Research Libraries, Chicago, 1956.
2. E. Garfield and I. N. Sher, "New Factors in the Evaluation of Scientific Literature through Citation Indexing," *Amer. Doc.* 14, 195–201 (1963).
3. I. M. Strieby, "Simplified Library-to-Dealer Purchasing," *Stechert-Hafner Book News* 9, 81–82 (March 1955).
4. W. A. Wilkinson, "A System for Machine-Assisted Serials Control," *Spec. Libr.* 58, 149–153 (1967).
5. H. W. Jones, "Computerized Subscription and Periodicals Routing in an Aerospace Library," *Spec. Libr.* 58, 634–638 (1967).
6. A. McCann, "Application of Machines to Library Techniques: Periodicals," *Amer. Doc.* 12, 260–265 (1961).
7. D. P. Hammer, "A Review of the ASTM Coden for Periodical Titles," *Libr. Resour. Tech. Serv.* 12, 359–365 (1968).
8. E. E. Wilkins, "Solving the 'Serials Record' Problem," *Spec. Libr.* 53, 258–261 (1962).
9. P. M. Strain, "A Study of Usage and Retention of Technical Periodicals," *Libr. Resour. Tech. Serv.* 10, 295–304 (1966).
10. C. V. Groos, "Less-Used Titles and Volumes of Science Journals; Two Preliminary Notes," *Libr. Resour. Tech. Serv.* 10, 289–290 (1966).
11. G. J. Orne, "Guest Editorial," *Amer. Doc.* 20, 185 (1969).

12. E. S. Proskauer, "Journals and Serials as Selective Information Filters," presented at the Symposium on the Journal and Patent Literature Explosion, Division of Chemical Literature, American Chemical Society, New York, September 8, 1969.

BIBLIOGRAPHY

American Society for Testing Materials, Special Committee on Numerical Reference Data, *Coden for Periodical Titles,* ASTM Data Series 23B ASTM, Philadelphia, Pa., 1966.

Barr, K. P., "Estimates of the Number of Currently Available Scientific and Technical Periodicals," *J. Doc.* **23,** 110–116 (1967).

Benton, M., "The Biological Serial Record Center," *Coll. Res. Libr.* **25,** 111–112, 1964,

Binnington, J. P., "Soviet Scientific Journals in English Translation," *Spec. Libr.* **48,** 28–30 (1957).

Cole, P. F., "Journal Usage Versus Age of Journal," *J. Doc.* **19,** 1–11 (1963).

Davinson, D. E., *Periodicals: A Manual of Practice for Librarians,* revised ed., Deutsch, London, 1964.

Grenfell, D., *Periodicals and Serials: Their Treatment in Special Libraries,* 2nd ed., Aslib, London, 1965.

Marty, J. and A. Gilchrist, *An Evaluation of British Scientific Journals,* Occasional Paper 1, Aslib, London, 1968.

Osborn, A. D., *Serial Publications: Their Place and Treatment in Libraries,* American Library Association, Chicago, 1955.

Paterson, G. M., "Aslib Exhibition of Methods for Preservation and Storage of Periodicals," *Asli Proc.* **12,** 202–207 (1960).

Scoones, M. A., "The Mechanization of Serial Records with Particular Reference to Subscription Control," *Aslib Proc.* **19,** 45–62 (1967).

Toase, M., Ed., *Guide to Current British Periodicals,* Library Association, London, 1962.

United States of America Standards Institute, American Standard for Periodical Title Abbreviations, USASI Z39.5-1963, USASI, New York, 1964.

Wall, R. A. and C. W. J. Wilson, "Codification of Periodical Titles: A Note on ASTM Coden Versus Standard Serial Numbers," *Libr. Assoc. Rec.* **72,** 188–190 (1970).

7

Technical Processes

Cataloging, Classification, and Subject Headings

The years since World War II have seen enormous growth in the publications available in the science-technology field. Coincidental with this growth has been the deviation from the traditional book as the general basis for the collection in the science-technology library. So great has been the output in all areas including reports, government documents, books, and such, that new means and devices have come into being to speed the flow of information from its source to its ultimate end and purpose, the user. This chapter deals with one phase of this flow of information, that is, classifying, assigning of subject headings, and cataloging of books, periodicals, and other materials.

This single chapter is not intended as a philosophical discussion of the basic principles of these subjects, but rather a guide for the less-experienced professional librarian confronted with the technicalities of technical processing in the complex fields of science and technology. The three processes mentioned above are usually carried on as a single unit in a small or medium-sized library, but for reasons of clarity they are discussed separately here. However, references to the cataloger or the classifier refer to the same person.

CLASSIFICATION

Classification, expressed in its most elementary terms, is placing like things together, but this simple concept so easy to express is extremely difficult to achieve. Two scientists in different disciplines may examine the same book and would probably make diverse classification decisions regarding it, and both could be approximately right. Frequently there is the temptation to build a new classification scheme rather than to adapt an old one. However, few librarians have sufficient background or experience to organize a whole field of knowledge so that subjects with their subdivisions will fall into logical and historical sequence. Therefore it is wise to consider the existing schemes and to choose the one which seems best suited to the needs of the situation involved.

Mann (1) has indicated that the following qualifications should be stressed in any system of classification:

1. It should be systematic, proceeding from the general to the special.
2. It should be as complete as possible, that is, cover the entire field of a subject.
3. It should be sufficiently detailed to represent all degrees of generality.
4. It should allow for the combination of ideas and for classifying from several points of view.
5. It should be logical, that is, show a sequence of ideas.
6. It should be explicit, but concise.
7. It should furnish a notation easy to write and to remember, which shall serve as a symbol for the books and determine their arrangement on the shelves.
8. It should be expansive and flexible in both plan and notation.
9. It should furnish a class for general books, and also provide for books treating subjects in any class or divisions of classes in a general way.
10. It should have an alphabetic index to facilitate use.
11. It should be printed in a form which will give one a quick survey of the field covered by the survey.

Two of the best known systems of classification are the Dewey Decimal Classification and the Library of Congress Classification. Both meet Mann's eleven points in some measure and both have advantages and disadvantages.

Dewey Decimal Classification

The Dewey Decimal Classification, named for its originator Melvil Dewey (2), has been through 17 editions since the first one in 1876. All knowledge in this scheme has been divided into the following 10 classes:

000	General Works
100	Philosophy
200	Religion
300	Social Sciences
400	Language
500	Pure Science
600	Technology
700	The Arts
800	Literature
900	History

Each of the ten groups above is further divided into classes which represent the main subdivisions of the subject. For example, 500 represents Pure Science and the subdivisions in this class are as follows:

500	Pure Science
510	Mathematics
520	Astronomy and Allied Sciences
530	Physics
540	Chemistry
548	Crystallography
549	Mineralogy
550	Earth Sciences
560	Paleontology
570	Anthropology and Biology
580	Botanical Sciences
590	Zoological Sciences

The 510 represents Mathematics and this is further subdivided into the various types of mathematics: 511, Arithmetic; 512, Algebra; 513, Geometry, and so on. Further subdivisions are possible by the use of decimal figures. The 511 represents Arithmetic; 511.1, Numeration Systems; 511.2, Fundamental Arithmetic Operations; 511.3, Prime Numbers and Factoring, and so forth. Throughout, the ten general classes are divided and subdivided in an attempt to bring related subjects together in a natural sequence. The sequence above looks as follows:

500	Pure Science
510	Mathematics
511	Arithmetic
512	Algebra
513	Geometry
513.1	Plane Geometry

| 513.2 | Curves |
| 513.3 | Solid Geometry |

A detailed index makes it possible to locate material in the body of the work easily. One of the physical advantages of the later editions is the fact that the index is published in a separate volume. One of the cardinal principles of classification is to put like things together through an understanding of the subject, but this cannot be effectively achieved merely by the use of an index; therefore, a classifier should be thoroughly familiar with the schedules.

Library of Congress Classification

This scheme (3) was originally developed for the books in the Library of Congress but has since been adopted by many other libraries. When the scheme was built, the books already in the Library of Congress were arranged by subject and a study made of their relationships; consequently, the final product is the result of the study of a large body of literature in each field. Inasmuch as over 3,000,000 books were in the Library of Congress collection when the main part of the work was done, there was a sound philosophical and scientific basis for the decisions made. The Library of Congress classification (LC) differs from the Dewey Decimal classification (DC) in many ways, but notably in two respects: (1) it is not a decimal system; and (2) the whole field of knowledge is divided into 21 groups using the letters of the alphabet to represent the classes. Provision is made in the LC for very minute subdivisions of a subject and for expansion. Four letters of the alphabet were left unused for later utilization in other classification schemes. The outline of the general scheme is as follows:

A	General Works; Polygraphy
B	Philosophy; Religion
C	Auxiliary Sciences of History
D	Universal History
E-F	American History
G	Geography; Anthropology
H	Social Sciences
J	Political Science
K	Law
L	Education
M	Music
N	Fine Arts

P	Language and Literature
Q	Science
R	Medicine
S	Agriculture
T	Technology
U	Military Science
V	Naval Science
Z	Bibliography; Library Science

It is seen from the outline above that the classes of greatest use in the science-technology field are Q, R, S, and T and to some extent H, J, U, V, and Z. The schedules above are published as separates, each with its own index, thus making it more convenient for the classifier needing only a part of the classification scheme. The LC uses a combination of letters and figures. The letter, as noted above, indicates the general class; an additional letter, the general divisions of a class; and Arabic figures, in numerical sequence, its smaller subdivisions. Using Q (Science) as an example, we find the following:

Q	Science
QA	Mathematics
QB	Astronomy
QC	Physics
QD	Chemistry
QE	Geology
QH	Natural History
QK	Botany
QL	Zoology
QM	Human Anatomy
QP	Physiology
QR	Bacteriology

Using mathematics as an example in the LC as a comparison with the DC the schedule gives the following:

Q	Science
QA	Mathematics
QA101	Arithmetic
152	Algebra
445	Geometry
447	Elementary Pure Geometry
501	Descriptive Geometry
529	Trigonometry
538	Analytic Geometry

The LC adapts itself more readily to the large collection needing minute subdivision, although it may also be adapted to the small collection having a variety of materials within its scope. The notation is somewhat more complicated than the DC, but it is flexible and provides for the practical subarrangement of many types of material. It does not have a general index, but each schedule has its own index, as mentioned above. If one is using the DC, the Library of Congress classification is a useful source of information regarding the content, arrangement, and sequence of a subject.

Medical Classifications

Several classification schemes have been developed over the years for medical collections but the most important one to date has been prepared by the National Library of Medicine (4) and covers the field of medicine and related sciences. It uses the letters QS–QZ and W which were left unused by the Library of Congress in their classification scheme. Following is a general outline:

Synopsis of Classes
PRECLINICAL SCIENCES

QS	Human Anatomy	QW	Bacteriology and
QT	Physiology		Immunology
QU	Biochemistry	QX	Parasitology
QV	Pharmacology	QY	Clinical Pathology
		QZ	Pathology

MEDICINE AND RELATED SUBJECTS

W	Medical Profession	WE	Musculoskeletal
WA	Public Health		System
WB	Practice of Medicine	WF	Respiratory System
WC	Infectious Diseases	WG	Cardiovascular
WD 100	Deficiency Diseases		System
WD 200	Metabolic Diseases	WH	Hemic and Lym-
WD 300	Diseases of Allergy		phatic Systems
WD 400	Animal Poisoning	WI	Gastrointestinal
WD 500	Plant Poisoning		System
WD 600	Diseases Caused by	WJ	Urogenital System
	Physical Agents	WK	Endocrine System
WD 700	Aviation and Space	WL	Nervous System
	Medicine	WM	Psychiatry

WN	Radiology	WU	Dentistry; Oral
WO	Surgery		Surgery
WP	Gynecology	WV	Otorhinolaryngology
WQ	Obstetrics	WW	Ophthalmology
WR	Dermatology	WX	Hospitals
WS	Pediatrics	WY	Nursing
WT	Geriatrics; Chronic	WZ	History of Medicine
	Disease		

Other Medical and Related Medical Classifications

Following are additional classification schemes which have been in use in various libraries. In choosing such a classification a word of caution is in order. It is important that the process of up-dating be continuous and this may present difficulties with special schemes; a problem not so acutely present in the NLM Classification which might make it the scheme of first choice particularly in the general medical field. It should be noted that the schemes listed below have all been kept up-to-date.

American Dental Association, Bureau of Library and Indexing Service; *Classification for Dental Literature; a Revision of the Classification,* devised by Arthur D. Black, D.D.S., The Association, Chicago, 1955; Addenda, 1964; Mimeographed.

Cunningham, Eileen R., *Classification for Medical Literature,* 5th ed., revised and enlarged by Eleanor G. Steinke and Mary Louise Gladish, Vanderbilt University, Nashville, Tenn. 1967.

National League for Nursing, Committee on the Nursing School Library, *The Bellevue Classification System for Nursing School Libraries* by Ann Doyle and Mary Casamajor; rev. by Constance Lima, 2nd ed., The League, New York, 1965. Originally published as part of *A Library Handbook for Schools of Nursing.*

Other General Classification Schemes

Bliss, H. E. A., *A Bibliographic Classification, Extended by Systematic Auxiliary Schedules for Composite Specification and Notation,* 2nd ed., Wilson, New York, 1952–1953, 4. v. in 3.

This classification was originally developed in the library of the College of the City of New York and was intended to be a bibliographic rather than a library classification. The scheme is divided into 35 main classes using the letters of the alphabet for notation. Taube (5) has said: "The classification has been recommended on the excellence and simplicity of its notation and the fact that being the latest system in a long series of similar attempts, it is more up to date and represents more adequately current fashions in the grouping of ideas and arrangement and subordination of various subjects." This statement, made in 1955, still remains substantially accurate.

Ranganathan, S. R., *Colon Classification*, 4th ed., Madras Library Association, Madras, India, 1952.

This scheme, the structure of which is quite different from those mentioned above, was developed at the Library of the University of Madras (6). "In it, Bliss's principle of composite specification is applied to the actual division of classes. The result is that the schedules consist mainly of a series of tables from which a composite symbol must be assembled in classifying specific topics."

It consists of 33 main classes and 10 generalia classes and uses a mixed notation of upper and lower case letters, numerals, Greek letters, and punctuation marks.

International Federation for Documentation, *Classification Decimale Universelle*, 5th ed., internationale, Editiones Mundaneum, Brussels, 1951-date.

The International Institute of Bibliography was organized as a result of a conference held in Brussels in 1895. One of its purposes was to devise a scheme to be used in indexing world literature. The Dewey Decimal Classification was used as the basis for this scheme since it was considered flexible enough to be expanded more or less indefinitely. The scheme has become variously known as the Universal Decimal Classification, or more popularly as the Brussels Expansion or simply as the UDC. The scheme was not developed primarily as a book classification, but for the purpose of indexing or arranging an enormous card bibliography which included not only books but also all kinds of documents, journal articles, patents, trade catalogs, abstracts, and such.

Publication of an English translation was begun in 1943, entitled *Universal Decimal Classification: Complete English Edition,* and designated as the fourth international edition (7). The British Standards Institution published the second edition of the abridged English edition, revised 1957 (8).

The following references are recommended for further study of the schemes above:

Aslib, *Handbook of Special Librarianship and Information Work*, 3rd ed., Aslib, London, 1967, pp. 79–140.
Tauber, M. F., *Technical Services in Libraries*, Columbia University Press, New York, 1953, pp. 199–202; 208–212.

HOW TO CLASSIFY

Sayers (9) gives the following rules for classifying:

1. Classify a book according to its subject, and then by the form in which the subject is presented, except in generalia and in pure literature where form is paramount.

2. In determining the subject, consider the predominant tendency or obvious purpose of a book, and its author's intention in writing it.

3. When a book appears to belong equally in two places in the classification, make a decision as to the one in which it is to go.

4. When a book deals with two (or three) divisions of a subject, place it in the one which appears to be the most important; or, if the parts seem of equal importance, in the first one treated. When more than two (or three) divisions of the subject are dealt with, place the book in the general heading which contains all or the majority of them.

5. When a subject arises for which no place is provided in the scheme of classification, find the heading to which it seems to be most nearly allied and make a place for it there.

6. Place a book in the most specific head that will contain it.

7. Avoid placings which are in the nature of criticism. Pros and cons of any subject go together.

8. Index all decisions to the scheme; that is to say, make your index exactly represent your practice.

9. Finally (to repeat) place a book where you think it will be most useful; and always have a reason for placing it there.

In the technical field, the place in the classification scheme for a book is often quite simple to locate; for example, Fieser and Fieser, *Experiments in Organic Chemistry* obviously belongs in 547, *Organic Chemistry* in the DC. However, it is frequently difficult to know just where to fit in a book, especially in a field with minute subdivisions. An examination of the table of contents will give one some idea of the scope of the book and some further reading in the body of the work will amplify this. The author's preface and the introduction may add further information, but the classification may still elude one, largely because the scheme used is not detailed enough. At this point, the classifier should examine the literature of the subject under consideration in an effort to fit the subject into its larger class in the scheme. A brief survey of the subject found in a textbook will often be helpful in placing material in its proper sequence in the larger field. An examination of the other expansions in the field will be useful, and if one is using the DC, the LC with its greater detail is often helpful. No scheme should be expanded on the basis of a few books; it is better to put them together into a larger class at first and when this has grown unwieldy to subdivide further. It is important to keep in mind that the classification must serve the special clientele. It is sometimes necessary to place a book in a seemingly unsuitable class because the material will be more useful so placed in a special situation.

BOOK NUMBERS

It is customary to assign an author symbol for each book within a class as a means of arranging books in alphabetical order. These symbols are also used to differentiate two titles as well as more than one edition of a work by a particular author. The Cutter-Sanborn (10) table which is supplied with a set of rules may be used to assign this author symbol. The small book collection may not need exact identification and differentiation for each work in any one class but as the collection grows larger it is a useful device.

A discussion and use of book numbers may be found in the following books:

Barden, Bertha, *Book Numbers; A Manual for Students with a Basic Code of Rules,* ALA, Chicago, 1937.
Akers, Susan Grey, *Simple Library Cataloging,* 4th ed., ALA, Chicago, 1954, Chapter 1, pp. 20–24.

SUBJECT HEADINGS

The functions of classifying and assigning subject headings are closely related. After material has been examined for content in order to assign it to its proper place in the classification scheme, it is logical to determine the subject or subjects under which it will be entered in the card catalog. The choice of subject headings under which books are to be entered in the catalog is a very significant action, since their accuracy determines the effective use of the books. Subject headings serve to supplement the title of a book and may be even more important than a nondescriptive title. Mann (1) in her discussion of subject headings says: "By subject entry, we mean the term or terms used in a dictionary catalog to express the subject or subjects of books. It is part of the cataloger's task to discover the topics with which books deal and then to select terms which express those topics briefly and exactly."

The two best known subject heading lists are *The Library of Congress List of Subject Headings* (11) and Sears, *List of Subject Headings for Small Libraries* (12). The former is designed for use in the larger library and the latter in the smaller one. A further distinction should be noted, however, that is, that the use made of the collection rather than its size may determine whether to use the more complete LC list or the less scientific Sears list. The LC list, because of its greater size includes a larger number of scientific terms and it also adds the LC classification number to each subject listed for use. In both lists, the subjects actually to be used are printed in boldface type while those subjects which refer from an unused form to the one chosen to represent the subject and known as "see" references are in light-face type.

Anderson (13) has said: "Subject headings do one or all of three things: they show where to find material on any specific subject; they show as nearly as possible in one place everything that is to be had on that subject; and, through cross-references, they indicate mention of the subject in places which would not be apparent immediately."

There are two kinds of cross references, "see" or final cross reference, and "see also" which is a related cross reference. The "see" reference refers from an unused heading to the one which has been chosen for use; for example, Carbonic acid see Carbon dioxide; or Activated charcoal, see Carbon, Activated. Since many subjects may be looked for under synonyms or under another form of the subject heading, this device directs the reader to the official heading. The "see also" cross reference refers the reader to additional related material. Each list indicates the related headings which the catalog may use and refer to provided the library already has material both on the subject to which he is referring and also the subject from which he is referring. This process involves keeping track of the subject headings which have been used and also the references which already have been made. For this purpose an authority list may be used, or the headings chosen and the cross references made may be checked in the subject heading list.

In assigning subject headings, several principles should be kept in mind:

1. Use as many subjects as necessary to describe the book. Many books can be described by a single subject heading, but in a small library a book discussing several subdivisions of a subject may be the only material in the library on these topics and they should be brought out under each one rather than lumped together into one larger subject.

2. Be specific. Never use a vague term or one capable of several interpretations. In case the latter is necessary, qualify it with a note indicating the type of material entered under it.

3. Make an authority list. This is essential if the cataloger is to achieve consistency, and particularly necessary in a library where subject headings must be chosen from several sources. This is usually made on cards, one subject to a card and filed alphabetically. References ("see" and "see also") are also made and entered in the subject authority file.

4. Use the shelf list as a guide to the material already placed in a subject. (The shelf list will be discussed more fully in the section on Cataloging.) If the class number has been determined, note the subject headings which have been used for the books classified in that number. Use the shelf list as your guide.

5. Be consistent. By the use of the authority list, shelf list, and other general aids, the same heading should always be used for the same type of material.

The real problem in the science-technology field is the matter of finding good up-to-date subjects to use. The LC list and Sears list were intended for the general library, large and small, respectively. They are brought up to date by new editions, and the LC list is kept current by monthly supplements. They are useful as guides and both lists could well be on the cataloger's shelf as reference tools whether they are being followed. However, for current usage special indexes should be examined. Some of these sources are as follows:

1. *Biological and Agricultural Index*
2. *Applied Science and Technology Index*
3. *Biological Abstracts*
4. *Chemical Abstracts*
5. COSATI Subject Category List
6. *Engineering Index*
7. *Index Medicus and Its Predecessors: Quarterly Cumulative Index Medicus and Current List of Medical Literature*
8. National Library of Medicine; Current Catalog
9. *Nuclear Science Abstracts*
10. *Physiological Abstracts*
11. Public Affairs Information Service

The list above is intended to be suggestive rather than definitive. A familiarity with the subject field of the individual library will lead one to abstracting and indexing services which will be useful.

Any abstracting or other service prepared by subject specialists in the area will be a valuable source of information for the field for which it has been prepared and should be used as a basis for decisions. There is not the space here to discuss subject headings fully, but a person working with subject headings generally would do well to read the instructions in the LC list (11) and Sears (12) as well as the chapters devoted to the subject in Mann (1) and the *Handbook of Medical Library Practice* (14). An additional discussion of subject headings which would be useful is Haykin, *Subject Headings* (15). Specialized thesauri are listed in Chapter 8.

It has been suggested earlier in this chapter that in general it is not wise to attempt to build a classification scheme. However, many individual schemes have been built by librarians who have been specialists in the fields with which they have been involved. The following publication may be useful to those looking for classification schemes and subject heading lists in special fields:

Denison, Barbara, comp., *Selected Materials in Classification; a Bibliography*, SLA, New York, 1968, 142 p. $10.50.

This publication replaces the *Guide to the SLA Loan Collection of Classification Schemes and Subject Heading Lists*, 5th ed., comp. by Bertha R. Barden and Barbara Denison, published in 1961.

Another project worthy of study in relation to the field of subject headings is the National Library of Medicine *Index Mechanization Project*, known as MEDLARS (Medical Literature Analysis and Retrieval System). A detailed discussion of the development of the project may be found in *Medical Library Association Bulletin* 49, No. 1, Part 2, January 1961.

ANALYTICS

Classification and assigning of subject headings in a science-technology library involve more than the ability to fit a book into an existing scheme or to find a specific subject for it. All indexing, particularly periodicals as found in *Chemical Abstracts* and *Index Medicus,* concerns itself with small units, so that each article contained in the journal indexed is brought out and made available. In the larger field of books, this has not always been true, for a book has of necessity been classified as a unit, and the subject headings have been assigned for the book as a whole. But in a library where minute information is of importance the material in books needs to be analyzed in greater detail, and the approach, especially in the matter of subject headings, should be on the level of the smaller units within each book. This will naturally vary with each library, but an example in point would be a general book on color which would fall into the general class, but a color chart may be a very useful item of information which is often difficult to locate; therefore, if this book contains such a chart and it is important in the situation an analytical entry should be made. Ranganathan (16) in *Special Librarianship —What It Connotes* defines this thought-unit process, which connotes the "special" in special librarianship, as "microscopic" rather than "macroscopic" in that it focuses attention upon parts of books and articles.

DESCRIPTIVE CATALOGING

Reduced to its simplest terms the card catalog is a record of the books in the library. Classification brings like things together and the subject headings indicate the topics under which books should be entered in the card catalog; but cataloging is the process by which one transfers certain technical information about the book to a card according to rule. It has already been suggested that reading the introduction and preface of a book and surveying its table of contents will help to give one a general idea of its scope and purpose. Much of the actual cataloging is the transference of the information found on the title page to the catalog card. The following items are listed on the card in the order mentioned and are found for the most part on the title page:

Call number
Author
Title
Edition
Translator
Imprint
Collation
Series note

The call number and the collation are not a part of the information found on the title page, and the series note, if the book happens to belong to a series, may or may not be found on the title page. These items are discussed in the sequence mentioned above and in order to make the information clearer, this discussion will be built around a single book. A sample title page of the book and an author or main entry card for it is included to illustrate the points made.

Items on the Main Entry or Author Card

1. *Call number.* The call number as mentioned earlier in the section on classification is made up of the classification number plus the book number and is placed in the upper left-hand corner of the card.

2. *Author.* The author's name appears in inverted form on the top line at first indention (eight typewriter spaces from the left edge of the card and the third line down from the top of the card) in as full form as is readily available. If the author entry is long and requires more than one line succeeding lines should be at the third indention (14 typewriter spaces from the left edge of the card.) If there is more than one author for a book, the first one named on the title page is used; additional authors are discussed later under Title and Added Entries. Some catalogers add the author's dates after his name, but this may not be considered important excepting in the case of persons whose names are identical.

3. *Title.* The title is entered on the line following the author's name at second indention (12 typewriter spaces from the left edge of the card) with succeeding lines at first indention and should be copied as it appears on the title page, including explanatory or alternative titles. If there is more than one author for a book they are all included as part of the title; but when there is only one author this information may be omitted from the title.

4. *Edition.* If the book has been brought out in more than one edition this should be noted. This is particularly important in the science-technology field.

5. *Translator.* When a book has been originally written in a foreign language and the information regarding the translation or translator appears on the title page this should follow the title. If this information appears in the preface or in a place other than the title page, it should be added in a note. Information regarding the edition or translator found on the title page follows the title and the information is separated from the title only by punctuation.

6. *Imprint.* This consists of place of publication, publisher, and date of publication and follows the title after four typewriter spaces.

7. *Collation.* The collation specifies the number of volumes if more than one or the number of pages if the book is in one volume plus information concerning illustrations, maps, plates, tables, and such. This latter information regarding illustrations, and so on may not be essential and may be omitted, or it may be added in note form following the collation. The collation is entered on the second line below the imprint at second indention with succeeding lines at first indention.

Scientific and Technical Libraries

Their Organization and Administration

Lucille J. Strauss

CHEMISTRY AND PHYSICS LIBRARIAN
THE PENNSYLVANIA STATE UNIVERSITY
UNIVERSITY PARK, PENNSYLVANIA

Irene M. Strieby

CONSULTANT IN ORGANIZATION OF
SPECIAL LIBRARIES AND COMPANY ARCHIVES
INDIANAPOLIS, INDIANA

Alberta L. Brown

ASSOCIATE PROFESSOR
WESTERN MICHIGAN UNIVERSITY
KALAMAZOO, MICHIGAN

Interscience Publishers

a division of John Wiley and Sons, New York • London • Sydney

Figure 1.

8. *Series note.* Series are of various kinds, that is, author, publishers, or monograph series. The collective title for a series may appear at the head of the title page, on the half title page, or on the cover of the book. The series note follows the collation in parentheses and is separated from it by four typewriter spaces.

9. *Special features.* For example, a bibliography which may be important to the reader is added in note form. Notes should be placed on the line after the collation beginning at second indention with succeeding lines at first indention.

10. *Contents.* Akers (17) advises that the card should "give contents of publications containing several works by the same author, or works by several authors, or works on several subjects, or a single work on a number of distinct subjects, especially if the collective title does not sufficiently describe them." Contents follow notes, if any, and are entered at second indention with additional lines at first indention.

The title page of the book chosen for this demonstration is shown in Figure 1.

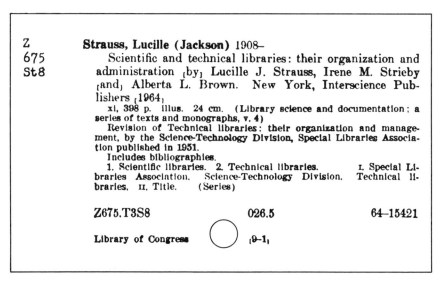

Figure 2.

Figure 2 is a sample LC card of the author or main entry card for the book.

Added-Entry Cards

Additional cards known as added-entry cards are exact copies of the main entry or author card which is also known as the unit card, except that the necessary heading is added at second indention above the author's name. If the heading is too long to be typed on one line succeeding lines are typed at third indention. If there is too much typing for one card, a second one should be used. Subject headings may be typed in red or in all black capitals; other entries are in black. Six added entries are necessary for the above book as follows:*

1. *Title card.*   Scientific and technical libraries.
2. *Subject cards.*   (a) Scientific libraries; (b) Technical libraries.
3. *Joint author cards.*   (a) Strieby, Mrs. Irene M.; (b) Brown, Alberta Louise.
4. *Series card.*   Library science and documentation, v. 4.

Tracing

This is a record of all added entries made for the book. It is usually entered on the back of the main author card, although it may be added to the shelf list (to be discussed later). Library of Congress traces added entries on the face of the card. The purposes of tracing are (*1*) to indicate the added cards that are to be made by the typist and (*2*) to show the cards that are to be removed if the work is later withdrawn, or if the cards later need correction. If the former, it is well to have headings for the added entries appear exactly as they are to be copied by the typist. Usually the cataloger decides on the order for the tracing to avoid confusion.

In tracing, a "t" indicates that a title card has been made; and "ser" is sufficient indication that a series card has been made. For subjects and other added entries the full heading is used. The tracing for Strauss' book used as an illustration is as follows:

       t
       jt a   Strieby, Mrs. Irene M.
                Brown, Alberta Louise
       s   Scientific libraries
                Technical libraries
       ser

* Library of Congress has omitted the added entries for joint authors; smaller libraries may wish to include them. The added entry (included on the LC card) is Special Libraries Association, Science-Technology Division. Technical libraries may be added as noted on the LC card if the library possesses this earlier edition and wishes to call attention to it.

Shelf List

The shelf list is a record of the books in the library arranged in the order of the books on the shelves. It is shorter in form than the main author card as it needs to contain only enough information to identify the book. It is usually kept near the cataloger's desk. According to Akers (17) the shelf list is used for the following:

1. To take the annual inventory to see if any books are missing. (Many libraries no longer take inventories, so this use may not be valid.)
2. To show how many copies of a given book the library owns.
3. To show what kind of books are in a given class as an aid to classifying.
4. To show the librarian who is making out book orders how many books the library already has in any given class.
5. To serve in a limited way as a classed catalog.
6. To give source, date, and cost if no accession record is kept.
7. To serve as a basis for a bibliography or reading list on a specific subject.

In addition, the shelf list, as mentioned above, may also be used for tracing. The shelf list is a unit or main author card except that notes, contents (and sometimes tracing) are omitted to shorten it. The accession number, if used, is added to the shelf list. If an accession record is not used, the source, acquisition date, and price are entered on this card.

There are many additional cataloging facts which are necessary equipment for any cataloger and a careful study of Akers (17), Mann (1), and the relatively new Anglo-American Cataloging Rules (18) will be helpful. Much material has of necessity been omitted here because of the brevity of the presentation. *A Manual of Form and Procedure for Typewritten Catalog Cards, and Anglo-American Descriptive Cataloging; A Compilation of 200 Exemplary Cards Indexed by Rule Number* will be useful both to the experienced and inexperienced cataloger. For the beginner it will be a guide to cataloging procedure particularly since it includes sample catalog cards. The second part of the manual will be particularly valuable to the experienced cataloger who is in the process of adapting the Anglo-American cataloging rules. It was compiled by D. J. Lehnus by whom it was published in Kalamazoo in 1969. The first part, the manual, provides a good, simple introduction to cataloging with step-by-step illustrations of the items on a catalog card. The second part reproduces 200 catalog cards exemplifying rules 130–191 of the Anglo-American scheme. An index by rule number makes it easy to consult. The author's address is 1822 Academy St., Kalamazoo, Mich. 49007, and the price of the book is $3.50.

In addition to this book, Mr. Lehnus is working on a new book tentatively entitled *Interpretation of the Anglo-American Rules with Cards.*

PERIODICALS

The treatment of periodicals deserves some discussion as it differs somewhat from that of books. Some libraries classify periodicals so that books and journals in the same field will be placed together on the shelves; that is, *Journal of Organic Chemistry* would stand in 547 in the DC and in QD in the LC. Other libraries arrange all periodicals together alphabetically by title. One variation of this latter arrangement is that journals which are the official organs of societies may be entered and shelved so that the *Journal of the American Medical Association* would file under American rather than under Journal and by the same rule the *Journal of Physiology* would file in the J's.

Rules for cataloging periodicals are discussed in the *Anglo-American Cataloging Rules* (18). For ease in determining the library's holding, it is sometimes advantageous to file the catalog cards for periodicals in a separate drawer. A subject index may also be added as there are times when it will be useful to know what journals are received in one subject field, especially if they are not classified.

LIBRARY OF CONGRESS PRINTED CARDS

The Card Division of the Library of Congress prints the cards used in its own catalogs and these may be purchased by other libraries. A unit card is used, and the purchasing library must add its call number, subjects, and other added entries to the set of unit cards received. By the use of boldface type combined with several other types of print somewhat more detailed information can be put on this card than on one which is typed, and furthermore, items of greater importance are emphasized. As mentioned above, added entries are traced on the back of the typed catalog card, but on the LC card these are indicated on the face of the card at the bottom. Libraries using LC cards usually check those which are to be used; any additional entries used must be added to those on the face of the card, or, preferable, typed on the back of the card. The LC and DC classification numbers are noted at the bottom of the LC cards and may be helpful as guides to the cataloger. In order to facilitate the ordering and use of these cards, the Library of Congress has issued two booklets explaining them: *Handbook of Card Distribution* (19) and *LC Printed Cards: How to Order and Use Them* (20). The latter is a somewhat briefer and less detailed explanation of the process. It will be seen from the facts above that the LC cards can save any cataloger considerable time; in general they possess a high degree of accuracy, and are particularly helpful to the less experienced person.

Sources to Consult to Locate Numbers for Library of Congress Cards

Booklist
Book review digest
Cumulative book index
Library journal
Publishers' Weekly
United States Catalog
U. S. Library of Congress, catalog of printed cards
U. S. Library of Congress, National Union Catalog
Verso of title page of books published during the past few years

It should be noted that fewer LC card numbers may be found in *Booklist* and *Book Review Digest* simply because they list fewer books in the science-technology field.

During recent years cataloging routines at the Library of Congress have fallen seriously behind, especially in the fields of science and technology. LC cards are frequently so slow in coming that the usefulness of the books in the above-mentioned fields is seriously hampered. Many publishers furnish catalog cards with books, but unfortunately, few of them are in the fields of science and technology. Vendors have entered the field and some do furnish catalog cards with books; but again most of their services are geared to public and school libraries.

Richard Abel and Co., P.O. Box 4245, Portland, Ore. 97208, is now providing computer-produced cataloging for all books purchased from them or sent on their approval plan. The service includes all titles listed in *Books for College Libraries,* and certain other limited fields. Although this service covers a lafger field, it still is not universal in its coverage. Following is a "card description" quoted from their description of their service.

Card Description

At the present we do not reproduce the following items from the Library of Congress card.

1. The full name entry at the foot of the card on those cards where the Library of Congress provides this information.

2. In some of the older cataloging, titles in the body of the card were preceded by an ellipsis (. . .). We omit this ellipsis.

3. At present we are providing only the primary classification number. Shortly we will be in a position to provide cards with either primary or secondary classification numbers. However, in the cases of analyzed series where the Library of Congress has given a secondary monograph classification, we have used this in preference to the analytic number.

4. We will correct printing errors on the Library of Congress cards where we can affirm that the misspelling is a simple typographical error on the card and not in the book. We also correct misspellings in the subject headings if they appear.

5. At the present we provide only Romanic lettering. In those cases where the card contains non-Romanic lettering such as Cyrillic, we will provide the information in transliterated form.

It would appear from this vendor's description of his service that LC cards are used as the basis for the cards reproduced. This means that the time problem has not been solved. Call numbers may be added as well as tracing on request, so that the service would appear to save typing time in the local library. It would also appear from the opening statement regarding the service that the field is limited, so that the library in specialized fields might well find that many cards are not available. "Customized cataloging" may not yet be a substitute for a good cataloger.

In addition to vendors who furnish catalog cards with books purchased from them cards may also be procured from processing centers. Some of the State Libraries as well as public libraries have set up such centers with some success, though the problem of timing seems to be a recurring one. For a somewhat complete discussion of this type of service which includes evaluations of processing centers, commercial centers, and so on, see

Piercy, Esther J. and Robert L. Talmadge, "Cooperative and Centralized Cataloging," *Libr. Trends* **16**:3–175 (1967).

MARC

The Machine-Readable Cataloging Project, better known by its acronym MARC, was a pilot project (November 1966–June 1967) of the Library of Congress. It was an experiment in the reproduction and distribution of machine-readable cataloging data which was later placed on a subscription basis as the MARC System. 1968 quotations are as follows: "The subscription price for the weekly service will be $600 a year. This price may be revised after the first year as the library gains experience in the production of tapes. A method by which tapes may be returned is under consideration and may be announced later. Payment in advance must accompany each order; the cost of tapes cannot be charged to Card Division deposit accounts."

The MARC System is divided into four major subsystems:

1. *The Input Subsystem* is concerned with the input, conversion, and formatting of bibliographic information into machine readable form.

2. *The Maintenance Subsystem* is concerned with the storage and maintenance of bibliographic records.

3. *The Retrieval Subsystem* is concerned with the retrieval of records.

4. *The Output Subsystem* is concerned with the arrangement, the printing, and the distribution of records and/or parts of records (Library of Congress Information Bulletin).

For an extensive bibliography on library automation which includes a section entitled "Cataloging (Project MARC)" see

Mason, Charlene, "Bibliography of Library Automation," *ALA Bull.* **63**:1117–1134 (September 1969).

ARRANGEMENT OF THE CARD CATALOG

When classifying and cataloging have been completed, the cards are filed in the card catalog. This card catalog may be of several kinds depending on the use made of it. The most common form is the dictionary catalog which has been defined as a catalog usually on cards, in which all the entries, for example, author, title, subject, and series, and their related references are arranged together in one general alphabet. A more complete discussion of the arrangement of cards in the card catalog may be found in the ALA rules for filing catalog cards (21) and in the Library of Congress filing rules for the dictionary catalogs of the Library of Congress (22). The sub-arrangement may vary from the strictly alphabetical. For a good discussion of this sub-arrangement which varies from the alphabetical consult Akers (17).

The author-subject catalog, also known as the divided catalog, is a variation often used in a special library. In this type of catalog, the subject cards are filed in one section and all other cards in another. This division makes it possible for different persons to use the sections at the same time. Also a person wishing to look for subject material is not bothered with other cards. Another common division in the science-technology library is to separate journal holdings from the rest of the catalog as this information is needed frequently. The idea of division can be used for any special collection such as microfilms and reprints. This type of catalog has been successfully used at the Library of the New York Academy of Medicine and also in the Library of the American College of Surgeons in Chicago.

The classified catalog differs from the previous two mentioned in that it is arranged by the class number rather than by the alphabetical entry on the catalog card. In this sense, it is similar to the shelf list; however, it is an expansion of the shelf list, for it includes cards for parts of books which have been analyzed and added to the catalog, pamphlet material, and other classified items. It is more useful in the large library where one may not go to the stacks to examine books first hand. It may also be useful to the research worker who wishes to visualize the entire content within a given class. The classified catalog must be supplemented by an alphabetical author and subject catalog and an index to the classes. Classified catalogs are in use in the John Crerar Library, Chicago; the Technology Department, Carnegie Library, Pittsburgh; and Engineering Societies Library, New York.

The horizontal catalog is useful in some libraries where material is important by date. In this catalog entries for books published during the last five or ten years are filed in separate sections from books published earlier. This is particularly useful in a medical library where current publications are of prime importance.

The filing of cards for all types of materials, both cataloged and indexed, in one central catalog is worthy of consideration. Variously colored cards can be used for each distinctive kind of publication represented so that it can be seen at a glance. The advantage of being able to find all the material in the library by looking in one place is obvious.

Another form is the "book catalog" that is advantageous because as many copies as may be required can be made for various locations. It is effectively produced by computer; one good system for doing this is outlined by Bregzis (23).

CONCLUSION

The technical processes discussed in this chapter are of great importance to the effective use of the library. Inefficient or incomplete cataloging may mean that valuable material is not available when most needed, thus the time expended to do competent cataloging is a good investment. Moreover a thorough knowledge of the principles of cataloging, classification, and subject headings gives one a sound foundation for the many kinds of indexing needed in the science-technology library. Whether one calls a subject a descriptor, or a "see" reference a link, is wholly unimportant, but an understanding of basic principles makes it possible to adapt these principles to the indexing world. Technical processing as discussed in this chapter describes one way of handling the flow of information from its source to its ultimate end and purpose, the user. For the large organization with unlimited funds the use of machines may be essential, but the smaller and financially limited organization must of necessity produce the same end results by the use of the traditional methods. At the end of this chapter is a selected list of books and articles dealing with this general subject for the benefit of those who may wish to pursue it further.

REFERENCES

1. Margaret Mann, *Introduction to Cataloging and Classification of Books,* 2nd ed., ALA, Chicago, 1943.

2. Melvil Dewey, *Dewey Decimal Classification and Relativ Index,* 17th ed., Forest Press, Lake Placid Club, N. Y., 1965, 2 vols.

3. Library of Congress, Subject Catalog Division, *Outline of Library of Congress Classification (1942),* rev. and enl. ed., U. S. Government Printing Office, Washington, D.C., 1942.

4. National Library of Medicine, *Classification; A Scheme for the Self Arrangement of Books in the Field of Medicine and Its Related Sciences,* 3d ed., U. S. Government Printing Office, Washington, D.C., 1964.

5. Mortimer Taube, "Bibliographic Classification." College and Reference Libraries; 14:453–455 (1955).

6. Aslib, *Handbook of Special Librarianship and Information Work,* 3rd ed., Aslib, London, 1967, p. 100.

7. *Universal Decimal Classification,* Complete English ed., 4th international ed., Keerberghen, Brussels, 1936–date.

8. *Universal Decimal Classification,* Abridged English ed., 2nd ed. rev., 1957, British Standards Institution, London, 1957.

9. W. C. B. Sayers, *Introduction to Library Classification,* 9th ed., Grafton, London, 1955.

10. C. A. Cutter and K. E. Sanborn, *Cutter-Sanborn Figure Alphabetic-Order Table,* Remington Rand Business Service, Library Bureau Division, Boston, n.d.

11. Library of Congress, *Subject Headings Used in the Dictionary Catalogs of the Library of Congress,* 7th ed., U. S. Government Printing Office, Washington, D.C., 1966.

12. Minnie Earl Sears, *Sears List of Subject Headings,* Ed., 9th ed., by B. M. Westby, Wilson, New York, 1965.

13. Medical Library Association, *Handbook of Medical Library Practice,* American Library Association, Chicago, 1943.

14. Medical Library Association, *Handbook of Medical Library Practice,* 3rd ed., ALA, Chicago, 1970.

15. D. J. Haykin, *Subject Headings; A Practical Guide,* U. S. Government Printing Office, Washington, D.C., 1951.

16. S. R. Ranganathan, "Special Librarianship—What It Connotes," *Spec. Libr.* **40:** 361–370 (1949).

17. Susan Grey Akers, *Simple Library Cataloging,* 5th ed., ALA, Chicago, 1969.

18. *Anglo-American Cataloging Rules,* prepared by the American Library Association, The Library of Congress, The Library Association and The Canadian Library Association; North American text, ALA, Chicago, 1967.

19. Library of Congress, Card Division, *Handbook of Card Distribution,* Library of Congress, Washington, D.C.

20. Library of Congress, Card Division, *Printed Cards; How to Order and Use Them,* U. S. Government Printing Office, Washington, D.C.

21. American Library Association, *A.L.A. Rules for Filing Catalog Cards,* 2nd ed., ALA, Chicago, 1968.

22. Library of Congress, *Filing Rules for the Dictionary Catalogs of the Library of Congress,* U. S. Government Printing Office, Washington, D.C., 1956.

23. R. Bregzis, "The Ontario New Universities Library Project—An Automated Bibliographic Data Control System," *Coll. & Res. Libr.* **26:** 4951508 (1965).

BIBLIOGRAPHY

Allen, Thelma and D. A. Dickman, Eds., *New Rules for an Old Game,* University of British Columbia, Publication Centre, Vancouver, B.C., 1967.

Batty, C. D., *An Introduction to the Seventeenth Edition of the Dewey Decimal Classification,* Archon Books, London, 1967.

Brodman, Estelle and Doris Bolef, "Printed Catalogs: Retrospect and Prospect," *Spec. Libr.* **59:**783–788 (1968).

Eaton, Thelma, *Cataloging and Classification: An Introductory Manual,* 4th ed., distributed by Edwards Brothers, Ann Arbor, Mich., 1967.

Gainer, E., "Large Municipal Library as a Network," *Libr. Quar.* **39:**41–51 (1969).

Henderson, J. W. and J. A. Rosenthal, Eds., *Library Catalogs: Their Preservation and Maintenance by Photographic and Automated Techniques,* M.I.T. Press, Cambridge, 1968.

Immroth, J., *A Guide to Library of Congress Classification,* Libraries Unlimited, Rochester, N.Y., 1968.

Kozumplik, W. A. and Lange, R. T., "Computer Produced Microfilm Library Catalog," *Amer. Doc.* **18:**67–80 (1967).

LaMontagne, L. E., *American Library Classification, with Special Reference to the Library of Congress,* Shoe String Press, Hamden, Conn., 1961.

Lehnus, D. J., "The Anglo-American Cataloging Rules; Their Teaching vs. Their Use," *Libr. J.* **93**:2975–77 (1968).

Melcher, D., "Cataloging, Processing and Automation," Amer. Libraries **2**: 701–713 (1971).

National Library of Medicine, *Current Catalog,* U. S. Government Printing Office, Washington, D.C., 1966.

Perreault, J. M., Ed., *Reclassification—Rationale and Problems,* University Student Supply Store, College Park, Md., 1968.

Schimmelfeng, R. H. and C. D. Cook, Eds., *The Use of the Library of Congress Classifications,* ALA, Chicago, 1966.

Shaw, R. R., Ed., *The State of the Library Art,* Graduate School of Library Science, Rutgers, New Brunswick, N. J., 1960–1961, Vol. 1, part 1: *Cataloging and Classification;* Vol. 1, part 2: *Subject Headings;* Vol. 2, part 3: *Classification Systems.*

Tauber, M. *et al.,* Eds., *The Dewey Decimal Classification,* N. Y. School of Library Service, Columbia University, N.Y., 1966.

Warheit, I. A., "Centralization of Library Processing," *Spec. Libr.* **56**:697–699 (1965).

Weber, D. C., "Book Catalog Trends in 1966," *Libr. Trends* **16**:149–164 (1967).

8

Indexing and Filing of Nonbook Materials

The indexing and filing of items other than books and periodicals requires much forethought to ensure that the information they contain can be found when it is needed. These materials, the acquisition of which is discussed in Chapter 5, comprise a most important part of the collection, and because they are unique to every situation, the indexing process must be developed to fit the subject area from the viewpoint of organizational interests. Among the possible categories represented may be the following: government publications, including technical reports; articles from periodicals; patents; trade literature, including catalogs; pictures and photographs, possibly slides; laboratory notebooks; engineering drawings; maps; reprints or preprints; archival items; and technical correspondence. These are in various forms, printed, typed, possibly handwritten, or as direct photocopies or microform. The indexing of such records is a process of documentation, the purpose of which is to provide a means for retrieving every bit of information they contain once they have been put into a filing location.

Because of the significant increase in the numbers of publications resulting from the expansion of scientific research activities in recent years, a consequent awareness of a need for more effective methods of locating the facts presented in every individual document has developed. The process has come to be known as "information retrieval," and special indexing schemes have been elaborated to meet requirements. For some purposes the newly devised methods are supplanting traditional procedures and are proving to be more effective. However, each indexing project requires study and individual decision as to what approach will adequately take care of it.

The intricate problems involved in the classification of subjects for indexing purposes are so diverse and complex that it is impossible to encompass them in such a brief chapter as this, and therefore only an introduction is outlined. Attention is directed to the numerous books and periodical articles that deal with the philosophy and processes relating to this intellectually demanding activity, some of which are cited at the end of the chapter. One of the best surveys, which includes an admirably provocative analysis of the newer systems for indexing, is the book by Metcalfe (1) entitled *Information Indexing and Subject Cataloging: Alphabetical, Classified, Coordinate, Mechanical*. This most scholarly presentation could be studied with profit by anyone seriously concerned with indexing problems, an opinion supported by Sharp (2) who states that this "work is the most penetrating analysis made to date of so much that is basic to the retrieval problem." Sharp's own book constitutes an extension of some of the same areas treated by Metcalfe, first defining the problem basic to information retrieval then tackling the elusive subject of classification. Vickery's (3) book on classification and indexing in science is a comprehensive review of all systems and theories, from the long established traditional patterns to the more recently developed ones designed for use in conjunction with automation. Much mental effort has been directed toward where to place and how to relocate large numbers of bits of information.

However, all indexing projects are not of such nature as to require the extensive analysis that the newer approaches entail, though warning must be expressed against a temptation to be too hasty in assessing an indexing problem. Today there are only a small number of research reports to be handled, but within five years there could be hundreds; thus the initial indexing should be done with as much perception as can be commanded. There will inevitably be some trial and error no matter how carefully the initial approach is made.

The introduction to procedures for indexing and filing items belonging in a scientific-technical collection presented in this chapter consists briefly of the simple, conventional methods that have long been, and still are, in use. This is followed by a short summary of the newer nonconventional methods with some attempt to suggest how to make a choice for a particular requirement.

GENERAL INDEXING CONSIDERATIONS

It can safely be assumed that in any library there will be a collection of materials that cannot be classified and cataloged as are books, yet they must be recorded and indexed, then filed in some orderly manner for ready location. The system to be adopted will be dictated by the broad nature or physical form of these items, their degree of complexity, and the use to be made of them. Every case is unique to some extent, and general principles can help to analyze an individual problem. Before making any decisions as to method, the content of the material must be studied to assess its significance, to try to anticipate how it will be used, and to foretell the eventual size of the collection. A small group of ephemeral papers not worth permanent retention will not merit the time and thought that many papers containing highly pertinent information must be accorded. The book by B. M. Weeks, *Filing and Records Management* (3rd ed., Ronald Press, 1964) is a good basic introduction to the subject of indexing and filing.

For a practical introduction to the more sophisticated methods, Jahoda's (4) book, *Information Storage and Retrieval Systems for Individual Researchers,* is as lucid and concise a presentation as has yet been written. Although the book is directed ostensibly to individual research workers, it is equally helpful for a larger scale project.

No matter what kind of system is adopted, conventional or nonconventional, a guide to the terminology to be used must be selected. If this method of controlling the vocabulary is not followed, chaos will ensue. Almost any field of science has such an authoritative list either as a thesaurus or as a subject index to a major abstracting or indexing publication from which terms can be chosen. Some of the thesaurusi are the following:

EJC Thesaurus of Engineering Terms, Engineers Joint Council, New York, 1964.
Thesaurus of DDC Descriptors, AD 632 600 Defense Documentation Center, Arlington, Va., 1966.
Thesaurus of Engineering and Scientific Terms (TEST), AD 672 000 U. S. Department of Defense, Washington, D.C., 1967.
U. S. Atomic Energy Commission, *Subject Headings Used by the U. S. AEC Technical Information Service,* U. S. AEC Technical Information Service, Oak Ridge, Tenn., 1951.
NASA Thesaurus: Subject Terms for Indexing Scientific and Technical Information, NASA–SP–7030 Scientific and Technical Information Division, Office of Technical Utilization, Washington, D. C., 1967; 3 vol.
ASM Thesaurus of Metallurgical Terms, American Society for Metals, Metals Park, Ohio, 1969.
AIChE Chemical Engineering Thesaurus, American Institute of Chemical Engineers, New York, 1961.
List of Subject Headings, 3rd ed., The Library of Congress, Technical Information Division, Washington, D. C., 1952.
FAA Thesaurus of Technical Descriptors, 3rd ed., Federal Aviation Agency, Washing-

ton, D. C., 1969; available from National Technical Information Service, Springfield, Va. 22151, as AD 686 837.

Thesaurus of Textile Terms Covering Fibrous Materials and Processes, S. Backer and E. I. Valko, Eds., M.I.T. Press, Cambridge, 1969.

COSATI Subject Category List, 1st ed., Committee on Scientific and Technical Information of the Federal Council for Science & Technology, Washington, D. C., 1964.

Indexing Terms of Announced Publications for Government Scientific and Technical Research Reports, W. Hammond, National Science Foundation, Washington, D. C., 1964, 2 vol.

Medical Subject Headings, 1965 revision, Part II of Index Medicus, National Library of Medicine, Bethesda, Md., January 1965.

Thesaurus of Pulp and Paper Terms, Pulp and Paper Research Institute of Canada, McGill University, Quebec, 1969?.

Thesaurus of Terms on Copper Technology, Copper Development Association, New York.

Petroleum Exploration and Production Thesaurus, University of Tulsa Petroleum Abstracts Advisory Committee, Tulsa, Okla.

Only some examples of the kinds of thesaurusi available for adoption or adaptation are listed here.

Because an indexing or abstracting publication requires careful attention as to choice of terms used for its subject indexes, these too can be utilized as authority lists. Among these are the following:

> *Applied Science and Technology Index*
> *Biological Abstracts*
> *Chemical Abstracts*
> *Engineering Index*
> *Metals Abstracts*
> *Physics Abstracts*

CONVENTIONAL INDEXING SYSTEMS

By conventional systems we mean those that basically make use of only two simple and universally known devices—the alphabet and numbers—to create an ordered framework. These can be manipulated to fit an extensive and complex subject area, but they do not suffice when a collection outgrows their limitations.

Any system of indexing is based upon an arrangement of topics in systematic order. It is usually necessary to provide some kind of specific listing or index as a guide to this array. The conventional systems are designated as (*1*) alphabetical, (*2*) numerical, (*3*) a combination of (*1*) and (*2*) called alpha-numerical, (*4*) classified, and (*5*) special. These are adaptable to readily managed collections of items, not too numerous and not highly complicated. These several systems are briefly described here with.

Alphabetical Indexing

The basis for this system is simply, and obviously, the alphabet. Metcalfe (1) is a strong proponent of this idea because it is familiar to every potential user, for one cogent reason. To initiate a system a list of topical words must be established, and it is recommended that this be developed from an already established authority such as has been mentioned previously. Of course, if the materials are of the simplest type, such as a group of manufacturers catalogs, these can be placed in alphabetical order by name, but this is not a true indexing situation. Where alphabetical indexing is applied, each item is reviewed and the appropriate terms from the authority list assigned to it, usually by preparing cards citing the reference with as many copies as there are topics assigned to it. The items must then be filed in some determined order, possibly by author or by issuing agent.

It is possible, of course, to develop a list of indexing terms that are considered to be unique to a particular situation. For example, a part of a list is shown here by permission of United Aircraft Corporation. Such a selection of terms would have to be updated to conform with usage.

Subject Headings

United Aircraft Corporation

Air Brakes (for aerodynamic brakes) *see also* Brakes; Drag Brakes (for Satellite & Space Vehicles); Propeller Brakes

Air Cleaners *see* Air Filters; Filters and Filtration

Air Compressors *see also* Compressed Air Equipment; Compressors

Air Conditioning *see also* Air Conditioning (specific item); Ventilation

Air Conditioning, Airplane

Air Conditioning, Building

Air Conditioning, Ship

Air Conditioning, Space Vehicle

Air Conditioning, Submarine

Air Currents

Air Cushion Vehicles

Air Cushion Vehicles (name)
Air Ducts *see* Ducts
Air Filters *see also* Filters and Filtration
Air Flow *see* Flow of Air
Air Flow Indicators *see* Flow of Air—Measurement
Air Inlets *see* Airscoops; Intake Systems
Air Lines *see also* names of Airlines
   Accounting
   Cost of Operation
   Countries
   Directories
   Finance
   Management
   Operation *see* Air Lines, Management
   Personnel
   Statistics
Air Lines, Feeder
Air Mail
   Countries
   Pickup Service

Numerical Indexing

The subjects to be used as topical words are listed in a chosen order, preferably in some logical sequence showing hierarchical relationships, and then these words are numbered in the order of the listing. If the subjects are few and acceptably broad such a scheme is adequate. Provision should be made for the insertion of new terms by leaving numbers open. As an item for indexing is analyzed, it is assigned an appropriate number, then filed with others carrying the same number. This file can be consulted directly. An alphabetical index to the list of subjects may be necessary.

It must be decided whether it is desirable to prepare index cards for each document, these to be interfiled in the card catalog or kept in a separate file.

Alpha-Numerical Indexing

A combination of the alphabet and numbers can be utilized in establishing an indexing system. Broad subjects are listed in alphabetical order, then the subdivisions numbered. No attention need be paid to the initial letter of the first word; there may be hierarchical significance.

This can take care of a limitless addition of subtopics. The documents are marked with the proper identification and filed accordingly. Within a group the order may be by author or corporate body.

Classified Indexing

In a classified system subjects are grouped in logical sequence according to the rational development of the field of knowledge represented. These subjects are assigned numbers, letters, or combinations thereof just as class identifications are given to books in such systems as the Library of Congress or Dewey Classifications. In fact, it is highly desirable to adapt the procedure used for books to the indexing of other materials. Only brief mention is made here of some of the principal book classification schedules. For a somewhat more detailed explanation of them Chapter 7 should be consulted.

The comprehensive classification schemes used for books are few, and it is rare that any other than the Dewey Decimal or the Library of Congress are considered for adoption, though these may be altered significantly to adapt to a special situation. It is possible and practical to use the broad divisions as framework and then expand to whatever degree of specificity is desired to apply them to indexing.

Expansion of the Dewey Classification is an actuality in the form of the Universal Decimal Classification (UDC). It is used for books much more widely in European countries than in the United States, although special study groups sponsored by the International Federation of Documentation have been studying it to determine whether it might be a desirable device when in the future the literature is handled internationally by automated procedures. Bradford (5) was a strong champion of the UDC in the 1940s and worked to instigate the practice of having every published item, including articles in periodicals, tagged with the appropriate UDC code. Points favoring the scheme are: first that the notation permits indication of more than one subject by the linking of two classes (or more) by a colon, and second the scheme is being revised continuously by subject specialists, a very important feature for the changing sciences. Furthermore, it is independent of language. The UDC is available in parts, each covering selected subject areas, from the British Standards Institution.

Another noteworthy system for classification that was designed originally for books is the one contrived by Bliss (6). From the discussion in Chapter 7 it is apparent that this system is amenable to detailed subject breakdown, making it useable for indexing. Its broad divisions are designated by letters, B for physics, C for chemistry, for example, and letters also denote subdivisions.

The system devised by Ranganathan is known as the Colon classification because the Colon is used to show subject relationships. It is often described as "completely synthetic," that is, based on principles that require the synthesis of a notation from a minimum of logical bases of the five fundamental categories of personality, matter, energy, space, and time. Application includes thorough preliminary study of the material to be indexed through which a group of applicable terms is collected and, as obvious similarities emerge, these are called "facets." Individually, each one is a "focus." When more than one concept is involved, two or more notations are strung together, connected by colons, hence Colon classification.

It is advisable to study Metcalfe (1) and Vickery (2) for exhaustive discussion and comparisons of this and other systems. Vickery includes some illuminating examples of representative classifications of science (23 in all) that have been proposed from the thirteenth century to the twentieth. It is an exercise certain to challenge as long as scientific investigation dictates that the subject matter be put in useful order.

Special Schemes

In certain situations it is expedient to adapt or devise a system of classification that is based upon some special aspect of the product or activity of the organization served by the library. For example, in some industries where the areas of activity are well-defined and the processes involved are so highly developed that major changes happen rarely, the flow sheets for the operations in the plant may be used as the basis for an indexing scheme. Because of the habit of the clientele to think in an already established pattern, it is advantageous to have the subjects for information files follow a similar order. As an instance, a metallurgical company might use these broad headings:

A. Geology and exploration
B. Mining
C. Ore beneficiation
D. Processing
E. Products: metals, alloys

However, instead of attempting to devise a scheme for metals, the possibility of adapting the one already developed by committees of the American Society for Metals and the Metals Division of Special Libraries Association might be considered. An important feature of this system is its accommodation to either manual or automated systems.

Many other classifications for various subject fields have been devised, and if one can be located for a particular area of interest it is certain to aid in an approach to the same field. A collection of such schedules had been collected by Special Libraries Association from which it was transferred to the School of Library Science, Western Reserve University, Cleveland, Ohio. A pamphlet entitled *Selected Materials in Classification: A Bibliography,* compiled by Dennison was published by SLA in 1968. The classifications may be borrowed from Western Reserve School of Library Science, Bibliographic Systems Center.

An historically significant indexing concept was proposed as early as 1910 by J. Kaiser. It is worthy of attention because it anticipated in principle some more recently propounded ideas, even though it was never accorded the merited recognition of widespread adoption. Kaiser's original publication has long since been out of print but Holmstrom (7), among others, provides a good description of it. Essentially it entails the selection of a group of broad terms applicable to the subject in hand, these being subjects termed "concretes" to be noted on the upper left-hand corner of a card. These are of such nature that they can be explicitly modified by terms identified as "process" that are noted on the upper right-hand corner of a card having a relevant "concrete" word. For example, a concrete term is "air" for which a "process" term might be "circulation." If the numbers for documents relating to the circulation of air are noted on this card, an index to information is developed. The system appears to be neatly logical and also permits subject additions when these are needed. Holmstrom designed a similar scheme with certain modifications. Similarity to the Uniterm system, discussed under nonconventional systems, is evident.

The foregoing presentation of conventional indexing methods is admittedly the barest introduction and will be helpful only as a start. However, there is no way of making an indexing project simple if the subject matter is at all involved. When the documents to be indexed number more than a few hundred and their content has complex interrelationships, recourse must be made to more efficacious systems.

NONCONVENTIONAL INDEXING FOR INFORMATION RETRIEVAL

When facing an indexing situation where the number of items is too great and their content too complex for conventional methods, one must select one of the established nonconventional systems. It is necessary first to become familiar with their broad characteristics in order to assess their suitability for the contemplated application.

To acquire background knowledge in the somewhat rarefied realm of information retrieval by nonconventional methods, the publications of authorities responsible for their development should be studied. Some of the important books are listed here followed by the periodicals in which articles that relate to even newer developments appear. Of the books, particular note should be taken of the *Annual Review of Information Science and Technology.*

Books

Annual Review of Information Science and Technology, C. A. Cuadra, Ed., Wiley-Interscience, New York, Vol. 1, 1966; Vol. 2, Britannia, Chicago, 1967; Vol. 3, 1968; Vol. 4, 1969; Vol. 5, 1970.

Punched Cards: Their Application to Science and Industry, R. S. Casey, *et al.,* Eds., McGraw-Hill, New York, 1958.

Information Retrieval Systems: Characteristics, Testing, and Evaluation, F. W. Lancaster, Wiley, New York, 1968.

Automatic Information Organization and Retrieval, G. Salton, McGraw-Hill, New York, 1968.

An Introduction to Computers in Information Science, S. Artandi, Scarecrow, Metuchen, N. J., 1968.

Information Storage and Retrieval: Tools, Elements, Theories, J. Becker and R. W. Hayes, Wiley, New York, 1963.

Punch-Card Methods in Research and Documentation with Special Reference to Biology, M. Scheele, translated by E. Holmstrom, Interscience-Wiley, New York, 1961.

Studies in Coordinate Indexing, M. Taube, Vol. 1, 1953; Vol. 2, 1954; Vol. 3, 1956; Vol. 4, 1957; Vol. 5, 1959, Documentation, Inc., Bethesda, Md.

Textbook in Mechanized Information Retrieval, A. Kent, 2nd ed., Wiley, New York, 1964.

IBM Reference Manual: Index Organization for Information Retrieval, Technical Publications Dept., IBM Corp., 112 East Post Road, White Plains, N. Y., n.d.

The State of the Library Art, R. Shaw, Ed., Vol. 4, Parts 1–5, Graduate School of Library Service, Rutgers—The State University, New Brunswick, N.J., 1961. Part 1, *Notched Cards,* F. Reichman; Part 2, *Feature Cards (Peek-a-Boo),* L. S. Thompson; Part 3, *Punched Cards,* R. Blasingame, Jr.; Part 4, *Electronic Searching,* G. Jahoda; Part 5, *Coding in Yes-No Form,* D. J. Hickey.

Methods of Information Handling, C. P. Bourne, Wiley, New York, 1963.

Periodicals

American Documentation, official journal of American Institute for Information Science, Washington, D.C.

Journal of Chemical Documentation, official journal of Division of Chemical Literature, American Chemical Society, Washington, D.C.

Journal of Documentation, official journal of Aslib (Association of Special Libraries and Information Bureaus), London.

Special Libraries, official journal of Special Libraries Association, New York.

Table 1   Some Representative Retrieval Systems

Device	Manufacturer	Remarks
Manual		
Edge-notched cards	Royal McBee, E-Z Sort, and Burroughs Zator Co.	For small-scale projects, needle for selecting
Peek-a-boo cards	Jonker (Termatrex), Find-It, and Wassell, Inc.	Based on principle of optical coincidence
Uniterm cards	Documentation, Inc. and American Institute of Chemical Engineers	Requires visual matching of document numbers
Systems Combining Document Image and Indexing Information		
Rapid selector	Developed by R. Shaw, prototypes only	Microfilm with code at side
Flip	Benson-Lehner	Microfilm with photographic indexing code
Filesearch	FMA, Inc.	Microfilm with photographic indexing code
Minicard	Eastman Kodak	Microfilm in minute bits, 0.6×1.3 inches, with photographic indexing code thereon
Miracode	Eastman Kodak	Cartridge microfilm with code on each frame
Magnavue	Magnavox Research Laboratories	Microfilm in chips, 3 inches, carrying image plus code
Equipment Storing Document Image, Separate Index		
Selectriever, Mosler 410	Mosler Safe Co.	Images on aperture cards, microfiche, or microfilm, wired to coded keyboard
Cypress, developed from Walnut	IBM	Images on film chips in cartridge controlled by computer, experimental only
Verac	Avco Corporation	Images on film sheets
Microcite	National Bureau of Standards	Images on sheet film, index on Termatrex cards
Mechanical Card Sorting Devices		
Card punchers and sorters	IBM, Remington Rand, and Burroughs	Useful for sorting and preparing lists of items

Table 1   (Continued)

Device	Manufacturer	Remarks
Electronic Calculating Equipment		
Computers	IBM, Remington Rand, Burroughs, Honeywell, G.E., and RCA	Versatile, wide range of applications, output on paper, cathode ray tube, microfilm

Abstracts

Information Science Abstracts, Documentation Abstracts, Inc., sponsored by American Society for Information Science, Division of Chemical Literature of the American Chemical Society, and Special Libraries Association.

Abstract Journal: Informatics, Institute of Scientific Information, State Committee for Science and Technology, Council of Ministers of the USSR, Academy of Sciences of the USSR, in English.

A logical query might be raised at this point as to what are the main types of nonconventional information retrieval systems. Table 1 shows some of the principal ones, somewhat updated since its original compilation in *Chemical and Engineering News* in 1961 (8). It will be noted that all of these systems involve some kind of manipulative device, ranging from the simple matching of a needle to holes in a card to the most ingenious electronic selectors.

Table 1 is a representative sample only of the kinds of systems that are adaptable for major indexing applications, all of which have been tested from seemingly every possible standpoint to judge from the copious literature pertinent to the subject. According to a survey by Holm (9) there were at least 100 projected ideas in varying stages of development in 1962; however, few of them ever reached the production stage.

Anyone seeking a quick introduction to this aspect of the art of information retrieval, involving particularly the use of computers, should be apprised of the warning stated by Gull (10) in his review of the volume of the State of the Library Art series that deals with this area. He expresses with authority the opinion that it is impossible to learn the complete story about any method from the published literature. Such additional sources as manufacturers' presentations and observation of equipment in operation must be diligently investigated. Nonetheless, the reports of actual experiences as published in articles in periodicals and books concerning various systems provide enough background to make intelligent inquiry possible.

The common primary purpose of the newer systems is to provide an indexing approach that will permit access to every bit of significant information in the documents covered. Some systems afford the added advantage of access to a copy of the whole item itself. Others are concerned only with the indexing aspect; while another combines the two and produces a copy in conjunction with the index entry.

In the following parts of this chapter the principal systems are discussed briefly. The presentation is purposely compressed because of the availability of detailed descriptions in many other sources. An excellent book by C. P. Bourne entitled *Methods of Information Handling* (Wiley, 1963) includes both explicit summaries and graphic illustrations of equipment with their resultant products in the form of unique listings and photocopies.

One of the first observations in first review of this group of systems is that some of them are completely manual or involve only such simple instruments as a long sorting needle—the kind used for knitting will do— whereas others require progressively complex equipment ranging to the most sophisticated electrical and electronic machines that were designed originally to manipulate the kinds of data involved in business and banking. Photographic processes are utilized also, usually for making copies of documents in greatly reduced size to store large numbers in a minimum of space.

In general, the manual systems are suitable for collections of intermediate size, the items too numerous for conventional methods but not great enough to warrant the cost and effort of automation. The complexity of the subject matter is an influencing factor also. Few estimates published suggest the sizes of the collections for which the various systems are intended, and their costs are very difficult to predict, partially because in many situations equipment can be shared with other departments, whereas others require total installations. Shaw (11) once advised that a collection should include at least 50,000 units and that there be concomitant need for many individual bits of information from each one before the use of a computer could be economic. A study made by Bourne and others (12) of information and retrieval systems included cost comparisons of three installations. They showed such wide differences that they cannot be considered conclusive. True cost assessments are elusive.

Manual Systems

Manual systems are those that employ only specially designed cards and, in some instances, very simple manipulative devices such as needles.

One of the most used is the one called the "notched," "edge-notched," or even "edge-punched" card. This has holes closely punched and accurately spaced around the periphery. A code is developed to assign specific terms to as many of the holes as necessary. Then an item such as a reference to an article from a periodical is written or typed on the card. For each bit of information a hole is selected according to the code, and this is punched to leave a V-shaped notch that permits the card to drop from the pack when a needle is inserted. Although the cards need not be filed in any order, the whole file must be handled in performing a search, a disadvantage if there are more than a few hundred. This can be a useful system, but it is best utilized for purposes that adapt well to it. For example, a file of chemical compounds whose uses and properties are of concern for a particular application might be handled on notched cards.

An example of a notched-card system that involves a unique coding principle known as "random" is sold under the trade name of Zator. Brenner and Mooers (13) describe a "Case History of a Zatacoding Information Retrieval System" in Chapter 15 of the book entitled *Punched Cards* edited by Casey *et al.* The unit is an edge-notched card of special design. For each application a list of subject terms must be developed; then the coding, which consists of a pattern of notches for each subject, all overlapping one another, is done. If the code patterns are properly manipulated the multiple use of holes is not chaotic and does permit the appropriate cards to emerge in response to queries.

Another system called "coordinate indexing" was developed by Taube (14) as a neat, logical process based on a relatively simple concept. It consists of establishing a vocabulary of broad but exact topics called uniterms, each one noted plainly at the top of a specially designed card marked off in columns. As documents are analyzed in numbered sequence, the appropriate terms are assigned to them and the document numbers are written on the cards bearing the matching uniterms. By visual mating of the numbers appearing on two or more cards, the documents relating to a topic being searched will be detected. A typical application of this system is outlined by Zerweckh (15) in the aforementioned book on punched cards edited by Casey. The capabilities of the coordinate procedure are enhanced by the introduction of modifying terms called links and roles that indicate such actions as "how" and "what" occur in a process, thus making possible more accurate searching. However, no indexing system is faultless, and Jonker (16) calls attention to some of the weak points of this one. The absence of hierarchical relationships and the dependence on the consequences of choosing terms in the order in which they present themselves can be disadvantageous.

A system based upon the principle of optical coincidence is engagingly called "peek-a-boo." The documents to be brought under control are studied to develop official index terms which are recorded on cards so designed that holes can be punched at numbered spots over the area to indicate the number of a document relevant to the index term at the top of the card. When the cards are stacked the documents matching a subject being sought are revealed by throwing light through the deck. The coincident holes permit passage of the beam, thus showing which cards carry the numbers of the documents wanted. A trade name for this system is Termatrex, and the best description of it is provided by its developer, Jonker (16). Thompson (17) published an excellent illustration of a procedure for developing an index for a broad-based subject collection, utilizing the Termatrex system.

Combination Indexing and Filing Systems

Certain of the nonconventional systems combine the filing and indexing operations, usually utilizing film copies of documents. Single frames of microfilm, for example, can be inserted in IBM-style punched cards with an opening of suitable size to accommodate the film. These are known as aperture cards and Filmsort is one of the trade names of a system utilizing this means of filing and sorting. Filmsort makes also an edge-notched card of similar design that can be searched manually.

Short lengths of film recording brief documents can be inserted in special card-size devices combining a half card and a plastic pocket or sleeve into which the film can be slipped for filing purposes. The upper section carries the typed legible identification.

A related procedure is the preparation of positive prints from microfilm on strips of printing paper especially made for this purpose. These strips have a backing paper that peels away to expose a sticky surface to adhere it to a filing card. Indexing information can be typed on the top edge of the card. Microstrip and Microtape are trade names for paper of this type. The copy can, of course, be read only with the aid of a reading device.

One of the earliest concepts for the simultaneous indexing and filing of a large file of documents was to microfilm them on reel-length strips and copy simultaneously a code consisting of a pattern of dots beside each frame. Subsequently as the film is run through a machine, an electronic scanning device selects those items that relate to a specific search, stopping them so that they can be read or photographed. The U.S. National Bureau of Standards has spent some effort in perfecting the original model first conceived by Vannevar Bush and developed by Ralph Shaw, then Librarian of the U.S. Department of Agriculture, who called this device the rapid selector. McMurray (18) reports an installation of the machine at the Bureau of Ships of the U.S. Naval Department. A similar system has been developed in France under the name Filmorex.

The Minicard device, a development of Recordak Corporation, has a feature in common with the Rapid Selector in that a copy of a document is put on film that carries also a code pattern. The film, however, is in discrete units, 16 by 32 mm in size, each of which is slotted for filing on a stick. Specially designed devices can select specific Minicards from the file and enlarged photocopies are made. Because this is so costly it is not likely that there will be many installations of this system, thus making it difficult to judge its potential effectiveness.

All of these systems are expensive, requiring from a few hundred to many thousands of dollars to install. This is a deterrent to experimentation, but it should not preclude all interest and investigation of possible applications for unique situations and for large-scale operations.

Systems Providing Separate Document Image File and Index

The retrieval systems listed on p. 194 includes Verac, made by Avco Corporation; Microcite, developed by National Bureau of Standards; and Walnut, an IBM product; each of these incorporates a unique method for recording micro images of documents to which a separate index is keyed. They all provide a method for reproducing copies of pages in greatly reduced size and storing them in such a way that any single one can be selected when it is wanted. The Verac utilizes sheet film, putting 10,000 pages on a 10 by 10 inch sheet. The fantastic Walnut prototype, later modified and renamed Cypress, is designed to produce microfilm copies of pages from the film copy in IBM aperture cards. Microcite uses sheet film in 15 by 15 inch sheets with accompanying index on a set of Termatrex (peek-a-boo) cards.

Another clever idea is embodied in the Command Retrieval Information System (CRIS) which was developed under sponsorship of the organization called Information for Industry. In this, photographic images are stored in long scrolls of microfilm of such dimensions that they carry 500,000 pages. Using a keyboarded instrument to make commands, an image of a page can be displayed on a screen in less than 30 seconds, and an aperture card produced as quickly.

Somewhat similar to CRIS is the CARD system, a product of HF Image Systems, Inc. This Compact Automatic Retrieval Display arrangement is based on the storage of copies of documents on Microfiche, 750 equivalent to 70,000 pages in one unit to which access is through a keyboarded code. An image is displayed in 4 seconds.

Machine Systems

By the term "machine systems" is meant those using the kind of electrical and electronic equipment that was designed initially for accounting and other data processing functions. Individual units of various types can perform operations related to the handling of information in libraries. They can sort cards, make lists, and select designated items. They can be used for an indexing purpose only, or they can record complete bibliographic references.

These machine operations can be classified as mechanical and electronic. The mechanical group includes the devices that use the punch card as an information-carrying unit; these can have tiny holes punched in vertical columns according to coded meaning, then scanned and sorted by electronically operated devices.

Information initially recorded on punch cards can be fed into a computer, an electronically motivated machine that is much faster than the merely mechanical card punchers and sorters. Information can be put into a computer store in various ways, such as typing on an electric typewriter to record on paper tape and then transferring this to magnetic tape or special disks for even more efficient storage. However, any kind of computer storage is expensive. A promising solution is to produce microfilm copy from tape stores.

In a complete computer system the chief operations for which provision must be made include the following:

1. Preparation of a code to encompass the subject area concerned for which a program must be written for processing by computer.

2. An input procedure to get information into the storage unit. This can be punched cards, paper tape, or magnetic tape.

3. An output procedure to deliver information as requested in a form that can be read by the human eye. This can be punched cards, tape from which typed copy is produced, a form to be photographed, a print-out, or display on a cathode ray tube (CRT).

4. A procedure to store all information that is fed into the system. The usual storage devices are magnetic drums, magnetic cores, magnetic tapes, magnetic disks, or special photographic processes, for example, microfilm.

5. A control operation to give instructions to the aforementioned units to cause them to execute the process of selecting from the store.

It is apparent that machines that can perform such functions are very complex, hence expensive. Therefore, their use is likely to be confined to major retrieval situations. However, computerized searching centers are now able to offer service for reasonable fees. Some of these are cited in Chapters 10 and 11.

One function that computing machines will perform well for library purposes is to produce lists of several types. One especially useful kind is the index known as KWIC, standing for Keyword in Context, and originally developed by P. Luhn. It is essentially a means for preparing quickly with minimum effort an alphabetized array by having the computer select the significant words from groups such as titles of reports or articles and arranging them so that each word falls into an alphabetically correct order.

FILING PROCEDURES

Once a group of documents are indexed, they must be physically placed in an orderly arrangement, except, of course for those that are stored as microfilm copies within a system. The two broad choices are to place them according to the indexing notation by topical word or code, or in sequential order of acquisition, marking with this number. The first system has the disadvantage of requiring good guessing as to space for varied growth rates in all parts of the file. If the other method is followed, all available space is used economically. However, there is complete dependence upon the most detailed and accurate subject indexing with no possibility of direct consultation of the items. Equipment for filing is suggested in Chapter 4.

The alternative to filing full size original copies of publications is to reproduce them photographically in one of the several possible microforms. The form chosen then determines the manner of filing.

KINDS OF PUBLICATIONS INDEXED

The foregoing brief discussion of indexing problems and procedures is followed by descriptions of the several types of materials that may have to be cared for in a science-technology library. Each has its own unique features with respect either to the character of the information or its physical form.

Pamphlets and Reprints

Pamphlets, a generic designation of publications consisting of few pages (sometimes specified as fewer than 64) are usually of less permanent significance than books; and reprints of articles from periodicals constitute a large part of the material in this category. They should be approached from the points of view indicated in the general discussion on indexing and the appropriate scheme used. Richardson (19) has provided a detailed description of the most simple of systems, that is, filing by author and indexing by subject. Index cards must be typed with the appropriate subject headings.

Pamphlets may be filed in drawers of standard filing cabinets (legal size may be necessary), possibly in manila folders or pockets for ease in handling. It may be preferable to house them in file boxes to stand on shelves, or even on divider-type shelving to hold them upright. A few will be given hard use and these should be fastened in pamphlet binders. The object of the method of storage is to have them as accessible as their use warrants.

Provision should be made for periodically weeding this file since material will inevitably accumulate that is not worth keeping indefinitely. However, only the individual situation can determine what may safely be discarded. Date of publication alone will not be a certain determining factor.

Government Publications

If only a few government publications, referring principally to United States or other nationally issued ones, need be acquired, they can either be cataloged as books if of permanent importance (fastened in pamphlet binders if small in size) or put into the pamphlet file and indexed. Many libraries, however, require extensive files of certain series, such as the *Bulletins* and *Technical Papers of the United States Bureau of Mines*. These should be kept together in numerical order. Where a fair representation of government documents from a number of agencies must be handled, a special scheme for indexing them should be adopted. An excellent one has been developed by Jackson (20) as presented in *A Notation for Public Document Classification*. The issuing agencies are utilized as a basis for classifying, and a combination of capital letters and arabic numbers is used for notations in a manner simple enough for ready comprehension.

At an E. I. duPont de Nemours & Company library an effective system for filing government documents separately from other pamphlets was developed and information concerning it supplied by Goff (21). Series publications are filed alphabetically by issuing bureau, then by title of the particular series in numerical order. In the catalog, cards with numbers 000 to 999 printed thereon are marked to show the holdings. Subject cross-reference cards are typed, using the official subject headings. The publications need only be stamped to show that they belong in the library collection, and the subjects under which they are entered in the card catalog are written inside the back cover. Special "out" cards are inserted in the file when an item is borrowed. The system is recommended as being both simple and adequate.

The preceding discussion applies chiefly to standard government publications that have been issued from the agencies that have been in existence for many years. The more recent type of publication known as the "report literature" that had its beginnings at the time of World War II has stimulated the necessity for somewhat different handling. Though these reports are usually in numbered series, the corporate authors are sometimes not simple to identify and several numbers on one document may appear, such as the contract number, the sequential number of the report issuing under that contract, and an overall series number. These documents are the results of government-sponsored research contracted chiefly by the Atomic Energy Commission, the Air Force, and other Armed Services agencies. In some libraries they are filed according to the series numbers, with special rules for the exceptions. In others, they are simply accessioned and filed in order of accession, the indexing serving as the guide for subsequent location. This latter procedure solves the problem of judging how much space to leave for a series, since each series grows at a different rate. Divider-type shelving is preferred for these reports.

The comprehensive work edited by Weil on *The Technical Report* (22) includes several chapters that give practical advice on the handling of government reports. Fry's chapter on "Cataloging Government Technical Reports" and Taube's "The Uniterm Coordinate Indexing of Reports" are examples of the kind of detailed instructions that the book provides.

Several of the government agencies supply important indexing aids. The Armed Services Technical Information Agency (ASTIA), since 1963 Defense Documentation Center (DDC), publication entitled Technical Abstract Bulletin (TAB) lists reports, and supplies indexing terms, or "descriptors," for each document preceding its abstract. For a number of years, through 1957, index cards were available also, and in 1962 tentative plans were in process to resume the preparation of cards and/or punched tape to be used by computers. Other agencies, such as the Naval Ordnance Laboratory, have had a card service. Because ASTIA (or DDC) has published thesaurusis of its indexing terms and these cover a broad range of scientific and technical fields now in active development, they are likely to be used extensively as authority lists.

Patents

Patents constitute a class of government publications that must be treated distinctively if they are a significant part of a library's resources. They should be indexed by assigning an adequate number of subject headings on cards to be filed conventionally if the number acquired does not exceed the limitations of this method. Where large numbers of chemical or electronics patents are needed, the Uniterm Index provided by Information for Industry, Inc. 1000 Connecticut Ave., Washington, D. C. 20006, can supplant this effort. Also, Documentation Inc. (since 1969 a division of Plenum Publishing Company), 4827 Rugby Ave., Bethesda, Md. 20014, has prepared an index to chemical patents on magnetic tape sold under the name Textape Service. Patent copies are in a reduced size called Docuform. The indexing information required usually includes the patentee, assignee, and subjects to cover those aspects of the contents that are pertinent. The copies can be filed either by number or Patent Office classification. When the files are used for direct searching, the latter method is preferable.

A special indexing procedure reported by Weinstein *et al.* (23) as applied to a collection of patents of countries other than the United States is effective in a situation where an abstract bulletin and the indexing of it became a problem for a small staff. The Peek-a-boo system using Remington Rand cards and a National Bureau of Standards punch was found to be completely satisfactory.

As for method of physical filing, patent copies may be kept in folders in filing cabinets, in boxes that stand on shelves, or in loose-leaf binders. In one library at least, the copies acquired for permanent reference are bound into volumes to assure their safe keeping.

All countries in which an extensive scientific research program is conducted have patent systems. They follow practices similar to those of the system of the United States Patent Office of numbering each patent in sequential order, classifying, and issuing to an inventor, although in some countries patents are issued directly to a company. Because of their general similarities, patents from all countries can be treated the same.

Trade Literature

Publications covered by the term "trade literature" may be pamphlets or even books. They are usually published by industrial firms. They may be catalogs of products. Some are issued as periodicals bearing volume numbers and dates, in which case they are treated like other serials if important enough to retain for any length of time. The pamphlet type will range from price lists likely to be of current significance only (though their possible eventual importance in market research should not be overlooked) to compilations of data not readily available from any other source. Items of temporary importance might be assigned to the pamphlet file and indexed accordingly. The more permanently valuable will merit full cataloging and a place on the shelves with the book collection.

A large collection of trade literature such as a group of product catalogs must be treated as an entity. The most obvious approach to it is by the names of the manufacturers. Moore and Holleman (24) have described in thorough detail a method for cataloging this type of material which has as its basis Cutter-Sanborn numbers for the names of commercial companies. This modified table was developed at the Boeing Airplane Company Library. General rules for indexing, using the *Thomas' Register of American Manufacturers* as authority for the company names, are presented. A significant feature is the cross-indexing of trade names to company names. The provision by Thomas of manufacturers catalogs on microfiche to accompany the *Register* provides a welcome solution to the problem of keeping such files in order. Details of this service are given in Chapter 5 of this book.

Another procedure for indexing technical trade literature has been outlined by O'Farrell (25). This system consists in filing alphabetically by company and possibly indexing by company, though this step may be omitted. The *Thomas' Register* can be used for the product index.

A unique aid is available for literature relating to electronic equipment. From Electronic Engineer Master, 6455 Stewart Ave., Garden City, L.I., N. Y., complete directions for establishing a filing system can be obtained for the asking. The complexity of the parts used in this kind of equipment makes this an important service.

Photocopies

The filing of photocopies will be dictated by the way their printed counterparts are handled. Photostats of items similar in nature to a file already in the library will simply be treated as are these originals, indexed as they are, and filed with them.

Microfilm copies present a special filing problem because of their physical difference from conventional printed publications. Long strips, such as are required for volumes of journals or complete books, must be kept on reels, preferably in individual boxes. Large collections should be kept in cabinets designed for the purpose. It had once been thought that microfilm had to be kept in a humidity-controlled atmosphere, but it has not been found to deteriorate as much as had been anticipated under ordinary atmospheric conditions. The contents of the reels must be marked on the boxes in which they are kept, and cards prepared with proper subject headings to file in the card catalog.

Short strips of film require their own methods of handling. Brown and Austin (26) developed a method of filing in cloth pockets, the strips being cut to uniform length to fit filing cabinet drawers. Dice (27) also devised a system involving the cutting of the film into strips, filing in standard stationery-size envelopes, and identifying the contents on the envelopes. Special filing equipment has been developed in which short pieces of film are filed in catalog-card size devices of which the top third is of plain card stock to which a clear plastic sleeve is attached. A piece of microfilm can be inserted in the lower part and the identifying information typed at the top. One example is known as "Sertafilm" and is available through Atlas Microfilming Service, 105 North Fifth St., Philadelphia 6, Pa. Another is "Filmsort," made by The Filmsort Company, Pearl River, New York.

An alternate procedure for dealing with short strips of film is to splice them and put them on a reel. The contents of the reel is then indexed.

The Recordak Corporation has prepared a pamphlet entitled *How to Index Your Microfilm Records,* which is free upon request to its Advertising Department, Wanamaker Place, New York, N. Y. 10003. Included in the pamphlet are its Kodamatic and Target systems, these being applicable chiefly to large-scale projects.

Evans and Goepp (28) developed a scheme for building a skeleton periodical file using both photostat and microfilm copies to be filed alphabetically by journal title, then chronologically just as a file of printed copies would be placed on shelves. In this system each item is put into a file folder which is lined with pockets to accommodate over 100 pages of microfilm copy. Only those parts of the periodical files that are pertinent to specific interests need be acquired.

Some photocopies in microprint form are on cards of standard catalog size. They cannot, however, be used to file in the card catalog but should be kept in a separate file or drawer and catalog cards provided to show holdings. Regular cataloging procedures can be followed. Microfiche copies should be filed in envelopes to avoid damaging.

Photographs and Pictures

When photographs and pictures comprise an important part of the library's resources they must be handled as a completely separate file. In few scientific libraries it is likely that they will be present in large number, but since a few collections do include them, their treatment is covered here. Strain (29) has reported the results of a study of methods of filing and indexing photographs that deal with scientific subjects. Photographs may be in the form of either positive prints or negatives. It is obvious that the latter must be treated from the point of view of their permanent preservation; a print can be replaced. Negatives should not be handled unnecessarily, and it is good practice to keep them in glassine envelopes. The usual arrangement is to file by accession number. Prints may be mounted on uniform-size cardboards to simplify their filing, or they may be put into loose-leaf binders of the special type that permits several to be on one page in a shingled position. There are some attendant disadvantages to this method, however, since individual pictures cannot be removed. Prints may also be kept in folders and filed in legal-size vertical files.

The indexing of photographs and other pictures is peculiarly difficult because the assigning of adequate captions may be largely a matter of personal judgment. Photographs that are records of information sought in the study of certain materials such as metals or textiles should be filed in accord with the system for keeping other research data and indexed with the research reports. A special system for indexing pictures has been described by Milhollen (30) who advocated the placing of microfilm copies of the pictures on the catalog card to aid in identification and also avoid undue handling of the prints. In general, the indexing procedures should conform to those used for other materials.

Slides

Photographic slides must obviously be housed in equipment especially designed for this purpose. It may be desirable to group them so that they are ready for special purposes such as lecture illustrations, or it may be preferable to maintain a single file from which they can be pulled as needed. They may be indexed in the same way as are other photographs with the attendant problem of descriptive terminology, although this should not be difficult for scientific subject matter. There is room on the cardboard mounting to inscribe an indexing designation.

Skoog and Evans (31) describe a system for classifying a collection of slides that is based on the Dewey Decimal system, an apt choice because it is so readily expanded. Although this application is for art subjects, the idea is readily adaptable to other areas.

Maps

Where maps constitute a significant segment of a collection, they too must be treated as an entity. Some types, such as the topographic sheets and folios of the United States Geological Survey, are easy to file and relocate because their ordering is obvious, alphabetically by state and quadrangle name; the Survey supplies the index maps. They do, of course, require specially designed map cases. If large numbers of different kinds of maps are to be filed, they must be approached from a broader point of view. The main objective, as in any classification scheme, is to bring like things together and, according to Lewis (32), this principle must be kept in mind when maps are put in filing order. He recommends placing the most used ones where they can be easily reached, however. The outstanding feature is usually the geographical area, but the subject classification should attempt to anticipate whatever call is most likely to arise in the particular library. If large numbers of maps are to be handled the pamphlet entitled *Cataloging and Filing Rules for Maps and Atlases,* edited by Drazniowsky (33) should be investigated.

Organization Reports

In many organizations reports of intramural activities are written for internal circulation only. They may be reports of engineering studies, product development, or laboratory research. Any or all of these may be assigned to the library or even to a special file room under supervision of the library. Since these documents constitute a unique record of developmental history, it is very important that their contents be indexed accurately and in adequate detail. Because the library staff is accustomed to handling the subject matter involved, it is logical that these reports be placed in its care.

It is likely that the greater volume of a company's reports will be those resulting from laboratory research. Most research activities follow a fairly standardized pattern; individual problems are assigned project numbers; research workers as individuals or teams undertake an investigation and periodically they write reports of progress until the project is terminated, at which time a final summarizing report is written. In the course of this process laboratory notebooks, progress reports, and final reports accumulate to be filed and indexed. To locate information contained in them a scheme must be developed relating it to the basic one used for classifying published information if at all feasible, though the pattern will be predetermined by the way in which the search is organized. Shorb (34) has provided an excellent description of the methods used in one large research library. The book edited by Weil (22) includes several chapters on their filing. Poland's chapter in the latter work on subject-classifying and alphabetical indexing presents a detailed analysis of all aspects, giving examples of procedures and advice concerning equipment.

Because laboratory notebooks precede the written reports, their treatment is considered a major responsibility. Bound blank notebooks have been generally adopted for this purpose, and in some instances the library has the task of issuing them to research workers, marking them with the project number for which they are to be used, and collecting them for filing when they are filled. Sometimes these notebooks are so designed that duplicate and even triplicate copies of the pages are made. The copy pages are perforated for easy removal. Where patents are likely to eventuate, all notebooks must be signed and witnessed as a regular procedure. Some of the data first set down in these notebooks are later included in reports so that their indexing need not be too detailed, though some guide to their content should be provided. This may be done by the person whose work is recorded in the book.

The notebooks must be filed in a manner such that they can be relocated when needed. However, because reference to them becomes increasingly rare with the passage of time, it may be satisfactory to have them microfilmed for permanent record if the organization's patent attorneys consent. Tylicki (35) describes such a procedure utilizing 16-mm film to be inserted in cassettes.

An organization's research reports are of two types, progress reports written at intervals during the course of an investigation and final reports summing the work at its completion. There must first be a system for numbering projects; each report issuing from a project will bear the project number and an additional serial number indicating its position in the file of reports for that project. It may also be desirable to assign a serial number in chonological order to each report and enter these in a record book which will show what reports from all projects have been issued in a certain period. If the research program is at all diversified, a system of classification of the projects may be used. This is preferable to filing alphabetically by subject.

Research reports should be indexed meticulously to reveal all work that has been done as insurance against its needless repetition. The person who assigns index entries should know thoroughly the subjects concerned. An individual card file, separate from any other, should be maintained. It is usually considered important that these reports be indexed by author as well as subject.

The foregoing suggestions apply where the volume of material is small enough to be treated adequately by conventional indexing methods. However, in a large organization where there are many projects in progress dealing with hundreds if not thousands of individual entities such as chemical compounds, traditional methods may not suffice. This kind of situation calls for the investigation of automated methods. Schulze (36) has published a detailed description of an example of a situation where a collection of research reports reached 28,000, many of them containing information about hundreds of chemical compounds. The solution consisted in installing an IBM punch-card system that coped with the mass of detail most satisfactorily.

Other applications of the newly created methods of indexing for information retrieval are reported in the comprehensive survey by *Chemical and Engineering News* (8) with special reference to company research reports. Some employ the manually sorted edge-notched cards of the Zator, Royal McBee, or E-Z Sort types. Others use the Peek-a-boo system developed by the National Bureau of Standards or the Uniterm system developed by Taube. Whaley (37) has written several very helpful papers telling how to analyze and code the kind of material that is contained in company reports for mechanized searching. Of particular interest is Jahoda's report of applying a combination manual and machine-based index to research and engineering reports (38).

The description by Kennedy (39) of an application of the special type of indexing by machine called "permutation indexing" showed that it can be effective and efficient for a collection of internal reports. It was done using in this instance the IBM 7090 computer to prepare a Key Word in Context (KWIC) index. This KWIC index form is an increasingly familiar device since it is used in such publications as *Chemical Titles*. It consists in setting up in columns the titles of items being indexed and manipulating them so that all of their key words appear in alphabetical order. The result is not a perfect index but it is good enough to serve a useful purpose in getting material into the hands of a large group very quickly.

For a final word concerning the handling of research reports, they must be regarded as meriting special handling in the library files. Because they are written as the result of costly research they must be treated as confidential material, subject to restricted circulation within the organization only to persons authorized to see them. They should be kept in locked files.

Correspondence Files

In many libraries correspondence files, particularly those relating to the scientific and development research activities, are assigned to the library for control. The system for filing and indexing can be adapted from the one used for published materials. Interoffice memoranda may be very important because ideas for possible laboratory investigation or conceptions of patentable ideas may be recorded in them. It is apparent that there will be a close relationship between some parts of this file and the content of the research reports. Good indexing will make possible the location of every piece of information that may ever be needed. Devlin (40) describes a system for microfilming all incoming correspondence on roll film to assure its safe retention and relocation when needed.

CONCLUSION

The problem of adequate indexing is one of the largest and most important that must be solved by the library staff. Judgment must be exercised in determining what areas require close control or indexing in depth, and which merit only cursory attention. Eventually, the indexing of published information will probably all be done by automated procedures on a national or even international scale, although it will be at least another decade before this happens. However, some beginnings are already in effect and these should be used when they suit purposes. There will always be some materials that will have to be handled in the individual situation.

REFERENCES

1. J. Metcalfe, *Information Indexing and Subject Cataloging: Alphabetical, Classified, Coordination, Mechanical,* Scarecrow, New York, 1957.

2. J. R. Sharp, *Some Fundamentals of Information Retrieval,* Deutsch, London, 1965.

3. B. C. Vickery, *Classification and Indexing in Science,* 2nd ed., Academic, New York, 1959.

4. G. Jahoda, *Information Storage and Retrieved Systems for Individual Researchers,* Wiley-Interscience, New York, 1970.

5. S. C. Bradford, *Documentation,* Crosby, Lockwood & Son, Ltd., London, 1948.

6. H. E. Bliss, *Bibliographic Classification,* 2nd ed., H. W. Wilson, New York, 1952–1953.

7. J. E. Holmstrom, *Records and Research in Engineering and Industrial Science,* 3rd ed., Chapman & Hall, Ltd., London, 1956.

8. C & EN Special Report, "Information Retrieval," *Chem. & Eng. News* **39**, 102–114, July 17, 1961; 90–100, July 24, 1961.

9. B. E. Holm, "Searching Strategies and Equipment," *Amer. Doc.* **13**, 31–42 (1962).

10. C. D. Gull, *Review of: State of the Library Art,* R. Shaw, Ed., Vol. 4, Rutgers—The State University, New Brunswick, N. J., 1961; *Coll. Res. Libr.* **23**, 269–271 (1962).

11. R. Shaw, "Parameters for Machine Handling of Alphabetical Information," *Amer. Doc.* **13**, 267–279 (1962).

12. C. P. Bourne, *et al., Requirements, Criteria, and Measures of Performance of Information Storage,* Report to NSF on Stanford Research Institute's project 3741, December 1961.

13. C. W. Brenner and C. N. Mooers, "A Case History of a Zatacoding Information Retrieval System," in *Punched Cards,* R. S. Casey, *et al.,* Eds., 2nd ed., Reinhold, New York, 1958, chap. 15.

14. M. Taube, *Studies in Coordinate Indexing,* Documentation, Inc., Bethesda, Md., 1953–1959, 4 vols.

15. C. E. Zerweckh, Jr., "A Uniterm System for Reports," in *Punched Cards,* R. S. Casey, *et al.,* Eds., 2nd ed., Reinhold, New York, 1958.

16. F. Jonker, *Indexing Theory, Indexing Methods, and Search Devices,* Scarecrow, New York, 1964.

17. M. S. Thompson, "Peek-a-Boo Index for a Broad Subject Collection," *Amer. Doc.* **13**, 187–197 (1962).

18. J. P. McMurray, "The Bureau of Ships Rapid Selector System," *Amer. Doc.* **13**, 66–68 (1962).

19. L. R. Richardson, "A Simple System for Reprint Filing," *Science* **104**, 181–182 (August 23, 1946).

20. E. Jackson, *A Notation for Public Documents Classification,* Oklahoma Agricultural & Mechanical College Library, Bulletin 8, July 1946.

21. M. S. Goff, *Technical Librarian,* E. I. du Pont de Nemours & Co., Technical Library, Wilmington, Del., private communication.

22. B. H. Weil, *The Technical Report,* Reinhold, New York, 1958.

23. S. J. Weinstein, *et al.,* "Abstract Bulletin of Foreign Patents and Index Preparation: A Combined Procedure," *J. Chem. Doc.* **1**, 28–32 (1961).

24. M. Moore and W. R. Holleman, "Cataloging Commercial Material," *Spec. Libr.* **38**, 295–297 (1947).

25. J. B. O'Farrell, "Indexing Technical Trade Literature," *Libr. J.* **70**, 467–469 (May 15, 1945).

26. H. P. Brown and J. A. Austin, "A Simple Method for Filing of Microfilm Records in Short Strips," *Science* **89**, 573–574 (January 13, 1939).

27. L. R. Dice, "A Simple Method for Filing Miniature Negatives and Microfilm Records in Strips," *Science* **89**, 39–40 (January 13, 1939).

28. E. Evans and R. M. Goepp, Jr., "Filing Photographic Copies of Articles," *Science* **91**, 248 (March 8, 1940).

29. P. Strain, "Photographs in Scientific and Technical Libraries," *Spec. Libr.* **39**, 77–82 (1948).

30. H. Milhollen, "Pictures Invade the Catalog," *Libr. J.* **71**, 803–804 (June 1, 1946).

31. A. Skoog and G. Evans, "A Slide Collection Classification," *PLA Bull.* **24**, 15–22 (1969).

32. D. C. Lewis, "Maps: Problem Children in Libraries," *Spec. Libr.* **35**, 75–78 (1944).

33. R. C. Drazniowsky, *Cataloging and Filing Rules for Maps and Atlases in the Society's Collection,* revised, American Geographical Society, New York, 1964.

34. L. Shorb, "Research Records in a Library," *Spec. Libr.* **40**, 12–16 (1949).

35. E. Tylicki, "Preparation of a Microfilm File of Company Technical Reports," *J. Chem. Doc.* **10**, 20–22 (1970).

36. E. L. Schulze, "Application of Automation in the Library: Indexing Internal Reports," *Spec. Libr.* **52**, 63–67 (1961).

37. F. R. A. Whaley, "Deep Index for Internal Technical Reports," in *Information Systems in Documentation,* J. Shera, *et al.,* Eds., New York, Interscience, 1957; and "The Manipulation of Nonconventional Indexing Systems," *Amer. Doc.* **12**, 101–107 (1961).

38. G. Jahoda, "The Development of a Combination Manual and Machine-Based Index to Research and Engineering Reports," *Spec. Libr.* **53**, 74–78 (1962).

39. R. A. Kennedy, "Library Application of Permutation Indexing," *J. Chem. Doc.* **2**, 181–185, 1962.

40. T. J. Devlin, "Use of Microfilm in Internal Mail Control," *J. Chem. Doc.* **10**, 22–25 (1970).

BIBLIOGRAPHY

Aitchison, J. and C. W. Cleverdon, *A Report on a Test of the Index of Metallurgical Literature of Western Reserve University,* College of Aeronautics, Aslib Cranfield Research Project, 1963.

Bloomfield, M. "Evaluation of Indexing; 1. Introduction," *Spec. Libr.* **61**, 429–432 (1970); "2. The Simulated Machine Indexing Experiments," *Ibid.,* 501–507; "3. A Review of Comparative Studies of Index Sets to Identical Citations," *Ibid.,* 554–561.

Caless, T. W. and D. B. Kirk, "An Application of UDC to Machine Searching," *J. Doc.* **23**, 208–215 (1967).

Cleverdon, C. W., "The Cranfield Tests on Index Language Devices," *Aslib Proc.* **19**, 173–194 (1967).

Cleverdon, C. W., F. W. Lancaster, and J. Mills, "Uncovering Some Facts of Life in Information Retrieval (Cranfield Project)," *Spec. Libr.* **55**, 89–91 (1964).

Collison, R. L., *Commercial and Industrial Record Storage*, Benn, London, 1969.

Collison, R. L., *Modern Business Filing and Archives*, John de Graft, New York, 1963.

Collison, R. L., *Indexes and Indexing*, Benn, London, 1969.

Engineering Societies Library, *Bibliography on Filing, Classification and Indexing Systems, and Thesauri for Engineering Offices and Libraries*, ESL Bibliography 15, Engineering Societies Library, New York, 1966.

Freeman, R. R. and P. Atherton, *Audacious—An Experiment with an On-Line, Interactive Reference Retrieval System Using the Universal Decimal Classification as the Index Language in the Field of Nuclear Science*, AIP/UDC-7, American Institute of Physics, New York, 1968.

Hagen, C. B., "A Proposed Information Retrieval System for Sound Recordings," *Spec. Libr.* **56**, 223–228 (1965).

Hines, T. H. and J. L. Harris, *Computer Filing of Index, Bibliographic, and Catalog Entries*, Bro-Dart Foundation, Newark, N. J., 1966.

Houwink, R. and H. Bouman, *Classification of High Polymers*, Butterworths, London, 1960.

Kyle, B., "Information Retrieval and Subject Indexing: Cranfield and After," *J. Doc.* **20**, 55–69 (1964).

Lancaster, F. W., *Information Retrieval Systems*, Wiley, New York, 1968.

Lundeed, D. A., *Methods of Handling Non-Book Materials in Chemical Libraries*, University of Wisconsin Library School, 1964.

Montague, B. A. and R. F. Schirmer, "DuPont Central Report Index: System Design, Operation and Performance," *J. Chem. Doc.* **8**, 33–41 (1968).

Pinches, M. F., *Subject Headings for Chemical Engineering*, University Microfilms, Ann Arbor, Mich., 1969.

Ready, W. B., "Punched Card and/or Computer Control of a Map Collection," *Spec. Libr.* **58**, 365–367 (1969).

Shaw, T. N. and H. Rothman, "An Experiment in Indexing by Word-Choosing," *J. Doc.* **24**, 159–172 (1968).

Skolnik, H. and M. H. Payson, "Designing an Author-Based Correspondence Information System," *J. Chem. Doc.* **6**, 240–244 (1966).

Slamecka, V., Ed., *Information Technology, Studies in Coordinate Indexing*, Vol. 6, Documentation, Inc., Bethesda, Md., 1965.

Sternberg, V., "Miles of Information by the Inch," *Pa. Libr. Bull.* **22**, 189–194 (1967).

Wilson, H. B., "SMART (Socony Mobil Automation Real Time) Computer System," *J. Chem. Doc.* **6**, 89–92 (1966).

9

Administration of Readers' Services

The major purpose in developing the book and periodical collection and the special files of unique materials, all cataloged and indexed with meticulous attention, is to provide those persons for whom the service is planned with whatever information they may require. This use must be administered through procedures that are adapted to the convenience of the clientele insofar as possible. All controlling routines should be established on the basic principle of keeping them as simple as expedience allows, the chief intention being to invite and encourage active consultation of the literature.

A good impression of efficiency is created if a staff member is always available to accept requests for information or assistance in locating specific publications. Facts, or the volume containing them, are often elusive, and time should not be lost in vain searching if an alert, ready information specialist could quickly locate the information. All inquiries should be treated with serious consideration, from the hesitant question of the young secretary who is not sure how to spell "benzaldehyde" to the senior scientist who must have the proceedings of the most recent symposium on plasma physics.

The several general types of readers' service are discussed in this chapter. They center on methods for putting publications into the hands of readers, sometimes at their request as in the lending of books, or as part of routine functions such as the routing of periodicals.

CIRCULATION OF BOOKS

Books have only potential value as they stand on the shelves; it is the use made of them that is the ultimate measure of their worth. Good books are those that are read, and as a means of promoting their use, circulation regulations should be as relaxed as possible. However, it is inevitable that there must be some rules governing the borrowing of books if all individuals in any group are to be served equitably. They should be recognized as mutually accepted policies established for the sole purpose of assuring the privileges of everyone concerned.

It is usually desirable to designate a definite loan period for the personal borrowing of books. Two weeks is the time limit commonly observed, with the understanding that this may be extended if there are no other calls. However, Strain (1) states that in one technical library at least (IBM Federal Systems Division, Space Guidance Center) this usual two-week or even one-month period is too short. Kennedy (2) reports that "about 30% of all loans result in overdue notices," a strong indication that the library clientele of the Bell Laboratories does not find this limit acceptable.

The situation could be such that there is no real necessity for establishing a specific loan period. This decision should be made cautiously, however, because borrowers are likely to take full advantage of it, the consequence of which will be that certain books will never be on the library shelves for others to discover, or the staff to consult in trying to answer queries. Even though the card catalog is an excellent guide to books on specific subjects, everyone who has used a library has experienced the satisfaction of finding something in a book on the shelf that, because he happened not to approach from the catalogers' point of view, he did not see in the card catalog. The book collection should ideally be in a fluid state with every volume as freely accessible as possible to all potential seekers of facts or ideas. Upon occasion it may tax the diplomacy of the staff member in charge to communicate the concept that the best interests of all readers are at stake.

The best means of coping with simultaneous demands for single copies of books is to provide duplicates. The alert librarian can usually anticipate that certain titles will be popular with the clientele and will be ready to circumvent potential dissatisfaction by having ordered multiple copies.

UNUSUAL LOANS

In some situations it is necessary to make arrangements to provide small collections of books to certain laboratories or offices. These will almost always be duplicates of titles held in the library, except, for example, a major data file such as is used in conjunction with spectra determinations that might be more convenient if placed near the instruments. This "splintering" of the collection should be kept to a minimum because such proliferation obviously weakens the service as a whole. It may be possible to arrange for semipermanent loans with the understanding that when there are no longer pressing needs for the books they will eventually return to the library.

It is usually good policy for an organization to control the purchase of all books through its library to preclude the spending of funds by individual departments that may want to have their own private libraries. If the library is functioning as it should be, this should not be necessary since strong efforts will be made to fulfill all reasonable requirements. However, if there is sufficient reason to place a significant number of volumes in an office or laboratory, there should be records of them in the library catalog. There are not many organizations that have unlimited funds.

NONCIRCULATING BOOKS

There are always certain books in a collection that should not be removed from the library by anyone at any time. Chief among these are the reference books that are usually consulted daily. Among these are handbooks, dictionaries, directories, encyclopedic works, abstracting journals, and indexes. Special compilations of data should also be kept for instant consultation. There may be other publications that patrons will request to be kept in the library. Reference works that are required as laboratory tools should be provided in duplicate if funds permit.

SYSTEMS FOR CIRCULATION CONTROL

There are several methods for recording of book loans, each of which has merit according to the requirements of a particular situation. Traditionally these are manual, but there is increasing application of automation for this purpose. This is one of the procedures studied and assessed in the overall analysis to determine how best to conduct the whole operation.

If the total circulation is not too large, the system adopted will be a manual one. One method uses a book card upon which the author, title, and call number are typed when the book is cataloged and which is kept in a pocket in the back of the book when not in circulation. The borrower signs this card, possibly adding his address if necessary, and card and book are dated with either the date borrowed or date due. These standard book cards are available in a variety of colors from library supply houses for use with different types of materials.

Another method is to use prepared slips in multiple copy, with inserted or self-carbon, upon which the borrower must write author, title, and call number or other identification in addition to his name and address. One advantage of this system is that slips can be filed by the names of borrowers as well as by call numbers of books. This record is helpful if there is a large turnover of resident borrowers.

Microfilm can be used for book charging with efficiency and satisfaction. A number of manufacturers of such equipment have developed such systems, among them Eastman Kodak who sells a unit called the Starfil Microfilmer which is inexpensive enough to warrant purchase by almost any size operation. The procedure is to film simultaneously a borrower's identity card, a slip showing due date, and either a book card or the inside cover of the book if it is marked with the essential information.

Notched cards of the McBee Keysort type can be used for book circu-

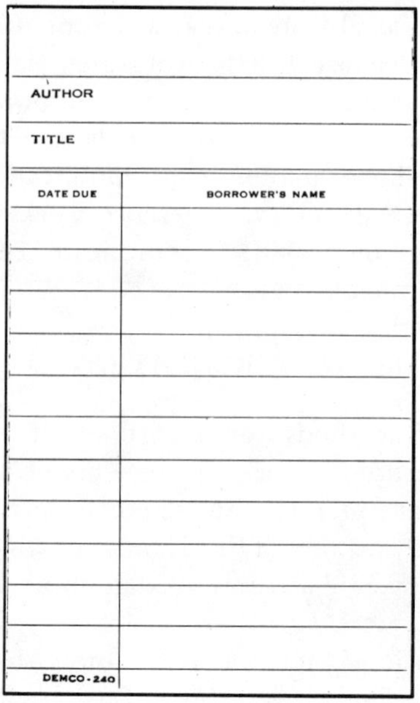

AUTHOR	
TITLE	
DATE DUE	BORROWER'S NAME
DEMCO-240	

Figure 1. Standard book circulation card.

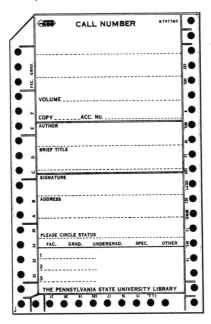

Figure 2. Mechanically sorting card.

lation with some advantages. The peripheral holes can be assigned to provide whatever information might be desired from circulation records. In addition to noting due dates, the names of borrowers can be coded, or relationships to reveal what groups of patrons borrow what categories of books can be determined by using the sorting needle.

When the volume of circulation attains a figure of well over 100,000 a year, and particularly where several branch locations are involved in the servicing, an automated system becomes practical. There are many detailed descriptions of automated book circulation systems giving convincing evidence of their effectiveness. Nolan, Cardinelli, and Kozumplik (3) tell of one based principally on simple electronic accounting machine equipment that resulted in an estimated savings of $38,000 a year for 177,700 transactions at the Lockheed Missiles and Space Company. Hazhedari and Voos (4) report an installation at the Technical Information Section of Picatinny Arsenal for which the monthly equipment costs (in 1964) were $755, and for which fewer personnel are needed than for a prior manual system.

One of the most sophisticated systems in existence by 1968 was known as BELLREL, which is now in operation at the Bell Telephone Laboratories, Inc. Its development and capabilities are outlined in the article

Figure 3. Routing slip for periodicals.

by Kennedy (2) referred to previously in this chapter. This is an "on-line, real-time computer network" that links two terminals in each of three locations (other libraries in the company) to a central computer. Lesser systems were considered but the final decision was that only the most capable one based on an IBM360-40 computer would answer present and foreseeable future requirements. This library's loans numbered 200,000 in 1968. Total costs were not reported although some indication was shown from the rental costs of the six terminals at $275 a month, and the library's assessment for its use of the transmission control unit at $1100 a month, figures that prove strong company support of the library. However, the wide range of potential transactions, 22 in the BELLREL system, show its effect on library efficiency. In addition to handling loans, it keeps record of returns, renewals, personal reserves, and questions concerning locations. In short, it is the answer to every well-financed library's requirements.

Examples of cards and forms used for the several circulations systems described are shown as Figures 1, 2, 4, and 5.

```
┌─────────────────────────────────────────────────────┐
│                                                       │
│                                                       │
│                                                       │
│                                                       │
│  AUTHOR                                               │
│                                                       │
│  TITLE                                                │
│                                                       │
│                                                       │
│  REPORT OR CALL NO.                    │ COPY  NO.    │
│                                                       │
│  PERIODICAL  DATE │ SERIES │ VOLUME    │ NO.          │
│                   │        │           │              │
│                                                       │
│         AERONUTRONIC LIBRARY                          │
│                                                       │
│         DATE DUE    ┌─────────────┐                   │
│                     │             │                   │
│                     └─────────────┘                   │
│                                                       │
│                                                       │
│                                                       │
│  BORROWER'S SIGNATURE                                 │
│                                                       │
│                                                       │
│  ROOM  NO.   │ BUILDING        │ PHONE                │
│              │                 │                      │
│  PLEASE PRINT LAST NAME                               │
│                                                       │
│                                                       │
│          LIBRARY          │ DATE                      │
│       CHECKOUT RECORD     │                           │
│                                                       │
│  LIBRARY  ARD-7198                                    │
│  APR   61                                             │
└─────────────────────────────────────────────────────┘
```

Figure 4. Library charge-out card, Aeronutronic Division, Ford Motor Co.

EXTRAMURAL LOANS

In addition to the usual services to people located in the immediate
vicinity of the library there may be need to serve personnel in other units

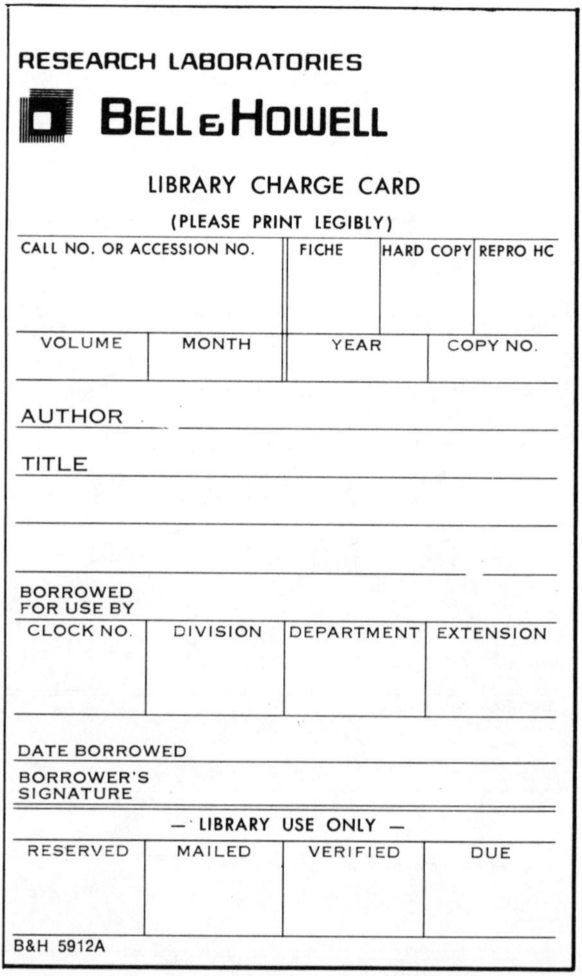

RESEARCH LABORATORIES

BELL & HOWELL

LIBRARY CHARGE CARD

(PLEASE PRINT LEGIBLY)

CALL NO. OR ACCESSION NO.		FICHE	HARD COPY	REPRO HC

VOLUME	MONTH	YEAR	COPY NO.

AUTHOR

TITLE

BORROWED
FOR USE BY

CLOCK NO.	DIVISION	DEPARTMENT	EXTENSION

DATE BORROWED

BORROWER'S
SIGNATURE

— LIBRARY USE ONLY —

RESERVED	MAILED	VERIFIED	DUE

B&H 5912A

Figure 5. Library charge card, Research Laboratories, Bell & Howell Co.

of the organization in far removed locations. Branch plants and scattered sales offices of industrial organizations or subunits of variously structured systems should be proffered the use of books if this is at all feasible. Ideally, there should be branch service at every location through which to handle requests.

There is also the extramural loan to an individual or library entirely outside the province of the intended service. Queries from other libraries should be considered seriously and loans granted if there is no chance that the library's own patrons will be inconvenienced. There is always the

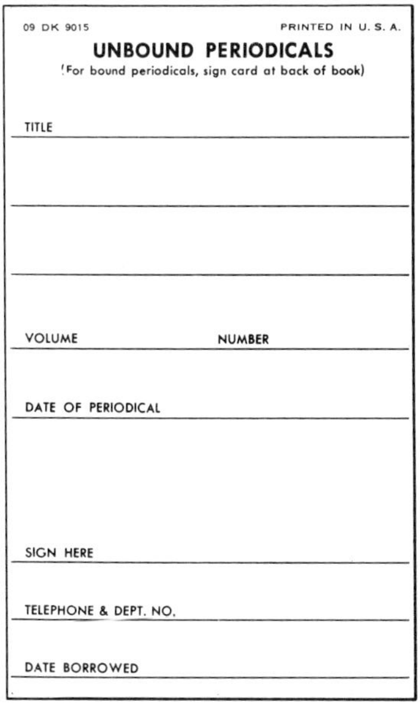

```
09 DK 9015                        PRINTED IN U. S. A.
            UNBOUND PERIODICALS
      (For bound periodicals, sign card at back of book)


TITLE _____




VOLUME              NUMBER _____

DATE OF PERIODICAL _____




SIGN HERE _____

TELEPHONE & DEPT. NO. _____

DATE BORROWED _____
```

Figure 6. Form used for circulating periodicals at Eli Lilly and Company Library.

possibility of reciprocity, and these courtesies are not likely to be abused. The good will they may engender is worth their little trouble. This idea is developed more fully in Chapter 12.

CIRCULATION OF MISCELLANEOUS MATERIALS

Provision should be made for the full use of the nonbook items such as pamphlets, reports, translations, patents, and all items normally housed in indexed files. Individual circumstances will determine what may safely be loaned outside the library. Administrative policy may require that certain research reports and laboratory notebooks, for example, should not leave the library.

The same type of form used for books may be suitable for records of nonbook loans if it is one such as is shown in Figure 1; another type, as shown in Figure 4, may be preferred. Whether is is necessary to stipulate specific loan periods is an individual decision, although it is usually wise to do so. For materials kept in vertical file drawers or on divider-type shelving, the standard "out" cards used in general office practice are satisfactory. One is simply signed by the borrower, the item removed

```
        PLEASE RELEASE AFTER 24 HOURS
     NAME                DEPT.  NC  SEND BACK
   AMERICAN DRUGGIST         C.3

    McDowell, J.L. Jr.       M-481

    DeHays, B.F.             M-483

    Meese, W.W.              M-495

    Schmitz, G.L.            M-490
    Sebald, C.W.             M-489

    King, B.H.               M-201
    Arnold, L.F.             M-223

    Sims, P.                 M-461

    Cromwell, L.G.           M-796

    Maze, N.                 M-781
    Rawlings, D.V.           M-781

    Nash, J.F.               M-741
    Market, H.L.             M-741

    Library                  M-789
```

```
 RELEASE AFTER 24 HOURS      21825      NC     RETURN

 CLIN EXPTL IMMUNOL                  01  M789      6

 06 PERIODICAL RACK
 10 HULL R N                             M787
 14 STONE R L                            M787
 18 BAKER R S                            M787
 22 PECK F B JR                          M783

 30 JOHNSON I S                          M592
 99 SCIENTIFIC LIBRARY                   M789
```

Figure 7. Periodical routing form used at Eli Lilly & Company Library.
Upper list is one formerly used, lower list is new.

from the file noted, and the card substituted in the file making sure it protrudes far enough to be noticed if it remains there too long.

In organizations that must handle classified government reports, special procedures must be instituted that conform to specific issuing office requirements. Only those persons who have proper security clearance may even see the documents, and their signatures must be affixed to a record for each item they borrow. Where many documents are used, this can be a time-consuming task that may well warrant the institution of automated control such as the one Berlin (5) outlines in detail, from the delivery of the documents to the borrower's signing in duplicate for them.

CIRCULATION AND ROUTING OF PERIODICALS

Because of the importance of the information they record and the vital necessity for its complete accessibility, the system for controlling periodicals should be carefully planned. Whether they should circulate is again a question to be answered for every library, according to the needs of patrons and the ability of the library to fulfill them, considering costs of multiple copies and perhaps heavy replacement. If duplicate subscriptions are possible, then one copy can be held in the library and used for binding. Very few libraries can afford the expense of both binding and providing shelf space for more than one copy of bound journals.

In a small, closely knit organization it may be entirely satisfactory to circulate bound volumes without special restrictions. However, complications arise where the group is large and much literature searching is done in the library. The absence of one volume, borrowed to use one paper, puts perhaps fifty other papers out of immediate reach. Also the character of the particular literature involved is a determining factor as to whether bound volumes should leave the library. If a reference work such as the Beilstein *Handbuch der organische Chemie* is used extensively, it would be a serious inconvenience not to have all of the volumes of the *Berichte* or the *Annalen* on the nearby shelves for immediate consultation. The question of the removal of bound volumes should therefore be weighed carefully, particularly if there are opposing points of view among patrons. Inasmuch as the majority of scientific libraries are oriented toward research activities, their most important resource, the periodical literature, ought to be available. However, if periodicals are to circulate a form such as Figures 3 and 6 is useful.

The solution to the journal circulation problem has been found in large measure in the availability of quick, easy-to-use copying equipment. Costs are so reasonable that any library can have at least one copying machine for both patrons or staff. The question of copyright has not been completely resolved and is in fact largely ignored despite specific warnings against photocopying printed in certain books and journals. Suggestions have been put forth to require payment by libraries for providing photocopies of copyrighted publications, but this would be almost impossible to enforce.

Many libraries find that one of their most appreciated services is the routing of current issues of periodicals. This is not a simple procedure, and for ultimate effectiveness it depends upon the conscientious cooperation of everyone on the routing lists. One scheme for coping with these persons who do not pass issues along promptly is to require returning the periodical to the library before going to the next person, but this is almost too much to handle expeditiously.

Once the decision has been made to route periodicals, it is necessary to determine which titles to circulate, to whom, and in what order of priority. An initial step will be to submit the list of titles to the group of persons interested and have them select those they would like to see regularly. Then the routing lists can be prepared.

Smith (6) describes an efficient system for the photocopying of routing slips using multilith plates to produce the required 12,031 slips needed each year to circulate 500 periodicals to 300 technical staff members at the Institute for Defense Analysis Library. Two hours of staff time were saved daily by eliminating the duplicate charge form, which had required the filing of the duplicate to show where an issue was, a good thing to have on record but found to be not essential.

Figure 7 shows a computer-produced routing list that is used by the Lilly Research Laboratories Scientific Library. The number 21825 identifies the journal, those in the left column indicate priorities, and those on the right are addresses. As an illustration of how developmental changes occur in an effective information center, a copy of the routing form formerly used in the same library is shown above the new one.

An alternative to routing copies of periodicals is to duplicate the tables of contents of single issues as they arrive for distribution. Readers can then determine which issues they really need to see. The Billerica Research Center Library of Cabot Corporation has an excellent procedure for sending notifications to individuals, using the self-explanatory form reproduced as Figure 8. At this library another good practice is to request individuals to sign a card attached to the journal if they want to

BILLERICA RESEARCH CENTER

LIBRARY

To:

This journal is now <u>ON RESERVE</u> in the
Billerica Library. A copy of the
contents page is attached.

If you wish to see the journal, you may:

    (a) Inspect it in the library anytime

    (b) Borrow it overnight

    (c) Borrow it for one week
        after _____

If you cannot come to the library, but
wish to see a particular article,
please mark the required pages on the
contents page, indicate whether you
wish to have:

☐ Journal on loan when available

☐ Photocopy or reprint for your file

and return the contents page with this
slip to the library.

The journal will be sent out on loan in
the order in which requests are received.

567-2-20 12/67

Figure 8. Notification sent with contents page of periodical, Billerica Library, Cabot Corporation.

read it at some future time when the issues are freed for circulation. The card is attached to the notice by perforations. See Figure 9.

RESERVE JOURNAL	TITLE:			
NOT TO BE REMOVED FROM				
BILLERICA LIBRARY	ISSUE DATE:			

	BORROWER	DATE REQUESTED	DATE SENT	DATE RETURNED
If you wish to *BORROW*				
this journal, please sign				
on the right. It will be				
sent on loan when the				
next issue arrives.				
Thank you!				
DO NOT REMOVE!				
833-7-21 10/67				

Figure 9. Notification asking for personal request to borrow periodical, Billerica Library, Cabot Corporation.

An interesting and significant by-product of analysis of circulation records is factual evidence of how the collection is used. Procedures can be instituted for sample periods to identify borrowers with respect to their locations in various departments in the organization as well as to determine what classes of books are loaned. Strain (1) reports such a study made at an IBM Federal Systems Division, Space Guidance Center Library, where 25% of the borrowers were from administration, 38.6% from operations, and 36.2% from the engineering department. Results of such a study can influence purchasing policies and also reveal where greater publicizing efforts should be directed.

PROVISION OF MATERIALS NOT OWNED BY THE LIBRARY

When there is urgent need for published material that is not owned by the library, such as articles in periodicals or books that cannot easily be procured by purchase, procedures must be initiated to discover where these are located in another collection. By the methods outlined in subsequent parts of this chapter, requests can be made to borrow material if a book or to supply photocopy if a periodical article. It is possible, too, to get photocopies of out-of-print books for moderate costs. University Microfilms is one such agent.

Before requesting an interlibrary loan, several facts concerning ethical practice in borrowing should be recognized. It is important that the Interlibrary Loan Code (7) developed by the American Library Association be read carefully. Most libraries operate their lending service in accord with these regulations which must be observed scrupulously if the system of interlibrary loan is to continue to function. It is likewise expedient to learn of any special restriction imposed by the library to which requests are addressed. Some libraries cannot render interlibrary loan service at all, and university libraries must give preference to the needs of students and staff members.

In general, requests for loans should be made to libraries that are in nearby locations. This is good practice because it is less expensive and is inevitably faster. It is also easier to become acquainted with the holdings and personnel of libraries within reasonable distances.

There is an increasing trend for groups of libraries in one geographical area to cultivate relationships to expedite loans among themselves. Evidence of the closeness among librarians in industry was confirmed by Strain (8) who surveyed the situation in upstate New York, finding that there are several kinds of interchange among special libraries, public libraries, and university libraries.

An example of an effective regional cooperative effort is the group known as the Associated Science Libraries of San Diego, Calif. (9). It consists of seven industrial libraries, three colleges and universities, three government agencies, and five research organizations. A booklet outlines its purposes and gives directions as to how to make use of the pooled resources.

Not only is it advantageous for libraries of individual organizations to share resources, but it should be apparent to those employed in large, complex, decentralized organizations with units in widely separated locations, such as corporations with various divisions or operations in several states and countries, that a system of intracompany cooperation might be fostered as a benefit to the whole enterprise. The several operating libraries will likely differ with respect to subject area emphasis. If acquisition policies recognize these subject limitations and there is agreement to depend upon an intralibrary loan system instead of calling upon outside sources, the corporate interests will be well served.

PROCEDURES FOR LOCATING BOOKS IN OTHER LIBRARIES

To be borrowed, an item must first be located. Since these procedures differ for books and periodicals, they are discussed separately. Finding a rare, out-of-print book can be a challenge, and discovery may require more than one letter of inquiry. The most likely source will be a library in which the subject field is represented that has been in existence long enough to have acquired a significant collection.

A first step might be to investigate special or university libraries in the immediate vicinity, locating them initially from directories of library associations or *Bowker's Guide to Subject Collections*. The Kruzas' *Directory of Special Libraries and Information Centers* is another possible source. Then the problem is to present a request in a manner that will reassure the owning library that the book will be safe.

If there is no local or nearby major collection from which to draw, a bibliographic center that maintains a union catalog of holdings in a large geographical region can be queried. There are several of these in the United States, and requests should be directed to the closest one. As a last resort, there is the Union Catalog of the Library of Congress which administers a system of circularizing for hard-to-find titles. It is conceivable that similar centers in other countries such as the National Lending Library in London or the Centre Nationale de Recherche Scientifique in Paris, for examples, could be approached. For detailed information on the development of the union catalogs and a listing of the smaller specialized projects, Downs (10) provides a detailed summary of the whole program. Some of the important union catalogs are the following:

Union Library Catalogue of Pennsylvania, University of Pennsylvania, Philadelphia, Pa.
Ohio Union Catalog, 1434 W. Fifth Ave., Columbus, Ohio
The Bibliographic Center for Research, Rocky Mountain Region, Denver, Colo.
The Union Catalog of the Library of Congress (The National Union Catalog), Library of Congress, Washington, D.C.
North Carolina Union Catalog, Louis Round Wilson Library, University of North Carolina, Chapel Hill, N.C.
State Union Catalog, California State Library, Sacramento, Calif.

Requests to borrow books should be typed on standard forms such as are available from library supply houses. They are designed to provide space for all necessary information that will make the transaction as convenient as possible for those processing the loan.

For emergency requests teletype service is preferable to telephoning. A written record is easier to interpret and is more likely to reach the correct department in a major library system. Telex installations are usually operative in most industrial organizations and are rapidly increasing in libraries.

PROCEDURES FOR LOCATING PERIODICALS IN OTHER LIBRARIES

Locating a periodical file is not usually as difficult as finding a book, except for some very obscure titles. It can happen, too, that a journal that would not seemingly be difficult to locate cannot be found anywhere, such as is known to be true for a reference in the *Bulletin Therapeutique Naturelle et de Renaissance de l'Art Medical* for the year 1891. Even the Bibliotheque Nationale possesses but one issue for that year!

To find a periodical one should first look in the published listings-with-locations, both local union lists if there are such, and the comprehensive ones. It is essential to be certain of the complete, exact title. Because references are usually cited as abbreviations, some problems can be encountered in correctly interpreting. Everyone cannot be relied upon to follow rules for official abbreviations; also the same rules are not used by even closely related disciplines. *Ann.*, for example, may stand for *Annalen, Annales, Annual* or even *Annals*. Sometimes the relationship between a date and volume number provides a clue for determining whether a citation is for one title or another. Complete unabbreviated titles must always be given when sending a request to avoid errors and unnecessary work for the library accepting the application. In fact, an inexact citation should be returned to the sender for verification. A detail that is too often ignored is indication of the source of the reference. When there is an inadvertent error the chance of correcting it is enhanced by providing this information.

To locate libraries that have files of periodicals certain of the major listings showing holdings must be consulted. These are provided in Chapter 6. One important reason for a library to acquire the *Union List of Serials in the United States and Canada,* and *Chemical Abstracts Service Source Index* is that they do indicate the libraries that have files of periodicals.

Once the elusive periodical has been located, the next step is to place an order for a photocopy of the pages required. Almost any library now has a copying service, but because it is costly not all libraries can handle a large volume of such business. Articles in periodicals will usually be short enough to warrant direct copying although there is an increasing tendency to make microfilm copies especially by some of the large-scale suppliers. It is good practice to use facilities located in the same geographical area. However, when local resources are not adequate, one of the following major libraries, all of them having extensive collections and good photoduplication departments, can probably provide what is needed:

New York Public Library, Photographic Service, Fifth Ave. & 42nd St., New York, 10017, accepts deposit accounts.

John Crerar Library, 35 W. 33rd St., Chicago, Ill. 60016

Technology Department, Carnegie Library of Pittsburgh, 4400 Forbes St., Pittsburgh, Pa. 15213

Engineering Societies Library, 345 East 47th St., New York, 10017

Linda Hall Library, 5109 Cherry St., Kansas City, Ka. 66104

U.S. National Library of Medicine, 8600 Rockville Pike, Bethesda, Md., 20014; orders may be placed through regional medical libraries, that is, for Pennsylvania the College of Physicians in Philadelphia.

There is available an inclusive listing that provides details of services located throughout the North American continent. This is the *Directory of Library Photoduplication Services in the United States, Canada, and Mexico,* compiled in 1966 by Cosby Brinkley, head of the service from which it can be purchased—Photoduplication Service, University of Chicago Library, Chicago, Ill.

AUXILIARY SERVICES

In any situation where an information service is in operation certain relevant activities will probably be instituted to augment those that are strictly within the bounds of usual library practices. Since these are not part of the conventional pattern it is not possible to suggest, except by a few examples, what these might be for a particular situation. By way of illustration, business services and institutional archives are described here in some detail. These may suggest others to those sufficiently alert to discern what might be appropriate in other organizations.

Business Services

Some scientific and technical libraries serve as a central information service for *all* components of an organization as was pointed out in Chapter 1. In case this situation exists, business information *per se* is integrated, being only one important facet of the administration of readers' services. As an industrial organization expands, there may be demand for a separate unit to provide aid not only to those having top responsibility for managing corporate affairs but also the legal, personnel, marketing, purchasing, and financial divisions and other divisions exclusive of research, development, and engineering. Information needs have been intensified by diversification of present product lines into new areas and by the establishment of branches abroad or increased development of foreign trade. In any event, competition has stepped up the need for information, but the collection of materials and the service performed by libraries are dictated by potential benefit to the individual organizations served.

Materials to be dealt with are largely nonscientific in nature even though they are pertinent to the work of those concerned with products based on science and technology. Plant operations require information on automation, materials handling, properties of materials, inventory control, new processes, labor relations, and employee activities, among others. Legal needs cover legislative matters affecting the organization and products, taxation, regulations, codes and ordinances of various types. Purchasing requires knowledge of sources and of availability of raw materials, price fluctuation, shipping regulations, and the like. Marketing is based upon commercial intelligence found in investment publications, governmental statistical agencies, sales personnel in the field, and customer inquiries directed to various segments of the organization. Public relations activities are discussed in Chapter 12. Obviously, the library may be only one source of the information needs cited here but the possibility of supplying many of them is likely to be at hand.

In regard to the development of a business section as an integral service of a company library, or only as a part of the science-technology unit activity efforts must be governed by management's reaction, encouragement, and approval. Once these are gained, many other factors receive consideration, such as plans for additional personnel, space, and communication techniques. The minimum result of the service should be elimination of needless duplication through centralizing materials, while the maximum would be increased profits from making hundreds of ideas available to the work force through access to business literature. One of the most successful and dedicated of business librarians, Vormelker (11) outlines specifics for organizing a company library; she also reports on good business service (12). Another article by Strieby (13), setting forth guiding principles in developing business service and what it can do has been influential in directing attention to this end.

In Minneapolis a new business service complex (14), called Northstar, operates in the twin cities area. Six special librarians, representing fields of finance, food, paper, and public utilities, share resources and exchange ideas. Another cooperative development is at Georgia Tech whereby services of the Price Gilbert Memorial Library (15) are made available to industrial research and off-campus users, especially those with no library facilities. Levesque (16) reports on the Technical Resources Center, an activity designed to make technological information more readily available to specific industries and business organizations in areas where such a need exists. A network, tying together the user-clientele with library resources to persons possessing pertinent expertise in a continuing interface, is the role, as well as the goal, of this plan, in a people-to-people atmosphere. Implementing the State Technical Services Act of 1965, this program is sponsored by the New York State Department of Commerce and the Syracuse University Research Corporation. These three examples of cooperation are undoubtedly indicative of the broader system of networks predicted for the future.

Institutional Archives

It is only within recent years that institutional archives have become a major concern of libraries—their accession, organization, maintenance, administration, and utilization. If a corporate records retention program is established, with emphasis on a reduction of paper work combined with preservation of documents having permanent business and/or legal significance, materials having an historical aspect may be needed. Very often the jurisdiction of these materials is entrusted to the library. If a comprehensive information center exists, a unified records program, historical and otherwise, may be administered as one of its many facets. Or a separate archival unit may be established for the institution it serves.

Since the primary purpose of administering institutional archives is to collect, preserve, and service records having an historical or reference value—official, functional, and even personal when personal achievements are tied directly with an organization's progress—it is logical for these materials to be a part of the library. Quite often the librarian has the experience and vision to preserve such items long before management recognizes their potential use. Provision should be made for housing and expansion. An archival collection may be any noncurrent record, written, audiovisual, or even memorabilia if associated with the particular institution. Simmons (17–18) discusses various categories of items that preserve an organization's historical record whether or not the items are distinctly archival in nature.

The collection is not always built around the traditional definition of institutional archives, often referred to as the "corporate memory." This designation may be narrowed to the life work and achievements of an individual, such as the theme of the Kettering Archives, a part of the General Motors Research Library (19). There the plan is to acquire a significant collection of historical material related to Charles F. Kettering, a distinguished engineer and scientist—the many-sided man who founded the GM Research Laboratories. Comprising the collection are copies of his 185 patents; his addresses and published articles; photocopies of his many honorary degrees, citations, and awards; significant photographs; and the Oral History Project which includes interviews with associates and friends—taped, transcribed, and indexed.

While many librarians do not have the time, space, funds, or staff to embark on institution-wide accession, housing, and organization of archival materials, it is never too early (and sometimes too late) for administrators with vision to plan ahead and at least make a beginning. For example, what began in 1934 with a few items shelved in a steel cupboard grew, with the support of management, into a full fledged archival unit with a small staff 25 years later in 1959. Materials, both documentary and museum type, poured in under an active accessions program, attracting hundreds of visitors. Ten years later, in May 1969, the archives were an important and integral part of the Lilly Center, a beautiful building dedicated to the reception of visitors who are guests of the company. On its opening day, one session of a midwest archival symposium was held there (20). Davidson (21), its archivist, has been responsible for several contributions to the literature relating to this activity.

In general, the objectives of preserving institutional records are to (*1*) make available any item of value in preparing a definitive history of the institution, (2) organize records of the past so that they will be helpful in guiding future policies, (*3*) provide a ready reference service for facts recorded in the materials preserved, (*4*) aid those responsible for preparing institutional publications, (*5*) furnish materials for exhibits inter- or intramural, (*6*) give management a useful tool to use in relationships with its publics (see Chapter 12), (7) supply adequate documentation of and for company activities. A by-product might be a laboratory for scholars engaged in economic research and the study of business history. It is evident that, with the objectives above in mind, many items whose historical significance is not easily recognized, may have important reference potential.

One of the many discussions that enumerates considerations of establishing archives and their organization, physical facilities, and reference value contains an annotated bibliography (22), which can easily be brought to date by a study of articles appearing in the 1960 decade. A few of these are included in the supplementary references of this chapter. The *American Archivist* should not be overlooked in a retrospective search for information. One of the most essential steps in planning an archival program is the adoption of a code of policies and practices pertinent to the scope, acceptance, and service of materials. The experience of others will help in forming this code. Leahy (23) says "records with the promise of an enduring reference and research value are those that will enlighten the future reader on the four P's of the company's past:

        Policy   Philosophy   Performance   People

Less than one per cent of the records produced by a company are needed to shed this light." But, as Davison (21) says, "How important that one per cent."

Record of Services—Statistics

In the day-to-day operation of the library, various services are rendered, and it is advisable to keep an accurate record of those that can be noted. A daily tally of the number of books circulated, reference questions asked and answered, requests for bibliographic searches, and any other noteworthy activity can be kept on a desk calendar. Details of significant reference queries should be kept in a notebook. When all of these activities are totalled daily, monthly, and annually they provide unquestionable evidence of the ways that the library as an information center is used to support the programs of the organization.

Statistics lead logically to the subject of an annual report because they should be featured prominently in it. Every library should produce a report of its operations at least once a year and submit it to key persons in management. The more simply it is done, the more it will likely be read. Even one page of a few of the most important facts and figures showing what has been accomplished, perhaps telling of future plans and raising questions about what might be done, will publicize and promote the effectiveness of the service.

REFERENCES

1. P. M. Strain, "The Circulation Patterns of One Technical Library," *Spec. Libr.* **56**, 312–317 (1965).
2. R. A. Kennedy, "Bell Laboratories Library Real-Time Loan System (BELLREL)," *J. Libr. Automat.* **1**, 128–146 (1968).

3. K. P. Nolan, F. S. Cardinelli, and W. A. Kozumplik, "Mechanized Circulation Controls," *Spec. Libr.* **59**, 47–50 (1968).

4. I. Hazhedari and H. Voos, "Automated Circulation at a Government Research and Development Installation," *Spec. Libr.* **55**, 77–81 (1964).

5. S. Berlin, "An Advanced Classified Document Control System," *Spec. Libr.* **58**, 160–165 (1967).

6. R. S. Smith, "Photocopying for Routing Slips," *Spec. Libr.* **58**, 54 (1967).

7. *National Interlibrary Loan Code, 1968*, Reference Service Division ALA, Chicago, 1968.

8. P. M. Strain, "The Industrial Librarian as Cooperator," *Spec. Libr.* **60**, 209–214 (1969).

9. Associated Science Libraries of San Diego, "Have you heard?" *Spec. Libr.* **54**, 653–654 (1963).

10. R. B. Downs, *Union Catalogs*, ALA, Chicago, 1946.

11. R. L. Vormelker, "The Company Library; What It Is and Does," *J. Indust. Training* **5**, 2–6, 13–16, 18–26 (1951).

12. R. L. Vormelker, "Fundamentals: How Is Good Library Service to Business Born and Bred?" *Southeastern Libr.* **13**, 135–144 (1963).

13. I. M. Strieby, "Looking Around: The Company Library," *Harvard Bus. Rev.* **37**, 35–36, 144–150 (1959).

14. T. Miller, "Six Minneapolis "Insiders" Build Unique Cooperative," *Spec. Libr.* **54**, 295–297 (1963).

15. "News from the Field," *Coll. Res. Libr. News* **30**, 47 (1969).

16. R. Levesque, "The State Technical Services Program—An Interface with Industry," *Spec. Libr.* **59**, 195–200 (1968).

17. J. M. Simmons, "Business in Company Archives," *Spec. Libr.* **59**, 20–23 (1968).

18. J. M. Simmons, "The Special Librarian as Company Archivist," *Spec. Libr.* **56**, 647–650 (1965).

19. *The Kettering Archives: General Motors Library*, descriptive leaflet, GM, Warren, Mich.

20. Archival symposium sponsored by the General Services Administration and the Society of American Archivists, afternoon session, Lilly Center, Indianapolis, Ind., May 12, 1969.

21. H. L. Davidson, "Business Archives and the Business Archivist," presented at the Twelfth Annual Conference Association of Records Executives and Administrators, New York, May 8, 1969, to be published.

22. I. M. Strieby, "All the King's Horses . . . ," *Spec Libr.* **50**, 3–12 (1959).

23. E. J. Leahy and C. A. Cameron, *Modern Records Management*, McGraw-Hill, New York, 1965.

BIBLIOGRAPHY

Anderson, J. W., "Improving the Validity of Comparative Technical Library Statistics," *Spec. Libr.* **58**, 697–702 (1967).

Cole, B. and H. Rowley, "Current Journal Routing," *Spec. Libr.* **35**, 324–327 (1964).

Corbett, E. V., "Focus on Charing Methods," *Libr. World* **63**, 1061–108 (1961).

Lewton, L. O., "The Silent Librarian: Linedex on a Stand for Locations," *Spec. Libr.* **57**, 658 (1966).

Midwest Interlibrary Center, *Rarely-Held Scientific Serials*, The Center, Chicago, Ill., 1963.

Millard, P., Comp. and Ed., *Directory of Technical and Scientific Translators and Services*, Crosby Lockwood, London, 1968.

H. G. Richardson, "The Proposed Houston Technical Information Center," *Spec. Libr.* **54**, 297–299 (1963).

Riggle, S. M., "Automatic Journal Routing Using IBM Punched Cards," *Spec. Libr.* **53**, 537–540 (1962).

Sewell, W., "The Needs of Industry for Library Services beyond That Expected of their Own Special Libraries and Resources Available to Them," *Libr. Trends* **14**, 226–235 (1966).

Simon, W. H., "This Works for Us: Periodical Handling with Photocopy System," *Spec. Libr.* **50**, 206–207 (1959).

Sloane, M. N., "The Validity of Comparative Technical Library Statistics," *Spec. Libr.* **58**, 692–696 (1967).

Strain, P. and W. Shawver, "An Automated Book Circulation System, Model II," *Spec. Libr.* **59**, 337–345 (1968).

Thornton, H., "Is the Circulation of Periodicals Desirable?" *Aslib Proc.* **11**, 106–107 (1959).

10

Dissemination of Currently Published Information

Library Bulletins—Other Methods

One of the most important functions of a library's information service in the areas of science and technology is the establishment of a system for reviewing publications immediately upon receipt, selecting information pertinent to the program of the organization served, and noting individual items to be brought to the attention, by one means or another, of those persons to whose work they are related. This is generally known as a "current awareness" service that is directed to the community of scientists as a whole or in groups. It involves a combination of processes including the selection of whatever is pertinent from periodicals, reports, patents, books, and announcements of various kinds, in fact, from all of the varied types of publications that are received. A systematic record is made of these significant references, and in many libraries they are accumulated for periodic distribution as bulletins. An important co-product is the development of a file of unique items that is an invaluable resource growing in importance as a continuous literature search. Innovative literature scientists have developed special methods of utilizing this operation for maximum benefits.

A refinement of the current awareness idea is the selective dissemination of information (SDI) procedure that is designed to serve the individual scientist directly. Profiles of personal interests are compounded by selecting relevant terms from a thesaurus, and only those facts that fit these choices are brought to attention. This is a feat that can be done most effectively by automation. Centralized services that perform this function are listed in this chapter.

The premise for the need to institute any kind of alerting activity is that the volume of publication in any field of science has increased to such magnitude that it is not possible for the scientist in management who determines the direction of future investigation, or even the research worker who tries to follow the literature closely, to review regularly and consistently the numerous publications that could be of importance to him. Although every individual develops his own methods for keeping abreast of personal areas of interest and does some regular reading, he cannot spend as much time as it would take to cover all of the possible sources that might contain facts that he should know. This is the situation open to perceptive analysis by the library staff member whose duty is to design a simple system for an operation of limited size and scope, or complex if a large diversified group must be apprised of developments of wide range.

There are several ways to get recently published information to those who should be made aware of it promptly. Some are more appropriate in one situation than in another. Procedures used in existing libraries are reviewed in this chapter and discussed in Chapter 12 from the standpoint of their use as a device for promoting good relations with the library's clientele.

METHODS FOR DISSEMINATION OF NEWLY PUBLISHED INFORMATION

As publications are received in the library their contents can be quickly scanned, and procedures instituted for selecting those items that are of pertinence to any possible interests, erring on the side of too much rather than too little. Another method is to subscribe to a centralized service that can supply material in a specified field, of which more is said later in the chapter. From either approach, a continuous flow of information must then be communicated in the most effective manner possible. In this process the most relevant material will be recorded for permanent retention in special files maintained in traditional card catalog format or, if sufficiently voluminous, by one of the so-called nonconventional systems, manual or automated.

Once the material is selected, ways of communicating it must be determined. The following methods are among those possible:

1. Telephoning to individuals
2. Noting references on slips and sending to individuals
3. Routing of periodicals, possibly marking certain articles for attention
4. Maintaining a card file of references in the library
5. Preparing a bulletin for wide distribution at regular intervals
6. Duplicating tables of contents of periodicals
7. Subscribing to centralized commercial services
8. Utilizing automation for selective dissemination

Each of these methods is described in detail with comments concerning its potential effectiveness.

Telephone Calls to Individuals

Personal telephone notifications cannot be used extensively because they take too much time. They are not fully effective for the obvious reason that not everyone is at his desk when the telephone rings. Only in small organizations can the telephone be used for this purpose with any degree of efficiency. However, there may be times when it is essential that certain information be communicated as quickly as possible and this is the way to do it.

Noting References and Sending to Individuals

Written personal notifications can be undertaken to a limited extent only; again it is too time consuming. This procedure will have a place, however, in almost any library where there is a close working relationship between the library staff and its patrons. In fact, card files for recording personal interests are often maintained to remember who should receive personal notice of subjects in an active state of development. An excellent opportunity is afforded for the library to show that it can participate fully in the program of the organization by apprising key persons of particularly significant publications. However, the broader purpose must be kept in perspective, and this means that the requirements of the many must not be disregarded in favor of the few in key positions. Examples of personal notification forms are shown as Figures 1 and 2.

Routing of Periodicals

The routing of periodicals might be considered a good way of getting their contents to those persons who can read and select for themselves

```
┌─────────────────────────────────────────────────────────────────────┐
│                                                                       │
│   LIBRARY MEMO                      YOUR FILING CODE: _____      │
│                                              DATE: _____         │
│                                                                       │
│   TO: _____                     │
│                                                                       │
│                                                                       │
│   CALLING YOUR ATTENTION TO _____      │
│                                                                       │
│   _____      │
│                                                                       │
│   _____      │
│                                                                       │
│   _____WHICH MAY INTEREST YOU.            │
│                                                                       │
│                                    _____          │
│   CEC 677                                     LIBRARIAN               │
│                                                                       │
└─────────────────────────────────────────────────────────────────────┘
```

Figure 1. Personal notification form used at Bell and Howell.

what they need. A serious drawback is their numbers. Who can cope with from 5 to 10 or more single issues in one day? Moreover, dissemination to a group is uneven because those whose names are at the head of the routing lists have an advantage over those below them. This matter is discussed in greater detail in Chapter 9.

Maintaining a Card File of References

As periodicals, chapters in books, patents, and other publications are reviewed, selected references can be typed on cards and adequate notations or abstracts appended. These can then be filed in accordance with a suitable subject classification scheme. Where such a file is sufficiently well publicized, kept up to date promptly, and kept adequate in its coverage, patrons will develop the habit of consulting it.

The maintenance of a continuous file of references can be achieved by using other than the conventional card file method. Such manual systems as the edge-notched card or the Peek-a-boo card device, both of which are described in Chapter 8, can be used for this purpose. Where the volume of items is in the thousands, only machines can cope. The drawback of the card file as a disseminating process is that there is only one copy, and it must be consulted in its permanent location. The exception, of course, is the automated system that can produce printed copies from its store.

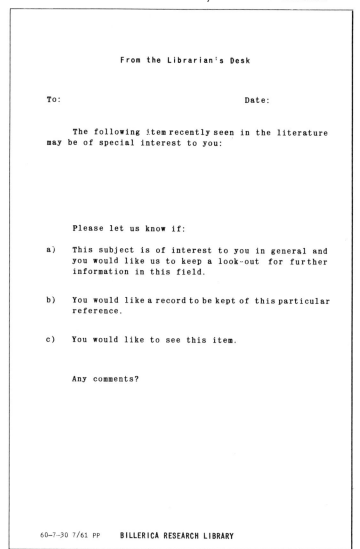

From the Librarian's Desk

To: Date:

     The following item recently seen in the literature
may be of special interest to you:

     Please let us know if:

a)   This subject is of interest to you in general and
      you would like us to keep a look-out for further
      information in this field.

b)   You would like a record to be kept of this particular
      reference.

c)   You would like to see this item.

     Any comments?

60-7-30 7/61 PP   **BILLERICA RESEARCH LIBRARY**

Figure 2. Personal notification form used at Billerica Research Laboratory, of Cabot Corporation.

Preparing a Library Bulletin

The most fully satisfactory way of publicizing information promptly upon receipt encompasses a combination of procedures just outlined. It consists, in brief recapitulation, of establishing a system for reviewing all publications as issued, noting pertinent items, collecting them, and as an ultimate step, issuing at regular intervals what is commonly called a Library Bulletin. All of these steps can be executed in various ways, and the material can even be selected by a group other than the library staff, but since it is essentially a library-oriented activity its processing and distribution should be directed from there. Because a bulletin of whatever sort is thought to be the most effective means for getting information to the greatest number of readers, procedures for preparation of one are described in some detail.

Several factors are involved in deciding to issue a bulletin. One of the strongest arguments in its favor is the fact that so many organizations do have them. Because the items selected for inclusion in a privately edited news medium emphasize internal interests, its audience does not have to scan a large volume of material of no possible pertinence as is the case with published services covering wide fields. Foreign language articles can be abstracted with particular care in deference to some scientists' impatience with other languages. All of these points indicate that reaching the right conclusion in the design of a bulletin for a particular situation merits the most serious consideration.

The subject of bulletins is large and important enough to have warranted the writing of a book entitled *Information Bulletins in Special Libraries* by Walker (1) that provides, as promised by the title, an excellent survey of background, problems, and practice. Although written from a British point of view, the coverage of the literature must be close to complete with a bibliography of almost 140 references. In it are detailed discussions of the various aspects treated briefly in this chapter.

Despite the acceptance of the idea as a good one, the economic factor must be rationalized because the whole process of preparing, duplicating, and distributing a bulletin does require significant budgetary provision. The amount of money involved will vary from a truly minor amount for a slight news sheet to a major expense for a publication of many pages, with full abstracts and a well-designed format. Walker (1) has little to offer concerning costs; thus it may still be of some value to cite some figures for their historical interest. Sewell (2) in 1954 reports one situation where costs were deemed by management as too high, $28,000 a year in 1951, to continue to issue what was a significant bulletin of such stature that it was distributed not only in the immediate organization but to the whole pharmaceutical industry and to schools of pharmacy and medicine as well. A decade later, in 1961, Mohlman (3) tells of another situation where the total number of abstracts for a year was

15,000 and the expense was estimated at $110,000. This included selection of items, abstracting, and processing the bulletin. Lesser publications, however, not as comprehensive in scope or as expensively reproduced, can be satisfactory for internal purposes. In a paper on library bulletins in 1955 Ford (4) observes that "figures mean little in this survey since so many variables must be taken into account."

One of the most distinctive features of the many private or in-house bulletins is their variety. Jackson (5) reports a detailed study of 50 representative examples from a cross-section of chemical companies, every one of which was in some way unique. Many differences are superficial since it is the content that is really important. However, certain of the observations made by Jackson are reaffirmed by Blair (6), who in 1961 published results of a survey of 123 bulletins produced in 94 engineering libraries. In a table comparing general characteristics Blair brought to light some differences and similarities of the two groups. These were reflections for the most part of variations of emphasis in certain directions among the industries represented. For instance, in the bulletins from chemical companies only one had research reports, whereas 69 of those from engineering firms included them. Here, however, there may have been some misunderstanding of what was intended, research reports from within the company or those issuing from government-sponsored research which comprise the so-called "report literature." More chemical company bulletins provided abstracts than did those in engineering fields.

The essential features of library bulletins are outlined in the following sections.

Content

With respect to what will be included in a bulletin a decision will have to be made first as to whether one comprehensive publication is desirable or whether subject breakdowns are needed, perhaps issuing at different frequencies. If there is to be one only, it must include all types of material.

The kinds of items most commonly presented are (1) articles from periodicals, with or without abstracts, (2) patents, with or without abstracts, (3) titles of newly acquired books, (4) pamphlets, (5) reports, from the organization or government-sponsored, (6) news items, (7) forthcoming meetings, and (8) staff publications. From the nature of these categories it is evident that there could be good reason to publish them in different groupings. If abstracts are used, they may be prepared by the staff or copied from a major abstracting journal, first negotiating for permission and paying for this privilege if necessary. There will be a longer delay if published abstracts are used, however, thus defeating the purpose of bringing information to attention quickly.

An alternative program followed by some organizations is to depend upon a centralized service (which is discussed later) and prepare only a brief news sheet for frequent distribution.

Style

Citations should be set down in an easy-to-scan style, as brief as possible but always giving complete bibliographic data. If abstracts or annotations are used, they should be as concise as possible. A too voluminous bulletin will not be read.

Format

The overall design for a bulletin should be as eye-catching as possible, using simple devices such as lines and a colored cover page. There is no point to employing costly printing processes for what is essentially a throw-away product. The size most commonly used is the standard 8½ by 11 inch commercial sheet. Blair (6) makes some good suggestions for effective design such as using elite type in preference to pica or micro and warns against crowding material too closely.

A distinctive cover or cover sheet to identify the publication should be designed with some care because it can be used without change for an unlimited period. There must be a title of some sort, short and direct, and there should always be a volume and issue number, plus the date of publication. The cover page can, if necessary, be a working sheet that carries the title at the top and informational items starting below it, or it can be used for a table of contents. If a bulletin is issued in several sections, different colors can be used for the covers.

An important feature is the inclusion of a request form to be used by readers to ask either for copies of specific items cited or the loan of others. A good spot for this is the last page because it can easily be removed without disturbing anything else.

Although such a publication is distributed only intramurally (with some few exceptions), it should carry the name of the organization on it. There are occasions when it is desirable for a copy to be used in some way outside the organization, and for this reason alone it should be identifiable. Also, if there is distribution to scattered units or plants, the name and location of the library from which it issues should be clearly shown.

Specific Procedures for Preparing a Bulletin

The complete process of producing a bulletin should be subjected to careful analysis in order to achieve the most effective production system. Some procedures will have to be executed daily, such as selecting items from materials received, and writing or dictating abstracts or notes. One staff member will have the responsibility of editing and will be aided by others to whom certain tasks are assigned. If the total staff consists of only two or three members, the head may consider this as one of his major duties. Essentially, the principal routines to be followed include the following:

1. Review of publications as they are received. The editor will have everything come to his attention daily for necessarily quick review. He may mark articles in periodicals that are to be cited by inserting slips, indicating classification if this is used.

2. Preparation of abstracts or annotation. If the editor prepares abstracts, he must do this immediately or he may pass this along to another staff member. A typist sets up the final copy in accord with a specified format. These items can be used for preparing the cumulative reference file, either as cards to be filed, or if paper tapes are made, for storage in a computer file.

An ideal method of preparing abstracts or annotations is to invite members of the research staff to write some of them. Certain journals can be assigned to individuals who express willingness to undertake this. However, unless there is cooperation of the kind reported by Hocken (7), this can result in more hindrance than help.

The selection of what to include in the bulletin requires the judgment of a person thoroughly acquainted with the whole program of organizational interests who knows the subjects well enough to recognize pertinent developments. It is helpful to keep a list of specific topics to watch for particularly.

Frequency

Blair (6) found from his study of a group of bulletins that an equal number were issued weekly and monthly. Some were semimonthly; very few were quarterly. Only one was a daily production. The decision as to how often to distribute is influenced by such factors as the need for its audience to be apprised of new information promptly, availability of staff to prepare it, and budget allowance.

Although Blair found that only one library had a daily issue, this can be a very effective practice. Hocken (7) reports the background situation that led to the initiation of the *IBM San Jose Technical Library News* that appears five days a week as a single $8\frac{1}{2} \times 11$ inch sheet, multilithed on both sides. In it are presented announcements of forthcoming meetings, abstracts of articles from periodicals, titles of newly acquired books, and any other newsworthy items received each day. This effort appears to be both appreciated and practical for the organization it serves.

Methods of Duplicating

The choice of method for duplication depends upon the equipment available and the number of copies needed for distribution. Mimeograph and Multilith are used most commonly. Multilith mats can be prepared advantageously on a Xerox machine. For a very large circulation of several thousand, photo offset or even print is occasionally employed. However, any duplicating method can be utilized if it is economic.

Material for an issue of a bulletin may be assembled for typing all at one time or a typist may do it daily as the material selected is marked or abstracts, either written by hand or recorded on a dictating machine. A Friden Flexowriter is a highly desirable machine for this purpose, particularly if computer equipment is accessible by means of which the co-produced paper tapes can be used to make a print-out of the individual items. These can then be assembled, photographed in slightly reduced size, and used to prepare pages for the bulletin. For any process, copy for reproduction must be made ready for the duplicating procedure.

Distribution Procedures

The list of names of persons to whom the bulletin should be addressed should be established with a view toward the widest possible distribution. Although the contents may be chosen primarily for the attention of the research scientists, it should be remembered that the ultimate objectives, in industrial organizations at least, are products for the open market. This means that the sales force may well have some concern with what is being developed, and management personnel should most certainly be aware of what is happening. The cost of extra names on the list will be very little compared with the total price of preparation. In a small organization, the library may undertake distribution, perhaps very simply by placing copies in mail boxes or on desks. Where hundreds of names comprise the list, a central mailing department will have to do the task. Sample pages of some representative bulletins are shown in this chapter as Figures 3–11.

One Alternative to a Bulletin

In a situation where there is insufficient staff to prepare a bulletin, a substitute might be to duplicate the tables of contents of periodicals as they are received. Any number of copies can be made, from a few to as many as may be required. They may even be routed instead of whole issues. Recipients can either come to the library to read the articles that they want to see or request copies. This system can operate with fair success.

MECHANIZED SYSTEMS

In organizations large enough to provide computer facilities that can be used by the information service, ways of applying such capabilities to the continuous process of disseminating just-published items should be explored. An excellent application is succinctly outlined by Skolnik and Curtis (8) or a system that produces "many outputs from one input" for the Hercules Research Center. Using IBM cards for the initial recording of references, current awareness bulletins are issued by means of an IBM 870. Furthermore, cumulative bibliographies and other selected information are available from magnetic tapes prepared from the cards. A similar system was designed by Wolfe and Herner (9) for the U.S. Public Health Service, Office of Pesticides. In this instance abstracts are first recorded on punch paper tape, then transcribed to magnetic tape for handling by computer. The system is used to produce selected lists of references to match profiles of interests designated by individuals, the procedure known as selective dissemination of information (SDI). User profiles are fed into a computer where the cumulated abstracts are stored by means of punched cards and a matching process produces the appropriate list. A monthly abstracting publication is produced also.

Instead of selecting items from the current literature and storing them in a computer file, an individual library can use a service that supplies a broad selection from periodicals in pertinent fields on magnetic tape at frequent intervals. These can be used in conjunction with individual interest profiles for an SDI process. Brannon et al. (10) tell of the automated literature alerting system developed at Eli Lilly and Company using at first *Chemical Titles* KWIC tapes and then switching to the

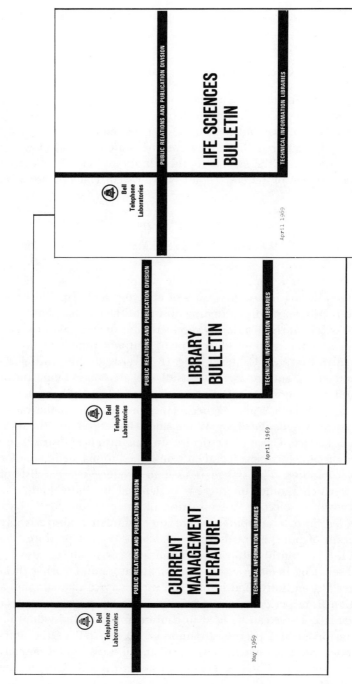

Figure 3. Covers of three Bell Telephone Laboratories Bulletins.

UNION TECHNIQUE INTERPROFESSIONNELLE DU BATIMENT ET DES TRAVAUX PUBLICS

DIRECTION GENERALE DE LA RECHERCHE

12, rue Brancion — PARIS 15ème

Téléphone : 828. 95-49 / 832. 21-69   Postes 348 & 426

BULLETIN SIGNALETIQUE

BIBLIOTHEQUE - DOCUMENTATION

MAI
1970

Figure 4

wider coverage provided by the Institute for Scientific Information in its ASCA service. Titles of an average 5600 articles are received weekly of which the nonpertinent can be deleted. For the profiles supplied to 82 registered participants from zero to 400 citations have been supplied from one week's batch, with a median of 70 to 80.

Where there is opportunity for the library to take advantage of using computer equipment, strong effort should be made to convince those in

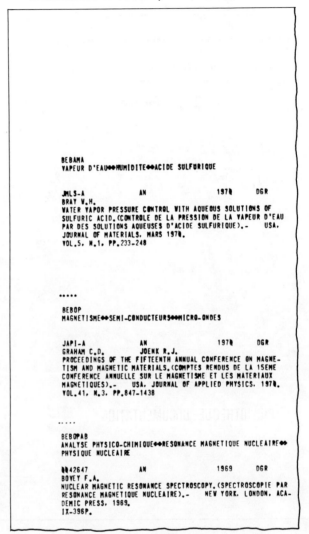

Figure 5. Sample page from bulletin shown as Figure 4.

authority that this is an excellent method for creating a store of selected information. However, the whole situation must be explored before undertaking something that may possibly be discontinued if other organizational activities eventually take precedence over this use of the computer. In this event traditional methods might be safer.

SCIENTIFIC LIBRARY BULLETIN

The Lilly Research Laboratories

March 3, 1969

SCIENTIFIC LIBRARY REMINDER
(Ninth in a series on services)

Special files available in the Library: (3) Copy Writers' Reference File. Direct mail advertising pieces of our competitors, as well as of Lilly, filed according to Lilly product with which they compete, or by pharmacological classification.

The following new books are being held for 60 days in the Scientific Library Reading Room for your examination:

ANNUAL REPORTS ON THE PROGRESS OF CHEMISTRY. V. 64B for 1967. London, The Chemical Society, 1968. (Periodical Stacks)

Dickens, F. CARBOHYDRATE METABOLISM AND ITS DISORDERS. V. 1 & 2. Academic Press, 1968. (QP 701 D5 1968)

Florkin, M. COMPREHENSIVE BIOCHEMISTRY. V. 23. Amer. Elsevier, 1969. (QP 509 F54 1968)

V. 23. Cytochemistry. Contents: Nucleus, by G. Siebert; The nucleolus, by H. Busch; Lysosomes, by A. L. Tappel; The cell-surface membrane, by R. Coleman and J. B. Finean; Microbial cytology, by M. R. J. Salton.

RECENT PROGRESS IN HORMONE RESEARCH. V. 24. Academic Press, 1968. (Periodical Stacks)

Eli Lilly & Co. was a sponsor. See attached pages for table of contents.

Teach, B.A. BIBLIOGRAPHY OF GERMFREE RESEARCH. (1885-1963). 1967 supp. (QH 324Z T4 1967)

REFERENCE AREA

PHARMACOPÉE FRANCAISE. 8th ed., lst Supplement. Moulins-les-Metz, Editions Maisonneuve S.A., 1968. [R] (RS 141.38 P5 1968)

Sax, N.I. DANGEROUS PROPERTIES OF INDUSTRIAL MATERIALS. 3d ed. Reinhold Publ. Co., 1968. [R] (T 55 S3 1968)

DEPARTMENTAL BOOK

Yates, M.L. THE SURFACE ENERGY OF PRE-CIPITATED PARTICLES. 1964. (Kept by L.C. Lappas)

TRANSLATION

Matsumoto, S., et al. Investigations of the ovulation suppressant action of 19-norsteroids in post-laparotomy patients. Geburtsh. Frauenheilk. 20:250-262, 1960. (Filed in Information File - Birth Control)

LILLY REPRINTS

Fuller, R.W. Influence of substrate in the inhibition of rat liver and brain monoamine oxidase. Arch. Int. Pharmacodyn. 174:32-37, 1968. (#1525)

Huber, F.M., Baltz, R.H. & Caltrider, P.G. Formation of desacetylcephalosporin C in cephalosporin C fermentation. Appl. Microbiol. 16:1011-14, 1968. (#1492)

NEW JOURNAL SUBSCRIPTION

FEBS LETTERS
V. 1- 1968-
See attached pages for first table of contents.

LOST OR MISPLACED

U. S. NATIONAL BUREAU OF STANDARDS, UNITS OF WEIGHT AND MEASURE. [R](B 32 U)

If anyone knows the whereabouts of this publication, please notify the Scientific Library.

Figure 6

Centralized Services

There are various special services designed to gather and supply at intervals collections of references from the literature published in

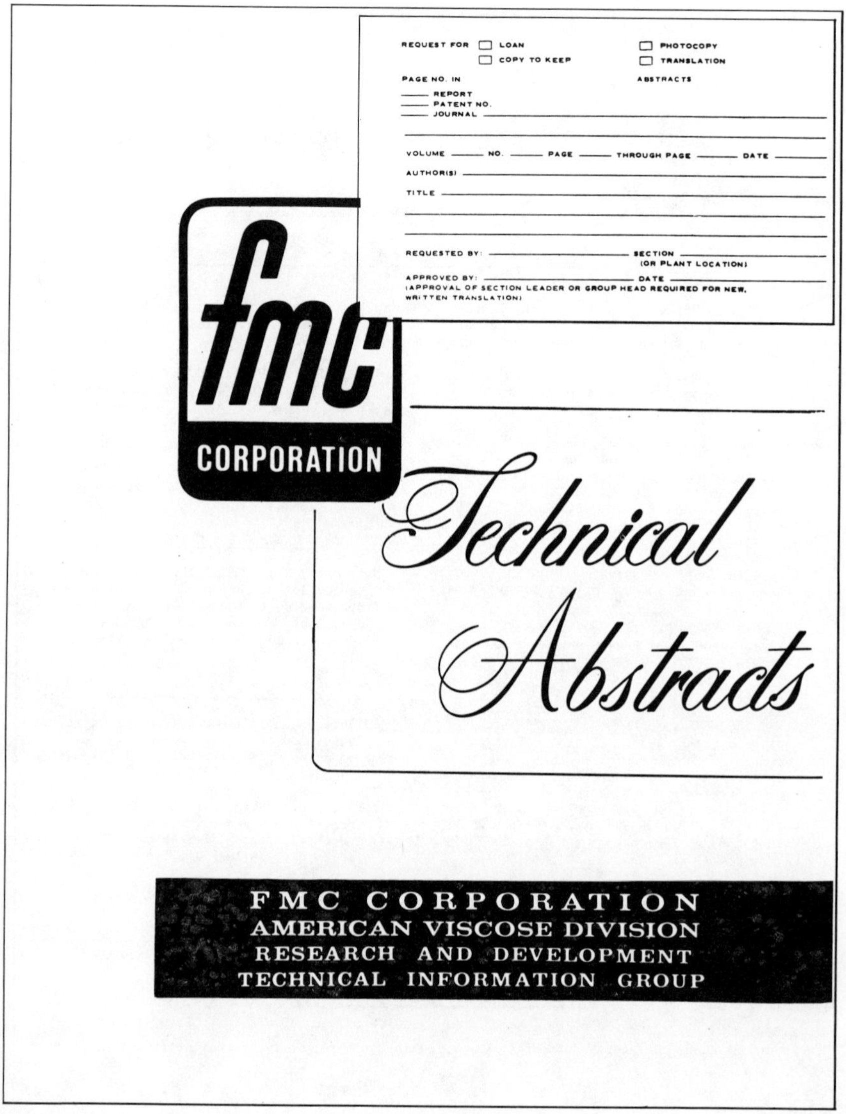

REQUEST FOR ☐ LOAN   ☐ PHOTOCOPY
                ☐ COPY TO KEEP   ☐ TRANSLATION
PAGE NO. IN   ABSTRACTS
_____ REPORT
_____ PATENT NO.
_____ JOURNAL _____

VOLUME _____ NO. _____ PAGE _____ THROUGH PAGE _____ DATE _____
AUTHOR(S) _____
TITLE _____

REQUESTED BY: _____ SECTION _____
                                         (OR PLANT LOCATION)
APPROVED BY: _____ DATE _____
(APPROVAL OF SECTION LEADER OR GROUP HEAD REQUIRED FOR NEW,
WRITTEN TRANSLATION)

fmc
CORPORATION

Technical Abstracts

FMC CORPORATION
AMERICAN VISCOSE DIVISION
RESEARCH AND DEVELOPMENT
TECHNICAL INFORMATION GROUP

Figure 7

specific subject areas. Some of these are so effective that they can supplant the need for an individually prepared bulletin or at least be relied upon for major coverage so that only some supplementary items are needed. Certain of these services are co-products of major abstracting publications; others utilize a number of data bases to provide selected informa-

Abstracts on
IRON AND STEEL MANUFACTURING

ESSO RESEARCH AND ENGINEERING COMPANY

This bulletin includes *Abstracts of Iron and Steel Manufacturing* that relate to the business of the Company. It is issued monthly by the Technical Information Section of Esso Research and Engineering Company's Analytical and Information Division, at Linden, N.J. Questions concerning circulation of this bulletin should be addressed to TIS Publications Distribution, ERC Building No. 8, Ext. 2636.

J. J. GWIRTSMAN, *Editor*

Volume 9	February 1969	Number 2

Table of Contents

HOW TO REQUEST DOCUMENTS

The services described below are available ONLY to New Jersey readers, except that New York City readers may borrow documents or longer abstracts already in the ERC Library. All other readers should direct their requests to local libraries.

LIBRARY DOCUMENT REQUEST forms (available from ERC and EEC stock rooms) must be used for requesting documents. *Complete bibliographical references must be filled in.* Send completed forms to the ERC Library (Linden) or the EIC Library (Florham Park).

ARTICLES, PREPRINTS, AND THESES abstracted in this issue are available in the ERC Library *unless* the abbreviation "abstr" precedes the last journal reference in the bibliographical listing or is part of the name of the last-cited journal. When this occurs, the ERC Library usually does not have the original document, but it will attempt to obtain a copy for you if you write "Order" after the abstract number. Otherwise, you will receive either an original document (or a "longer abstract") if the Library has it, or a notice that it doesn't, asking for exact further instructions. *U.S. GOVERNMENT REPORTS* are also not uniformly available, and *ORIGINAL PATENT SPECIFICATIONS* are available only when cited without a journal reference. For either, mark "Order" when you must have the original. Foreign patents take 2-4 weeks or more to obtain, however.

LANGUAGES OF THE ORIGINAL DOCUMENTS are given in parentheses at the end of the literature abstracts for non-English documents, and for English documents in foreign-language journals. *On-the-spot interpretations* of available documents may be requested at Linden by asking for the translations librarian (ERC Ext. 2351); *for complete, written translations,* send her a purchase order. *At Florham Park,* all translations should be requested through the EIC.

Figure 8

tion from a broad range of sources. Most of the selective dissemination provisions began operation in the mid-1960s; at least this is true for those offering computerized searching. In 1969 the Reference Services Division of the American Library Association published an initial

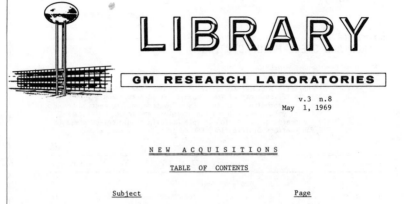

Figure 9

survey of what was being offered in a pamphlet entitled *A Guide to a Selection of Computer-Based Science and Technology Reference Services in the U.S.A.*

A number of these SDI services are listed here to indicate the types

65 North Atlantic Treaty Organization. Advisory group for aerospace & development AIR
Properties of air and combustion products with kerosine POLLUTION
and hydrogen fuels. Bristol, England. Bristol Siddeley
Engines Ltd., 1967. 13 volumes. (541.3600 N862 1967)
Volume titles: v.1 Thermodynamic properties and
equilibrium composition -- Air; v.2: Thermodynamic properties
for fuel-weak mixtures -- C_nH_{2n}/Air; v.3 Equilibrium composition for fuel-weak mixtures -- C_nH_{2n}/Air; v.4 Equilibrium
composition for fuel-weak mixtures -- C_nH_{2n}/Air; v.5 Thermodynamic properties for stoichiometric and fuel-rich mixtures --
C_nH_{2n}/Air; v.6 Equilibrium composition for stoichiometric and
fuel-rich mixtures -- C_nH_{2n}/Air; v.7 Equilibrium composition
for fuel-rich mixtures -- C_nH_{2n}/Air; v.8 Thermodynamic properties
for fuel-weak mixtures -- Hydrogen/Air; v.9 Equilibrium composition for fuel-weak mixtures -- Hydrogen/Air; v.10 Equilibrium
composition for fuel-weak mixtures -- Hydrogen/Air; v.11 Thermodynamic properties for stoichiometric and fuel-rich mixtures --
Hydrogen/Air; v.12 Equilibrium composition for stoichiometric
and fuel-rich mixtures -- Hydrogen/Air; v.13 Equilibrium composition for fuel-rich mixtures -- Hydrogen/Air.

Figure 10. Sample item from bulletin shown as Figure 9.

that are available. Some offer broad coverage in one subject area; others, as has already been indicated, are prepared to meet specific "profile of interest" requirements. Preliminary investigation is recommended before contracting with any such supplier to be certain that they fulfill require- ments. A list of representative ones follows:

Major Abstracting or Indexing Publication Projects

API Abstracts of Refining Literature, and *API Abstracts of Refining Patents,* Amer- ican Petroleum Institute, Central Abstracting Service, 50 West 50th St., New York, 10020. Weekly issues as bulletins and on cards. Also on film. For production litera- ture: *Petroleum Abstracts,* University of Tulsa, Department of Information Ser- vices, Tulsa, Okla.

Biological Abstracts, Biosciences Information Service, 2100 Arch St., Philadelphia, Pa. 19103. Offers abstracts and bioresearch index on tape. BA Previews. Tapes avail- able five weeks in advance of printed version.

Chemical Abstracts Service, P.O. Box 1378, Columbus, Ohio 43216. Additional services include *Chemical Titles,* printed or on magnetic tape. Also *Chemical-Biological Activities* and *Polymer Science & Technology* on tape.

Engineering Index, Inc., 345 East 47th St., New York, 10017. Weekly card service called Card-A-Lert, selected subject fields possible. Also weekly tapes, designated as Compendex.

Excerpta Medica, 2 East 103d St., New York, 10029. Current references on magnetic tapes.

Index Medicus, National Library of Medicine, Bethesda, Md. Also from NLM, *MEDLARS (Medical Library Automated Retrieval System)* selective searching ser- vice.

Institute for Scientific Information, 325 Chestnut St., Philadelphia, Pa. 19106. Pub- lishes four *Current Contents* titles: *Life Sciences; Physical & Chemical Sciences;*

$\mathcal{A}$merican $\mathcal{H}$ospital $\mathcal{A}$ssociation

840 NORTH LAKE SHORE DRIVE   CHICAGO, ILLINOIS 60611

TELEPHONE 312 645-9400 / CABLE ADDRESS: AMHOSP

RECENT ACQUISITIONS
* IN THE
LIBRARY OF THE AMERICAN HOSPITAL ASSOCIATION
ASA S. BACON MEMORIAL

February 1969

ACCOUNTING
  Geaney, Michael Joseph, Jr. Determination of the effect of size
  variation on hospital departmental expenses in Connecticut. (Thesis)
  New Haven, Conn., Department of Epidemiology and Public Health, Yale
  University, 1968. 56p. (HF5687 G29)

ADMINISTRATION
  National Industrial Conference Board. Developing managers in the
  smaller company. (Managing the moderate-sized company, no. 8) New
  York, The Board, 1968. 33p. $1.00 to members, $5.00 to nonmembers
  (HF5500 N26 M8)

  Odiorne, George S. Management decisions by objectives. Englewood
  Cliffs, N.J., Prentice-Hall, Inc., 1969. 252p. $8.95 (HF5500 O24)

AUTOMATION
  British Medical Bulletin. Computing in medicine. (BRITISH MEDICAL
  BULLETIN, v.24, no.3, September 1968) London, Medical Department,
  The British Council, 1968. $6.50 per single issue (HD6331 B86)

COST OF MEDICAL CARE
  U.S. Dept. of Health, Education, and Welfare. Secretary's Regional
  Conference on Health Care Costs; summary, Washington, The Depart-
  ment, 1968. (RA410 U66r 1968)

DISASTER SERVICE
  Rowe, Bobby G. Application of computer simulation techniques to an
  Air Force Casualty Staging Flight. (Thesis) New Haven, Conn., Department of Epidemiology and Public Health, Yale University, 1968.
  130p. (HV556 R87)

> RECENT ACQUISITIONS should be considered a "buying" rather than a
> "borrowing" guide. Order through your local book dealer or direct
> from the publisher whose address your librarian will help you find.
>
> If you wish to borrow rather than buy any of these titles, please
> use local and regional library resources whenever possible. The
> Library of the American Hospital Association cannot acquire copies
> in sufficient quantity to meet the demand created by the inter-
> national distribution of this list. And remember, please--our loan
> service is limited to staff and members of the Association.

Figure 11

Agricultural, Food & Veterinary Sciences; Engineering & Technology. Each is weekly. Offers also the store of cumulated references on magnetic tape, and a searching service tailored to individual interest profiles called ASCA, Automatic Subject Citation Alert.

Institute of Electrical and Electronics Engineers, Inc., **IEEE** Information Services, 345

E. 47th St., New York, 10017. Monthly tape service, covers own publications and all other publications relating to the relevant subjects.

Physics Abstracts, American Institute of Physics, 335 East 45th St., New York, 10017. Monthly magnetic tape service. Also for quick dissemination, *Current Physics Titles.*

Derwent Publications Ltd., Rochdale House, 128 Theobalds Road, W.C.1, England. Provides several selective subject field services printed and on tapes: *Patents Abstracts Publications, FARMDOC (Pharmaceutical Patents Documentation), AGDOC (Agricultural Patents Documentation), PLASDOC (Plastics and Polymers Patents Documentation), ORGANODOC (Organic Chemicals Patents Documentation), RINGDOC (Pharmaceutical Literature Documentation), VETDOC (Veterinary Literature Documentation), RINGDOC.* Profiles 42 subject areas in chemicomedical sciences.

Automated Services Utilizing Several Data Bases

Computer Search Center, Illinois Institute of Technology Research Institute, 10 West 35th St., Chicago, Ill. 60616. Uses tapes from *Chemical Abstracts, Biological Abstracts, Engineering Index,* and *Institute for Scientific Information.*

Information Science, Computer Center, University of Georgia, Athens, Ga. 30601. Uses tapes from *Biological Abstracts, Chemical Abstracts,* and *Nuclear Science Abstracts.*

Knowledge Availability Systems Center, University of Pittsburgh, Pittsburgh, Pa. 15213. Searches tapes from NASA (National Aeronautics and Space Administration), Chemical Abstracts Service, DDC (Department of Defense Documentation Center), and *Engineering Index.*

CONCLUSION

Each situation must be analyzed to determine the best method of keeping the clientele informed of pertinent information as it is published. Any method can be used, or as is more likely, a combination, ranging from personal notifications to a universal bulletin, will be utilized by an alert library staff. It may take some experimenting to determine the most effective methods for bringing the facts to those who can advance the work of the organization.

REFERENCES

1. J. R. A. Walker, *Information Bulletins in Special Libraries: Backgrounds. Problems. Practice.,* The Library Association, London, 1966.
2. W. Sewell, "Problems of Issuing a Company Pharmaceutical Abstract Bulletin," *Spec. Libr.* **45**, 63–66 (1954).
3. J. W. Mohlman, "Costs of an Abstracting Program," *J. Chem. Doc.* **1**, 64–67 (1961).
4. K. G. Ford, "Use of Library Bulletins," *Spec. Libr.* **46**, 451–455 (1955).

5. L. Jackson, "Some Observations on Fifty Technical Library Bulletins," *Spec. Libr.* 44, 366–369 (1953).

6. K. G. Blair, "Engineering Library Bulletins," *Spec. Libr.* 52, 175–182 (1961).

7. S. Hocken, "Disseminating Current Information," *Spec. Libr.* 53, 93–95 (1962).

8. H. Skolnik and R. E. Curtis, "Mechanized Information System for Many Outputs from One Input," *J. Chem. Doc.* 8, 41–45 (1968).

9. M. A. Wolfe and S. Herner, "SDI System for the U.S. Public Health Service, Office of Pesticides," *J. Chem. Doc.* 7, 138–147 (1968).

10. P. B. Brannon, D. F. Burnham, R. M. James, and L. E. Bertram, "Automated Literature Alerting System," *Amer. Doc.* 20, 16–20 (1969).

BIBLIOGRAPHY

Bennett, R. E. and S. J. Frycki, "Internal Processing of External Reference Services," *J. Chem. Doc.* 11, 76–83 (1971).

Costello, M. A. and H. Voos, "Preparation of an Information Bulletin," *Spec. Libr.* 50, 454–455 (1959).

Friedenstein, H., "Alerting with Internal Abstract Bulletins," *J. Chem. Doc.* 5, 154–157 (1965).

Frome, J., "An Experimental Approach to Current Awareness," *J. Chem. Doc.* 7, 135–137 (1967).

Hanson, C. W., "Deciding What to Read to Keep Informed," *Engineering* 190, 378–379 (September 16, 1960).

McKenna, F. E., "An Abstract Bulletin for Corporate R & D Reports," *Spec. Libr.* 56, 318–322 (1965).

Moss, W. R., "Individual Abstracts Versus Bulletins," *Aslib Proc.* 11, 102–105 (1959).

Page, S. B., "The Production of Library Publications," *Aslib Proc.* 16, 165–175 (1964).

Skolnik, H. and W. R. Paulson, "A New Posting Method for the Preparation of a Cumulative List," *J. Chem. Doc.* 3, 21–24 (1963).

"Symposium on Methods of Alerting Chemists to New Developments," *J. Chem. Doc.* 5, 123–172 (1965).

11

Reference Procedures and Literature Searches

The previous chapters in this book were concerned primarily with methods of organizing a library service, the development of a well-selected collection of source materials, and effective administrative procedures. All of this is in preparation of the foundation from which the real purpose of supplying information can proceed. Efficiency in the establishment of the groundwork will affect both major groups of users, the library staff as it is called upon to produce information, and the clientele that either tend to request assistance for all requirements or find it satisfying to consult directly the inviting stocks of materials arranged for easy access to read, borrow, or copy.

However, the collection that can be assembled in any one library cannot be adequate to supply answers to all potential queries, and there must be an awareness of the whole vast record of scientific and technical information diffused in countless repositories, small and large, in all countries where scientific investigation is of concern. The term "information retrieval," so pervasive in the literature of recent years, can truly be applied for any action taken to locate particular specified information. It has, in fact, come into popular usage concurrently with the employment of computers and other mechanized systems for the literature searching process. All possible methods of approach should, of course, be utilized in searching for whatever is requested legitimately by any person whom the library is to serve.

The reference information service of the library is divided into two categories: (*1*) the answering of relatively simple requests for brief facts or simple data, usually called "reference questions;" and (*2*) the supplying of either complete or selected information on specified subjects requiring a methodical search of the literature. A staff member must always be available to fulfill either type of request. In large organizations where many diversified projects involve investigation, provision must be made for full-time literature searchers.

A reference specialist in action is illustrated in Figure 1.

It is common practice to have as member of a research team pursuing scientific investigation one person whose chief assignment is to do whatever consultation of the literature is necessary to aid the project. This person may be a member of either the library or laboratory staff. The number of such literature scientists required will obviously depend upon the scope and diversity of the research program. Kent and Perry (1) describe some ways in which literature specialists function on research teams. They illustrate graphically the possible organizational relationships where the literature scientists are placed in both types of situations.

In this chapter the scientific literature is discussed in its broadest aspects with a view toward providing a guide for organizing reference procedures and literature searches. Various aids for finding the source publications of· specific fields are cited. The patent literature is considered separately. Finally, some methods of achieving the answers to the questions asked in a science library are suggested.

THE LITERATURE OF SCIENCE AND RELATED TECHNOLOGIES

The literature of science, theoretical and applied, is voluminous, and much of it is remarkably well organized for locating specific subject information. There are many guides to the contents of thousands of periodicals. There are classified listings of reference publications. As might be expected, some subject fields are better served by existing indexing and abstracting publications than others while continuous efforts are being made to improve methods of communicating information in all areas. It is toward this end that mechanical and electronic devices are being designed in a grand attempt to make all knowledge accessible.

However difficult the situation may seem now, it is possible to locate much information without undue cost or effort. In viewing broadly the whole scientific literature, it becomes apparent that there are relatively few basic types of publications in each subject area. These include (*1*)

Figure 1. Reference librarian with user. (Charles C. Lauritsen Library, Aerospace Corp.)

periodicals in which results of original research are reported and applications described, (2) abstracting and indexing periodicals, (3) books as texts and monographic works, (4) technical reports from government- and industry-sponsored research, (5) compilations of data or handbooks, (6) dictionaries, (7) encyclopedic works, (8) comprehensive treatises, (9) patents and (10) standards and specifications. The chapters of this book that deal with the selection of books, periodicals, and other unique publications should be helpful in developing a perspective of the literature to provide answers to reference questions.

Viewed as a whole this literature is enormous in volume, and therefore, if its potential value is to be realized, ways of locating every piece of factual information must be provided. This involves the problems of selecting, classifying, indexing, and filing in an individual library that is developing its own collection as well as those of those professional and governmental bodies that assist in coping with the literature. This situation has been a subject for attention at least since the 1940s; Ditmas (2) reviewed the efforts directed toward bibliographic control on an international scale. Studies of the state of the art as it stood in 1948 were summarized in the *Royal Society Scientific Information Conference Report* (3) in which extensive analyses of the difficulties attending the publication and subsequent retrieval of scientific information were presented.

The international situation was reviewed again in 1958 at an International Conference on Scientific Information held in Washington, D.C. (4). Many cogent papers were presented, analyzing all aspects of the increasingly complex problems, but the consensus was that in the years since the 1948 conference progress had been chiefly in gaining a better understanding of the difficulties rather than in finding their solutions. In the intervening years, because of the ever expanding growth of the scientific literature, the concomitant efforts to control it have not diminished. One major investigation sponsored in the United States resulted in a report issued in 1969 entitled *Scientific and Technical Communication: A Pressing National Problem and Recommendations for Its Solution* (5). While it presents a perceptive delineation of every possible phase of the situation, the suggestions for resolving matters are not likely to produce discernible results quickly in light of the varied reactions expressed in *Scientific Information Notes* (6) subsequent to its publication.

At the same time that the problems of the literature are considered in terms of an ultimate solution, actual publications must be used with the help of the existing guides. Despite the imperfections of the situation it is possible to locate with some ease the most significant information that has been published on most subjects investigated extensively. However, it is admitted that there are areas lying between broader fields, topics that are neither exactly physics nor engineering, for instance, yet related to both, for which information can be elusive.

To use the scientific and technical literature effectively, it is necessary to become thoroughly familiar with the abstracting publications, or indexes, and any special aids dealing with the area that a searcher is called upon to investigate. He must have enough knowledge of the subject to recognize its terminology. How many connotations are there for the word "sandwich?" Continuous reading of the literature keeps one aware of changing usage.

In the Appendix to this book lists of publications cover certain subject fields. The abstracting or indexing publications pertaining to broad areas are cited first, followed by those concerned with certain specific, narrow fields. There is some overlapping of coverage by the indexing publications. Experience alone can reveal exactly what should be consulted for effective coverage of a desired purpose.

There are many guides to the literature relating to specific scientific fields. They can be very helpful as introductions to sources if their existence is discovered at the right time by an inexperienced literature searcher. The most comprehensive compilation of such guides was published in 1958 by G. Schutze, 801 Crotona Park North, New York, 10060, and was entitled *Bibliography of Guides to the S-T-M (Science-Technology-Medicine) Literature,* which was followed by a supplement in 1962.

The sources to be consulted for the selection of books cited in Chapter 5 include some guides to the literature. Additional ones are cited in the Appendix of this book. Others are listed here because they provide advice and suggestions as to how to approach a literature searching project.

Some Guides to the Scientific-Technical Literature

American Chemical Society, *Advances in Chemistry Series* No. 30, *Searching the Chemical Literature,* Washington, D.C. (1961); No. 78, *Literature of Chemical Technology,* Washington, D.C. (1968). Based on two symposia held in 1963.

American Society for Engineering Education, Engineering School Libraries Division, Suite 400, One Dupont Circle, Washington, D.C. 20036. *Guide to Literature on Computers,* K. T. Quinn, 1970; *Guide to Literature on Electrical & Electronics Engineering,* R. L. Funkhauser, W. L. Corya, and J. M. Lucas, 1970; *Guide to Literature on Environmental Sciences,* R. McDonald, 1970; *Guide to Literature on Industrial Engineering,* E. Finley, 1970; *Guide to Literature on Mechanical Engineering,* J. K. K. Ho, 1970. Additional Guides in prospect on mining engineering, nuclear engineering, transportation engineering, and chemical engineering.

Blake, J. R. and C. Roos, *Medical Reference Books, 1679–1966,* Medical Library Association, Chicago, 1970.

Blanchard, J. R., and H. Ostvold, *Literature of Agricultural Research,* University of California Press, Berkeley and Los Angeles, 1958.

Bottle, R. T., *Use of the Chemical Literature,* 2nd ed., Butterworths, London, 1969.

Crane, E. J., A. Patterson, and E. B. Marr, 3rd ed., *A Guide to the Literature of Chemistry,* Wiley, New York, 1957.

Dalton, B. H., *Sources of Engineering Information,* U. of California Press, Berkeley and Los Angeles, Calif., 1948.

Gibson, E. B., and E. W. Tapia, Eds., *Guide to Metallurgical Information,* 2nd ed., SLA Bibliography No. 3, SLA, New York, 1965.

Goldman, S., *Guide to the Literature of Engineering, Mathematics, and the Physical Sciences,* The Johns Hopkins University Applied Physics Laboratory, Baltimore, Md., 1959.

Herner, S., *A Brief Guide to Sources of Scientific and Technical Information,* Information Resources Press, Washington, 1969.

Holm, B. E., *How to Manage Your Information*, Reinhold, New York, 1968. Includes information systems for the engineer, chemist, physicist, doctor, architect, archivist.

Holmstrom, J. E., *Records and Research in Engineering and Industrial Science*, 3rd ed., Chapman and Hall, London, 1956.

Houghton, B., *Technical Information Sources, a Guide to Patents, Standards, and Technical Reports*, Archon Books, Hamden, Conn., 1967.

Interscience Guides to Information Sources in Science and Technology, Vol. 1, *Space Science and Technology*, B. M. Fry and F. E. Mohrhardt, Interscience-Wiley, New York, 1963; Vol. 2, *Mining, Minerals, and Geosciences*, S. R. Kaplan, Interscience-Wiley, New York, 1965.

Jenkins, F. B., *Science Reference Sources* 5th ed., MIT Press, Cambridge, Mass., 1969.

Landuyt, M., *Bibliography of Engineering Abstracting Services*, SLA Bibliography No. 1, SLA, New York, 1955.

Malinowsky, H. R., *Scientific and Engineering Reference Sources: A Guide for Students and Librarians*, Libraries Unlimited, Rochester, N. Y., 1967.

Mellon, M. G., *Chemical Publications: Their Nature and Use*, 4th ed., McGraw-Hill, New York, 1965.

Parke, N. G., III, *Guide to the Literature of Mathematics and Physics*, 2nd ed., Dover, New York, 1958.

Pearl, R. M., *Guide to Geologic Literature*, McGraw-Hill, New York, 1951.

Randle, G. R., *Electronic Industries: Information Sources*, Gale Research Co., Detroit, 1968.

Sternberg, V. A., *How to Locate Technical Information*, Prentice-Hall, Englewood Cliffs, N.J., 1964.

Whitford, R. H., *Physics Literature, A Reference Manual*, 2nd ed., Scarecrow, Metuchen, N. J., 1968.

Wright, J. K., *Aids to Geographical Research: Bibliographies, Periodicals, Atlases, Gazetteers, and Other Reference Books*, Columbia University Press, New York, 1947.

Yates, B., *How to Find Out About Physics*, Pergamon, New York, 1965.

Unusual Resources

In the process of considering resources for supplying needed information, the immediate collection is not the only source to be consulted; if answers are not to be found there, other possible aids may be tapped. Libraries in the same geographic area can be called upon, especially if there is a developed awareness of the benefits of fostering interrelations among special libraries, as Budington (7) has outlined so perceptively. As the idea of national networks expands, proposals for which are discussed by Knox (8) and Weinstock (9), there will be an even wider prospect to which to resort.

Additionally, there are two important nationally centralized services that have been established in the United States that are unique. One is the record maintained at the Smithsonian Institution in Washington, D.C. described by Freeman (10), and called Science Information Exchange. This consists of a register of research planned or in progress as reported by many organizations willing to reveal their activities. Such a service can sometimes provide information not found in print. The second of these services is the National Referral Center for Science and Technology, sponsored by the Library of Congress. As the name implies, the procedure is to supply a requester with the names of places where information relating to his problem may be forthcoming. Thus it is possible to reach some basic sources by taking advantage of these well-administered offices. The Center is providing published compilations such as the *Directory of Information Resources in the United States: General Toxicology,* which is available from the Government Printing Office, Washington, D.C. 20402 (1970).

A somewhat novel method of locating information relevant to a subject is through the tracing of citations. If one or two good articles are known, and the succeeding articles that refer to them subsequently can be located, theoretically a web of interrelating facts can be disclosed. The proponents of this idea of citation indexing defend it against the direct search by indexed subjects. Chief of the defenders and active propagator is Eugene Garfield whose confidence has led to the publication of the *Science Citation Index,* which first appeared in 1963 and by the late 1960s was being issued quarterly. Garfield (11) supports this thesis of interconnection as a "new dimension in indexing," but Mathews (12) reveals some inherent problems. For one example, significant references could be lost from the literature store if for some reason they are not cited by others. Other ensuing difficulties happen for such simple reasons as differences in the representation of authors names, for example, Muller, Müller, or Mueller can refer to the same individual.

It is possible to evolve an individual search using the citation technique by taking advantage of the bibliographies appended to a few known authoritative papers. Rafter (13) reports a detailed investigation of citation patterns by this procedure.

PROCEDURES FOR RECORDING REQUESTS FOR INFORMATION

It is good practice to establish a system for recording reference requests in a uniform manner, with provision for noting all relevant details when questions are presented. This is not necessary for the quickly answered reference question, although it is advisable to have a record of everything that requires some intellectual effort to fulfill. Notation in a notebook is adequate, and it is particularly important to enter immediately those elusive queries that are not answered satisfactorily. Consultation with other members of the staff can sometimes bring to mind another approach that will produce the needed facts. The volume and nature of this record prove the need for additional staff.

In the case of requests for extensive literature searches, it is ˙helpful to both the inquirer and the person who is to execute the search to have a written record of what is required. The information that is wanted must be clearly defined, the period of coverage indicated if there is a possible limiting date, sources to be searched may be suggested, and any other aids noted that the requester can supply. A form such as the following might be used for this purpose.

Library Search Request

Requested by
Date
Subject of search
To be reported as:
  Specific facts, citing sources
  Complete bibliography
  List of selected references only
  Annotations or abstracts
  Pertinent quotations
  Summarized report
Sources to be searched:
  Books
  Abstracting and indexing publications
  Information files
  Laboratory reports
  U. S. patents (or other countries)
  Computer store (on premises or outside sources)
Name of staff member accepting request
To be completed by
Delivery Date

After the search has been completed, the request sheet should be added to a permanent file. Questions sometimes recur or follow a pattern, and knowledge of this can be useful. This file can even be helpful as an aid to new staff members who will become oriented more quickly if they can review a representative selection of information requests.

There are situations where only information that is being published currently or was published just prior to the time is of concern. It is in these instances that the centralized services are likely to be of particular help. They can be used either on a continuing subscription basis or for individual searches. Many of them operate from computerized stores so that they can supply bibliographies on computer tape, if this can be utilized on the purchaser's equipment, or a printout in legible form or on microfilm. Among these searching services are the following:

American Institute of Physics, 334 East 45th St., New York, 10017. Monthly magnetic tapes; bibliographies in specific subject areas.

American Petroleum Institute, 555 Madison Ave., New York, 10016. *API Abstracts of Refining Literature* and *API Abstracts of Refining Patents*, both since 1961. Weekly, printed as bulletins and on cards. *API Abstracts of Air and Water Conservation Literature* and *API Abstracts of Air and Water Conservation Patents*, since 1970.

Biological Abstracts, Biosciences Information Service, 2100 Arch St., Philadelphia, Pa., 19103. Previews as tapes available five weeks in advance of printed version. Search service from January 1968.

Chemical Abstracts Service, The Ohio State University, Columbus, Ohio 43210. Available on magnetic tape are *CA Condensates*, the complete *Chemical Abstracts; Chemical Titles; CBAC, Chemical-Biological Activities; POST, Polymer Science and Technology; SSS, Substructure Search System*, from 1968.

Engineering Index, Marketing and Business Service Division, 345 East 47th St., New York, 10017. Service called Compendex, monthly on tape or cards, from 1969.

Excerpta Medica, New York Academy of Medicine Bldg., 2 East 103rd St., New York, 10029. Magnetic tape service, from 1969.

Institute for Scientific Information, 325 Chestnut St., Philadelphia, Pa. 19106. Bibliographic searches provided on computer tape or in print. Current service called Automatic Subject Citation Alert (ASCA).

Highway Research Information Service (HRIS), Highway Research Board, 2101 Constitution Ave. N.W., Washington, D.C. 20418. Bibliographies, copies of items supplied from computer store, from 1967.

National Library of Medicine, Bethesda, Md., Search service called Medical Literature Analysis and Retrieval System (MEDLARS). Computerized searching for professional individuals and groups in the health field.

Water Resources Scientific Information Center (WRSIC), Office of Water Resources Research, U. S. Dept. of the Interior, Washington, D.C.

National Aeronautics and Space Administration (NASA), Computerized search service in conjunction with its abstracting publication *STAR*.

Nuclear Science Abstracts, U. S. Atomic Energy Commission, Division of Technical Information. Since 1969 abstracts on tape, printouts of selected bibliographies.

International Nuclear Information System (INIS), sponsored by International Atomic Energy Agency. Bibliographies supplied on magnetic tape or microfilm. Service to start 1970.

Centers Providing Searching Service from Several Data Banks

In addition to the centers providing searching service from a single data bank encompassing their own resources only (usually limited to one subject area), others contract with several of the original producers of selected bibliographic items on computer tape in order to offer bibliographies from more than one source. Among those in operation in 1970 were the following:

United States

Aerospace Research Applications Center (ARAC), Indiana Memorial Union, Bloomington, Ind. 47401

American Petroleum Institute, Central Abstracting and Indexing Service, 1271 Avenue of the Americas, New York, 10020

Greater Louisville Technical Referral Center, University of Louisville, Speed Scientific School, Louisville, Ky. 40208

IIT Research Institute, Computer Search Center, 10 West 55th St., Chicago, Ill. 60616

University of Georgia, Computer Center, Athens, Ga. 30601

University of Iowa, Special Services, University Computer Center, East Hall, Iowa City, Iowa 52240

University of Pittsburgh, Knowledge Availability Systems Center (KASC), Pittsburgh, Pa. 15213

Canada

Alberta Information Retrieval Association, Research Council of Alberta, 11315 87th Ave., Edmonton 7, Alberta, Canada

National Science Library, Library Systems Analyst, National Research Council of Canada, 100 Sussex Drive, Ottawa 2, Ontario, Canada

KINDS OF REFERENCE QUESTIONS

Reference questions may be classified according to the nature of the information requested. In general, these are as follows:

1. For specific factual information. A single item or a group of related facts may be wanted. It may take a few seconds to locate a formula, a publication date, an address, or a physical constant. Such facts may also be elusive and require lengthy pursuit.
Examples:

Melting point and composition of beeswax
Address of the editor of the *Physical Review*
Price of naphthalene, C.P. grade
Composition of sterling silver
First metal spring, when and where made

2. For a few selected references concerning a specific subject. Background information regarding the development of a product or a process may be supplied in a brief list of selected references.

Examples:

Methods in current use for producing streptomycin
Applications of iodine as a tracer element
Publications by Dr. X of Y University for the past five years
Methods for removing ink from news print
Designs for a 3-phase electric melting furnace

3. For a comprehensive bibliography. A request may require the preparation of a systematic bibliography representing all information that can be found on a specific subject. Book and periodical references with only incidental patents may be adequate, or it may be necessary to do a complete patent search also. The procedure for executing an exhausive literature search as a process of compiling such a bibliography is outlined in a later section of this chapter.

Examples:

All published information on the coloring agents used in glass
Methods for the preparation of titanium metal
Drugs used for controlling blood pressure
Designs for television tubes
Pollutant controls for gasoline combustion engines
Methods for detecting residues of pesticides in animals

RESOURCES FOR ANSWERING REFERENCE QUESTIONS

In seeking to supply the answer to a reference question, one that requires an on-the-spot delivery of the specific bit of information, the possible sources for its location should first be reviewed mentally if it is at all devious. There must first be complete understanding of what is wanted, and this can sometimes be elicited only by asking further questions of the inquirer. He may ask, for example, for a certain kind of directory and not be aware that even though the library does not own such a publication, his information may be available in something else at hand.

As the approach to the answer is being sought, the potentially helpful directories, handbooks, encyclopedic works, special compilations, and such reference works that have been procured and assembled in an accessible place should be considered. One of the most important resources to be considered at this time are the files and indexes of information pertinent to the immediate interests of the organization. This file can be developed only over a period of time; the longer the library is in existence, the more significant the cumulation becomes. Items put in it are not easily located even though they are in print. Such facts as trade names, changed addresses, statistics, and the like will be added to the file when they are noted from current publications. Strieby (14) has provided a detailed description of the kinds of files that serve active demands in a pharmaceutical library. Here the accumulated records of selected abstracts of articles, remedies, names of companies, names of organizations, miscellaneous pamphlets, trade catalogs, telephone directories, and picture and history files provide facts that may be needed quickly. However, all queries cannot be anticipated in this way, and a question can make it necessary to ponder the most likely source for its answer.

The major types of reference works to be considered include the following; the order in which they are brought to mind will be determined by the nature of the question.

> Scientific dictionaries and encyclopedias
> Directories
> Handbooks
> Special compilations in specific subject fields
> Treatises and texts
> General reference works
> Bibliographies
> Telephone directories
> Compilations of statistics

Answers can sometimes be found in books whose titles do not reveal or even suggest all that they contain. Therefore, knowledge of the contents of the books in the collection as well as of the subjects involved is necessary if the materials at hand are to be used to their fullest extent. For example, a book on insecticides contains information about a trademarked aerosol needed in connection with a problem on mineral flotation. A book on chromatography tells something about the filtration of viruses. These possibilities are not apparent from the card catalog and the kind of personal knowledge that leads to such answers will be invaluable.

Some examples of questions that have been asked in a science-technology library have been supplied by Lane (15) who outlined the exact procedures followed for locating their answers:

Question. Information on the design of pumps for dredges.
Procedure to Answer. The word "dredges" led to "gold dredges" in the initial mental attack. This led to an entry in an index "pumps in

hydraulic service" which brought to mind a book entitled *Fire Service Hydraulics*. This contained designs of the type of pump required.

Question. A book or possibly an article in a journal by Taylor on the mechanics of compressible fluids.

Procedure to answer. Not knowing Taylor's initials precluded a search in an author index. Hence it was thought best to look in books on hydraulics. The index of Rouse's *Fluid Mechanics for Hydraulic Engineers* gave a reference to Taylor on page 367. On this page there was a footnote referring to mechanics of compressible fluids in Vol. 3, p. 217 of Durand's *Aerodynamic Theory*. Upon consultation of this volume it was found that the right Taylor had written the section.

Question. What is shot clay?

Procedure to answer. The term was not found in several dictionaries. However, in a volume of the *Agricultural Index* there was an entry under "clays" citing an article on "buckshot soil." This article was not in the library. In the *Index to Publications of the U.S. Dept. of Agriculture,* there was reference to a report in 1908 of the Office of Experiment Stations in which there was mention of drainage of buckshot soil near a small town in Georgia. The *Postal Guide* gave the county in which this town is located. By referring again to the *USDA Index,* a soil survey of the county was found, and in this it was stated that buckshot soil belonged to the Sharkey series.

Business problems may sometimes draw upon aspects of art and science before a search is completed. An illustration of this is reported by Jackson (16): "Two years ago I had to make extensive searches into pipe organ literature to find information that bore on the resonance of ram jet engines—both fields concerned vibrations in pipes, which phenomena were subject to the same physical laws." In another instance he (17) tells about GM designers asking for authentic Indian color and shape for the figure of a firebird to be placed on the prow of an experimental gas turbine automobile. The colored drawing for this was supplied when the librarian brought together the designer and an engineer whose hobby was Indian lore. Thus cross fertilization takes place in the library.

Swenson (18), in conformity with trends to systematize all library operations, has prepared a good chart to illustrate literature searching techniques. The several types of publications are shown in order of possible consultation. A further intention was to indicate their locations in the library as an added help.

The fastest way of supplying answers to reference questions, once they are located, is to make photocopies of the pertinent pages. In addition to being quick this eliminates the chances of errors in copying, particularly where tables of data are involved.

THE COMPREHENSIVE LITERATURE SEARCH

Before initiating a major literature search it may be advisable to determine whether the project is one that should be performed by the library staff. There are times when it may be wise to contract for it with an outside agency employing skilled professional searchers or with someone who works on a free-lance basis. Charges are usually by the hour. In busy times the expenditure is justified. A comprehensive guide to such services is the publication *Specialized Science Information Services in the United States: A Directory of Selected Specialized Information Services in the Physical and Biological Sciences,* which was issued by the National Science Foundation in November 1961. This was out of print by 1970 but copies are available in major libraries for consultation. It will probably be replaced by publications issuing from the National Referral Center at the Library of Congress. Examples of some literature searching services are the following:

John Crerar Library, Research Information Service, 10 West 35th St., Chicago, Ill. 60616

Engineering Societies Library, 345 East 47th St., New York, N. Y. 10017

The University of Akron, Center for Information Services, 302 East Buchtel Ave., Akron, Ohio 44304. Specializing in polymer and rubber chemistry.

Except for the one at the University of Akron, these searching services can undertake assignments in a broad range of subjects, and for as far back in time as may be needed; this is in contrast to those listed earlier in this chapter which are prepared to cover publications for only as far back as the early or mid-1960s.

However, it may well be that most serious literature searches will be done by members of the library staff. Systematic methods for doing them should be established.

PROCEDURES FOR A COMPREHENSIVE LITERATURE SEARCH

There are two main reasons for making a comprehensive search of the literature. One is to bring together all of the published information than can be found on a subject. The other is to locate certain specific facts concerning it. In either case coverage must be thorough if the results of the effort are to be submitted as conclusive. It may be adequate for some purposes to cover the book and periodical literature primarily and include patent references only incidentally, or it may be necessary to make an independent patent search. The two kinds of searches require different techniques and are discussed separately in this chapter. Either one results in a bibliography which may be presented in several ways. The organization of bibliographies is considered following the discussion of search procedures.

In setting up the plan of procedure for a search, the first step is to define what is to be sought, the necessity being greater when much time and effort are to be expended. Before any start is made a conference should be held between the person scheduled to perform the search and the one requesting it. There must be mutual understanding as to the scope of the investigation, points to be emphasized, and the possibility of related material that might be pertinent. The known history of the development of an art may be sufficiently definite to make it safe to establish a limiting date beyond which it would be unrewarding to go. Other factors such as patent situations will suggest relevant clues. Once the problem is defined, the outline for the search can be made.

Despite the fact that one of the chief characteristics of science is that of being systematic, the execution of a good literature search is an art. Though there are the obvious guides to the literatures of the several distinct subject fields of the physical and biological sciences, there are also reference aids that are unique to each one, some of which are not so readily discerned. Every expert searcher develops his own techniques, but certain general procedures are commonly followed. Berolzheimer (19) recommended that as a beginning the searcher acquaint himself with the subject upon which he is going to work by reading an article concerning its broadest aspects in a scientific or technical encyclopedia, making mental note of the terminology as a guide in using the indexes of abstracting publications.

Singer (20), another literature searcher of wide experience, has provided a well-documented warning of the pitfalls in scientific publications that the novice should heed, thereby avoiding stumbling into them as much as possible. The two attitudes that Singer considered to be imperative were imagination and scepticism. He cited examples of such traps as the use of varying terminologies, a practice certain to break the spirit of the most redoubtable electronic scanner, to say nothing of the patience of the human searcher.

Most literature searches are made in the organization's own library, but occasionally it will be desirable to know where unusual collections in certain fields are located. These may be in libraries freely accessible to public use, or if they are in private special libraries, permission to use them may be granted. There are several papers in the book, *Searching the Chemical Literature*, cited in the list of guides to the literature in this chapter that tell of the collections of chemical publications in some of the major chemical libraries. An invaluable source for the location of libraries in special subject fields is the compilation *Guide to Subject Collections*, published by Bowker, though some judgment must be exercised in detecting whether all collections cited can be of such size as to merit being rated as significant. Another is *Special Libraries and Information Centers* edited by Kruzas and published by Gale Research Company, 2nd edition, 1968.

If a particular search requires that all of the information published in books, periodicals, pamphlets, and any other source, published and unpublished, be found, the search should be carried forward through the following steps. (N. B. Advantage should be taken of any bibliographies that may be discovered in the course of the search.)

1. *For summarized information in comprehensive works.* These reference publications include the handbooks, dictionaries, and encyclopedias. One or two will be consulted initially for the searcher's own orientation. Specific data and other information may be found in them also. A little browsing in these compilations is likely to be rewarding.

2. *For information in texts, monographs, and special studies.* Assuming that the library acquires all books published that are pertinent to its interests, the card catalog will be the first place to look for the books dealing with the subject. Annual reviews and other serials, major treatises, and monographic works in the subject field should be sought. The information in these sources may be more up-to-date than that in the comprehensive works.

3. *For all relevant articles in the periodical and report literature.* This entails a complete search of the appropriate abstracting and indexing publications. It must be done in a rigidly systematic manner, keeping exact record of the sources consulted with note of the subject entries used in the indexes of each publication, and taking into account differences in indexing practice from one publication to another. This latter point is more important than it first appears. Sometimes it becomes necessary to alter the course of a search or to review it in the light of subsequent developments, and it is therefore expedient to be able to learn from the index search record exactly what topics have been covered thoroughly.

A form for keeping a proper record of a search in an abstracting periodical was developed by Lewton (21), which is shown as Figure 2. Though it is designed specifically for use with *Chemical Abstracts,* the scheme is adaptable to other publications of similar type. As a rule the best approach is to start with the most recent index to the abstracting or indexing publication that is available and work back. Reviews which include comprehensive bibliographies that may expedite the search will thereby be discovered and used. Furthermore, the perspective of the development of the subject is more revealing than when viewed from the forward direction.

Another form designed for use in the Cabot Corporation library is shown also as Figure 3.

Before starting a search in the abstracting publications, it is advisable to determine which ones cover the subject to be investigated most fully. In some areas there is a significant amount of duplication of periodicals abstracted, whereas others are not caught completely by any

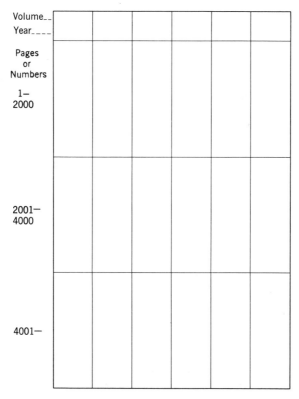

Figure 2. Form for page notations from *Chemical Abstracts Indexes.*

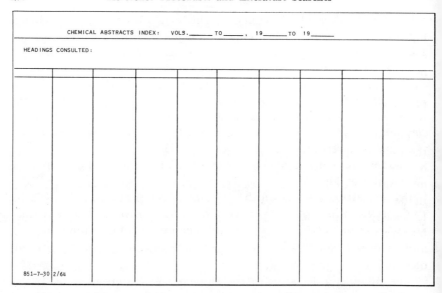

CHEMICAL ABSTRACTS INDEX: VOLS. _____ TO _____ ,   19 _____ TO   19 _____

HEADINGS CONSULTED:

851–7–30 | 2/64

Figure 3.   Index   Search   Record.   Cabot   Corp.   Billerica   Research   Center.

abstracting journal. When approaching a field in which the searcher has not had prior experience, he should first investigate the guides to the literature to determine which abstracting and indexing publications are indicated, then test them by sampling their coverage, thus deciding which ones to use. Those recommended for searches in the subject fields represented in the Appendix to this book are listed with the other pertinent publications.

After the appropriate abstracting publications have been determined, one must decide whether to consult first the comprehensive one encompassing a broad area and subsequently verify and expand the coverage by ultimately searching one dealing with the specific field only. For example, if the topic is concerned with a ferrous metallurgical process, *Chemical Abstracts* might be used first, after which the abstracts in the *Journal of the Iron and Steel Institute* could be searched for possible references not included in the first. Perhaps it might even be necessary to go as far as a third source such as the American Society for Metals' *Review of Metal Literature* before being satisfied that all possibilities have been exhausted. By 1970 these two metallurgical abstracting publications had merged as *Metals Abstracts*. Or the opposite procedure could be pursued, namely, to start with the specialized abstracts and then consult the comprehensive one. There is no other way of comparing their scope.

An important point to be considered in searching is the question of how far back in time to carry the investigation. If it is necessary to find everything that may ever have been published on the subject, attention must be given to the vagaries of the older literature. The field of chemistry, at least, has had an excellent guide into these less well-marked paths. Dyson's (22) paper on searching the older chemical literature is invaluable for tracing publications prior to 1875.

The effective use of indexes requires an analytical approach to discern the indexing pattern. It is an absolute necessity to follow the same line of thought, even though there might be disagreement with it, if maximum information is to be retrieved. Indexes to abstracting publications in the same field such as *Chemical Abstracts* and *Chemisches Zentralblatt*, for example, differ in indexing procedure. All aspects of a subject must be kept in mind when using an index, if the subject is at all complex, and changes in terminology accompanying developments over a period of time must be recognized.

The inherent difficulties in the indexing of scientific subjects have not been circumvented by any systems developed to this date. It may be that eventually a mechanical system will produce more interrelated facts, but the possibilities must always be anticipated while producing the code involved.

Another small difficulty to be kept in mind in using indexes is the various ways of transliterating the alphabets of foreign languages. The German umlaut must be regarded in detecting the alphabetizing procedure. A Russian language consonant may be indicated either as *Ts* or *Ch* and is found in both forms in different indexes.

As an example of the kind of imagination that must be brought into play in using indexes, Lewton (21) cited the following in a paper concerned with the art of searching the scientific literature:

For instance, a search was recently made on Rates of Diffusion of Swelling Agents and Reactants Through Cellulose Fibers. Upon consulting the indexes of *Chemical Abstracts* no entries were found under Cellulose or under Fibers using the words rates or penetration. To make an adequate survey of this subject it was necessary to search the following key words under both the main heads of Cellulose and of Fibers: 1) absorption, 2) dyes and indicators, penetration of, 3) structure, 4) grinding effect, 5) reactivity, 6) water sorption, 7) swelling, 8) degradation, 9) hydrolysis, as well as the commonly known reagents for cellulose, viz. NaOH (mercerization), cuprammonium, nitric acid, acetic acid (acetylation), carbon bisulfide (Xanthation), and to inspect all such abstracts, selecting only work with a kinetic approach, discarding that which was qualitatively descriptive. Thus, ability to analyze the subject into constituent aspects furnished the clues.

Some information published in certain journals is not noted in the indexing and abstracting publications. This is sometimes of possible concern for some search projects and it is difficult to locate. Even though an article is abstracted its full content is not always caught. This may be due to certain policies established by the publication rather than error on the part of abstracters. Rose (23) has observed, for example, that in one of the major chemical abstracting publications, chemical processes have not been covered with the same thoroughness as have compounds. Brief news items, announcements of the marketing of a new product, preliminary announcements of developments of one kind or another are the types of things that may not be considered worthy of being abstracted, yet may have great importance in certain kinds of searches.

4. *For information from miscellaneous sources.* Much potentially significant information is all but hidden in several types of publications. It can be found only if the searcher is acquainted with their possibilities. As he gains experience he develops a special sense that leads him to the facts needed, no matter how obscure their location. Among these special kinds of publications are the following.

Trade Literature

These publications issued by companies to advertise their products may be serials issued regularly and possibly indexed, or occasional pamphlets. Most company libraries maintain files of competitors' literature and index the most important items. Some of the large reference libraries, such as the Technology Department of Carnegie Library in Pittsburgh, have been collecting advertising literature for a long time, and their collections are invaluable. If it is known that a company manufactured a product some years back, or it is suspected that it might have, such a file will verify this. Part of this literature is noted by some of the abstracting publications; much of it is not.

Another approach is to inquire directly of a company that manufactures a certain product. This should be done only if permission is obtained from the person responsible for requesting the search.

Dissertations and Theses from Academic Institutions

These records of directed research done by students as part of the requirements for an advanced degree have already been cited in Chapter 5 of this book. Some Ph.D. dissertations are abstracted by the regular abstracting publications; no masters theses are abstracted though some information appearing in them may appear in journal articles. A periodical titled *Dissertation Abstracts International,* Section B, Sciences and Engineering (1957 to date), published by University Microfilms, provides abstracts of dissertations written at a large number of selected universities in the United States.*

Some institutions publish listings of their own dissertations and theses, and these may be consulted in university or major public libraries if they are not used enough to be purchased. The publication, *Doctoral Dissertations Accepted by American Universities,* 1933–1955, issued by H. W. Wilson Company, is a helpful source for the years it covered. In 1940 Palfrey and Coleman (24) published a *Guide to Bibliographies of Theses, United States and Canada,* 2nd edition.

Certain specific subject fields are served by important comprehensive publications. For physics there is *Dissertations in Physics, an Indexed Bibliography of All Doctoral Theses Accepted by American Universities, 1861–1959,* compiled by M. L. Marckworth and published by Stanford University Press in 1961. For chemistry there is the American Chemical Society's biennial, since 1957, publication, *Directory of Graduate Research: Faculties, Publications, and Doctoral Theses in Departments of Chemistry, Biochemistry, and Chemical Engineering at United States Universities.*

Universities in countries other than the United States also produce these academic publications. There are some national listings such as the *Catalogue des Thèses et Écrits Académiques* published annually in France, from 1884 to 1943, followed by *Bibliographie de la France,* 1930 to date. In Germany there is the annual, since 1885, *Jahres-Verzeichnis der an den deutschen Universitaten und Hochschulen erschienen Schriften.* In Great Britain Aslib publishes an annual *Index to Theses Accepted for Higher Degrees in the Universities of Great Britain and Ireland.* Other countries have published listings also. Many of these were cited by Stephens (25) in a paper on the subject of searching this literature.

Government Publications

Some publications issued either by government agencies or as a consequence of government-sponsored research are indexed in the standard indexing and abstracting sources. The best direct approach to those of the major, long-established agencies is through the *Monthly Catalog of United States Government Publications.* Also, such bodies as the National

---

* In 1969 a new approach to the contents of these scholarly publications was made available through a service called DATRIX, a computerized retrieval system that permits access through key words occurring in titles.

Bureau of Standards, the U. S. Bureau of Mines, the U. S. Department of Agriculture, and the U. S. Geological Survey provide cumulative lists of their own publications. Investigation of these compilations will reveal their potential usefulness in a particular area of inquiry.

In the years since World War II a new type of government publication, known as the "report literature," has become so voluminous that it is very difficult to locate the significant information presented in reports written as a result of investigations sponsored and supported by government funds. Work is done in industrial, educational, and professional organizations under contract with such governmental agencies as the Air Force, Atomic Energy Commission, and Office of Naval Research. There are thousands of projects and concomitantly, hundreds of thousands of reports, most of which are not cited by the standard indexing publications. Consequently, ways of making this mass of information available were necessary, and several publications are issued primarily as guides to the report literature. The most important ones are as follows.

Nuclear Science Abstracts, U. S. Atomic Energy Commission, 1944– . Published initially as *Abstracts of Declassified Documents.* Includes both reports and articles in periodicals.

United States Government Research & Development Reports, Clearinghouse for Federal Scientific and Technical Information, 1945– , Springfield, Va. 22151. Abstracts reports from many government sponsored sources.

Technical Abstracts Bulletin, Defense Documentation Center for Scientific and Technical Information, 1944– . Available only to those engaged in classified research.

Scientific and Technical Aerospace Reports (STAR), National Aeronautics and Space Administration, 1963– . Abstracts reports concerned with aeronautical and space research.

Discerning the scope of these publications is not easy. Certain reports have been found in at least three of them, others in two, some in only one. It is relatively easy to procure copies of the originals, particularly now that they are provided on microfiche.

Identifying a reference as a technical report is not difficult because it is designated usually by a combination of letters, such as HW, NYO, or BNL followed by numerals. There may be more than one set of identifying indicators. As a help in determining what these codes mean a very helpful *Dictionary of Report Series Codes* was compiled by Redman and Godfrey and published in 1962 by Special Libraries Association. It was in process of revision in 1970. Another aid is the cumulative index of report numbers that is issued in conjunction with *Nuclear Science Abstracts.* The situation concerning reports is not simple, but increasing familiarity with them makes it possible to locate whatever information they may contain that might be of use in a literature search.

Patents constitute a type of government publication that is so specialized and important to technical development that they are treated separately and in detail in a later section of this chapter.

Government agencies in countries other than the United States issue publications that may contain information of importance to a particular research problem if they can be located. In some instances there are bureaus such as the Department of Scientific and Industrial Research in Great Britain in which the divisions correspond to similar U. S. Government scientific research bureaus. The United Kingdom Atomic Energy Research Authority is a source in recent years of documents like those issuing from the U. S. Atomic Energy Commission (AEC). In fact, some British documents are listed in AEC abstracts and bibliographies.

Business Publications

Precise facts and figures pertinent to major business interests are necessary decision aids in most components of an industrial organization. Obvious reasons for this are discussed in Chapter 9. Business literature is as varied as business itself. Sources for its acquisition appear continuously; all need scanning regularly as timeliness is an important factor. Daniels (26) has revised an important annotated bibliography which should be consulted. Coman's (27) well-known book on business information sources has its special place on the reference shelf for quick consultation. Alexander (28) lists 1125 pamphlets, reprints, and paperbacks which contain useful data. Many articles on various categories of special files can be read, such as Billingsley's (29) paper on manufacturers' literature which she regards as an "information goldmine" for engineers as well as management groups.

Although there is no single indispensible comprehensive reference tool for all of the various aspects of the field, *Business Periodicals Index* (30) does cover subjects appearing in books and pamphlets as well as periodicals. It is especially useful for reference work if the library has storage facilities for the important periodicals indexed. As for books, if housing space is not available some titles might be obtained by interlibrary loan or ordered for different individuals; however, each method has its drawbacks. Another general source of information is *Management Index* (31). Two others listing current materials under special topics are *Business Literature* (32) and *Business and Technology Sources* (33). The current indexes of the *New York Times* and *Wall Street Journal* are major sources of business news. *Public Affairs Information Service* with a different emphasis is helpful in listing government publications of interest to business activities. Directories and one or two investment services may be needed. Even periodicals of general interest such as *Business Week* and *Fortune* can be good sources for needed facts, as well as those dealing directly with administration such as the aforementioned *Management Week*. The publisher of this latter title, the American Management Association, also is cognizant of problems of information science for business, the subject of some special reports.

Personal Sources

The acquaintance of persons in positions where they have access to information in the subject fields of interest should be cultivated. Librarians, research workers, statistical analysts, information scientists, and any other professional experts should be called upon for advice at times when help is needed. Of course the situation must be a reciprocal one with the inquirer ready to be of assistance too. It is usually wise, however, to obtain approval before asking for information outside the organization in case the subject is confidential.

Recording of References

When making a literature search it is vital that whatever notes are made of the selected citations be legible, complete, and amenable to arrangement in whatever order may ultimately be desired. These notes may be taken by hand, read into a dictating device for later transcription, or photocopied. Another procedure is for the searcher to prepare the record of the search by noting only the index entries, these to be given to a typist for location and copying the references.

Another method for locating and recording abstracts was introduced by Chemical Abstracts Service in 1965 when the file was made available on microfilm. The actual searching must still be done in the printed indexes, although there is suggestion that even these might eventually be filmed. The individual references are read by placing the film cartridges in a reader-printer, running it to the page upon which the abstract appears, then either reading it or making an immediate copy. Weil (34) was one of the first to adopt this system and reported its enthusiastic acceptance at Esso Research Laboratories. Actually, it is not always faster to locate an individual abstract by this means, and a procedure is needed to handle a sheaf of copied pages, each of which bears only one abstract of concern.

Every literature searcher will develop his own way of taking notes of references. He will soon appreciate the necessity for being systematic and careful, especially if he has had the frustrating experience of having to relocate citations because complete identification was not noted when they were first read. An error or omission can cause much wasted time as it always seems to take twice as long to relocate what was once found so easily.

For an article in a journal the complete reference includes the author, title of the article, title of the journal, volume number (if used), issue number (if necessary), inclusive pages, and date. Indication of the indexing or abstracting source is usually a good safety factor. For a book, the author, title, publisher, edition, and date of publication are all significant. The test of a citation is whether it provides adequate identification for anyone else to relocate it. Some examples of references are shown here.

Articles from Periodicals

1. "Self-Induced Relief of Airframe Loads," Anon, *Engineering* **190**, 458 (September 30, 1960); *Appl. Sci. Tech. Ind.* **49**, 2 (1961).

2. Carroll, J. G., and R. O. Bolt, "Radiation effects on organic materials," *Nucleonics* **18**, No. 9, 78–83 (1960); *C.A.* **55**, 85.

3. Phillpott, J., "Irreversibility in Interacting Spin Systems," *Phys. Rev.* **119**, 1803–1807 (1960).

Books

1. Stevens, G. W. W., *Microphotography*, 2nd ed., Wiley 1968, Chap. 9, "Microphotographic Technique."

2. West, W., "Spectroscopy and Spectrophotometry in the Visible and Ultraviolet," in *Technique of Organic Chemistry*, Vol. I, Part 3, A. Weissberger, ed., Interscience, 1959.

Pamphlets

Gibson, K. S., *Spectrophotometry*, U. S. Natl. Bur. Standards Circ. 484, 1949.

These are only a few examples of ways in which citations might be made. Several points are matters of personal preference; whether to put author or title first may be important only to the person making the compilation.

References may be noted on plain cards or slips of uniform size, always being consistent in the manner of taking notes. In some libraries colors are used for different types of sources searched. Where many important bibliographic searches are undertaken, printed forms such as are illustrated in Figures 4–7 are used. They can be set up in any way that suits a particular situation. Cards for use with sorting devices are shown as Figures 8–10. These are the type known as "punched" cards. The

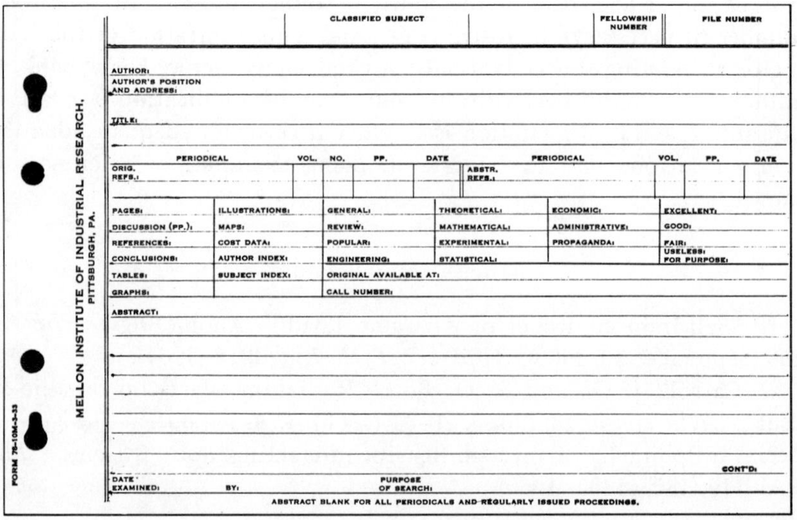
FORM 75-10M-3-33
MELLON INSTITUTE OF INDUSTRIAL RESEARCH, PITTSBURGH, PA.

CLASSIFIED SUBJECT | FELLOWSHIP NUMBER | FILE NUMBER

AUTHOR:
AUTHOR'S POSITION AND ADDRESS:
TITLE:

PERIODICAL | VOL. | NO. | PP. | DATE | PERIODICAL | VOL. | PP. | DATE
ORIG. REFS.: | ABSTR. REFS.:

PAGES: | ILLUSTRATIONS: | GENERAL: | THEORETICAL: | ECONOMIC: | EXCELLENT:
DISCUSSION (PP.): | MAPS: | REVIEW: | MATHEMATICAL: | ADMINISTRATIVE: | GOOD:
REFERENCES: | COST DATA: | POPULAR: | EXPERIMENTAL: | PROPAGANDA: | FAIR:
CONCLUSIONS: | AUTHOR INDEX: | ENGINEERING: | STATISTICAL: | USELESS: FOR PURPOSE:
TABLES: | SUBJECT INDEX: | ORIGINAL AVAILABLE AT:
GRAPHS: | CALL NUMBER:

ABSTRACT:

CONT'D:
DATE EXAMINED: BY: PURPOSE OF SEARCH:
ABSTRACT BLANK FOR ALL PERIODICALS AND REGULARLY ISSUED PROCEEDINGS.

Figure 4. Reference record form (Mellon Institute).

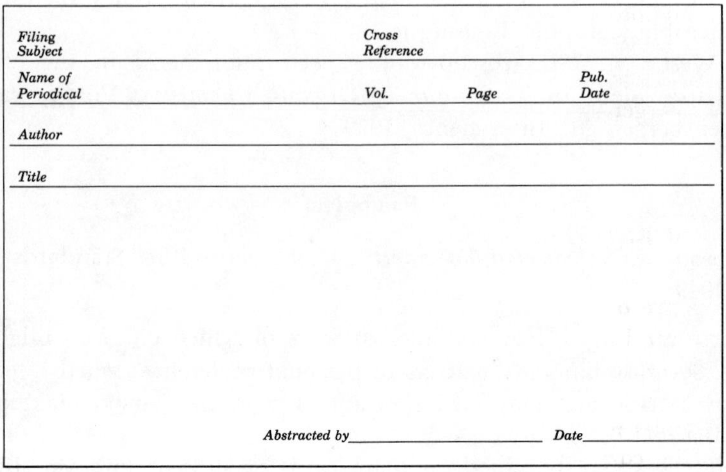
Filing Subject | *Cross Reference*
Name of Periodical | *Vol.* | *Page* | *Pub. Date*
Author
Title

*Abstracted by*________ *Date*________

Figure 5. Reference record form.

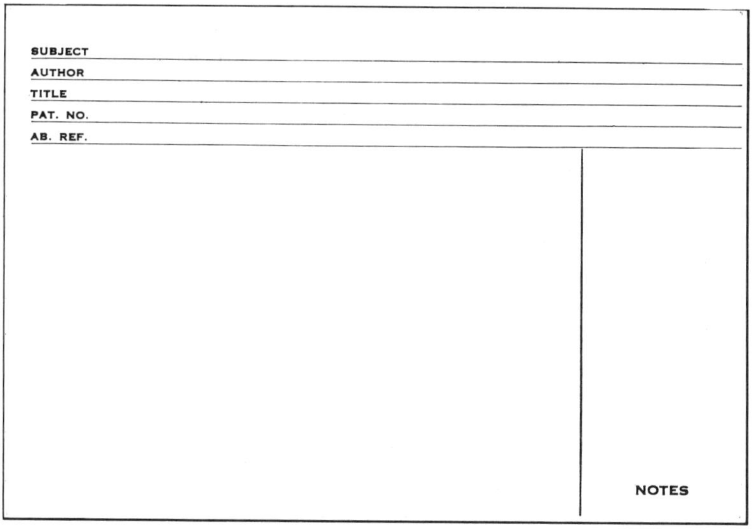

SUBJECT

AUTHOR

TITLE

PAT. NO.

AB. REF.

NOTES

Figure 6. Reference record form.

results of extensive and possibly continuing searches can be filed in special binders to provide a permanent record of the work done.

Although this discussion is directed primarily toward the specific literature search performed by a member of the library staff in response to a specific assignment, it is nonetheless pertinent to cite here the excellent survey and summary by Jahoda (35) in the book *Information*

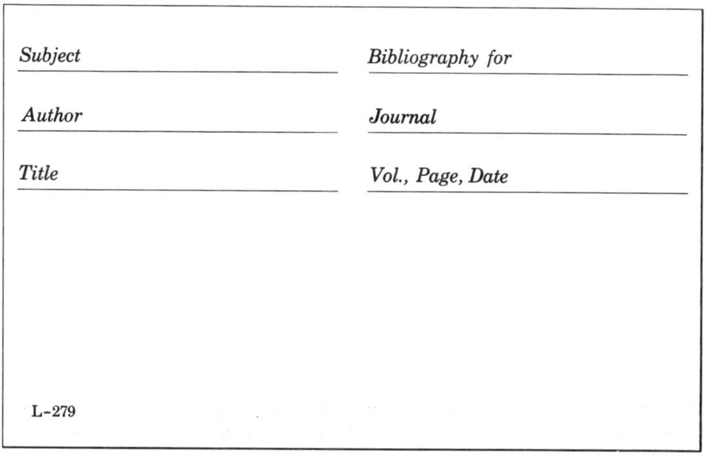

Subject _____   Bibliography for _____

Author _____   Journal _____

Title _____   Vol., Page, Date _____

L–279

Figure 7. Reference record form.

Figure 8. Punched card for bibliographic use.

Storage and Retrieval Systems for Individual Researchers. It consists of a concise review of methods available and in use for managing ongoing literature searches that could well be employed by library staff searchers. The various types of indexes, conventional, coordinate, keyword, and

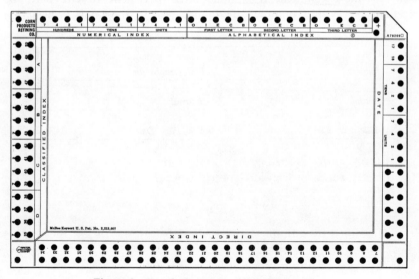

Figure 9. Punched card for bibliographic use.

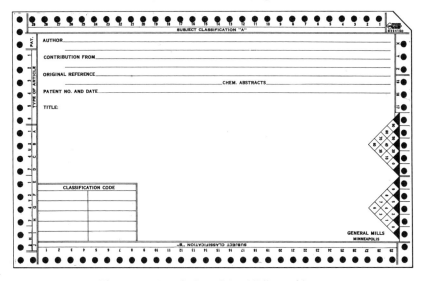

Figure 10. Punched card for bibliographic use.

citation are discussed from the point of view of their uses for bibliographic organization.

ORGANIZATION OF BIBLIOGRAPHIES

After the references pertinent to the subject being searched have been gathered, the next step is to organize them so that they constitute a good bibliography, easy to consult and giving assurance of a job well-executed. Schrero (36) provides an excellent guide for the organization of scholarly bibliographies in his article "Bibliographic Technique." He stresses the necessity for accuracy, completeness, consistency, and effective final arrangement. If there are only a few references, an alphabetical order by author is likely to be adequate, but a large number requires a breakdown into classified groups. The following are these possibilities for the sequential order of references comprising a bibliography:

1. Alphabetical by author
2. Chronological
3. Classified by subtopics, alphabetical by author within these groupings
4. By types of publications
5. By source, as by titles of journals

Combinations of these main kinds of groupings are also possible. For instance, references may be arranged chronologically, then alphabetically by author for each year. Within the groups, no matter which type of general arrangement is followed, it is usually desirable to keep together the references from each main type of source if the total number is at all large, for example, books, periodical articles, and patents may each be kept together. As the references concerning a subject accumulate during the search, a logical order for their arrangement usually becomes apparent. The chief influencing factor should be the intended use of the finished work. For most bibliographies in scientific fields, a grouping by subdivisions of the broad subject with an outline indicating the subdivisions is the most useful system, unless the person requesting the information is interested in a chronological development or the publications of certain authors. Such a bibliography can be used if it is kept only on the original cards or other forms, but it is often desirable to have the references typed as a report and as many copies made as might be needed.

When a bibliography is completed, an introductory preface should be written to accompany it. The sources searched and the dates covered ought to be indicated prominently because they can show at a glance the value of the search for certain purposes. It is helpful, too, to number the pages and provide a table of contents. The completed bibliography should be signed by the person responsible for executing it.

ANNOTATIONS AND ABSTRACTS

In the process of compiling a bibliography the searcher should make some note of the content of each reference, selecting those points that pertain to the problem prompting the investigation. He may make only brief annotations or fully informative abstracts may be required. Instead of writing complete sentences, a style of noting the most telling phrases as tersely as is compatible with retaining correct meaning may be used. McClelland (37) stated that the purpose of an annotation is simply to characterize an article as an aid to the reader to determine whether he should read the original publication. An abstract should summarize information so well that there will be need in rare instances only for the complete article to be consulted.

The preparation of good abstracts requires a special skill. Hopp and Howell (38) discuss the problem of abstracting primarily from the standpoint of preparing current library bulletin material, but their advice is generally applicable to the writing of abstracts of scientific publications for any purpose. They emphasized the point that the abstracter must think from the point of view of the potential reader, be as brief as possible, yet be certain to include essential information. Dyson (39) has outlined and discussed the main points to be considered in writing an abstract, and even mentioned the easily overlooked value of including negative results.

MECHANICAL AIDS FOR BIBLIOGRAPHIC CONTROL

As the literature of science grows in volume, the problem of making literature searches that can be relied upon as being complete in their coverage by using conventional indexing publications becomes increasingly difficult. The results are contingent on the matching of wits between the searcher and indexers-abstracters. Since the 1950s methods of meeting this problem by using devices such as the Uniterm indexing process developed by Taube, Mooers' Zatacoding, and mechanical aids utilizing data processing equipment have been developed. Reference has already been made to these procedures, particularly in Chapter 8 concerning indexing of information. Mention has been made in Chapter 10 and earlier in this chapter of services that supply information indexed by such methods. Consideration will be given to the matter of indexing for retrieval in any library that has serious need to be able to locate facts and data as regular literature searching procedures. If equipment is installed in the organization for other purposes the library may be able to make use of it, especially if it can procure bibliographies already on computer tape; for example, those the Defense Documentation Center for Scientific and Technical Information has instituted. Development in this area is in such a fluid state that it must be watched closely to recognize what can be utilized effectively in a particular situation.

THE PATENT LITERATURE

Patents constitute a distinct division of the literature, and they are of particular importance to an enterprise concerned with technological developments. As records of scientific advances, they sometimes constitute the only source of detailed descriptions of new processes. Some of the information revealed in them is eventually incorporated in books and journal articles, but much never reaches these more accessible publications, and it is sometimes available at an earlier date in the patents. Therefore this literature cannot be ignored, though it is of greater significance to certain types of developmental activities than others.

The collection of patents may be confined to a separate patent department, which may in fact maintain its own patent library, or it may be part of the main library collection to be used by anyone concerned with any phase of patent investigation, including prosecution. In many scientific and technical libraries the staff is expected to furnish patent information, including the execution of comprehensive searches of the literature as a part of the organization's developing patent program.

This section of the chapter is concerned with the handling of patents as a source of information, how to locate pertinent ones, and typical questions involving them are illustrated. For more detailed coverage, such guides as Crane, Patterson, and Marr's *A Guide to the Literature of Chemistry* (40) or Newby's *How to Find Out About Patents* (41) should be consulted. Some of the papers presented at meetings of the Chemical Literature Division of the American Chemical Society and published in the Society's *Advances in Chemistry Series* and in the Division's *Journal of Chemical Documentation* are concerned with patent searching problems.

What Patents Are

Since patents generally are not as familiar as are other types of publications, the essential facts concerning them are presented briefly. Patents are individual documents representing agreements between a national government and an inventor. In return for disclosing his invention for the benefit of the public good, the inventor is granted the right to exclusive exploitation of his invention for a definite period ranging in various countries from 15 to 20 years. In the United States the term is 17 years. All countries in which scientific research is conducted have a patent system, though the greatest number of patents, as might be suspected, are granted in the United States. Because the bulk of the patent literature issues in the United States, this discussion is centered chiefly on the situation in this country. However, the systems in other countries are somewhat similar, and there are trends toward international cooperation.

In brief, a patent is awarded in the United States to an inventor who proves that he has brought forth any "new and useful process, machine, manufacture, or composition of matter, or any new and useful improvement thereof." When his patent is granted, printed copies of the complete document are made available to the public. The essential features of a printed patent are the following.

1. *The patent number.* Consecutive numbers are assigned to patents as they are issued, and they are listed in this order within the three subject groupings in the weekly issues of the *Official Gazette of the United States Patent Office.* This number serves as complete identification for the document, for example, U.S. 2,192,624.

2. *Date of issue.* The Tuesday upon which a patent is officially granted is the date from which the time of protection is calculated.

3. *Application date and serial number.* The date upon which an application for a patent is made to the Patent Office is shown on the printed copy. A serial number is given to the application when it is received by the Office, and this too is carried on the copy.

4. *Title.* The title of a patent is often so general that it does not adequately identify the contents. Particularly is this true for older patents, and, since the index entries in the annual index are made from the title, they may be difficult to detect using this as an approach.

5. *Patentee.* The name of the inventor or inventors to whom the patent is issued is cited below the title on the copy. N.B. In the United States a patent is always issued to individual persons, whereas in some other countries it may be issued directly to a company.

6. *Assignee.* The patentee may immediately assign his invention, usually to a company by which he may be employed, though occasionally it is assigned to another individual, at the time of issue. If he assigns it at some later date it is difficult to determine because the only record of this subsequent transaction will be in the Patent Office.

7. *Classification.* A patent is assigned to a specific class in the Patent Office System of Classification when it is granted. This notation is indicated on the printed copies of those issued since about 1930.

8. *Specifications.* The body of a patent is in two parts, the first of which is called the specifications. This is the statement of the argument for the invention. In some instances there are reviews of the technology involved that provide valuable expositions of the state of the art.

9. *Claims.* The other part of the body of the patent comprises the claims which are exact statements of what the invention covers. Since each claim must be stated in one sentence, they are sometimes very involved.

10. *File wrapper.* The complete history of a patent application is held in a file wrapper, available for consultation in the Patent Search Room. Copies may be obtained through Washington agents.

11. *Reissue.* If a patent must be revised after it has already been issued, it is reissued in corrected form.

12. *Disclaimer.* When the validity of the claims of a patent are questioned and cannot be defended, disclaimers are published in the forepart of an issue of the *Gazette.* Needless to say, these can be elusive.

Location and Selection of Patents

To some extent the selection of patents has already been dealt with in Chapter 5 of this book. For those issued currently the *Official Gazette of the United States Patent Office* should be scanned each week, and patents of interest either ordered or notations made for indexing record. If subscriptions are carried to certain classes, the *Gazette* need not be read so carefully. All relevant patents are entered in the library's card index to information which, as it is carefully maintained over the years, becomes a major source to be searched when inquiries are made. Shaler (42) has shown how the development of such a file provides a series of continuous records in certain subject areas. Some patents, particularly those in the field of chemistry, are cited in the abstracting publications, but complete coverage in any area cannot be achieved unless the official journals are read, or subscriptions carried for all classes of possible interest.

As an aid to the "non-patent oriented scientist, engineer or businessman," quoting from the announcement flyer, the Patent Office has instituted a new journal titled *Patent Abstracts Section* issued since January 1968. It provides only the readily intelligible abstract with a drawing, if applicable, to bring the essential information to a wider public.

It is sometimes necessary, particularly in organizations where products and processes are dependent upon patent protection, to make complete searches of the patent literature pertaining to a specific art that has not been of interest prior to the time of the request for the investigation. A first step at this point will be to consult the Patent Office's *Manual of Classification* to determine the classes in which patents covering pertinent information will be included. After the classes are determined, one procedure might be to go to the search room of the United States Patent Office in Alexandria, Va., to examine the files or to request a professional patent searcher, usually associated with a patent attorney, to do this. This is the only place where a complete, classified file of patent copies is maintained, although the office is, in 1970, preparing to make available microfilm copies on aperture cards in a number of centers in the United States and possibly other countries.

Another procedure is to obtain from the Patent Office lists of the numbers of patents in the classes of interest, then either purchase copies, thus building a classed file for permanent referral, or to take the numbers to a library where there is a numerical file for consultation.

In each issue of the weekly *Gazette* the classes of patents contained in it are listed, thereby making a search by classes theoretically possible. However, this would be much too tedious a procedure to be practical.

There are several services designed to provide assistance in the location of patents. One is the *Uniterm Index to U.S. Chemical and Chemically Related Patents* developed by Information for Industry and subsequently marketed by IFI/Plenum Data Corporation, 1000 Connecticut Avenue N.W., Washington, D.C. 20036. Using the coordinate indexing concept a dictionary (in duplicate) of terms permits the selection of documents relevant to a search through the matching of terms. Coverage is back to 1950 and is kept up to date. Service on magnetic tape is offered also. Plenum Publishing Corporation in 1969 acquired Sigmadoc, publisher of an index of European patents in chemical fields, in anticipation of issuing a World Chemical Patent Index.

A similar approach, even more restricted in subject coverage is the American Petroleum Institute's abstracts of patents relating to the refining of petroleum. This, too, employs the coordinate indexing procedure implemented by a dual dictionary of terms. The beginning date is 1961 and carries forward to the present.

In 1962 *The National Catalog of Patents* was announced as a very significant aid to patent literature research. This is a compilation of U. S. patents in the fields of chemistry and electricity, including communications and radiant energy, arranged by Patent Office Classification. Although the *Catalog* gives only the representative claim for each patent as it appears in the *Gazette,* it should prove to be a valuable searching tool. The plan was to publish in six series, each one to cover a span of ten years, except for number one which includes all years prior to 1900. This project is being undertaken by Rowman and Littlefield, Inc., New York.

Another effort to enhance the accessibility of patents is their publication in microform, a publishing program of Microcard editions, 901 26th St. N.W., Washington, D.C. A beginning was made with French chemical patents in 1961.

For a complete, international patent search the ultimate source is the service provided by the International Patents Institute (Institut International des Brevets) located at the Hague in the Netherlands. The most complete files of patents from every country that cooperates in the international patent system are maintained at this center.

If a complete search of the patent literature is not required, it will be adequate to cite as references only those patents that are located in the abstracting publications. The subject area that includes good coverage of this aspect of the literature is chemistry, because *Chemical Abstracts* has long considered it important, as has *Chemische Zentralblatt*. Since 1947 particularly, *Chemical Abstracts* has covered patents more intensively than was the case in earlier years. Certain periodicals list or abstract patents in their restricted fields as, for example, do the *Journal of the Acoustical Society of America, Hydrocarbon Processing*, and the *Journal of the Society of Dyers and Colourists*.

In addition to the periodicals that publish information about patents, there are some specialized compilations that are sufficiently thorough in their coverage to warrant their use for background searching. Some of these are the following:

Alterthum, H., *Fortschritte der Chemischen Apparatewesens Elektrische Ofen*, Akademische Verlagsgesellschaft M.B.H., Leipzig, 1936. This is a classified listing of patents relating to electric furnaces. Only the German ones are abstracted.

Berkman, S., J. C. Morell, and G. Egloff, *Catalysis*, Reinhold, New York, 1940.

Egloff, G., and G. Hulla, *Alkylation of Alkanes*, Vol. 1, *Patents*, Reinhold, New York, 1948.

Gmelin, *Handbuch der anorganischen Chemie*, Patentsammlungun, Berlin, Verlag Chemie, G.m.b.H. A series of inclusive compilations covering alloy compositions. Iron and steel (1932), supplement (1935), aluminum (1936), supplement (1939), platinum (1937), and magnesium (1937).

Where patents are a major concern the unique world wide service provided by Derwent Information Service, Rochdale House, Theobalds Road, London, W.C. 1 England, should be investigated. They publish a *Derwent Patents Manual*, 2nd ed., 1964, that describes the scope of this remarkable service. Among the compilations available on subscription are *Fine Chemicals Patents Journal, Netherlands Patents Report, Petrochemicals Patents Journal, British Patents Gazette, German Patents Gazette*, and others.

Patent Searching

Patent searching is a highly specialized art; it can be done reliably only by those whose attention is devoted almost exclusively to patents, and who have made a protracted study of them. However, it is possible for the library staff to render significant assistance on patent problems if there is some understanding of the principles involved. Particular help can be given in the preliminary investigation of subjects upon which research is contemplated. Hoffman (43) has provided an excellent description of the procedure followed in a library serving the patent department of a petroleum company, an example of an industry in which there is much concern with patents. Some of the parts of the procedure could be readily incorporated in a library where a patent situation is only an occasional problem. An example of a form for keeping record of a patent search is shown as Figures 11 and 12. A less elaborate one that may be quite satisfactory is suggested as Figure 13.

A patent search may have one of several purposes. In general it is concerned with the finding of specific information relating to a technological device or process. This information may exist in either patents or other kinds of publications so that books, periodicals, and patents must all be investigated in a complete search. If a fact can be shown to be in print in any kind of publication, no matter how obscure, a patent position may be invalidated. Specific terms are used to designate the usual types of patent searches, the more common being the following.

1. *Patentability search.* This is also called the "preliminary search" which is made to determine whether an idea is patentable, that is, whether it is novel and has not been available for public use for more than two years. It is assumed that the invention fulfills the other requisite of being useful. Hoffman (43) has indicated that this search

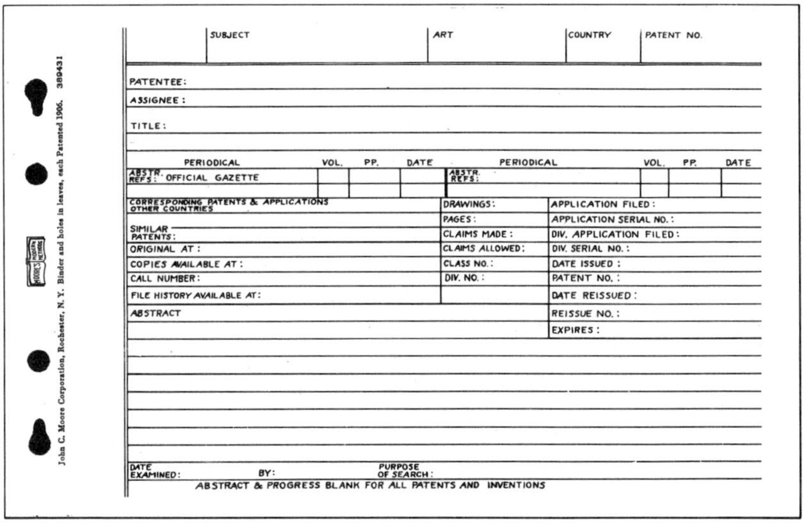
John C. Moore Corporation, Rochester, N. Y. Binder and holes in leaves, each Patented 1906. 389431
MOORE'S MODERN METHODS
SUBJECT
ART
COUNTRY
PATENT NO.
PATENTEE:
ASSIGNEE:
TITLE:
PERIODICAL VOL. PP. DATE
ABSTR. REFS: OFFICIAL GAZETTE
PERIODICAL VOL. PP. DATE
ABSTR. REFS:
CORRESPONDING PATENTS & APPLICATIONS OTHER COUNTRIES
SIMILAR PATENTS:
ORIGINAL AT:
COPIES AVAILABLE AT:
CALL NUMBER:
FILE HISTORY AVAILABLE AT:
ABSTRACT
DRAWINGS:
PAGES:
CLAIMS MADE:
CLAIMS ALLOWED:
CLASS NO.:
DIV. NO.:
APPLICATION FILED:
APPLICATION SERIAL NO.:
DIV. APPLICATION FILED:
DIV. SERIAL NO.:
DATE ISSUED:
PATENT NO.:
DATE REISSUED:
REISSUE NO.:
EXPIRES:
DATE EXAMINED:
BY:
PURPOSE OF SEARCH:
ABSTRACT & PROGRESS BLANK FOR ALL PATENTS AND INVENTIONS

Figure 11. Form for patent search.

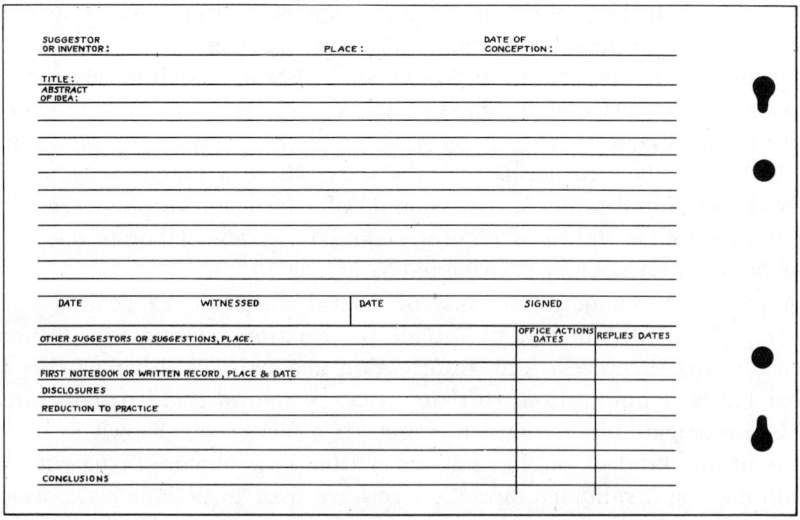
SUGGESTOR OR INVENTOR: PLACE: DATE OF CONCEPTION:
TITLE:
ABSTRACT OF IDEA:
DATE WITNESSED DATE SIGNED
OTHER SUGGESTORS OR SUGGESTIONS, PLACE. OFFICE ACTIONS DATES REPLIES DATES
FIRST NOTEBOOK OR WRITTEN RECORD, PLACE & DATE
DISCLOSURES
REDUCTION TO PRACTICE
CONCLUSIONS

Figure 12. Form for patent search.

may be either a brief preliminary review, or it may be comprehensive and consist in locating all published information on the subject in books, journal articles, patents, and any other possible sources.

2. *State-of-the-art search.* A full survey of all patents and other publications relating to the art involved is required to determine the precise state of progress of a technological development. It is an extension of the patentability search.

3. *Infringement search.* A study of the claims contained in all patents concerned with the subject under investigation for a prior period of 17 years is made to determine whether there has been an encroachment on an idea. Patents are, in some respects, closely akin to politics.

4. *Validity search.* This, the most exhaustive of all searches, is called for when it is necessary to gauge the strength of an existing patent. The patent may be one blocking an activity in which a company wishes to participate, or it may be a patent involved in an infringement suit. Every possible reference must be investigated and, as in other patent searches, publication date is of paramount importance.

5. *Index search.* A routine investigation of all patents issued to a certain individual or assigned to a company, rarely requiring exercised judgment with respect to subject matter. It can be done from the annual indexes to the *Gazette,* or from the inventor and assignees files often maintained in a library where there is a large collection of patents.

Patent No. __________
Date __________

Patentee:

Assignee:
Title:

Abstract:

Figure 13. Simple form for patent search.

Trademarks

Trademarks are closely allied to patents, though handled officially as a separate kind of agreement. Those granted each week were until 1971 illustrated in the forepart of the *Gazette*. Since February 1971 they appear in a separate publication. They are indexed annually, but the only complete index to them is in the Patent Office Search Room. Some of general interest are included in scientific dictionaries, and a few are cited in current periodicals. Several cumulative indexes have been published, but so many new trademarks are granted continuously that no list can be complete. Many libraries develop their own index record of those of interest to them, noting them from the *Gazette* as it is read weekly.

Types of Patent Questions

Requests that concern or involve patents vary, although most of them fall into several main categories. As in any search, efficiency of approach to it depends upon understanding what is wanted, and in the case of subject searches there must be knowledge of the subject field. Discussion of patent requests may be presented most directly by citing examples of typical ones, with suggestions for locating the answers to them. As was suggested for general reference questions, it is advisable to keep a systematic record of requests, taking care to establish the habit of noting complete citation in a uniform manner. In libraries where much patent work is done, it is important to have all requests for searches submitted in writing, perhaps on a special form for the purpose.

Some examples of patent questions follow. (Note that it is assumed that the answers are not to be found in the library's own index files.)

Question. Locate United States Patents known to have been assigned to Company X within the past five to ten years concerned with a process for removing phosphorus from copper ores.

Procedure. Since the name of the company is known, the annual indexes to the *Official Gazette of the United States Patent Office* may be consulted and likely titles noted. If there is any doubt, the exact contents of the patents may be verified from the claims cited in the *Gazette*. Should the *Gazette* not be at hand and the subject be chemical, there is a good chance of locating abstracts in *Chemical Abstracts* by consulting the indexes from 1937 to date. Prior to 1936 they were not indexed by number, but a special index covering the years 1907–1936 has been prepared by the Science-Technology Group of Special Libraries Association. *A Collective Numerical Patent Index,* 1937–1946, and another for 1947–1956 have been issued by *Chemical Abstracts.*

Question. Locate all patents assigned to Company Y having to do with the dyeing of nylon.

Procedure. Again, since the name of the company is known, the annual indexes to the *Gazette* will supply the titles of all patents assigned to the company at the time of their issue. There is also the possibility that the company may hold others that may have been acquired subsequent to the time of their being granted, which fact may be of particular importance, but it should be kept in mind, as these can be located only from Patent Office Records. Another point to be aware of is that patents may be assigned to a company affiliated with Company Y, and if no patents appear to be assigned to Y, a study of the corporate structure as shown in Moody's *Industrials* or Standard and Poor's *Register* may reveal other companies whose patents on the dyeing of nylon should be investigated.

Question. Locate all patents on the dyeing of nylon.

Procedure. This necessitates a subject search which should start with the *Manual of Classification of Patents* from which the likely classes will be selected. The files of the pertinent ones must either be read in the Patent Search Room or copies purchased. It may be economic to purchase copies in view of the cost of a trip to Washington. However, if the organization already has an arrangement with patent searchers in Washington, the assignment can be made to them. The aforementioned *National Catalog of Patents* might be consulted for this purpose.

Question. Locate some representative patents on the dyeing of nylon.

Procedure. A search in *Chemical Abstracts* will show which references are to patents; the page number is preceded by "P" in the index. Unfortunately, subject fields other than chemistry are not abstracted as effectively.

Question. Locate the patent covering a composition trademarked as XYZ.

Procedure. The name of the company will probably be known, or it may be discovered readily in trademark indexes. If it is not, it can be found only from the files in the Patent Search Room in Washington. The patents assigned to the company should then be located from the assignment record in the Patent Office, and the likely ones read until the correct one is identified. This can be a troublesome item to locate, especially if a company has had issued to it a large number of patents. Sometimes the patents covering an invention are cited with the trademark.

Question. Locate the British patent corresponding to a specific United States one.

Procedure. If the subject is chemical, it may be possible to locate the patent fairly easily by investigating those granted and abstracted at the same period that the United States one was issued. The patent index of *Chemisches Zentralblatt* is particularly useful for finding equivalent patents issued in other countries. However, if this is not rewarding the next step is to consult the British Office *Journal;* this failing, the files of British patents in the Patent Office Search Room must be investigated.

CONCLUSION

The ultimate service that can be rendered in the science-technology library is to supply factual information in response to requests. If the preliminary preparations of assembling files of materials and indexes are thorough and they are kept up to date, a majority of the questions brought to the library should be answerable from the resources at hand.

The introduction to the use of the literature provided in this chapter is admittedly brief, but it should afford an adequate start into the maze. The source publications themselves must be studied as they are used; there is no substitute for this educational experience. A good literature searcher has a deeply inquisitive attitude and an open mind and is always on the alert for new resources to augment his mental stock. The literature and methods of approach are not static; continuous effort must be made to follow the shifting advance of science and its resultant technologies as it is recorded and indexed.

REFERENCES

1. A. Kent and J. W. Perry, "The Library and the Research Team," *Spec. Libr.* **47**, 156–161 (1956).

2. E. M. R. Ditmas, "Co-ordination of Information, a Survey of Schemes Put Forward in the Last Fifty Years," *J. Doc.* **3**, 209–221 (1948).

3. The Royal Society Information Conference, June 21–July 2, 1949, The Royal Society, London, 1948.

4. *International Conference on Scientific Information,* Washington, D.C., 1958, *Proceedings* National Academy of Sciences-National Research Council, Washington, D.C., 1959.

5. Committee on Scientific and Technical Communication of the National Academy of Sciences-National Academy of Engineers, *Scientific and Technical Communication: A Pressing National Problem and Recommendations for its Solution,* National Academy of Sciences, Washington, D.C., 1969.

6. "News: Special Feature: Comments on the SATCOM Report," *Sci. Inf. Notes* **1**, No. 5, 189–200 (September–October, 1969).

7. W. S. Budington, "Interrelations among Special Libraries," *Libr. Quart.* **39**, 64–77 (January 1969).

8. W. T. Knox, "National Information Networks and Special Libraries," *Spec. Libr.* **57**, 627–630 (1966).

9. M. Weinstock, "Network Concepts in Scientific and Technical Libraries," *Spec. Libr.* **58**, 328–334 (1967).

10. M. E. Freeman, "The Science Information Exchange as a Source of Information," *Spec. Libr.* **59**, 86–90 (1968).

11. E. Garfield, "Science Citation Indexing—A New Dimension in Indexing," *Science* **144**, 649–654 (1964).

12. G. M. Mathews, "Citation and Subject Indexing in Science," *Libr. Resour. Tech. Serv.* **9**, 478–482 (1965).

13. S. Rafter, "Citation Patterns: Analysis and Summary," presented at American Chemical Society Meeting, September 1966.

14. I. M. Strieby, "Reference Files in a Pharmaceutical Library," *Med. Libr. Assoc. Bull.* **34**, 101–115 (1947).

15. B. B. Lane, personal communication.

16. E. B. Jackson, "The Information Explosion and Its Implications for Management," presented at the College of Business Administration and Center for Executive Development, Arizona State University, Tempe, March 4, 1969.

17. "Business Libraries Multiply," *Wall Street J.* **149**, 1 (Monday, May 20, 1957).

18. S. Swenson, "Flow Chart on Library Searching Techniques," *Spec. Libr.* **56**, 239–242 (1965).

19. D. D. Berolzheimer, "Searching Chemical and Allied Literature," *The Chemist* 13, 426–433 (February 1936).

20. T. E. R. Singer, "Need for Imagination and Skepticism in Making Literature Searches," *Rec. Chem. Prog.* 18, No. 1, 11–29 (1957).

21. L. O. Lewton, "I. Search for on-the-Spot Information," *J. Chem. Educ.* 28, 487–491 (1951); "II. The Literature Survey Proper," *ibid.*, 539–543.

22. G. M. Dyson, "Searching the Older Chemical Literature," in Advances in Chemistry Series, No. 30, *Searching the Chemical Literature,* The American Chemical Society, Washington, D.C., 1961, pp. 38–91.

23. E. G. Rose, Applied Science Laboratories, State College, Pa., personal communication.

24. T. R. Palfrey, and H. E. Coleman, compilers, *Guide to Bibliographies of Theses, United States and Canada,* 2nd ed., ALA, Chicago, Ill., 1940. Additions and corrections by R. P. Rosenbery, *Bull. Bibliogr.* 18, 181, 203 (1946).

25. I. R. Stephens, "Searching for Theses, Dissertations, and Unpublished Data," in *Searching the Chemical Literature,* 2nd ed., Advances in Chemistry Series, No. 30. American Chemical Society, Washington, D.C., 1961, pp. 110–120.

26. L. M. Daniels, Ed., *Business Literature; An Annotated List for Students and Businesses,* Baker Library, Harvard School of Business Administration, Cambridge, Mass., 1968. Reference List No. 25.

27. E. T. Coman, Jr., *Sources of Business Information,* Revised ed. University of California Press, Berkeley, 1964.

28. R. Alexander, *Business Pamphlets and Information Sources: A Guide to Currently Available Pamphlets,* Exceptional Books, New York, 1967.

29. S. V. Billingsley, "Manufacturers' Literature . . . ," *Sci.-Tech. News* 14, 8–9 (1960).

30. *Business Periodicals Index,* H. W. Wilson Co., New York.

31. *Management Index,* monthly. Keith Business Library, Box 453, Ottawa, Canada.

32. *Business Literature,* monthly, Newark Public Library, Newark, N. J.

33. *Business and Technology Sources,* four to six issues a year, Business Information and Science & Technology Departments, Cleveland Public Library, Cleveland, Ohio.

34. B. H. Weil, W. G. Emerson, W. Bolles, and C. F. Lewerz, "Esso Research Experiences with Chemical Abstracts," *J. Chem. Doc.* 5, 193–200 (1965).

35. G. Jahoda, *Information Storage and Retrieval Systems for Individual Researchers,* Wiley-Interscience, New York, 1970.

36. M. Schrero, "Bibliographic Technique," *Spec. Libr.* 30, 302–306 (1939).

37. E. H. McClelland, "Abstracts and Annotations," *Spec. Libr.* 34, 362–372 (1943).

38. R. H. Hopp, and W. W. Howell, "Abstracting Has its Own Techniques," *Libr. J.* 72, 1578–1580 (1947).

39. G. M. Dyson, "Relation of an Abstract to its Original, in *Searching the Chemical Literature,* Advances in Chemistry Series, No. 30, American Chemical Society, Washington, D.C., 1961, pp. 33–37.

40. E. J. Crane, A. M. Patterson, and E. B. Marr, *A Guide to the Literature of Chemistry,* 2nd ed., Wiley, New York, 1957.

41. F. Newby, *How to Find Out about Patents,* Pergamon, New York, 1967.

42. C. Shaler, "Techniques of Meeting the Information Needs of a Patent Department of an Industry," *Spec. Libr.* 34, 270–273 (1941).

43. T. Hoffman, G. Wohlauer, and R. Cross, "Techniques Employed in Making Literature Searches for a Patent Department," in *Searching the Chemical Literature,* Advances in Chemistry Series, No. 30, American Chemical Society, Washington, D.C., 1961.

BIBLIOGRAPHY

American Chemical Society, Advances in Chemistry Series, No. 16, *A Key to Pharmaceutical and Medicinal Chemistry Literature,* Washington, D.C. (1956)); No. 30, *Searching the Chemical Literature,* Washington, D.C., 1961.

Anthon, L. J., *Sources of Information on Atomic Energy,* Pergamon, New York, 1966.

Artandi, S., *Information Science and Technology,* Scarecrow, Metuchen, N.J., 1969.

Besterman, T., *Index Bibliographicus. Directory of Current Periodical Abstracts and Bibliographies,* Vol. 1. 4th ed., "Science and Technology," Unesco & FID, Paris, 1959.

Bottle, R. T. and H. V. Wyatt, *The Use of Biological Literature,* Shoe String Press, 1967.

Bottle, R. T., *The Use of the Chemical Literature,* 2nd ed., Butterworths, London, 1969.

Brunn, A. L., *How to Find Out in Pharmacy,* Pergamon, New York, 1969.

Campbell, G. A. and R. Brown, *How to Find Out about the Chemical Industry,* Pergamon, New York, 1969.

Cohan, L., *The International Information Network Series;* Vol. 1, "Directory of computerized information in science and technology;" Vol. 2, "Directory of Computer Programs," Science Associates International, Inc., 23 East 26th St., New York 10010, 1968.

Committee on Chemical Information, Division of Chemistry and Chemical Technology, National Research Council, *Chemical Structure Information Handling, a Review of the Literature,* 1962–1968, National Academy of Sciences, Washington, D.C., 1970.

Cox, N. S. M., J. D. Daws, and J. L. Dolby, *The Computer and the Library: The Role of the Computer in the Organization and Handling of Information in Libraries,* Archon, Hamden, Conn., 1967.

Dyke, F. H., Jr. *How to Manage and Use Technical Information,* Industrial Education Institute, Boston, 1968.

Foskett, D. J., revised by J. B. Whitehead, *Information Service in Libraries,* Library Association, London, 1967.

Frank, N. D. *Data Sources for Business and Market Analysis,* 2nd ed., Scarecrow, Metuchen, N. J., 1969.

Grogan, D. J. *Science and Technology: An Introduction to the Literature,* Archon, Hamden, Conn., 1970.

Haydock, E., *A Guide to the Literature of Electronics,* Western Canadian Contributions to Librarianship, No. 1, School of Librarianship, University of British Columbia, Vancouver, 1963.

Henderson, M. M., *Tentative Bibliography on Evaluation of Information Systems*, National Bureau of Standards, Research Information Center and Advisory Service on Information Processing, Government Printing Office, Washington, D.C., 1965.

Henderson, M. M. et al., *Cooperation, Convertibility, and Compatibility among Information Systems: A Literature Review*, National Bureau of Standards Miscellaneous Publication No. 276, Government Printing Office, Washington, D.C., 1966.

Houghton, B., *Technical Information Sources: A Guide to Patents, Standards, and Technical Reports Literature*, Archon, Hamden, Conn., 1967.

Keenan, S., "Abstracting and Indexing Services in the Physical Sciences," *Libr. Trends* **16**, 329–336 (1968).

Koch, H. W., "A National Information System for Physics," *Phys. Today* **21**, 41–49 (1968).

Martyn, J., *Coverage, Overlap and Indexing of Abstracts Journals*, Aslib, London, 1960.

National Science Foundation, *Current Research and Development in Scientific Documentation*, No. 14, National Science Foundation, Washington, D.C., 1966.

Schultz, L., "New Developments in Biological Abstracting and Indexing," *Libr. Trends* **16**, 337–352 (1968).

Sternberg, V. A., *How to Locate Technical Information*, Prentice-Hall, Englewood, N. J., 1964.

Schutze, G., *Documentation Source Book*, Scarecrow, Metuchen, N. J., 1965; supplement, 1970.

Sternberg, V. A., *How to Locate Technical Information*, National Foremans' Institute, Waterford, Conn., 1964.

Swenson, S., "Flow Charts on Library Searching Techniques," *Spec. Libr.* **56**, 239–242 (1965).

Taylor, F. R., "Library Service to Industry in Great Britain and on the Continent," *Libr. Trends* **14**, 306–331 (1966).

Vickery, B. C., "Technique of Information Retrieval," Shoe String Press, Hamden, Conn., 1970.

Wilson, B. J., Ed., *Aslib Directory*, Vol. 1, "Information Sources in Science, Technology, and Commerce, Aslib, London, 1968.

Yescombe, E. R., *Sources of Information on the Rubber, Plastics and Allied Industries*, Pergamon, New York, 1968.

Patents

Derwent Patents Manual, 2nd ed., Derwent Publications, London, 1964.

Newby, F., *How to Find Out about Patents*, Pergamon, New York, 1967.

Pfeffer, H., *Information Retrieval among Examining Patent Offices*, Spartan, New York, 1964.

Searching British Patent Literature, British Patent Office, 25 Southampton Bldgs., London, 1968.

12

Interpreting Services to the Library's Publics

A science-oriented organization depends upon all types of specialized information pertinent to its needs. This may be recorded in books, journals, pamphlets, reports, government documents, and occasionally it may be information which has not yet found its way into print, thus necessitating tapping individual expertise. To develop the potential value of available facts, hundreds of special libraries have been established. Their staffs must be alert to clientele problems, then strive to meet them courteously, accurately, efficiently, skillfully, and creatively, using knowledge of source material to extract pertinent information for transfer from media to minds.

The preceding chapters covered many aspects of the development and administration of the special library in the fields of science and technology regardless of its location—in an academic or research institution, a subject department of a public library, a manufacturing organization, a hospital, or the headquarters of a professional or trade association. There now remains the further need to emphasize the librarian's responsibility to interpret library service for his many publics—the publics which are points of contact for his relationships with people. It is left for the future to demonstrate whether computerization, tied in with geographically distributed networks, will strengthen or lessen the effectiveness of these relationships.

Public relations is an umbrella term with many definitions, most of them attempting to convey the same meaning although the words used are not always synonymous. Some of the expressions are exceedingly simple such as "human engineering," "a way of life," "the art of getting along with people," and "the science concerned with the relationship of an organization to the people it involves." The broad spectrum of these interrelationships is indicated by the definition found in Webster's Dictionary, the library's most frequently used reference tool (1), which characterizes public relations as:

The promotion of rapport and goodwill between a person, firm, or institution, and other persons, special publics, or the community at large through the distribution of interpretative material, the development of neighborly interchange, and the assessment of public reaction.

Canfield (2) defines public relations as "a social philosophy of management expressed in policies and practices which are communicated to the public to secure its understanding and goodwill." In an earlier edition, he (3) presented a definition chosen as one of the best by a majority of specialists in the field:

Public relations is the continued process of keying policies, services, and actions to the best interests of those individuals and groups whose confidence and goodwill an individual or institution covets; and secondly, it is the interpretation of these policies, services, and actions to assure complete understanding and appreciation.

The librarian has a ready-made opportunity to cooperate in programs such as the ones encompassed by these definitions. In fact, public relations is an integral factor of every library system.

Wright and Christian (4) explain that the number of publics in any community is theoretically the number of distinct combinations of people possible there. They prepared a chart, "the composition of publics," with examples of groups bound together by common interests such as professional, economic, fraternal, political, educational, patriotic, and geographical. Underlying all is the common denominator of *people,* people who compose a specific public, each capable of forming its own opinion. Such a chart may be useful to the librarian in analyzing his publics; this he must do before he decides why he should reach them, upon what he needs to place emphasis, and how he will communicate— face to face, by telephone, by memorandum, or indirectly through other media. Under no circumstances can the librarian assume that his publics have complete information about library operations and resources, especially in terms of potential use. Thus reaching the unreached are a goal and role of the librarian in his interrelationships.

Kobre (5) also thinks in terms of groups who compose the publics of various types of institutions and classifies them accordingly. Lesly (6) outlines factors that influence public relations, with specialists treating the classifications in ten basic categories of organizations. At first thought it may seem fairly simple for librarians of collections based on science and technology to identify, as distinct audiences, the separate groups of people with whom they have contact. The diverse types of institutions with which libraries are connected, however, prevent formation of an outline equally applicable to all. For example, there is a striking difference between the publics of two types of technical libraries, one in the science department of a public library with its ever-changing clientele, another in a multidivisional or multiproduct manufacturing company with clientele relatively stable though geographically dispersed.

Contrast in publics can also be indicated by the intrarelationships of the departmental librarian of a technical library in a decentralized university library system who must deal with the faculty, with the students, and with his own staff, as well as with the director of the university libraries. The latter may need the help, at times, of the departmental librarian in budget justification, or, if connected with a state-supported institution, the director may need aid in keeping a weather eye on the legislature, farm interests, or some other public, especially if the university offers extension work. Reck (7), in analyzing a university's constituency, said the number of off-campus publics is likely to approach, if not pass, thirty. Schoenfeld (8) lists media suited to contacting them, many of which are acceptable in other types of libraries.

This chapter emphasizes an industrial librarian's working relations within an organization, the library of which serves a particular clientele. It is in this type of library that it is possible to identify and to discuss at least four specific publics. Arranged for the sake of convenience, they are (1) the library staff, (2) the clientele, or users of the library, (3) the many-sided one of overall management, and (4) the members of the librarian's profession whom he contacts for help.* Various channels of communication open to the librarian and the motivation for using them are discussed under these four categories. While they are inter-dependent and sometimes overlap, all need consideration in planning a balanced program for an industrial library. Many of the suggestions are applicable to other types of special libraries; if not, alternatives can be developed.

The librarian first acquires a perspective of the value of the library to his organization, not only by acquainting himself with the historical background and operation of the parent institution, but also with those

---

* Publisher relations has also been suggested as a distinct public for the librarian—a logical one which is not specifically covered by any of the four categories above unless it is considered a part of (3), management's public. The nurturing of good relations with book publishers is an important aspect of SLA's Publisher Relations Committee [*Spec. Libr.* **58**, 186 (March 1967)]. Although this is an association activity, it has significance for individual librarians.

of the industry of which it is a part. Taking the second step, he works out with management the areas of library service for which he is to be held responsible. Duncan (9) reviews the factors necessary to establish an information activity geared to an institution's needs. With this method of study in mind, the organizational location of the library to meet its objectives can be determined. Although subject to change, the box on Duncan's chart has probably been predetermined before the employment of the librarian. His status and title are usually related to the placement of the information group within the parent structure. This subject is discussed more fully in Chapter 2 and Refs. 10–12 in this chapter. Although the points covered in this paragraph are primarily aspects of library administration, they often have a direct bearing on the successful interpretation of services.

LIBRARY STAFF IS A PUBLIC

In his chapter on "Managements Nearest Public—Employees," Hill (13), a pioneer in public relations, says the following:

Its every communication must build management's status as an honest, farsighted leadership to which employees can always look for the truth—and even for real inspiration and guidance, too, in making life a good experience.

Any one of the library staff members can contribute toward the creation of a favorable image of the library in the minds of its users; he avoids creating one that is unfavorable.

Effective communications are necessary whether the staff consists of two, ten, or twenty or more members who serve a clientele located in one geographic area or one scattered among components in various parts of the country. It is impossible to state where staff administration *per se* ends and public relations begins. In any case, it is the librarian's task to foster the realization that good internal relationships precede sound external ones. The librarian, therefore, has the obligation to staff members who work with him to prepare the climate for a rewarding and satisfying career. Lincoln Filene, the department store executive, emphasized this responsibility when he said, "If we were to create contentment in front of the counter we had first to create contentment behind."

With objectives of library service outlined, the librarian explains them to his staff and, with aid of its members, develops policies for carrying out the objectives. Each must know the goal and how his job contributes toward it. It is also the librarian's privilege to interpret the parent organization's overall corporate philosophies, relating the library's function to each, thus strengthening pride in its mission. Likewise the librarian has responsibility to state clearly organization policies and practices such as those having to do with employment, pay plans, progress reviews, and promotion. Future relations of the librarian with his staff depend on how carefully he takes these steps.

During this same orientation period it is also wise to emphasize the importance of good staff-clientele relationships. *Feedback methods* to measure services must be devised in order to know what adjustments are needed to keep pace with innovations in information programs. Walkey (14) has warned that in an age of frequent business mergers, realignment of management, cost reduction, and reevaluation of corporate activities and services, the wise librarian accelerates his normal continuing analysis of library operations. To this end he also uses all talents available to work amicably and constructively with his immediate supervision. He is also consistent in carrying out his administrative function.

The staff looks to the librarian for direction of effort. When effort is effectively coordinated, each staff member will submerge his own interests in contributing to the total operation of library service. Staff members must understand what is to be done, when it is to be done, and how it is to be done—in other words, the librarian, in order to train, must give clear and concise instructions. To guide staff members in putting knowledge to work, he must work with them and help them understand the problems to be met separately and together. The efficiency of the entire staff will be increased if and when many of the library operations are described in a *staff manual,* complete with flow charts (see also Chapter 2). Not only does a manual provide the medium for the recording of experience gained in solving problems pertinent to the job at hand, but also it proves to be excellent insurance against failure to remember correctly. It is also invaluable in training staff replacements; therefore, it must be kept up to date.

There are many other ways of accomplishing effective staff rapport. If there is a small *bulletin board* for his exclusive use, no member of the staff lacks a medium to reach others working in the same unit. It may have a hodgepodge appearance but it is never ignored. Where staff members are scattered, circulation of memoranda which may concern only the staff or cover announcements of general interest may be used. To secure immediate reactions and results, the *staff meeting* is most effective. Some problems, however, are more easily solved if committees are appointed to investigate all angles and to propose a solution or possible alternatives for further discussion. Lage (15), in a still worthwhile summary, lists a variety of ways in which staff members are encouraged to develop professionally on the job and, at the same time, gain more knowledge for their day-to-day work in order to guard against obsolescence, both professional and technological.

An effective method of library staff orientation, for the new employee as well as for the clientele, is an *audiovisual presentation* of library operations. (See also next section.) Many librarians also take advantage of invitations to *lectures* concerned with their subject fields, particularly if presented intramurally. Not only is the individual educated but also his attendance fosters good relationships both within and without the library's walls. In a large information service, a *staff news sheet* often serves as an excellent information medium and, at the same time, aids in the unification of the working group. Most special library staffs are so small, however, that good liaison prevails without this aid.* A summary of suggestions, as well as additional ideas for staff development, appear at the end of this chapter.

Often referred to in past decades as "management's hidden asset," the special library is fast gaining recognition as a creative participant in research and development. In fact, as Jackson (16) points out, "information is clearly a vital asset of the firm and, if properly employed, should rank in importance with the organization's personnel resources, physical facilities, and financial resources." Not always is this reflected in the company organization chart. Regardless of its position here, Sable (17) emphasizes that the librarian can exert a natural leadership role; "he will be vested with authority granted by the users of the service providing the service is of high quality and influential in guiding the direction of the company program." An important aspect of the *staff as a public* is, therefore, the fostering of informal organizational relationships which have no place on a chart. It is the challenge of this responsibility that the librarian brings to his staff so that each one realizes that a corollary to information transfer is a keen sense of participation in its eventual use.

Atmosphere of the Library

Lying somewhere between the areas of responsibility of the librarian to the staff and the staff to the clientele is consideration of the library's atmosphere and its impact on their working relations—an important

---

* In developing this chapter, recognition is given to the fact that there are some "one man" technical libraries operating effectively. Many of the suggestions for group action are not practicable unless there is a minimum of five staff members. However, many adaptations of suggestions contained herein can be made as the changing needs of the library demand.

interface. Many new buildings are now designed with the recognition that an easily accessible location for the library is an added factor in the economical use of time which, in turn, enhances good relations with users. Even a less desirable location can be made attractive and comfortable with due attention paid to lighting, ventilation, and adequate, well-equipped quarters. The location of study tables, abstract bars, and carrels within easy access to stack areas promotes satisfaction. Pleasant, courteous, and well-groomed staff members, perceptive of the user's needs, lend an air of assurance which will be reflected not only in the initial approach of the clientele to the library but also in the continuous use of its service and facilities.

THE CLIENTELE IS A KEY RELATIONSHIP

Of paramount importance is the librarian's responsibility for interpretation of information services to those who use the library and who, by their actual physical presence, greatly outnumber its other publics. Little wonder then that it is this public, frequently referred to as the "consumer public," to whom the principal services are aimed. The scope of the latter varies from library to library whether offered on a company-wide basis or only, for example, to the research and development function. In addition to special collections and staff publications, Southern (18) lists fifteen distinct services offered by the Science Information Service he heads such as translations, personal book orders, and computerized services. Eight regularly issued service publications and six issued less frequently are described in a list issued by the Technical Information Libraries of the Bell Telephone Laboratories (19). A return request form is attached to the list and any of the various publications can be circled. Three of them are computer-printed and indexed; more will be computerized later. Several specific practices in various libraries for enhancing good relationships are outlined in the following.

Library Committee

The most important function of the library is to give adequate and imaginative service; in so doing, the information function may, in time, be recognized as a major resource of the business just as are manpower, money, materials, and machines. To this end, as well as to guide staff efforts along the most productive lines, a *library committee* is often helpful if organized so that its duties will be purely advisory in nature rather than supervisory; its liaison function is discussed briefly in Chapter

1. Such a committee should be representative of major interests of the organization, or at least of the function in which the library operates. Within the personal experience of one of the authors (IMS), it has been observed that middle-management men have more interest in serving on such a committee than executives whose time is at a premium for other types of meetings and conferences.

Library Handbook

Staff collaboration is necessary to prepare a handbook for the clientele. At the outset it is wise to get the points of view of the users as to what needs emphasis and explanation. Since a handbook is a guide to the use of the library, it should be kept up to date. It usually contains library policies and rules for circulation of materials, library hours, floor plans, and telephone numbers; explains the classification system in use; tells how to use the card catalog, especially noting variations from the traditional; describes special services, files, and indexes; and may give the names of staff members who are in charge of special duties such as microfilming and interlibrary loans.

The impressive illustrated booklet issued by the library of the Aerospace Corporation (20) is one which graphically describes its organization and sets forth its objectives. Details of the collection and services are given together with organization charts, floor plans, and user statistics in the first section. In the second, one finds the text of the *Library Guide,* and in the third part, a series of twenty flow charts which make an important addition to a staff manual. This item supplements the general information contained in the extremely well illustrated library handbook of the same organization. Other attractive handbooks, presenting an adequate amount of information in a readable and eye-catching manner, are issued by libraries; a few are shown in Figure 1 in a composite arrangement.

Librarians willing to contribute professional-level assistance and on-the-job teaching can aid the newly employed bench scientist in improving his own working relations because he must learn during the early part of his professional career how to find, use, and communicate information. For example, he may not know how to copy a bibliographical reference correctly or he may not know how to use an indexing service. He may learn by trial and error that one requests a reprint from the author rather than the publisher. Many of these problems may be anticipated and the necessary information incorporated in the *library handbook,* thus recognizing its instructional value. If more time were available for preparation of handbooks, many librarians of industrial organizations

Figure 1. Library Handbooks

could utilize the talents of their in-plant visual aids department in presenting readable and attractive booklets.

Audiovisual Orientation

A communications problem compounded by a large number of services provided by an information center, is described by Keller (21). It was determined that a *sound-slide presentation* may serve the threefold purpose of (1) relieving personnel from routine orientation of new employees, allowing more time for other duties; (2) presenting facilities in a form readily understood; and (3) making possible reorientation when the user has a problem. Here a "split frame" technique was used to prepare slides with colored backgrounds to maintain a cohesive explanation and then the script was modified to describe the slides. Slide mounting was followed by turning on both units, tape on the recorder and slide tray on the projector, for viewing. Two units describing Monsanto's Information Center containing a total of 145 slides are available from the Headquarters of the Special Libraries Association.

Bulletin Boards

Even the smallest of libraries, both in staff and in space, can well use a bulletin board. If placed in a prominent spot near the main entrance, those using the library unconsciously form the habit of looking at it, either upon entering or leaving. Here the clientele may see notices of notable achievements in its fields of interest, scientific meetings, academic courses scheduled in the area, and forthcoming publications. Reprints of papers presented by staff members at recent meetings please both the author and his associates if placed on the bulletin board. Announcements of personnel changes and news stories released by the company's press relations department, including those of honors and awards to individual employees, are likewise appreciated. Vacation folders, road maps, and competitive advertisements can always be used if and when technical news items are scarce.

In at least one library, pertinent science items from *The New York Times* and other daily papers are clipped regularly for the bulletin board. This practice occasioned favorable comment to the extent that other scientific spot news was noted by readers and sent to the library. The bulletin board may be changed frequently, and those clippings which promise to be of some lasting interest may be preserved in the information or picture files. Even an occasional cartoon attracts attention and may aid getting back lost books! A shelf built below the bulletin board affords a choice spot for displaying new books before placed in the stacks or circulated to individuals. A comfortable chair close at hand enhances the invitation to examine new books and thus pays dividends in reader comfort and satisfaction. If acquisition of a new book has been recommended by a library user, advance notice to him that the book is available will be welcomed.

Exhibits

Some libraries are fortunate in having the space and cases for eye-catching exhibits. Initiative and careful planning are necessary in order to produce displays that are timely and pertinent to the interests of the organization. Archival material, especially photographs, never fails to arouse interest, not only on the part of the newcomers to the organization, but also of the older members who have contributed to its growth. Visitors to the library also carry away with them a favorable and lasting impression if something tangible focuses their attention directly upon a phase of current research.

Rare books of historical interest in the field of the organization's activities are in the possession of many libraries. Although they are usually hidden away in the stacks, the exhibit case offers an opportunity to display them occasionally. Materials borrowed from various units of the organization may prove interesting; a collection of raw ores or crude drugs might be used in a metallurgical and pharmaceutical library, respectively. To be effective "people-stoppers," *exhibits* must be varied from time to time and tied in whenever possible with the organization's calendar of events. Their subjects are limited only by the imagination of and time available to the librarian and his staff.

Annual Report

A readable summary of the year's activities draws specific attention to what is being accomplished, thus providing the readers with an opportunity to evaluate library services. It is also valuable as an historical record. Examples of services inaugurated such as a new file of trade names, compilation of a comprehensive bibliography covering an important company product, contribution of the library staff to a professional journal,—all are grist for an annual report. A joint effort by staff members responsible for various area activities of a special library might serve the double purpose of incorporating variety and increasing staff interest in its preparation. Or one might show the effectiveness of a specific service by charting, for example, the increase in daily circulation of materials over a decade from a mere 50 in 1960 to 250 in 1970. One of the most succinct statements covering the purpose, audience, contents, preparation, and style of an annual report appeared as an editorial in a professional publication some time ago (22). It is well worth the brief reading time required.

If it is not usual procedure to make *annual reports* to management, another time span may be chosen. In fact, quarterly reports are customary in some organizations. A summary of library operations submitted from time to time can conceivably be more attention-getting than a routine report, especially if some unusual items are included such as a "good story" illustrating effective reference work. One illustrated report examined, summarizing achievements during a fiscal year and touching on highlights and trends to bring it to the end of the calendar year, is both unique and comprehensive (23). Whether brief or full, accompanied or not by charts and illustrations, the report is a legitimate means of telling the library's story not only to top management but to anyone who is either a habitual or potential user. In any case, the report must compete for the reading time of its recipients; therefore, it must be both stimulating and interesting in content and presentation.

Library Bulletin

Dissemination of information pertinent to the organization's specific interests is the main purpose of a library bulletin. It is discussed in detail in Chapter 10. Aside from its primary objective, its value as a medium for communication (two-way when a return card is attached) of other items is recognized. The first or last page is often utilized for booklists, bibliographies, or news items. The bulletin offers a way to publicize a new file or staff service which may be of special interest—in fact, it always provides an opportunity for issuing supplementary material when the need for it is indicated. Many libraries have supplanted their bulletins with a *table-of-contents service,* either purchased commercially or prepared by the staff. When "user-oriented systems" become more generally employed and after national networks of information systems in science and technology are fully developed, special libraries will depend more and more on them, leaving the bulletin as the medium for intramural communication of news.

House Organs

Exercising one's imagination in showing the library's "wares" through print is an effective way to reach potential users. Many organizations have one or more publications issued at regular intervals, the columns of which are usually open to the librarian. Appropriate contributions might include reviews, lists of new books, or selected abstracts of articles having an organization-wide interest if editorial policy permits their inclusion. By far the most welcome type of news in a publication intended solely for distribution within the organization is an account of unusual service rendered by the library provided it is of a nonconfidential nature; many such stories are available if a library staff member develops a "nose for news." From a public relations point of view an experience which created interest outside the organization was one of a chemist who found a letter from Liebig to Faraday, dated 1842, among the pages of an old volume of the *Journal of the Chemical Society* which had been purchased by the library a century later (24). The letter, which was reproduced to illustrate the story, has since been laminated for permanent preservation.

Special Files and Indexes

To supplement the printed reference tools in a subject field, special files and indexes are often prepared if and when time permits. For example, files of college catalogs and competitors' price lists will be useful. The philosophy of such supplementary service has been discussed elsewhere (25). When the library staff generates finding aids which will answer reference questions on subjects not covered in commercially prepared indexes such as a complete and current alphabetical list by author of journal articles published by the firm's research personnel, a search through printed annual indexes can be eliminated. Not only do these special aids facilitate information transfer; their availability also gains the confidence and appreciation of the library's major public which, as a rule, needs prompt answers. If nonconventional and specialized materials are integrated in a centralized cataloging system, their use will be further increased.

Reprography

Equipment is used to best advantage by both staff and clientele if housed in the library but, because of the expense factor, it may be necessary to use that located elsewhere. One of the best builders of goodwill is an on-the-spot method of reproducing one copy of a bibliography, a complete article, or possibly only an abstract. This is usually done for or by the person who has an immediate use for the item and who would be inconvenienced if required to wait for procurement by some other method. *Photocopying* also reduces extended loans of material needed for projects which do not end in a month and sometimes not within a year. Both the expense of repair service and copyright are problems still to be resolved. In some situations reader-printer copies from microfilm, facsimile transmission, also printout service via the computer are innovations which supplement photocopy service, equipment for which is discussed in Chapter 4. Dickson (26) describes a simple desk top reader for microfiche users in checking 500 duplicate copies of documents supplied weekly with reader-printers conveniently located to supply enlargements. Ultrafiche, an advanced type of microfilming system, is undergoing studies for library use.

Enclosures

Limited only by the imagination of staff, items attached to or enclosed in materials circulated may be announcements, bookmarks, cartoons, flyers, or other *"separates"* conveying a message. They are designed to accompany the book, periodical, or report as it leaves the library either by messenger or in the hands of the borrower. Colored and eye-catching are the series of eight cards, 1¾ by 3 inches in size, bearing messages on both sides which cannot be overlooked. These clever enclosures, used at the Lincoln Laboratory Library of the Massachusetts Institute of Technology, are varied as to the messages carried, such as "printed request-for-reprint forms, on stamped postcards, are available at the Library's circulation desk;" "the Library has current telephone directories for most major U.S. cities;" "quick comprehensive computer service;" "current awareness service on foreign language articles;" and other pertinent announcements. One card even bears an apt quotation while another has a timely cartoon.

Individualized Service

The librarian has an unusual opportunity to learn the special interests of his clientele through personal conversation; noting subjects of papers presented at meetings; checking reports of contact trips; and attention to the reference questions directed to the library. The ideal situation is brought about when the librarian is informed of research projects to be undertaken, either through actual attendance at research staff meetings when the projects are in the planning stage or by reports and memoranda circulated by the director of research and development. Still another opportunity is opened to the librarian when he first is asked to make a preliminary search on a subject which holds promise for investigation. Credit to the library for assistance given in preparation of scientific articles is especially rewarding since it indicates information transfer is a "two-way street."

The tempo of work in a scientific library does not allow for unlimited and flexible interchange of duties nor do the specialist positions on the staff. There have been situations, however, wherein professional staff members spend part time at the information desk in order to keep informed of special interests of the clientele, thus placing staff in a position to relate any pertinent article coming to their attention, immediately upon its receipt, to the work interests of the specific individual who might use information contained in the publication. Once informed, in one way or another, staff members are in a strategic position to catch items of interest as they appear in current publications. Although limitations of time may dictate the use of printed forms, a telephone call expedites personal service. In selective dissemination of information (SDI), *interest profiles of clientele* are prepared to be used with computerized service described in Chapter 10.

In establishing relationships and balancing time to be allocated, service to potential users should not be overlooked; in fact, the development of a simple "user-interest" file will often prove rewarding. There are always employees, too, who will be grateful for help with a personal problem such as how to identify a termite or take an ink spot out of a rug if time permits a staff member to guide inquirers to the proper reference source which they can use for themselves. Although not to be encouraged since the library cannot be "all things to all men," occasional help with identifying a portrait of a scientist in a popular contest will gain a staunch supporter for the library; the mail boy may someday rise to the position of division manager. Particularly rewarding is the time given to acquainting secretarial employees with library resources for it is they who often remember where to go for the answer when "the boss" forgets.

Other Media

Among the many unclassified items collected in preparing this chapter are the publications compiled by Washburn (27) for members of a professional association; they include a classification of dental literature, names of librarians of dental schools, dental organizations of the United States, and lists of new books and periodicals. A special service, which began experimentally in 1940, became a full fledged one five years later when the library staff of Eli Lilly and Company cooperated with the Indianapolis Public Library in manning a station library of the latter twice weekly. Another station was established in a second location of the company at the end of the decade. A unique service of the Aerospace Corporation's library (20) is a bookstore operated on the mall behind the library during lunch hour periods for the convenience of employees. Here the latest scientific and technical books are available at a discount from the stock of a local bookseller immediately after publication.

Since not all of the librarian's public relations activities can be described in detail, a checklist of media and techniques available for use is appended to this chapter. They are applicable to plant-wide service if management encourages service to all components of its organization. Furthermore, many are adaptable to other types of libraries whether applied to a hospital, technical society, or departmentalized subject library since the principles are basically the same for all. It will be judicious for the librarian to select only those media and techniques most likely to produce results and thereby gain the support of management. If impediments exist, a resourceful librarian usually meets the challenge to circumvent or to overcome them. He never forgets that good *service to the clientele* is his messenger of good will, and one of his best means of interpreting service is the time given to introducing the new employee to the library and learning the latter's needs.

RESPONSIBILITY TO MANAGEMENT'S PUBLIC

Because direct contact is so often lacking, the third area of the librarian's individual responsibility for good public relations is perhaps the most difficult for him to recognize. In an article reviewing various statements of prominent business leaders as to how and why they are striving to reach their publics, Buchanan (28) quoted an insurance executive:

Every employee is a public relations emissary. If you multiply the number of employees by individuals in their circle of family and friends, that will represent a substantial section of the public, even with a moderate-sized firm. All of these people are getting their ideas about the company and what it stands for through what the employees are saying about it.

As pointed out earlier in this chapter, the library staff has an unusual opportunity to build and to keep the good will of the many interests represented in management's public.

What groups compose a corporation's complex public? Still assuming that emphasis is placed here primarily on an industrial library, the public of its overall management will usually fall into major divisions such as (a) employees who desire steady employment, good working conditions, friendly human relations, and high wages; (b) stockholders who wish their assets protected and a fair return on investment; (c) suppliers, dealers, distributors, competitors, and others with whom there are business relations; (d) consumers of the manufactured product who expect the best and most for their money; (e) government, because of its multiplicity of regulations affecting business operations; and (f) the community of which the organization is a part—sometimes referred to as the "grass roots" public. Many of these publics overlap because they are made up of people who represent more than one group. Burton's (29) recent book listed most of the techniques used in communicating with them.

In many industrial companies the *house organ* serves a dual purpose and therefore receives both external and internal distribution. In others, separate publications are directed to potential users of products manufactured; they serve an educational purpose and likewise are messengers of good will. By giving thoughtful study to the purpose of the publications, an alert library staff has much to offer the editors. Suggestions may include creative ideas for cover designs, a series of illustrated biographical articles, or bibliographies on products developed by the organization. The experiences of individual librarians in creating good will for and understanding of their organizations would make an interesting research project for a student of information science.

Another type of contribution to management's public was the result of a request of the story of library service in a pharmaceutical organization as an educational aid for sales representatives in Latin America. Whatever physical form was to be used, it had to be small enough to carry in a brief case because of weight limitations of plane travel. A series of 20 colored slides was made showing library staff members providing information by means of reference work, bibliographies, interlibrary loans, microfilm, maps, special files, weekly abstracts, as well as by routine circulation of journals. An appropriate script accompanied the slides which required a viewing time of 15 minutes. With this audiovisual presentation, company representatives were better prepared to explain to members of the health professions whom they contacted how their questions could be handled on a referral basis. It also demonstrated the library phase of the careful search preceding the development of company products.

It is in this same area, responsibility to management's publics, that the librarian's sense of public relations sometimes undergoes a severe test. Some students, in their eagerness to acquire information for term papers, try to think of quick and easy ways. They may address an inquiry to the sales department of an organization. More often than not, the letter is referred to the library. Averse to doing the actual work, the librarian has difficulty in deciding on the minimum amount of information to assemble for the student, a potential customer. The final decision, usually shared with an official of the sales department, might be to send a review article or a bibliography which may lead the student further in his quest for information.

From *company archives* come ideas and information for speeches, institutional advertising, anniversary celebrations, and material for the company history which, sooner or later, everyone wants. Early production, payroll, and utility records make intriguing statistics when compared with the present. Old pictures showing interior and exterior views of the plant furnish excellent subjects for articles in company publications; pictures of people and products of a century ago are likely to create even more interest. Price lists and advertisements are often useful to the legal department. The value of archival material in planning exhibits is mentioned elsewhere in this chapter and in Chapter 9.

The technical librarian in industry, in fact the librarian working within any institution, is a captive professional rather than an independent operator such as are many engaged in professional occupations. Fortunately for the special librarian, he is usually connected with an organization that recognizes the worth of good public relations; therefore he does not need to waste time contending with misunderstood concepts of its value. More often than not he has ready-made support for his efforts. His problem, however, is to comprehend the breadth and significance of *management's public* and to mesh his own program with the overall program. Within the range of his own duties he must keep in mind that each telephone conversation, each letter written, each purchase negotiated, and each questionnaire answered represent his organization in the eyes of the public. As a matter of fact the library staff member *is* the organization in each of his contacts.

PROFESSIONAL RELATIONSHIPS FORM ANOTHER PUBLIC

A fourth area of responsibility for good public relations is that which lies between the library staff and the professional sources outside the library upon which it relies for aid. For example, information is often needed to supplement the resources of the special library for none is complete within itself. An experienced librarian realizes that there is scarcely a problem in any field of human endeavor for which there is not at least a partial answer recorded somewhere. Always optimistic, he will try to produce needed facts from whatever source available; if the source is neither the printed nor written page, a search may lead him to subject specialists in specific fields who have not yet put their ideas on paper. However, in the process of seeking personal help outside his own organization, a librarian depends primarily upon members of his own and related professions but is always careful to give credit when and where it is due.

Information can often be obtained locally by telephone, trips to other libraries, or borrowing needed items by special messenger service. The librarian knows that his efficiency and enthusiasm are increased when he is fully informed of the significance of the item sought as well as the end use to be made of it—another step in successful public relations. So, too, he must recognize that those from whom he, in turn, seeks help will work more intelligently if they know why their aid is sought. Certainly confidential information must be kept as such, but there are usually reasonable limits within which a librarian can work and still impart to others that desire for cooperation with which he is imbued. Furthermore, the *ethics* of professional librarianship encompass the treatment of requests for information as a trust.

The following incident illustrates skillful professional relations. A special librarian was called upon periodically for illustrations to be used in a publication distributed to scientists. Exhausting his own resources, he occasionally asked for help from the reference and art departments of the local public library. At first, these department staffs saw no connection between the special librarian's area of interest and the item requested; in fact, once or twice they questioned the need. Upon one occasion, to their surprise, they received marked copies of the completed publications in which appeared the illustrations based upon those originally loaned from their files. This tangible evidence of their help led to enthusiastic cooperation when future requests came from this same librarian whose organization represented one of the city's largest taxpayers.

Special libraries, and especially those with limited resources, depend upon interlibrary loans to supplement service (see Chapter 9). When items are obtainable within the immediate vicinity, responsibility falls upon the librarian to encourage his staff to become familiar with resources of other libraries and to know the personnel administering them. Even if he is in the position of borrower more often than that of lender, he may have much with which he can reciprocate. Lists of new books and periodicals, with borrowing privileges, are the minimum means to accomplish this end. He can also offer, if his organization's policies permit, to help with a specialized reference question. In relations with academic institutions, he might make available specialized materials for study within the library, if space permits, provided the student presents a note from the professor assigning the work. In fact, management's community service policy may emphasize the librarian's obligation to maintain good relationships.

When needed items must be obtained from without the local area, *professional relationships* are just as important to cultivate and to preserve. The obligation of clearly stating requests, giving complete bibliographic references, and observing the rules of interlibrary loan is unquestioned. The borrowing librarian can always be on the alert to cooperate in contributing to union lists of holdings as well as to devise other means of reciprocal courtesy to librarians of collections containing items which supplement his own library's holdings. Specialization in libraries can be shared more economically with others than independently striving for completeness.

Instantaneous transmission of reference materials is at hand in some locations. Budington (30), in his excellent review of interrelations among special librarians, reviews the objectives, etiology, and requirements of the *library network* as it "overtakes and embraces cooperation." He feels the shift is due to two factors—first, the application of systems thinking, analysis, and techniques and second, current technology identified most readily in two areas, mechanization or computerization, and communication procedures. He quotes from another writer who defines a network as a circumstance where more than two people are dealing with a common pattern of information exchange by means of communication links.

Further channels of communication are open to the librarian who encourages his staff to become members of professional library associations, to attend their meetings, to share in joint projects likely to be of lasting usefulness, to contribute articles to periodicals which enrich professional literature, and, in other ways, to enhance the exchange of useful methods and techniques of disseminating information. Beltran (31) issues a challenge when he writes: "In becoming a professional librarian he drew upon the discipline's fund of knowledge. He is now expected to replenish and advance this knowledge that others may in turn draw upon it." Participation in National Library Week pinpoints another opportunity; not only will it foster cooperation at the local level but it also will contribute toward the goals of all librarians. It is also important that librarians share in activities of professional societies concerned with their subject specialties.

Today's special librarian does not lack opportunity to continue his education by reading, by enlarging his circle of contacts, or by registering in institutes, workshops, and formal courses of varying lengths in information management. Lists of these appear frequently in professional journals such as the one contributed by Klassen (32). Financial assistance is often available from library associations, state library agencies, foundations, and library schools in accordance with their programs. With more and more attention directed toward subject specialization and library systems, *continuing education* need not be restricted to library-oriented activities but, even in these areas, new and imaginative approaches are recognized. Aware of the necessity for maintaining good relationships in every aspect of business, management will support professional contacts and activities of the library staff but the staff must assume the initiative.

SUMMARY

In this chapter concepts of service of the technical librarian and his staff to their principal publics are discussed. His channels of communication with each of them are pointed out. They involve human relations, business relations, professional relations, and even community relations, all of which are facets of public relations—good, bad, or indifferent. Equipped with knowledge of the expenditure of time and effort needed in developing good relationships, the librarian will have the incentive to analyze the background necessary to develop a program geared to his own situation and needs. The suggested methods included both in the text and the checklist can be selected in the order of their relative significance. In every situation it is obvious that there are limitations of budget and manpower in work to be undertaken. It is important, therefore, to recognize their complexity in order not to "oversell" library service beyond what is practicable.

A most excellent and perceptive survey by Crum (32) of the relationships between management and the head of the library appeared in 1970. He reviews, as a by-product of his own experience and suggestions, some of the views of others as set forth in professional articles published in recent years. This list is an important supplement to the bibliography accompanying this chapter. Concepts for making the relationship of the manager-librarian more dynamic and creative within the organizational climate are considered by the author after first analyzing the division of authority and responsibility to make the interaction more effective. See Figures 2 and 3.

The parent administrative authority expects services of a highly specialized nature from the librarian it employs. To be effective, the interpretative process of the services cannot be sporadic such as issuing only an occasional list of new books or preparing a report once in a decade. The program must be planned carefully, possess continuity, and reach the specific group for which it is intended. Lacking such direction, a haphazard program is likely to develop with obvious areas of responsibility overlooked. Added to tangible efforts made as a result of planning are the subconscious acts that reflect a helpful attitude on the part of the library staff; good service is always contagious. Since "public relations

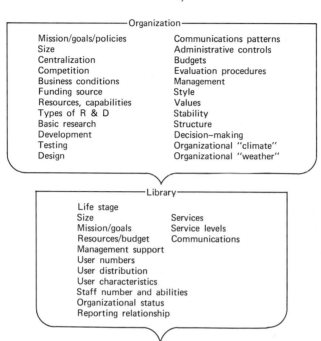

Figure 2. Organization and library variables. Reprinted from *Special Libraries* **61,** No. 9, 487 (November 1970), copyrighted by the Special Libraries Association.

begins at home" and each contact made presents its own opportunity for building good will, it clearly becomes the duty of each library staff to interpret and to communicate its services adequately to its multiple publics.

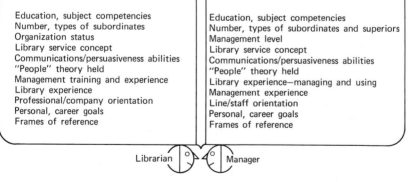

Figure 3. Librarian and manager variables. Reprinted from *Special Libraries* **61,** No. 9, 487 (November 1970), copyrighted by the Special Libraries Association.

CHECKLIST OF SUGGESTED MEDIA AND TECHNIQUES FOR
PUBLIC RELATIONS ACTIVITIES IN
SPECIAL LIBRARIES*

1. Numerous media exist, in addition to the usual communications in person, by telephone, and in memoranda, which can be used effectively such as:

Information counter
Suggestion receptacle
Daily messenger service
Weekly library bulletins
Open house—annual events
Bookmarks for announcements
Feature articles in house organs
Use of organization bulletin boards
Moving pictures of library operations
Pictorial posters of library in action
Tours of library for all new employees
Information section in employee handbook
Library columns in organization newspaper
Library exhibits at employee's hobby shows
Attractive brochure to introduce the library

2. Some techniques of communication in addition to reference and literature search service are as follows.
   a. With clientele who depend upon the library

Translations assistance
Informal personal contacts
Attention to specific interests
Calendar of employee activities
Assistance with editorial problems
Application of computer techniques
Cheerful consideration of criticism
Bibliographies prepared upon request
Careful attention to recommendations
Displays of organization news releases
"Extra touch" such as comfortable chairs
Aid in acquisition of personal library items

* Revised with permission from "Public Relations Activities in Special Libraries," *Libr. Trends,* October 1958, a publication of the University of Illinois Graduate School of Library Science.

Suggestions for binding of personal periodicals
Use of information networks system when available
Presentation of library service at research seminar
Reproduction of tables of contents of current journals
Duplicating and/or copying machines available in library

b. With management

Annual   library   reports
Material   for   sales   talks
Regular   intelligence   digest
Daily   news   clippings   service
Indexing   company   publications
Participation   in   community   goals
Archival   preservation   and   operation
Aid in organizing department collections
Good working relationships with supervision
Provision for employee's recreational reading
Library orientation for management's secretaries
Participation in organization's educational plans
Cooperation in plant-wide public relations program
Understanding relationships with library committee
Advice in classification of personal book collections

c. With the library staff

Imaginative   planning
In-service   preparation
Equitable promotion policy
Staff manual kept up-to-date
Recognition for accomplishment
Develop pride in the profession
Communicate effectively and clearly
Invite ideas for library bulletin boards
Staff participation in employee activities
Staff meetings in which members participate
Encourage additional educational preparation
Bulletin board for exclusive use of library staff
Suggest contributions for professional periodicals
Man station library maintained by local public library

3. Media and techniques useful outside the organizations
a. With professional colleagues

Exchange of duplicate materials
Attendance at professional meetings
Adherence to rules of other libraries

Cooperation with professional projects
Participation in National Library Week
Visits to library facilities in local area
Widen interest in librarianship as a career
Report help gained through interlibrary loan
Arrange for professional meetings in company library
Participation in development of information networks
Consultation regarding library development in the area

b. With potential library employees

"Librarian-for-the-day" project
Library summer work-study program
Vocational talks to high school pupils
Acquaint library schools in area with work
Picture of library in company's recruiting folder
Open house for students interested in librarianship
Keep schools informed of career progress of graduates

In using this checklist it should be kept in mind (1) there are several overlapping items in the categories above; (2) not every library will find it practicable or even desirable to consider all of them; and (3) many of the suggestions may already be incorporated not only in programs of special libraries but in those of other types as well—school, college, and public.

Institutes such as the one sponsored by the Public Relations Section of LAD, American Library Association, and the Graduate School of Library Science at Drexel, in Atlantic City, June 20–21, 1969 advance new ideas, some of which will supersede older ones. The Library Public Relations Council [see *Libr. J.* **93**, 698, (1968)] collects samples of the most effective library public relations items for distribution to their members.

REFERENCES

1. *Webster's Third New International Dictionary of the English Language*, unabridged, Merriam, Springfield, Mass., 1966.
2. B. R. Canfield, *Public Relations: Principles, Cases, and Problems.* 5th ed., R. D. Irwin, Homewood, Ill., 1968, p. 4.
3. *Ibid.*, Revised ed., 1956, p. 19.
4. J. M. Wright, and B. H. Christian, *Public Relations in Management*, McGraw-Hill, New York, 1949, p. 12, 17.
5. S. Korbe, *Dynamic Force of Public Relations Today*, Brown, Dubuque, Iowa, 1964, Chapts. 5, 10, 11, 14.

6. P. Lesly, Ed., *Public Relations Handbook,* 3rd ed., Prentice-Hall, Englewood Cliffs, N.J., 1967, Chapts. 1, 5, 6, 9, 11, 12, 13, 16, 17, 23.

7. W. E. Reck, "Public Relations for Educational Institutions," in *Public Relations Handbook,* 3rd ed., Prentice-Hall, Englewood Cliffs, N.J., 1967, Chap. 23, p. 386.

8. C. A. Schoenfeld, *Publicity Media and Methods: Their Role in Modern Public Relations,* Macmillan, New York, 1963, pp. 47–49.

9. "Administration of Technical Information Groups," *Ind. Eng. Chem.* **51,** 48A–61A (1959). Contains abstract of G. W. Duncan's paper, "Establishing an Information Group."

10. *Ibid.,* contains abstract of "Organizational Relations of Information Groups," Preprint of paper reproduced ten organization charts showing group location.

11. I. M. Strieby, "Organizational Relations of Special Librarians," *Libr. Trends,* **1,** 173–188 (1952).

12. "The Place of the Library in the Organization," *Proceedings* (of the) *Executive Conference on Organizing and Managing Information,* University College, University of Chicago, 1957, pp. 42–56.

13. J. W. Hill, *Corporate Public Relations; Arm of Modern Management,* Harper, New York, 1958, p. 93.

14. E. M. Walkey, "Communicating with Management," *Spec. Libr.* **57,** 565–568 (1966).

15. L. Lage, "A Program for Library Staff Development," *Bull. Med. Libr. Assoc.* **40,** 37–42 (1952).

16. E. B. Jackson, "The Information Explosion and its Implications for Management," presented at the College of Business Administration and Center for Executive Development, Arizona State University, Tempe, Ariz., March 4, 1969.

17. E. M. Sable, "A Management Concept of the Modern Special Library," *Spec. Libr.* **55,** 23–25 (1964).

18. *Science-Patent-Business Information Services,* booklet describing Abbott's Science Information Service (received by authors April 1969); see also W. A. Southern, "Information Services at Abbott Laboratories," *Ill. Libr.* **45,** 493–498 (1963).

19. Library Publications, booklet describing fourteen publication services of the Technical Information Libraries, Public Relations and Publication Division, Bell Telephone Laboratories, Murray Hill, N. J., received by authors May 1969).

20. *The Charles C. Lauritsen Library: Library Services,* Aerospace Corporation, Los Angeles, Calif., 1969.

21. C. W. Keller, "Monsanto Information Center's Audio-Visual Orientation Program," *Spec. Libr.* **57,** 648–651 (1966).

22. Editorial, "The Annual Report," *Bull. Med. Libr. Assoc.* **42,** 503–504 (1954).

23. Illustrated library report, 1966–1967, Chicago College of Osteopathy, Chicago, March 1968.

24. "The Mystery in the Lilly Library; Missing 110 Years," *Lilly Revi* **12,** 4–5 (November 1952).

25. I. M. Strieby, "Reference Files in a Pharmaceutical Library," *Bull. Med. Libr. Assoc.* **35,** 107–115 (1947).

26. R. R. Dickson, "The Scholar and the Future of Microfilm," *Amer. Doc.* **17,** 178–179 (1966).

27. *Books and Package Libraries for Dentists,* Bureau of Library and Indexing Services, American Dental Assoc., Chicago, 1967, monthly supplements.

28. M. B. Buchanan, "The Crow's Nest," *Wilson Libr. Bull.* 32, 304–305 (1957). Traditionally this publication, now the Wilson Bulletin, devotes one issue periodically to public relations, e.g., see 40, 509–512 (1966) and 42, 270–311 (1967). Earlier issues also contain good suggestions.

29. P. Burton, *Corporate Public Relations,* Reinhold, New York, 1966, pp. 65–67. Lists of techniques supplied by the Raytheon Manufacturing Co. appear in National Industrial Conference Board's *Studies in Business Policy,* No. 80.

30. W. S. Budington, "Interrelations among Special Libraries," *Libr. Quart.* 39, 64–77 (1969).

31. A. A. Beltran, "Professionalism and SLA Publications," *Sci-Tech. News,* 22, 4–6 (1968).

32. N. J. Crum, "Head Librarian and Manager," *Spec. Libr.* 61, 486–491 (1970).

33. R. Klassen, "Institutes for Training in Librarianship: Summer 1969 and Academic Year 1969–70," *Spec. Libr.* 60, 185–189 (1969).

BIBLIOGRAPHY

Annual Review of Information Science and Technology, Vol. I. C. A. Cuadra, Ed., for the American Documentation Institute, Wiley, New York, 1966. Various articles in this and later volumes.

Aspnes, G., "Committee Control of the Industrial Research Library," *Libr. Trends* 11, 74–81 (1962).

Behling, O. and K. Cudd, "A Library Looks at Itself," *Coll. Res. Libr.* 28, 416–422 (1967).

Boaz, M., "Evaluation of Special Library Service for Upper Management," *Spec. Libr.* 59, 789–791 (1968).

Bozone, B., "Staff Manuals for Reference Departments in College and University Libraries," *Coll. Res. Libr.* 22, 19–20, 34 (1961).

Bundy, M. L. and P. Wasserman, "Professionalism Reconsidered," *Coll. Res. Libr.* 29, 5–26 (1968).

"Can We Commit Ourselves to a Code of Ethics?" Committee report, *ALA Bull.* 62, 511–514 (1968).

Chamis, A. Y., "The Design of Information Systems: The Use of Systems Analysis," *Spec. Libr.* 60, 21–31 (1969).

Crookston, M. E., "Public Relations for the Special Library," *Spec. Libr.* 55, 283–285 (1964).

Crum, N. J., "The Librarian-Customer Relationship," *Spec. Libr.* 60, 269–277 (1969).

Cutlip, S. M., *A Public Relations Bibliography,* 2nd ed., University of Wisconsin Press, Madison, 1965.

Davis, R. A., "Continuing Education: Formal and Informal," *Spec. Libr.* 58, 27–36 (1967). Entire issue devoted to this subject.

Delzell, R. F., "The Administrative Assistant—Pragmatic Job Description," *Coll. Res. Libr.* **28**, 382–386 (1967).

Dougherty, R. M. and F. J. Heinritz, *Scientific Management of Library Operations,* Scarecrow, New York, 1966.

Feinler, E. J. *et al.*, "Attitudes of Scientists toward a Specialized Information Center," *Amer. Doc.* **16**, 329–337 (1965).

Forman, S., "Innovative Practices in College Libraries," *Coll. Res. Libr.* **29**, 486–492 (1968).

Gardner, J. L., "The Library as a Partner in Scientific Creativity," *Libr. Assoc. Rec.* **67**, 84–5 (1965).

Gibson, E. B., "An Industrial Research Library: View through a Library Staff Manual," John Cotton Dana lecture presented at the University of Toronto, October 19, 1962, 19 p. Available on loan from Special Libraries Association.

Griffith, A. B., "Library Handbook Standards," *Wilson Bull.* **39**, 475 (1965).

Kenney, L. A., "Public Relations in the College Library," *Coll. Res. Libr.* **25**, 263–266 (1964).

Lamkin, B. E., "Systems Analysis in Top Management Communications," *Spec. Libr.* **58**, 90–94 (1967).

Lee, L. E., "Basic Communication Tool—the Bulletin Board," Circles of Communication-Working Papers for General Session No. 3, Special Libraries Association, Minneapolis, May 31, 1966, pp. 26–28.

Lowry, W. K. and R. A. Kennedy, "The Services of Technical Information at Bell Telephone Laboratories, *Akt. Probl. Inf. Dokum.* **14**, 1–6 (1969).

Meltzer, M. F., *The Information Center,* American Management Association, New York, 1967.

Moore, E., "Systems Analysis: An Overview," *Spec. Libr.* **58**, 87–90 (1967).

Peak, W. J., "Community Relations," in *Public Relations Handbook,* chap. 9 (see #6 in References under Lesly).

Phipps, B. H., "Library Instruction for the Undergraduate," *Coll. Res. Libr.* **29**, 411–423 (1968).

Pings, V. M., "Development of Quantitative Assessment of Medical Libraries," *Coll. Res. Libr.* **29**, 373–380 (1968).

Pizer, J. H. and A. M. Cain, "Objective Tests of Library Performance," *Spec. Libr.* **59**, 704–711 (1968).

Raburn, J., "Public Relations for a 'Special' Public," *Spec. Libr.* **60**, 647–650 (1969).

Randall, G. E., "Special Library Standards, Statistics, and Performance," *Spec. Libr.* **56**, 379–386 (1965).

Rathbun, L. R., "The Company Professional Librarian . . . ," *Spec. Libr.* **54**, 210–213 (1963).

Scientific and Technical Communication, a report by the Committee on Scientific and Technical Communication of the National Academy of Sciences—National Academy of Engineering, National Academy of Science, Washington, D.C., 1969, publication 1707.

Sewell, W., "The Needs of Industry for Library Services beyond That Expected of Their Own Special Librarian . . . ," *Libr. Trends* **14**, 226–235 (1966).

Simon, B. V., "The Need for Know-How in Libraries," *Bull. Med. Libr. Assoc.* **57**, 160–170 (1969).

Stebbins, K. B., *Personnel Administration in Libraries*, 2nd ed. reviewed by F. E. Mohrhardt, Scarecrow, New York, 1966.

Williams, G. R., "Library Cooperation—Key to Greater Resources," *Spec. Libr.* **56**, 565–570 (1965).

Appendix

BASIC REFERENCE PUBLICATIONS

The following list of reference tools is intended to cover the basic essentials in establishing a new library, irrespective of the type of library or the subject field involved. Books are grouped under general subject categories, such as Dictionaries and Encyclopedias, in order to facilitate their use. Generally several works in each class are listed to provide choice. Every effort has been made to provide the latest edition in each case and all books, insofar as ascertainable, that were in print May 1, 1970. In general, books printed during the 1960s are given preference; however, standard works of an earlier date are also included.

The following is a selection of guides to reference material, both general and scientific in nature, as well as some book selection aids that provide added bibliographic sources.

Jenkins, F. B., *Science Reference Sources,* 5th ed., The M. I. T. Press, Cambridge, Mass., 1969.

Malinowsky, H. R., *Science and Engineering Reference Sources (Library Science Text Series)* Libraries Unlimited, Inc., Rochester, N. Y., 1967.

Walford, A. J., Ed., *Guide to Reference Material,* 2nd ed., *Science and Technology,* Vol. 1, Library Association, London, 1966.

Winchell, C. N., *Guide to Reference Books,* 8th ed., ALA, Chicago, 1967. Section 12. The bibliographic aids in this list will be a useful supplement to *Guide to Reference Material.*

The following are miscellaneous selection aids.

Technical Book Review Index (TBRI), SLA, New York.

New Technical Books, New York Public Library.

Off the Press: New books in science, technology, business and medicine from all publishers. Palo Alto, Calif., Stacey's, a Division of Bro-Dart, Inc.

Brandon, A. N., "Selected List of Books and Journals for the Small Medical Library,
  Med. Libr. Assoc. Bull. **57**, 130–149 (1969). Quarterly supplements published in
  the Bulletin.

Medical books in print, Palo Alto, Calif. Stacey's, a Division of Bro-
  Dart, Inc.

The material in this section is arranged as follows:

A. General

1. ENCYCLOPEDIAS

The Encyclopedia Americana, international ed., Americana Corporation, New York, 1964, 30 vols.

Encyclopaedia Britannica; A New Survey of Universal Knowledge, Encyclopaedia Britannica, Chicago, 1969, 24 vols.

The Columbia Encyclopedia, 3d ed., Columbia University Press, New York, 1963.

2. DICTIONARIES

The Oxford English Dictionary, Clarendon Press, Oxford, 1933, 12 vols.

Random House Dictionary of the English Language, unabridged ed., Random House, New York, 1966.

Webster's Third New International Dictionary of the English Language, unabridged, Merriam, Springfield, Mass., 1966.

Random House Dictionary of the English Language, college ed., Random House, New York, 1968.

Webster's Seventh New Collegiate Dictionary, Merriam, Springfield, Mass., 1965.

Webster's Dictionary of Synonyms; A Dictionary of Discriminated Synonyms with Antonyms and Analagous and Contrasted Words, Merriam, Springfield, Mass., 1951.

Roget's International Thesaurus, 3rd ed., Crowell, New York, 1962.

Words and Phrase Index, Vol. 1– , Pierian Press, Ann Arbor, Mich., 1968. (An index that supplements the *Oxford English Dictionary.*)

3. ALMANACS

World Almanac and Book of Facts, New York World Telegram, New York, annual.

Canadian Almanac and Directory, Copp Clark, Toronto, annual.

4. TRAVEL INFORMATION

Official Airline Guides, Donnelley, New York, monthly.

Official Guide of the Railways, National Railway Publication Co., New York, monthly.

Rand McNally New Cosmopolitan World Atlas, Rand McNally, New York, 1968.

Rand McNally Road Atlas: United States, Canada, Mexico, Rand McNally, New York, annual.

Hotel & Motel Red Book, American Hotel Association Directory Corporation, New York, annual.

Official Hotel & Resort Guide, OHRG, Montreal and Quebec, annual.

International Hotel Directory, International Hotel Directory, Inc., Ft. Lauderdale, Fla., semiannual.

5. MISCELLANEOUS

Bartlett, John, *Familiar Quotations,* 14th ed., Little, Brown and Co., Boston, 1968.

Doris, Lillian, and B. M. Miller, *Complete Handbook for Secretaries,* 2nd ed., Prentice-Hall, New York, 1960.

Fowler, H. W., Ed., *A Dictionary of Modern English Usage,* 2nd ed., Oxford University Press, Fairlawn, N. J., 1965.

U. S. Post Office Department, *Directory of Post Offices,* revised annually.

U. S. Post Office Department, *National Zip Code Directory,* P.O.D. Publication 65, biennial.

Holy Bible, suggested new translations: *The Jerusalem Bible,* Doubleday, Garden City, N. Y., 1966; The New English Bible, Oxford University Press, Oxford, 1970.

B. Manuscript Aids

1. STYLE MANUALS

Fieser, L. F. and Mary Fieser, *Style Guide for Chemists,* Reinhold, New York, 1960.

Hawkins, C. F., *Speaking and Writing in Medicine; The Art of Communication,* C. C. Thomas, Springfield, Ill., 1967.

Conference of Biological Editors, committee on form and style, *Style Manual for Biological Journals,* 2nd ed., American Institute of Biological Sciences, Washington, D.C., 1964.

Seeber, E. D., *Style Manual for Authors,* Indiana University Press, Bloomington, Ind., 1965.

Strunk, William and E. B. White, *The Elements of Style,* trade ed., Macmillan, New York, 1959.

U. S. Government Printing Office, *Style Manual,* revised ed., Washington, 1967; supplement, 1968.

U. S. Government Printing Office, *Style Manual,* abridged revised ed., Washington, 1967.

University of Chicago Press, Eds., *A Manual of Style,* revised 12th ed., Chicago, 1969.

2. TECHNICAL AND REPORT WRITING; EDITING

American Standards Association, *American Standards for Periodical Title Abbreviations,* Z39.5–1963, New York, 1963.

Arnell, Alvin, *Standard Graphical Symbols; A Comprehensive Guide for Use in Industry, Engineering & Science,* McGraw-Hill, New York, 1963.

Ehrlich, E. H. and D. J. Murphy, *The Art of Technical Writing; A Manual for Scientists, Engineers, and Students,* Crowell, New York, 1964.

Hicks, T. G., *Writing for Engineering Science,* McGraw-Hill, New York, 1961.

Philler, T. A. *et al., Selected Bibliography on Technical Writing, Editing, Graphics and Publishing, 1950–1965,* Society of Technical Writers and Publishers, Columbus, Ohio, 1966.

Rhodes, F. H., *Technical Report Writing,* 2nd ed., McGraw-Hill, New York, 1961.

Trelease, S. F., *How to Write Scientific and Technical Papers,* 3rd ed. Williams & Wilkins, Baltimore, 1958.

UNESCO, *Bibliography of Publications Designed to Raise the Standard of Scientific Literature,* Paris, 1963.

U.S.A. Standards Institute, Committee Z39, *U.S.A. Standards for Indexes,* 1968 ed., New York, 1968.

C. Biographical Data

1. GENERAL

Who's Who, Macmillan, New York, annual.

Who's Who in America, Marquis, Chicago, revised and issued biennially.

Who's Who of American Women, Marquis, Chicago, revised and issued biennially.

International Who's Who, 33rd ed., Europa Publications, London, 1969–1970.

2. SCIENCE

American Men of Science, 11th ed., Bowker, New York, 1965; supplements, 1966– .

Asimov, Isaac, *Asimov's Biographical Encyclopedia of Science and Technology . . . ,* Doubleday, Garden City, N. Y., 1964.

Dictionary of Scientific Biography, Scribner, New York, 1970, projected 12 vols., Vol. 1–2 in 1970.

Directory of British Scientists, Benn, London, annual.

International Directory of Research and Developmental Scientists, Institute for Scientific Information, Philadelphia, 1967– , Vol. 1– .

Ireland, N. O., *Index to Scientists of the World; From Ancient to Modern Times; Biographies and Portraits,* Faxon, New York, 1962.

National academy of sciences, *Biographical Memoirs,* Vol. 1– , Washington, 1877/79– , annual.

Royal Society of London, *Biographical Memoirs of Fellows of the Royal Society,* Vol. 1– , London, 1955– .

Turkevich, J., *Soviet Men of Science; Academicians and Corresponding Members of the Academy of Sciences of the U.S.S.R.,* Van Nostrand, Princeton, N. J., 1963.

Who's Who in Science in Europe, International Publications Service, New York, 1968.

5. MISCELLANEOUS

Addressbuch Deutscher Chemischer, 1959/60, Weinheim, 1960.

Chemical Who's Who, 4th ed., biography in dictionary form of the leaders in chemical industry, research and education, Lewis Historical Publications, New York, 1956.

Who's Who in Atoms, Valleny Press, London, 1962.

Who's Who in Engineering, a biographical dictionary of the engineering profession, 9th ed., Lewis Historical Publications, New York, 1964.

Hooper, Alfred, *Makers of Mathematics,* Random House, New York, 1958.

Bell, E. T., *The Men of Mathematics,* 2nd ed., Simon & Schuster, New York, 1945.

Who's Who in Commerce and Industry, 16th ed., Marquis, Chicago, 1969.

Poor's Register of Directors and Executives, Poor's Corporation, New York, annual.

Membership Directories of Professional Societies.

D. Directories

1. TRADE DIRECTORIES AND ASSOCIATIONS

Canadian Trade Index, Canadian Manufacturers Association, Montreal, annual.

Colgate, Craig, Jr., Ed., *Directory of National Trade and Professional Associations of the U. S.,* Columbia Books, Washington, 1966–1970, 5 vols.

Federation of British Industries, *FBI Register of British Manufacturers,* The Federation, London, annual.

Gale Research Company, *Encyclopedia of Associations,* 5th ed., Gale, Detroit, 1968, 3 vols.

Industrial Research in Britain, 6th ed., Harrop Research Publications, London, 1968.

International Bibliography of Directories, new ed., Bowker, New York, 1970.

Moody's Investor's Service, Moody, New York, annual. Kept up-to-date with semi-weekly supplements.

Stanford Research Institute, *Directory of Chemical Producers,* The Institute, Menlo Park, Calif., 1961– , 7 vols., loose-leaf.

Thomas Register of American Manufacturers, Thomas Publishing Co., New York, annual.

Trade Directories of the World, Croner, Queens Village, N. Y., annual. Kept up-to-date by an amendment service.

The World of Learning, 20th ed., Europa Publications, London, 1969–1970.

2. FOUNDATIONS

The Foundation Directory, 3rd ed., M. O. Lewis, Ed., Russell Sage Foundation, New York, 1967.

3. INDUSTRIAL RESEARCH LABORATORIES

American Council of Independent Laboratories, Inc., *Directory,* 8th ed., Washington, 1961.

Industrial Research Laboratories in the United States, 13th ed., Bowker, New York, 1970.

4. SCIENTIFIC ORGANIZATIONS

Annuaire des Organizations Internationales, 8th ed., 1960–1961, Palais d'Egmont, Bruxelles, 1961.

Bates, R. S., *Scientific Societies in the United States,* 3rd ed., M.I.T. Press, Cambridge, Mass., 1965.

Battelle Memorial Institute, *Directory of Selected Scientific Institutions in the U.S.S.R.,* Merrill, Columbus, Ohio, 1963.

Buttress, F. A., *World List of Abbreviations of Scientific, Technological, and Commercial Organizations,* 3rd ed., Leonard Hill, London, 1966.

Directory of Scientific Directories; A World Guide to Some 1800 Scientific Directories, A. P. Harvey, Ed., Francis Hodgson, London, 1969.

International Chemistry Directory; 1969–1970, W. A. Benjamin, New York, 1970, annual up-dating.

National Research Council, *Scientific and Technical Societies of the United States and Canada,* 8th ed., Washington, D.C., 1968.

Research Centers Directory, 3rd ed., Gale, Detroit, 1968, *New Research Centers: A Periodic Supplement to Research Centers Directory,* no. 1– , 1968– .

5. UNIVERSITIES AND COLLEGES

American Universities and Colleges, 10th ed., American Council on Education, Washington, 1968.

Commonwealth Universities Yearbook, Association of Universities of the British Commonwealth, London, annual.

International Handbook of Universities, 4th ed., International Association of Universities, Paris, 1968.

U. S. Office of Education, *Education Directory,* Part 3, *Higher Education.* Government Printing Office, Washington, D.C., annual.

6. MISCELLANEOUS

Aslib, *Aslib Directory; A Guide to Sources of Information in Great Britain and Ireland,* Aslib, London, 1957, 2 vols.

Directory of Special Libraries and Information Centers, 2nd ed., Gale, Detroit, 1968.

UNESCO, *World Guide to Science Information and Documentation Services,* Paris, 1965.

Wales, A. P., *International Library Directory,* 3rd ed., Wales, London, 1968.

World Guide to Libraries, 1968, Bowker, New York, 1968; *Internationales Bibliotheks-Handbuch.*

For a list of Directories see: *Directories* in Public Affairs Information Service.

E. Technical Dictionaries and Encyclopedias

1. GENERAL

Ballentyne, D. W. G. and L. E. O. Walker, *A Dictionary of Named Effects and Laws in Chemistry, Physics and Mathematics,* 2nd ed., Macmillan, New York, 1961.

Flood, W. E. and Michael West, Comps., *Elementary Scientific and Technical Dictionary,* 3rd ed., Longmans, London, 1962.

Graham, E., Ed., *The Basic Dictionary of Science,* Macmillan, New York, 1966.

Harper Encyclopedia of Science, rev. 2nd ed., Harper and Row, New York, 1967.

McGraw-Hill Encyclopedia of Science and Technology, 2nd ed., McGraw-Hill, New York, 1965, 15 vols.

Van Nostrand's Scientific Encyclopedia, 4th ed., Van Nostrand, Princeton, N. J., 1968.

2. ACRONYMS, ABBREVIATIONS, CODE NAMES, AND SUCH

De Sola, R., *Abbreviations Dictionary,* revised ed., Meredith, New York, 1967.

Gale Research Company, *Acronyms and Initialisms,* 2nd ed., Detroit, 1965.

Gale Research Company, *New Acronyms and Initialisms, 1968–1969,* Detroit, 1969.

Goldsmith, Milton, *Dictionary of Modern Acronyms & Abbreviations,* H. W. Sams, Indianapolis, 1963.

Moser, R. C., *Space-Age Acronyms, Abbreviations and Designations,* Plenum Press, New York, 1964.

Ruffner, F. G. and R. C. Thomas, *Code Names Dictionary,* Gale, Detroit, 1963.

Wohlauer, G. E. and H. D. Gholston, *German Chemical Abbreviations,* SLA, New York, 1966.

3. CHEMISTRY

Clark, G. L. and G. G. Hawley, Eds., *Encyclopedia of Chemistry,* 2nd ed., Reinhold, New York, 1966.

Hawley, G. G., Ed., *Condensed Chemical Dictionary,* 8th ed., Reinhold, New York, 1971.

Flood, W. E., *Dictionary of Chemical Names,* Littlefield, Totoma, N. J., 1967.

Grant, J., *Hackh's Chemical Dictionary,* 4th ed. rev., McGraw-Hill, New York, 1968.

International Encyclopedia of Chemistry, Van Nostrand, Princeton, N. J., 1963.

Krauch, Helmut, and W. Kunz, *Organic Name Reactions; A Contribution to the Terminology of Organic Chemistry, Biochemistry and Theoretical Organic Chemistry,* Wiley, New York, 1964.

Miall, L. M., *New Dictionary of Chemistry,* 4th ed., Wiley, New York, 1968.

Van Nostrand's International Encyclopedia of Chemical Science, Van Nostrand, Princeton, N. J., 1964.

Williams, R. J. and E. M. Lansford, *Encyclopedia of Biochemistry,* Reinhold, New York, 1967.

4. CHEMICAL TECHNOLOGY

Chambers' Technical Dictionary, 3rd ed., revised with supplements, Macmillan, New York, 1958.

Encyclopedia of Chemical Process Equipment, Reinhold, New York, 1964.

Encyclopedia of Chemical Technology, 2nd ed., Vol. 1– , Wiley Interscience, New York, 1963– (Known as *Kirk-Othmer Encyclopedia*).

Snell, F. D. and C. T. Snell, *Dictionary of Commercial Chemicals,* 3rd ed., Van Nostrand, Princeton, N. J., 1962.

Snell, F. D. and D. L. Hilton, Eds., *Encyclopedia of Industrial Chemical Analysis,* Vol. 1– , Interscience, New York, 1966– .

Thorpe's Dictionary of Applied Chemistry, 4th ed., Longmans, New York 1937–1956, 12 vols.

Modern Plastics Encyclopedia, Vol. 1– , 1941– (An annual supplement to the periodical *Modern Plastics*).

Simonds, H. R. and J. M. Church, *Concise Guide to Plastics,* 2nd ed., Reinhold, New York, 1963.

Simonds, H. R., Ed., *Encyclopedia of Plastics Equipment,* Reinhold, New York, 1964.

Whittington, L. R., *Whittington's Dictionary of Plastics,* Technomic Publishing Co., Stamford, Conn., 1968.

Merriman, A. D., *Concise Encyclopedia of Metallurgy,* American Elsevier, New York, 1965.

Encyclopedia of Polymer Science and Technology; Plastics, Resins, Rubbers, Fibers, Interscience, New York, 1964– , Vol. 1– .

Encyclopedia of Textiles, 2nd ed., Prentice-Hall, Englewood Cliffs, N. J., 1966.

Fairchild's Dictionary of Textiles, I. B. Wingate, Ed., Fairchild Publications, New York, 1967.

5. MATHEMATICS

Baker, C. C. T., *Dictionary of Mathematics,* Hart, New York, 1966.

International Dictionary of Applied Mathematics, Van Nostrand, Princeton, N. J., 1960.

James, Glen and R. C. James, Eds., *Mathematics Dictionary,* 3rd ed., Van Nostrand, Princeton, N. J., 1968.

Kandall, M. G. and W. R. Buckland, Eds., *A Dictionary of Statistical Terms*, 2nd ed., Hafner, New York, 1960.

Merritt, F. S., *Mathematics Manual; Methods and Principles of the Various Branches of Mathematics for Reference, Problem Solving, and Review*, McGraw-Hill, New York, 1962.

Universal Encyclopedia of Mathematics, Simon and Schuster, New York, 1964.

6. PHYSICS AND NUCLEAR SCIENCE

Besançon, R. M., *The Encyclopedia of Physics*, Reinhold, New York, 1966.

Clark, G. L., *Encyclopedia of Spectroscopy*, Reinhold, New York, 1960.

Encyclopedic Dictionary of Physics, James Thewlis, Ed., Pergamon, New York, 1961–1964, 9 vols.; supplementary volumes, 1966– .

Handbuch der Physik, 2nd ed., Springer, Berlin, 1955– , Vol. 1– .

Hix, C. G., *Physical Laws and Effects*, Wiley, New York, 1958.

International Dictionary of Physics and Electronics; 2nd ed., Van Nostrand, Princeton, N. J., 1961.

International Encyclopedia of Physical Chemistry and Chemical Physics, Pergamon, New York, 1960– (A series of monographs planned in about 100 vols.).

Zimmerman, O. T., *Industrial Research Service's Conversion Factors and Tables;* 3rd ed., Industrial Research Service Co., Dover, N. H., 1961.

Caidin, Martin, *The Man-in-Space Dictionary; A Modern Glossary*, Dutton, New York, 1963.

Concise Encyclopedia of Nuclear Energy, Chemical Rubber Co., Cleveland, 1967.

Del Vecchio, Alfred, Ed., *Concise Dictionary of Atomics*, Philosophical Library, New York, 1964.

Encyclopedia of Space, Maurice Allward, Ed., Hamlyn, London, 1968.

Hogerton, J. F., *The Atomic Energy Deskbook*, Reinhold, New York, 1963.

McLaughlin, Charles, *Space Age Dictionary*, 2nd ed., Van Nostrand, Princeton, N. J., 1963.

NASA, *Dictionary of Technical Terms for Aerospace Use*, Washington, D.C., 1965, NASA Sp–7.

National Research Council Conference on Glossary Terms in Nuclear Science and Technology, ASME, New York, 1957.

Nayler, J. L., *Dictionary of Astronautics*, Hart, New York, 1964.

7. BIOLOGICAL SCIENCES

a. BIOLOGY

Abercrombie, Michael, *et al.*, Eds., *Dictionary of Biology*, 5th ed., Aldine, Chicago, 1964.

Clark, G. L., *Encyclopedia of Microscopy*, Reinhold, New York, 1960.

Encyclopedia of the Life Sciences, Doubleday, Garden City, N. Y., 1964–1967, 8 vols.

Gray, Peter, *Dictionary of the Biological Sciences*, Reinhold, New York, 1967.

Gray, Peter, Ed., *Encyclopedia of the Biological Sciences*, 2nd ed., Reinhold, New York, 1969.

Henderson, I. F. and W. D. Henderson, *A Dictionary of Biological Terms*, 8th ed., Van Nostrand, Princeton, N. J., 1963.

Shilling, C. W., Ed., *Atomic Energy Encyclopedia in the Life Sciences*, Saunders, Philadelphia, 1964.

b. ZOOLOGY

The Larousse Encyclopedia of Animal Life, McGraw-Hill, New York, 1967.

Leftwich, A. W., *Dictionary of Zoology*, 2nd ed., Van Nostrand, Princeton, N. J., 1967.

Pennak, R. W., *Collegiate Dictionary of Zoology*, Ronald, New York, 1964.

c. MEDICAL SCIENCES

Dorland's Illustrated Medical Dictionary, 24th ed., Saunders, Philadelphia, 1965.

Durham, R. H., *Encyclopedia of Medical Syndromes*, Harper & Row, New York, 1960.

Medical Terms for the Scientist, 2nd ed., Noyes Press, Pearl River, N. Y., 1964.

National Conference on Medical Nomenclature, *Standard Nomenclature of Diseases and Operations*, 5th ed., Blakiston, Philadelphia, 1961.

Skinner, H. L., *The Origin of Medical Terms*, 2nd ed. Williams and Wilkins, Baltimore, 1961.

Stedman, T. L., *Medical Dictionary; A Vocabulary of Medicine and its Sciences, with Pronunciations and Derivations*, 21st ed., Williams and Wilkins, Baltimore, 1966.

Steen, E. B., *Dictionary of Abbreviations in Medicine and Related Sciences*, 2nd ed. Cassells, London, 1963.

Taber, C. W., *Cyclopedic Medical Dictionary*, 10th ed., F. A. Davis, Philadelphia, 1965.

Young, C. G. and J. D. Barger, *Learning Medical Technology Step by Step*, Mosby, St. Louis, 1967.

8. ENGINEERING

American Institute of Chemical Engineers, *Chemical Engineering Thesaurus*, New York, 1961.

Audel's New Mechanical Dictionary for the Technical Trades, Theo Audel, New York, 1960.

Baumeister, Theodore and L. S. Mark, *Standard Handbook for Mechanical Engineers*, 7th ed., McGraw-Hill, New York, 1967.

Carter, Harley, *Dictionary of Electronics*, 2nd ed., Hart, New York, 1967.

Cooke, N. M., *Electronics and Nucleonics Dictionary*, McGraw-Hill, New York, 1960.

Del Vecchio, Alfred, *Dictionary of Mechanical Engineering*, Philosophical Library, New York, 1961.

Dictionary of Computer and Control Systems Abbreviations, Signs and Symbols, Odyssey, New York, 1965.

Engineers Joint Council, *Thesaurus of Engineering and Scientific Terms*, New York, 1967.

Jones, F. D. and P. B. Shubert, *Engineering Encyclopedia*, 3rd ed., Industrial Press, New York, 1963.

Markus, John, *Electronics and Nucleonics Dictionary*, 3rd ed., McGraw-Hill, New York, 1967.

Nayler, J. L. and G. H. F. Nayler, *Dictionary of Mechanical Engineering*, Hart, New York, 1967.

Weinstein, R., *et al.*, *Nuclear Engineering Fundamentals*, McGraw-Hill, New York, 1964.

9. MISCELLANEOUS

Institut International de Froid, *International Dictionary of Refrigeration*, Pergamon-Macmillan, New York, 1963.

Winburne, J. N., *A Dictionary of Agricultural and Allied Terminology*, Michigan State University, East Lansing, Mich., 1962.

F.   Foreign Language Dictionaries

1. BIBLIOGRAPHIES

Collison, R. L., *Dictionaries of Foreign Languages; A Bibliographical Guide to the General and Technical Dictionaries of the Chief Foreign Languages, with Historical and Explanatory Notes and References*, Hafner, New York, 1955.

Stechert-Hafner, Inc., *The World's Languages; Grammars, Dictionaries: General, Specialized, Scientific, Technical*, Stechert-Hafner, New York, revised semiannually.

UNESCO, *Bibliography of Interlingual Scientific and Technical Dictionaries*, 4th ed. rev., Paris, 1961, supplement, 1965.

2. CHINESE

Chu, Chi-Shiun, Ed., *Applied English-Chinese and Chinese-English Chemical Dictionary*, Oriental Publication Service, Thousand Oaks, Calif., 1965.

Modern Chinese—English Technical and General Dictionary, McGraw-Hill, New York, 1963.

Yang, P., *et al.*, *English-Chinese Dictionary of Chemistry and Chemical Engineering*, Oriental Publication Service, Thousand Oaks, Calif., 1965.

3. FRENCH

DeVries, Louis, *French-English Science Dictionary*, 3rd ed., McGraw-Hill, New York, 1962.

Lepine, Pierre, *Dictionnaire Francais-Anglais, Anglais-Francais des Terms Medicaux et Biologique*, Flammarion, Paris, 1952.

Patterson, A. M., *French-English Dictionary for Chemists*, 2nd ed., Wiley, New York, 1954.

4. GERMAN

DeVries, Louis and W. E. Clason, *Dictionary of Pure and Applied Physics*, Elsevier, New York, 1963–1964, 2 vols.

DeVries, Louis, *German-English Medical Dictionary*, McGraw-Hill, New York, 1952.

DeVries, Louis, *German-English Science Dictionary*, 3rd ed., McGraw-Hill, New York, 1959.

DeVries, Louis and T. M. Herrman, *German-English Technical and Engineering Dictionary*, 2nd ed., McGraw-Hill, New York, 1965.

Dorian, A. F., Comp., *Dictionary of Science and Technology; English-German.* Elsevier, New York, 1967.

Herland, L. J., *Dictionary of Mathematical Sciences,* 2nd ed. revised, Harrop, London, 1965–1966, 2 vols.

Macintyre, S. and E. Witte, *German-English Mathematical Vocabulary,* 2nd ed., Interscience, New York, 1966.

Neville, H. H., *et al., New German-English Dictionary for Chemists,* Van Nostrand, Princeton, N. J., 1964.

Patterson, A. M., *German-English Dictionary for Chemists,* 3rd ed., Wiley, New York, 1950.

Polanyi, Magda, *Technical and Trade Dictionary of Textile Terms; German-English; English-German,* 2nd revised and enlarged ed., Pergamon, New York, 1967.

Rau, H., *Dictionary of Nuclear Physics and Nuclear Chemistry,* 2nd ed. Pitman, London, 1965.

Webel, A., *German-English Dictionary of Technical, Scientific and General Terms,* 3rd ed., Dutton, New York, 1953.

5. ITALIAN

Denti, R., *Dizionario Technico; Italiano-Inglese, Inglese-Italiano,* 6th ed., Hoepli, Milan, 1965.

Gatto, Simon, *Dizionario Tecnico Scientifico Illustrato; A Dictionary of Technical and Scientific Terms; English-Italian, Italian-English,* Casa Ceschina, Milan, 1960.

Marolli, Giorgio, *Technical Dictionary; English-Italian, Italian-English,* 8th ed., Heineman, New York, 1964.

6. RUSSIAN

American Mathematical Society, *Russian-English Dictionary of the Mathematical Sciences,* Providence, R. I., 1961.

Blum, A., *Concise Russian-English Scientific Dictionary for Students and Research Workers,* Pergamon, New York, 1965.

Burlak, J., *Russian-English Mathematical Vocabulary,* Interscience, New York, 1963.

Callaham, L. I., *Russian-English Chemical and Polytechnical Dictionary,* 2nd ed., Wiley, New York, 1962.

Dumbleton, C. W., Comp., *Russian-English Biological Dictionary,* Plenum, New York, 1965.

Emin, I., *et al., Russian-English Physics Dictionary,* Wiley, New York, 1963.

Jablonski, Stanley, *Russian-English Medical Dictionary,* Academic, New York, 1958.

Karpovich, E. A., *Russian-English Biological and Medical Dictionary,* Technical Dictionaries Co., New York, 1958.

Karpovich, E. A. and V. V. Karpovich, *Russian-English Chemical Dictionary,* 2nd ed., Technical Dictionaries Co., New York, 1963.

Kotz, S., *Russian-English Dictionary and Reader in the Cybernetical Sciences,* Academic, New York, 1966.

U. S. Library of Congress, *Soviet Russian Scientific and Technical Terms; A Selected List,* Government Printing Office, Washington, 1963.

Usovsky, B. N., *et al.*, *Comprehensive Russian-English Agricultural Dictionary*, 1st English ed., Pergamon, New York, 1967.

Zimmerman, M. G., *Russian-English Translators Dictionary; A Guide to Scientific and Technical Usage*, Plenum, New York, 1967.

7. MULTILINGUAL

Elsevier's Dictionary of Aeronautics in Six Languages, Elsevier, New York, 1964.

Elsevier's Dictionary of Industrial Chemistry in Six Languages, Elsevier, New York, 1964, 2 vols.

Elsevier's Dictionary of Nuclear Science and Technology in Six Languages, Elsevier, New York, 1958.

Elsevier's Medical Dictionary in Five Languages, Elsevier, New York, 1964.

Fouchier, Jean and Fernand Billet, *Chemical Dictionary*, 2nd ed., Netherlands University Press, Amsterdam, 1961.

Lettenmeyer, Lou, *Dictionary of Atomic Terminology*, Philosophical Library, New York, 1959.

Librarian's Practical Dictionary (Worterbuch des Bibliothekars), 3rd ed., Bowker, New York, 1969.

Wittfoht, Annemarie, *Plastics Lexicon (Polyglot)*, American Elsevier, New York, 1963.

Zalucki, H., *Dictionary of Russian Technical and Scientific Abbreviations; With Their Full Meaning in Russian, English and German*, Elsevier, New York, 1968.

G. Handbooks

1. GENERAL

Gieck, Kurt, *A Collection of Technical Formulae*, English translation by F. B. Catty, S-H Service Agency, Inc., New York, 1967.

International Union of Pure and Applied Chemistry, *Nomenclature of Organic Chemistry*, 2nd ed., Buterworths, London, 1965–1966, 3 vols.

International Directory of Radioisotopes, 3rd ed., International Publishers, New York, 1964.

Kaye, G. W. C., Comp., *Tables of Physical and Chemical Constants and Some Mathematical Functions*, 13th ed., Wiley, New York, 1966.

National Research Council, *International Critical Tables of Numerical Data, Physics, Chemistry and Technology*, McGraw-Hill, New York, 1926–1933, 7 vols. and index.

2. CHEMISTRY

CRC Handbook of Biochemistry with Selected Data for Molecular Biology, Chemical Rubber Co., Cleveland, 1968.

CRC, *Handbook of Chemistry and Physics*, Chemical Rubber Co., Cleveland, annual.

Frankel, Max and Saul Patai, Comps., *Tables for Identification of Organic Compounds*, 2nd ed., Chemical Rubber Co., Cleveland, 1964. (reprinted from *CRC Handbook*)

Handbook of Biochemistry and Biophysics, H. C. Damm, *et al.* Eds. World Publishing Co., Cleveland, 1966.

Lange, N. A., Ed., *Handbook of Chemistry*, revised 10th ed., McGraw-Hill, New York, 1967.

Meites, Louis, Ed., *Handbook of Analytical Chemistry*, McGraw-Hill, New York, 1963.

Seidell, Atherton, *Solubilities of Inorganic and Metal Organic Compounds*, 4th ed., W. F. Linke, Ed., Van Nostrand, Princeton, N.J., 1958–1968, 2 vols. (Vol. 2 published by American Chemical Society)

Syzmanski, H. A., Ed., *Infrared Band Handbook*, Plenum, New York, 1963, supplements, 1964– .

3. PHYSICS

American Institute of Physics, *Physics Handbook*, 2nd ed. McGraw-Hill, New York, 1963.

Atomic Handbook, Vol. 1– , Morgan Bros., London, 1965– .

Condon, E. U. and Hugh Odishaw, Eds., *Handbook of Physics*, 2nd ed., McGraw-Hill, New York, 1967.

Frisch, O. R., Ed., *Nuclear Handbook*, Van Nostrand, Princeton, N. J., 1958.

Menzel, D. H. *Fundamental Formulas of Physics*, revised ed., Dover, New York, 1960, 2 vols.

U. S. National Bureau of Standards, *The ISCC-NBS Method of Designating Color Names*, Washington, D.C., 1955 (NBS Circular 553).

Zimmerman, O. T. and Irvin Lavine, *Industrial Research Service's Conversion Factors and Tables*, 3rd ed., Industrial Research Service, Dover, N. H., 1961.

4. MATHEMATICS

Burington, R. S., *Handbook of Mathematical Tables and Formulas*, 4th ed., McGraw-Hill, New York, 1965.

CRC Standard Mathematical Tables, 15th ed., Chemical Rubber Co., Cleveland, 1965.

Fletcher, Alan, *et al.*, *An Index to Mathematical Tables*, 2nd ed., Addison-Wesley, Reading, Mass., 1962, 2 vols.

Huskey, H. D., *Computer Handbook*, McGraw-Hill, New York, 1962.

Korn, G. A. and T. M. Korn, *Mathematical Handbook for Scientists and Engineers; Definitions, Theorems and Formulas for Reference and Review*, 2nd revised ed., McGraw-Hill, New York, 1968.

Mathematical Tables from Handbook of Chemistry and Physics, 2nd ed., Chemical Rubber Co., Cleveland, 1964.

5. BIOLOGY

Altman, P. L. and D. S. Dittmer, Eds., *Biological Data Book*, Federation of American Societies for Experimental Biology, Bethesda, Md., 1964. (Revised ed. of Spector, W. S., Ed., *Handbook of Biological Data*, 1956)

Altman, P. L. and D. S. Dittmer, Eds., *Environmental Biology*, Federation of American Societies for Experimental Biology, Bethesda, Md., 1966.

6. ENGINEERING

a. GENERAL

Collins, A. T., *Newnes Engineer's Reference Book*, Newnes, London, 1965.

Eshbach, O. W., *Handbook of Engineering Fundamentals*, 2nd ed., Wiley, New York, 1952.

Perry, R. H., Ed., *Engineering Manual; A Practical Reference of Data and Methods*, 2nd ed., McGraw-Hill, New York, 1967.

b. CHEMICAL

Perry, J. H. *et al.*, *Chemical Engineers Handbook*, 4th ed., McGraw-Hill, New York, 1963.

c. CIVIL

Abbett, R. W., *American Civil Engineering Practice*, Wiley, New York, 1956–1957, 3 vols.

Seelye, E. E., *Data Book for Civil Engineers*, 3rd ed., Wiley, New York, 1957–1960, 2 vols.

d. ELECTRICAL

Clifford, M., *Electronics Data Handbook*, Gernsback, New York, 1964.

Electrical Engineer's Reference Book, 11th ed., Newnes, London, 1964.

National Electrical Code Handbook, 11th ed., McGraw-Hill, New York, 1963.

Standard Handbook for Electrical Engineers, 10th ed., McGraw-Hill, New York, 1968.

e. MECHANICAL

American Society of Mechanical Engineers, *ASME Handbook*, 2nd ed., Vol. 1– , Mc-Graw-Hill, New York, 1965– .

Standard Handbook for Mechanical Engineers, 7th ed., McGraw-Hill, New York, 1967.

f. MISCELLANEOUS

The following is a miscellaneous list of handbooks. The key word in each entry is in boldface type to indicate the subject area.

Society of **Automotive Engineers**, *S.A.E. Handbook*, New York, 1926– , annual.

American Society for **Metals**, *Metals Handbook*, vol. 1– , Metals Park, Ohio, 1960– .

Etherington, Harold, Ed., **Nuclear Engineering** Handbook, McGraw-Hill, New York, 1958.

Henney, Keith, **Radio Engineering** Handbook, 5th ed., McGraw-Hill, New York, 1959.

American Society of **Heating, Refrigeration and Air-Conditioning** Engineers, *ASHRAE Guide and Data Book*, 2nd ed., New York, 1966–67, 2 vols.

Strock, Clifford and R. L. Koral, Eds., *Handbook of **Air-Conditioning**, Heating and Ventilating*, 2nd ed., Industrial Press, Totowa, N. J., 1965.

American Home Economics Association, **Textile handbook**, 3rd ed., Washington, D.C., 1966.

American Welding Society, **Welding** Handbook, New York, 1962–1967, 5 vols.

H.   Standards and Specifications

American Society for Testing and Materials, *ASTM Standards*, annual, 32 parts. (Title, number of parts, and frequency may vary)

American Society for Testing and Materials, *Index to ASTM Standards,* annual.

American Standards Association, *American Standards,* New York, 1923– .

American Standards Association, *Catalog of American Standards,* New York, 1923– .

British Standards Institution, *Yearbook,* London, 1937– .

Struglia, E. J., *Standards and Specification Information Sources; A Guide to Literature and to Public and Private Agencies Concerned with Technological Uniformities,* Gale, Detroit, 1965.

U. S. General Services Administration, *Federal Standardization,* Government Printing Office, Washington, D.C., 1965.

U. S. National Bureau of Standards, *Publications of the National Bureau of Standards,* 1901 to June 30, 1947, Washington, D.C., 1948; supplementary lists, 1958– .

I.   Market Data and Statistics

1.   MARKET DATA

Croner's Basic Data for Overseas Market Research, R. K. Bridges, Comp. and Ed. Croner Publications, Queens Village, N. Y., 1969.

Exporter's Encyclopedia, Dun and Bradstreet New York, (bi-monthly amendment service).

Rand McNally Commercial Atlas and Marketing Guide, Chicago, 1969, annual.

Reference Book for World Traders, Croner Publications, Queen's Village, N. Y., 1949. (Up-dated by monthly supplements.)

Special Libraries Association, *Sources of Commodity Prices,* New York, 1960.

Stanford Research Institute, Dept. of Business and Industrial Economics, *Chemical Economics Handbook,* Stanford, Calif., 1951–1964, 7 vols. and index. (Kept up-to-date with loose leaf supplements.)

Wheeler, L. J., Ed., *International Business and Foreign Trade,* Gale, Detroit, 1967, Gale's Management information guide series, no.14.

2.   STATISTICS

Economic Almanac for 1967/68– , A handbook of useful facts about business, labor and government in the United States and other areas, published for the National Industrial Conference Board by Newsweek, New York, 1967/1968– .

Gale Research Co., *Statistics Sources; A Subject Guide to Data on Industrial, Business, Social, Educational, Financial and Other Topics,* 2nd ed., Detroit, 1966.

Harvey, J. M., *Sources of Statistics,* Archon, Hamden, Conn., 1969.

Quality Control and Applied Statistics, Vol. 1– , Interscience, New York, 1956– (abstract service).

The Statesman's Year-Book; Statistical and Historical Annual of the State of the World, Macmillan, New York annual.

Statistical Theory and Method: Abstracts; Vol. 1– , published by Oliver & Boyd for International Statistical Institute, *Edingurgh,* 1959– .

United Nations, Statistical Office, *Statistical Yearbook,* United Nations, New York, annual.

United Nations, *World Trade Annual,* world trade annual, New York.

U. S. Office of Business Economics, *Business Statistics,* Government Printing Office, Washington, D.C., biennial, (statistical supplement to *Survey of Current Business*).

U. S. Bureau of the Census, *Statistical Abstract of the United States.* Government Printing Office, Washington, D.C., annual.

J. Trade Names Information

1. GENERAL

Thomas Register of American Manufacturers, Thomas Publishing Co. New York, annual; Vol. 8, *Trade Names: Commercial Organizations.*

U. S. Patent Office, *Index of Trademarks,* Government Printing Office, Washington, D.C. annual.

2. CHEMISTRY

Chemical Week, buyers guide issue, annual.

Oil, Paint, and Drug Reporter; Green Book Buyer's Directory, Schnell, New York, annual.

Synthetic Organic Chemical Manufacturers Association, *SOCMA Handbook: Commercial Organic Chemical Names,* American Chemical Society, Washington, D.C., 1965.

3. DRUGS

Accepted Dental Therapeutics, American Dental Association, Chicago, annual.

American Drug Index, Lippincott, Philadelphia, annual.

Modern Drug Encyclopedia and Therapeutic Index, 10th ed., R. H. Donnelley, New York, 1965; monthly supplement: *Modern Drugs.*

Unlisted Drugs, Vol. 1– , Pharmaco-Medical-Documentation, Chatham, N. J., 1949– .

4. PROCESS INDUSTRIES

CEC, Chemical Engineering Catalog; The Process Industries Catalog, Reinhold, New York, annual, includes trade names index.

Electrical Products Guide; Company and Trade Names in Electrical Construction and Maintenance, annual issue.

Electronic Industries Directory; Brand and Trade Names in Electronic Industries, annual issue.

Zimmerman, O. T. and Irvin Lavine, *Handbook of Material Trade Names,* 2nd ed., Industrial Research Service, Dover, N. H., 1953; supplements 1–4, 1956–1965.

K. Abstracting and Indexing Publications

1. COMPREHENSIVE ABSTRACTING SERVICES

Biological Abstracts, Vol. 1– , Biological Abstracts, Philadelphia, 1927– .

British Abstracts, 1926–1953, Bureau of Abstracts, London, 1926–1953, Section A:I: *General, Physical, and Inorganic Chemistry;* Section A.II: *Organic Chemistry;* Section A.III: *Physiology, Biochemistry, Anatomy;* Section B.I: *Chemical Engineering and Industrial Inorganic Chemistry, Including Metallurgy;* Section B.II: *Industrial Inorganic Chemistry;* Section B.III: *Agriculture, Foods and Sanitation;*

Section C: *Analysis and Apparatus.* Sections A.I and A.II continued in *Current Chemical Papers,* Chemical Society, London, 1954–1969. Section A.III continued in *International Abstracts of Biological Abstracts,* Vol. 1– , Pergamon, New York, 1954– . Sections B.I & B.II continued in the *Journal of Applied Chemistry,* Abstract section. Section B.III continued in the *Journal of the Science of Food and Agriculture.* Section C continued in *Analytical Abstracts,* 1954– .

Chemical Abstracts, Vol 1– , American Chemical Society, Easton, Pa., 1907– .

Chemisches Zentralblatt, Vol. 1–140, Verlag Chemie, Berlin, 1830–1969.

Chemisches Zentralblatt: Schnellreferate, 1967– , Verlag Chemie, Berlin, 1967– .

Dissertation Abstracts International: Section B—*The Sciences and Engineering,* Vol. 27– , University Microfilms, Ann Arbor, Mich., 1966– .

Excerpta Medica; The International Medical Abstracting Service, Vol. 1– , Excerpta Medica, Amsterdam, (published in 32 parts).

International Abstracts of Biololgical Sciences, Vol. 1– , Pergamon, New York 1954.

International Journal of Abstracts: Statistical Theory and Method, Vol. 1– , International Statistical Institute, London, 1959– .

Referativnyi Zhurnal, Akademiia Nauk, Moscow, SSSR, 1953– .

Science Abstracts, Vol. 1– , Institution of Electrical Engineers, London, 1898– . Section A: *Physics Abstracts;* Section B: *Electrical Engineering Abstracts. Physics Abstracts* and *Electrical and Electronic Abstracts* each published separately, 1966.

U. S. Library of Congress, Science and Technology Division, *Guide to the World's Abstracting and Indexing Services in Science and Technology,* NFSAIS, Washington, D.C., 1963.

2. INDEXES

Agricultural Index, Vol. 1–49, Wilson, New York, 1916–1964. (Continued as *Biological & Agricultural Index.*)

Applied Science and Technology Index, Vol. 46– , Wilson, New York, 1958– . (Supersedes *Industrial Arts Index,* Vol. 1–45, 1913–1957.)

Biological and Agricultural Index, Vol. 50– , Wilson, New York, 1964– . (Continues *Agricultural Index,* Vol. 1–49.)

Bioresearch Index, Vol. 1– , Biological Abstracts, Philadelphia, 1965– .

Engineering Index, Vol. 1– , Engineering Index, Inc, New York, 1884– .

Index Medicus, Vol. 1– , National Library of Medicine, Washington, D.C., 1960– .

Pandex, CCM Information Sciences, New York, 1967– . (Microfiche; quarterly with annual cumulations)

Pandex Current Index of Scientific and Technical Literature, a biweekly printed version of *Pandex.*

Public Affairs Information Service, Vol. 1– , P.A.I.S., New York, 1915– .

Science Citation Index, Institute for Scientific Information, Philadelphia, 1963– . *Permuterm Subject Index,* 1967– , annual.

3. BIBLIOGRAPHIES

Ulrich's International Periodicals Directory, 14th ed., Bowker, New York, 1971. 2 vols.; annual supplement. (List of abstracts and abstracting services may be found under classified list of periodicals.)

World Health Organization, current indexing and abstracting periodicals in the medical and biological sciences, an annotated list, 2nd ed., WHO, Geneva, 1959.

L. Bibliographic Aids

1. BOOKS

Ash, Lee and Denis Lorenz, Comps., *Subject Collections: A Guide to Special Book Collections and Subject Emphasis by University, College, Public and Special Libraries in the United States and Canada*, 3rd ed., revised and enlarged, Bowker, New York, 1967.

Blake, J. B. and Charles Roos, *Medical Reference Works, 1679–1966; A Selected Bibliography*, Medical Library Association, Chicago, 1967.

Bonn, G. S., *Science-Technology Literature Resources in Canada*, National Research Council, Ottawa, 1966.

Houghton, Bernard, *Technical Information Sources; A Guide to Patents, Standards and Technical Reports Literature*, Archon, Hamden, Conn., 1967.

Maichel, K., *Guide to Russian Refrence Books*, Vol. 5: *Science, Technology, and Medicine*, Hoover Institution, Stanford University, Stanford, Calif., 1967.

Schutze, Gertrude, *Bibliography of Guides to the Literature of Science-Technology-Medicine*, privately printed, Woodhaven, N. Y., 1958; supplements, 1–2, 1962, 1966.

2. PERIODICALS

American Society for Testing and Materials, *CODEN for Periodical Titles*, Philadelphia, 1967, 2 vols. (supplement covers publications in the physical and biomedical sciences)

Andrews, Theodora, *World List of Pharmacy Periodicals*. American Society of Hospital Pharmacies, Washington, D.C., 1963.

Ayer Directory: Newspapers, Magazines and Trade Publications, Ayer, Philadelphia, annual.

Chemical Abstracts Service Source Index, formerly *Access: Key Source Literature of the Chemical Sciences*, American Chemical Society, 1969, Columbus, Ohio (Replaces *Chemical Abstract List of Periodicals*)

Current Contents, Institute for Scientific Information. Philadelphia; *Life Sciences*, Vol. 1– 1958– ; *Physical & Chemical Sciences*, Vol. 1, 1958– ; Vol. 1– , 1961– ; *Behavioral, Social and Management Sciences*, Vol. 1, 1969– ; *Agricultural, Food and Veterinary Sciences*, Vol. 1, 1970; *Engineering and Technology*, Vol. 1– , 1970– .

Directory of Canadian Scientific and Technical Periodicals, National Research Council, Ottawa, 1961.

Fowler, M. J., *Guides to Scientific Periodicals; Annotated Bibliography*, Library Association, London, 1966.

Guide to Latin American Scientific and Technical Periodicals; An Annotated List, Pan American Union, Washington, D.C., 1962.

Half a Century of Soviet Serials; 1917–1968, a bibliography and union list of serials published in the USSR, Rudolf Smits, Comp., Library of Congress, Washington, D.C., 1968, 2 vols.

International Association of Agricultural Librarians and Documentalists, *Current Agricultural Serials, A World List of Serials in Agriculture and Related Subjects* (excluding forestry and fisheries), current in 1964, Alden, Oxford, 1965–1967, 2 vols. (Supplementary listings in the *Quarterly Bulletin* of the association.)

Irregular Serials and Annuals; An International Directory, Emery Koltay, Ed., 1st ed., Bowker, New York, 1967.

John Crerar Library, Chicago, *List of Current Serials*, 1965.

Medical Library Center of New York, *Union Catalog of Medical Periodicals*, 2nd ed., 1968.

New Serial Titles, 1950–1960, Library of Congress, Washington, D.C., 1960, supplement, 1961–1965, Bowker, New York 1966. *Subject Index to New Serial Titles, 1950–1965*, Pierian Press, Ann Arbor, Mich., 1968.

The Standard Periodical Directory, 2nd ed., Oxbridge, New York 1967.

Ulrich's International Periodicals Directory, 14th ed., Bowker, New York 1971. Updated by supplements.

U. S. Library of Congress, *Aeronautical and Space Serial Publications; A World List*. Washington, D.C., 1962.

U. S. Library of Congress, *Biological Science Serial Publications; A World List, 1950–1954*, Washington, D.C., 1955.

U. S. National Agricultural Library, serial publications indexed in *Bibliography of Agriculture*, revised ed., Washington, D.C., 1965.

U. S. National Library of Medicine, *Biomedical Serials*, 1950–1960, a selective list of serials in the National Library of Medicine, Washington, D.C. 1962.

Wall, C. E., *Periodical Title Abbreviations*, Gale, Detroit, 1969.

World List of Scientific Periodicals Published in the Years 1900–1960, 4th ed. Butterworth, London, 1963–1965, 3 vols. Supplemented by *British Union-Catalogue of Periodicals*, incorporating *World List of Scientific Periodicals; New Periodical Titles*, 1964– ; quarterly with annual cumulations.

World Medical Periodicals, 3rd ed., World Medical Association, New York, 1961. reprinted in 1968 by *British Medical Journal*, supplement, 1968– .

Lists of periodicals abstracted in the following:
Biological Abstracts
Chemical Abstracts
Excerpta Medica
Index Medicus

M. Miscellaneous

1. SCIENTIFIC MEETINGS; CONFERENCE PAPERS

Scientific Meetings, Vol. 1– , SLA, New York, 1957– .

World Meetings: USA and Canada, CCM Information Corporation, New York, 1963– .

World Meetings: Outside USA and Canada, CCM Information Corporation, New York, 1963– .

Current Index to Conference Papers in Chemistry, CCM Information Sciences, Inc., New York, 1969– , monthly.

Current Index to Conference Papers in Engineering, CCM Information Sciences, Inc., New York, 1969– , monthly.

Current Index to Conference Papers in Life Sciences, CCM Information Sciences, Inc.,
New York, 1969– , monthly.

2. *TRANSLATIONS*

Consolidated Index to Translations in English compiled by the staff of the National
Translations Center, The John Crerar Library, SLA, New York, 1969.

Himmelsbach, C. E. and G. E. Boyd, Comps., *Guide to Scientific and Technical Journals in Translation,* SLA, New York, 1968.

Translations Register-Index 1967–   SLA Translations Center, Chicago, 1967–
(located at the John Crerar Library).

Translators and Translations: Services and Sources in Science and Technology, 2nd ed.,
F. E. Kaiser, Ed., SLA, New York, 1965.

World List of Scientific Translations, Vol. 1–   , Stechert-Hafner Book News, New York,
1967– , quarterly.

SUBJECT BIBLIOGRAPHIES AND BASIC GUIDES TO
REFERENCE MATERIAL IN THE FIELDS OF
SCIENCE AND TECHNOLOGY

The following subject bibliographies were prepared for the most part
during the first half of 1970. Every attempt has been made to cite material in print as of June 1970 and to include the latest edition of the
books listed. Books published in the United States or by well-known
publishers in other countries have been checked against *Books in Print,
1969: An Author, Title-Series Index to Publishers Trade List Annual,*
Bowker, New York, 1969.

Complete bibliographic information regarding comprehensive abstracting and indexing tools is given in Basic Reference Publications, Section
K. Full information for this type of material is included in each section
when not found in Section K.

A selected list of periodicals has been chosen for each subject; these
have been checked against either *Ulrich* or *Access* (see Section L, 2 of
Basic Reference Publications for complete bibliographic information).
Spelling, starting date, and such are quoted from these sources.

The material in each subject field is arranged under the following
headings; either singly or in combination, depending on the amount of
material available:

Bibliographies
Guides to the literature
Abstracts and indexes
Special reference works

Review serials
Periodicals

No actual cut-off date was used in preparing the following bibliographies, though current material is in preponderance. Rather, a basic guide to the literature in print was the objective. Consequently some older material in print is included. Arrangement has been under two general subjects, Pure Science and Applied Science. Following is an outline of the subdivisions covered in the two areas:

A. Pure Science

1. ASTRONOMY

Bibliographies and Guides to the Literature

Astronomischer Jahresbericht, Vol. 1–68, G. Reimer, Berlin, 1899–1968.

Bibliography of Natural Radio Emission from Astronomical Sources, Vol. 1– , Cornell University Press, Ithaca, N. Y., 1962– .

Brown, H. S., *Bibliography of Meteorites,* University of Chicago Press, Chicago, 1953.

Glasstone, Samuel, *Sourcebook on the Space Sciences,* Van Nostrand, Princeton, N. J., 1965.

Abstracts and Indexes

Astronomy and Astrophysics Abstracts, Vol. 1. Springer Verlag, Berlin, 1969.

Astrophysical Abstracts, Vol. 1– , Gordon and Breach, New York, 1969– .

Mathematical Reviews, 1940– .

Meteorological and Geoastrophysical Abstracts, Vol. 1– , American Meteorological Office, Washington, D.C., 1950– (Formerly: *Meteorological Abstracts and Bibliography*).

Physics Abstracts, 1898– (Formerly Section A: *Science Abstracts*).

Referativnyi Zhurnal, Astronomiya, 1953– .

Special Reference Works

Bowditch, Nathaniel, *American Practical Navigator,* Government Printing Office, Washington, D.C., 1958.

Dictionary of Astronomical Terms, Natural History Press, New York, 1966.

Directory of Meteorite Collections and Meteorite Research, UNESCO, New York, 1968.

The Flammarion Book of Astronomy, Simon & Schuster, New York, 1964.

Handbuch der Astrophysik, Springer, Berlin, 1928–1936, 7 vols. in 10.

Kleczek, Jospi, *Astronomical Dictionary; In Six Languages: English, Russian, German, French, Italian, Czech,* Academic, New York, 1962.

Kuiper, G. P. and B. M. Middlehurst, *The Solar System,* University of Chicago Press, Chicago, 1953– .

Kuiper, G. P. and B. M. Middlehurst, *Stars and Stellar Systems,* University of Chicago Press, Chicago, 1960– .

Larousse Encyclopedia of Astronomy, Prometheus Press, New York, 1959.

Nayler, J. L., *Dictionary of Astronautics,* Hart, New York, 1965.

Space Encyclopedia; A Guide to Astronomy and Space Research, new revised ed., Dutton, New York, 1960.

U. S. Nautical Almanac Office, *American Ephermeris and Nautical Almanac,* Washington, D.C. 1855– , annual.

Weigert, Arnold and Helmut Zimmermann, *A Concise Encyclopedia of Astronomy,* American Elsevier, New York, 1968 (Translation of *ABC der Astronomie,* 2nd ed.).

Atlases

Ernst, Br. and Tj. E. DeVries, *Atlas of the Universe,* translated by D. R. Welsh, Ed. by H. E. Butler, Nelson, London, 1961.

Kopal, Z., *et al., Photographic Atlas of the Moon,* Academic, New York, 1965.

Kuiper, G. P., Ed., *Photographic Lunar Atlas,* University of Chicago Press, Chicago, Ill., 1960.

Sandage, Allan, *The Hubble Atlas of Galaxies,* Carnegie Institution of Washington, Washington, D.C., 1961 (publication No. 618).

Smithsonian Institution, Astrophysical Observatory, *Star Atlas of Reference Stars and Nonstellar Objects,* M.I.T. Press, Cambridge, Mass., 1969.

The Times Atlas of the Moon, The Times of London, 1970.

Wilkins, H. P., *Moon Maps,* Macmillan, New York, 1960.

Review Serials

Advances in Astronomy and Astrophysics, Vol. 1– , Academic, New York, 1962– .

Advances in the Astronautical Sciences, Vol. 1– , American Astronautical Society, New York, 1957– .

Annual Review of Astronomy and Astrophysics, Vol. 1– , Annual Reviews, Stanford, Calif., 1963– .

Comments on Astrophysics and Space Physics, Vol. 1– , Gordon and Breach, London, 1969– .

Vistas in Astronomy, Vol. 1– , Pergamon, New York, 1955– .

Yearbook of Astronomy, Norton, New York, 1963– .

Periodicals

Acta Astronomica, 1925– .

American Astronomical Society, *Bulletin,* 1969– .

Annales d'Astrophysique, 1938–1969, (merged with *Bulletin Astronomique* and *Journal des Observateurs* to form *Astronomy and Astrophysics*)

Astronomical Institutes of Czechoslovakia, *Bulletin,* 1949– .

Astronomical Journal, 1849– .

Astronomical Society of Japan, *Publications,* 1949– .

Astronomical Society of the Pacific, *Leaflets,* 1925– .

Astronomical Society of the Pacific, *Publications,* 1889– .

L'Astronomie, 1887– .

Astronomy and Astrophysics, 1969– .

Astronomy and Astrophysics, supplement series, 1970– .

Astrophysical Journal, 1895– .

Astrophysical Journal, supplement series, 1954– .

Astrophysical Letters, 1967– .

Astrophysics, 1965– (translation of *Astrofizika*).

Astrophysics and Space Science, 1968– .

Astrophysics and Space Science, comments, 1969– .

British Astronomical Association, *Journal,* 1890– .

Celestial Mechanics, 1969– .

Icarus (U. S.), 1962– .

Irish Astronomical Journal, 1950– .

Meteoritica, Vol. 23– , 1963– (translation of *Journal Meteoritika*).

Moscow, *University Physics Bulletin,* 1966– (translation of *Vestnik Moskovskogo Universiteta,* Series II: *Fizika, Astronomii*).

The Observatory, 1877– .

Planetarium, 1900– .

Planetary and Space Science, 1959– .

Royal Astronomical Society, *Monthly Notices,* 1827– .

Royal Astronomical Society, *Quarterly Journal,* 1960– .

Sky and Telescope, 1941– .

Smithsonian Contributions to Astrophysics, 1956– .

Solar Physics, 1967– .

Solar System Research, 1967– (translation of *Astronomicheskii Vestnik*).

Soviet Astronomy A.J., 1957– (translation of *Astronomicheskii Zhurnal*).

Space Life Sciences, 1967– .

2. CHEMISTRY

Bibliographies

American Chemical Society, *Bibliography of Chemical Reviews,* Washington, D.C., 1958– .

American Chemical Society, *Literature of Chemical Technology,* Washington, D.C., 1968, (*Advances in Chemistry Series,* no. 78)

American Chemical Society, Division of Chemical Literature, *Literature Resources for Chemical Process Industries,* Washington, D.C., 1954 (*Advances in Chemistry Series,* no. 10).

Bolton, H. C., *Select Bibliography of Chemistry, 1492–1902,* Smithsonian Institution, Washington, D.C., 1893–1904, 4 vols.

Book Buyer's Guide: Books on Display at the Chemical Education Book Exhibit, published annually in the September issue of the *Journal of Chemical Education.*

Cahn, R. S., *Survey of Chemical Publications and Report to the Chemical Society,* Chemical Society, London, 1965.

Guides to the Literature

American Chemical Society, Division of Chemical Literature, *Searching the Chemical Literature,* revised and enlarged ed., Washington, D.C., 1961 (*Advances in Chemistry Series,* no. 30).

Bottle, R. T., *Use of Chemical Literature,* 2nd ed., Butterworths, London, 1969.

Burman, C. R., *How to Find Out in Chemistry,* Pergamon, New York, 1965.

Crane, E. J., *Chemical Literature,* in G. L. Clark, *Encyclopedia of Chemistry,* Reinhold, New York, 1957, pp. 215–220.

Crane, E. J. *et al., A Guide to the Literature of Chemistry,* 2nd ed., Wiley, New York, 1957.

Mellon, M. G., *Chemical Publications; Their Nature and Use,* 4th ed., McGraw-Hill, New York, 1965.

Nomenclature

American Chemical Society, *Chemical Nomenclature,* Washington, D.C., 1953 (Advances in Chemistry Series, no. 8).

American Chemical Society, *Naming and Indexing of Chemical Compounds,* Washington, D.C., 1957. (published in 1945; revised in 1957).

Cahn, R. S., *Introduction to Chemical Nomenclature,* 3rd ed., Plenum, New York, 1968.

Christiansen, J. A., "Manual of Physico-Chemical Symbols and Terminology," (in *J. Amer. Chem. Soc.* **82:** 5517 (1960).

International Union of Pure and Applied Chemistry, *Nomenclature of Inorganic Chemistry; Definitive Rules for Nomenclature of Inorganic Chemistry,* Butterworths, London, 1959.

International Union of Pure and Applied Chemistry, *Nomenclature of Organic Chemistry,* 2nd ed., Butterworths, London, 1965–1966, 3 vols.

International Union of Pure and Applied Chemistry, *Rules for I.U.P.A.C.; Notation for Organic Compounds,* Longmans, New York, 1961.

Patterson, A. M. *et al., The Ring Index; A List of Ring Systems Used in Organic*

Chemistry, 2nd ed., American Chemical Society, Washington, D.C., 1960; supplements, 1963– .

Tinley, E. H., *Naming Organic Compounds; A Guide to the Nomenclature Used in Organic Chemistry,* Noyes Press, Pearl River, N. Y., 1962.

Abstracts and Indexes

Analytical Abstracts, 1954– .

British Abstracts, 1926–1953, parts AI–AII.

Chemical Abstracts, 1907– .

Chemical Titles, 1960– (available both in print and on magnetic tape).

Chemisches Zentralblatt, 1830–1969.

Chemisches Zentralblatt: Schnellreferate, 1967– .

Current Abstracts of Chemistry and Index Chemicus, Vol. 1– , Institute for Scientific Information, Philadelphia, 1970– .

Current Chemical Papers, 1954–1969.

Index chemicus, Vol. 1–35, Institute for Scientific Information, Philadelphia, 1960–1969 (followed by *Current Abstracts of Chemistry and Index Chemicus,* 1970–).

Referativnyi Zhurnal, Khimiya, Akademiia Nauk SSSR, Moscow, 1953– .

Special Reference Works

Organic Chemistry

Beilstein, F. K., *Handbuch der Organischen Chemie,* 4th ed., Springer-Verlag, Berlin, 1918–1940, 31 vols., supplement 1, 1928–1939, 27 vols., supplement 2, 1941–1957, 29 vols., supplement 3, 1958– .

Elsevier's Encyclopedia of Organic Chemistry, Vols. 12–14, Elsevier, New York, 1940–1961.

Encyclopedia of Polymer Science and Technology, Vol. 1– , Wiley-Interscience, New York, 1964– .

Heilbron, I. M. and H. M. Banbury, Eds., *Dictionary of Organic Compounds; The Constitution and Physical, Chemical and Other Properties of the Principal Carbon Compounds and Their Derivatives, Together with Relevant Literature References,* 4th ed., Oxford University Press, New York, 1965, 5 vols, supplement, 1965– .

Houben-Weyl's Methoden der Organischen Chemis, 4th ed., Vol. 1– , 4th ed., Stuttgart, Thieme, 1952– .

Organic Reactions, Vol. 1– , Wiley, ,New York, 1942– .

Organic Syntheses, Vol. 1– , Wiley, New York, 1921– , annual.

Rodd, E. H., Ed., *Rodd's Chemistry of Carbon Compounds; A Modern Comprehensive Treatise,* 2nd ed., Elsevier, New York, 1964– .

Theilheimer, W., *Synthetic Methods of Organic Chemistry,* Vol. 1– , Interscience, New York, 1942– , annual since 1951.

Weissberger, Arnold, Ed., *Technique of Organic Chemistry,* 3rd ed. completely revised and augmented, Vol. 1– , Interscience, New York, 1959– .

Inorganic Chemistry

Brauer, G., *Handbook of Preparative Inorganic Chemistry,* 2nd ed., translated by

Scripta Technica, Inc., Academic, New York, 1963–1965, 2 vols. (translated from the *German Handbuch der Preparative Anorganischen Chemie*).

Gmelin, L., *Gmelin's Handbuch der Anorganischen Chemie*, 8th ed., Vol. 1– , Verlag Chemie, Berlin, 1927– .

Inorganic Syntheses, Vol. 1– , McGraw-Hill, New York 1939– .

Jacobson, C. A., Ed., *Encyclopedia of Chemical Reactions*, Reinhold, New York, 1946–1959, 8 vols.

Jonassen, H. B. and Arnold Weisberger, Eds., *Technique of Inorganic Chemistry*, Vol. 1– , Interscience, New York, 1963– .

Mellor, J. W., *Comprehensive Treatise on Inorganic and Theoretical Chemistry*, Longmans, New York, 1922–1937; supplements, 1956– .

Pascal, P. V. H., Ed., *Traité de Chimie Minérale*, 2nd ed., Masson, Paris, 1956.

Sneed, M. C., *et al.*, *Comprehensive Inorganic Chemistry*, Vol. 1– , Van Nostrand, Princeton, N. J., 1953– .

Analytical Chemistry

Jolly, S. C., Comp., *Official Standardized and Recommended Methods of Analysis*, Heffer, Cambridge, 1963.

Kolthoff, I. M. and P. J. Elving, *Treatise on Analytical Chemistry*, Vol. 1– , Interscience, New York, 1959– .

Standard Methods of Chemical Analysis, 6th ed., Vol. 1– , Van Nostrand, Princeton, N. J., 1962– .

Wilson, C. L., Ed., *Comprehensive Analytical Chemistry*, Vol. 1– , Van Nostrand, Princeton, N. J., 1959– .

Biochemistry

Florkin, Marcel and H. S. Mason, Eds. Vol. 1–7, *Comparative biochemistry*, Academic, N. Y., 1960–1964.

Florkin, Marcel and E. H. Stotz, Eds., *Comprehensive biochemistry*, Vol. 1– , Elsevier, N. Y., 1962– .

Methods of biochemical analysis, Vol. 1– , Interscience, N. Y., 1954– .

National Research Council, *Specifications and Criteria for Biochemical Compounds*, 2d ed., Washington, D.C., 1967. (NAS-NRC Pub. No. 1344).

Williams, R. J. and E. M. Lansford, Jr., eds., *Encyclopedia of Biochemistry*, Reinhold, N. Y., 1967.

Physical Chemistry

Hampel, C. A., Ed., *Encyclopedia of Electrochemistry*, Reinhold, New York, 1964.

Handbook of Thermophysical Properties of Solid Materials, Pergamon, New York, 1961.

Partington, J. R., *Advanced Treatise on Physical Chemistry*, Wiley, New York, 1949–1954, 5 vols.

Porter, M. W. and R. C. Spiller, *The Barker Index of Crystals; A Method for the Identification of Crystalline Substances*, Heffer, Cambridge, 1951–1964, 3 vols. in 7.

Purdue University, Thermophysical Properties Research Center, *Thermophysical Properties of High Temperature Solid Materials*, Macmillan, New York, 1967– .

Review Serials

Advances in Alicyclic Chemistry, Vol. 1– , Academic, New York, 1966– ; supplement 1, 1968.

Advances in Analytical Chemistry and Instrumentation, Vol. 1– , Interscience, New York, 1960– .

Advances in Carbohydrate Chemistry, Vol. 1– , Academic, New York, 1945– .

Advances in Catalysis and Related Subjects, Vol. 1– , Academic, New York, 1948– .

Advances in Chromatography, Vol. 1– , Dekker, New York, 1965– .

Advances in Free Radical Chemistry, Vol. 1– , Academic, New York, 1965– .

Advances in Heterocyclic Chemistry, Vol. 1– , Academic, New York, 1963– .

Advances in High Temperature Chemistry, Vol. 1– , Academic, New York, 1967– .

Advances in Inorganic Chemistry and Radiochemistry, Vol. 1– , Academic, New York, 1959– .

Advances in Macromomolecular Chemistry, Vol. 1– , Academic, New York, 1968– .

Advances in Organic Chemistry, Vol. 1– , Interscience, New York, 1960– .

Advances in Organometallic Chemistry, Vol. 1– , Academic, New York, 1964– .

Advances in Physical Organic Chemistry, Vol. 1– , Academic, New York, 1963– .

Advances in Polymer Science, Vol. 1– , Springer-Verlag, Berlin, 1958– .

Advances in Protein Chemistry, Vol. 1– , Academic, New York, 1944– .

Advances in Quantum Chemistry, Vol. 1– , Academic, New York, 1964– .

Annual Review of Physical Chemistry, Vol. 1– , Annual Reviews, Stanford, Calif., 1950– .

Macromolecular Reviews, Vol. 1– , Interscience, New York, 1967– .

Organometallic Chemistry Reviews, Vol. 1– , Elsevier, Amsterdam, 1966– .

Preparative Inorganic Reactions, Vol. 1– , Interscience, New York, 1964– .

Progress in Analytical Chemistry, Vol. 1– , Plenum, New York, 1968– .

Progress in Boron Chemistry, Vol. 1– , Macmillan, New York, 1964– .

Progress in Inorganic Chemistry, Vol. 1– , Interscience, New York, 1959– .

Progress in Organic Chemistry, Vol. 1– , Academic, New York, 1952– .

Progress in Physical Organic Chemistry, Vol. 1– , Interscience, New York, 1963– .

Survey of Progress in Chemistry, Vol. 1– , Academic, New York, 1963– .

Topics in Stereochemistry, Vol. 1– , Interscience, New York, 1967– .

Transition Metal Chemistry, Vol. 1– , Dekker, New York, 1966– .

Periodicals

Acta Chimica Scandinavica, 1947– .

Accounts of Chemical Research, 1968– .

The Analyst, 1876– .

Analytica Chimica Acta, 1947– .

Analytical Chemistry, 1929– .

Angewandte Chemie, 1948– .

Angewandte Chemie, international English ed., 1962– .

Annalen der Chemie, Justus Liebigs, 1832– .

Annales de Chimie, 1714– .

Annual Reports on the Progress of Chemistry, 1904– .

Bulletin de la Société Chimique de France, 1858– .

Bulletin des Sociétés Chimiques Belges, 1887– .

Bulletin of the Academy of Sciences of the U.S.S.R., Division of Chemical Science, 1952– (*Trans of Izvestiya Akademii Nauk S.S.S.R.,* Otdélène Technichskikh Nauk).

Bulletin of the Chemical Society of Japan, 1926– .

Canadian Journal of Chemistry, 1929– .

Chemical Communications, 1965– .

Chemical Instrumentation, 1968– .

Chemical Reviews, 1924– .

Chemische Berichte, 1868– .

Chemistry in Britain, 1965 .

Chromatographia, 1968– .

Collection of Czechslovak chemical communications, 1929– .

Comptes-Rendus, Académie des sciences, 1835– .

Doklady chemical Technology, English translation 1956– .

Doklady Chemistry, English translation 1956– .

Doklady Physial Chemistry, English translation, 1959– .

Fresnius' Zeitschrift für Analytische Chemie, 1945– (formerly *Zeitschrift für Analytische Chemie*).

Industrial Laboratory, V. 24, 1958– .

Helvetica Chimica Acta, 1918– .

Inorganic Chemistry, 1962– .

Journal of Analytical Chemistry of the U.S.S.R., 1952– (translation of *Zhurnal Analiticheskoi Khimii*).

Journal of Chemical Physics, 1933– .

Journal of General Chemistry of the U.S.S.R., 1949– (translation of *Zhurnal Obschei Khimii*).

Journal of Inorganic and Nuclear Chemistry, 1955– .

Journal of Organic Chemistry, 1936– .

Journal of Organometallic Chemistry, 1963– .

Journal of Physical Chemistry, 1896– .

Journal of Research of the National Bureau of Standards, Section A: *Physics and Chemistry,* 1959– .

Journal of the American Chemical Society, 1879– .

Journal of the Chemical Society, 1841– , Sections A: *Inorganic, Physical, Theoretical;* Section B: *Physical;* Section C: *Organic.*

Nature, 1869– .

OMR Organic Magnetic Resonance, 1969– .

OMS Organic Mass Spectrometry, 1967– .

Organic Preparations and Procedures, 1970–   ceased 1970.

Organometallics in Chemical Synthesis, 1970–   .

Proceedings of the Chemical Society, 1957–1964 (continued as *Chemistry in Britain*).

Proceedings of the Royal Society, Series A: *Mathematical and Physical Sciences,* 1800–   .

Quarterly Reviews, 1947–   .

Radiochemical and Radioanalytical Letters, 1969–   .

Radiochimica Acta, 1962–   .

Revue de Chimie Minerale, 1964–   .

Science, 1880–   .

Steroids, 1963–   .

Synthesis, 1969–   .

Talanta, 1958–   .

Tetrahedron, 1957–   .

Tetrahedron Letters, 1959–   .

Theoretica Chimica Acta, 1962–   .

Transactions of the Faraday Society, 1905–   .

Zeitschrift für Analytische Chemie, Vols. 1–127, 1862–1944 (new title: *Fresnius' Zeitschrift für Analytische Chemie,* Vol. 128–   , 1945–   ).

Zeitschrift für Anorganische und Allegemeine Chemie, 1892–   (formerly *Zeitschrift für Anorganische Chemie*).

Zeitschrift für Physikalische Chemie, neue folge, 1954–   (original series, 1887–January 1954.

3. EARTH SCIENCES

a. GEOLOGY

Bibliographies and Guides to the Literature

Annotated Bibliography of Economic Geology, Vol. 1–   , Economic Geology Publishing Co., Urbana, Ill., 1929–   .

Bibliography and Index of Geology, Vol. 33–   , Geological Society of America, Washington, D.C., 1969–   (supersedes Nickles and Miller, *Bibliography and Index of Geology Exclusive of North America,* Vols. 1–32, 1934–1968).

Bibliography of North American Geology, Vol. 1–   , Government Printing Office, Washington, D.C., 1919–   (U. S. Geological Survey, *Bulletin*).

British Geological Literature, Vol. 1–   , Coridon Press, Bourne End, Bucks, England, 1964–   .

Bulletin Signalétique, Centre National de la Recherche Scientifique, Paris, 1956–   ; part 11: *Sciences de la Terre; 2. Physique du Globe; Geologie; Paleontologie.*

Catalog of the United States Geological Survey Library, Department of the Interior, G. K. Hall, Boston, 1965, 25 vols.

Chronic, John and Halka Chronic, *Bibliography of Theses Written for Advanced Degrees in Geology and Related Sciences at Universities and Colleges through 1957,* John Chronic and Halka Chronic and Petroleum Research Corporation, Pruett Press, Boulder, Colo., 1958.

Corbin, J. B., Comp., *An Index of State Geological Survey Publications Issued in Series, Scarecrow,* New York, 1965.

Long, H. K., *Bibliography of Bibliographies on the Geology of the States of the United States,* (in *GeoScience Abstracts* 7:115–125, 1965).

Mason, Brian, *Literature of Geology,* American Museum of Natural History, New York, 1953.

Nickles, J. M. and R. B. Miller, *Bibliography and Index of Geology Exclusive of North America,* Vols. 1–32, Geological Society of America, Washington, D.C., 1934–1968 (continued by *Bibliography and Index of Geology,* Vol. 33– , 1969– .

Pearl, R. M., *Guide to the Geological Literature,* McGraw-Hill, New York, 1951.

U. S. Geological Survey, *Publications of the Geological Survey, 1879–1961,* Government Printing Office, Washington, D.C., 1964, annual; supplements: 1962– .

Ward, D. C., III, *Geological Reference Sources,* University of Colorado Press, Boulder, Colo., 1967.

Abstracts and Indexes

Abstracts of North American Geology, Vol. 1– , Government Printing Office, Washington, D.C., 1966– (supersedes *Geoscience Abstracts,* 1959–1966).

Applied Science and Technology Index, 1913– .

Chemical Abstracts, 1907– .

Engineering Index, 1884– .

Geological Abstracts, Vols. 1–6, Geological Society of America, New York, 1953–1958 (superseded by *Geoscience Abstracts,* 1959–1966 and *Abstracts of North American Geology,* 1966–).

Geological Society of America, *Abstracts,* 1961– , New York, 1962– , annual.

Geoscience Abstracts, 1959–1966, Geological Institute, Washington, D.C., 1959–1966 (superseded by *Abstracts of North American Geology,* 1966–).

Zentralblatt für Geologie Paleontologie, Vol. 1– , Schweizerbart'sche Verlagsbuchhandlung, Stuttgart, 1950– .

Special Reference Works

General

American Geological Institute, *Dictionary of Geological Terms,* Doubleday, Garden City, N. Y., 1962 (Dolphin books).

American Geological Institute, *Glossary of Geology and Related Sciences,* 2nd ed., Washington, D.C., 1960.

Challinor, John, *Dictionary of Geology,* 3rd ed., Oxford, New York, 1967.

Compton, R. R., *Manual of Field Geology,* Wiley, New York, 1962.

Handbook of Physical Constants, revised ed., Geological Society of America, Washington, D.C. 1966 (Memoir 97).

Larousse Encyclopedia of the Earth, Pergamon, New York, 1961.

Lehrbuch der Angewandten Geologie, Vol. 1– , Enke, Stuttgart, 1961– .

Lexicon of Geologic Names of the United States for 1936–1960, Government Printing Office, Washington, D.C., 1966 (U. S. Geological Survey, *Bulletin,* 1200).

Lexique Stratigraphie International, Vol. 1– , Centre National de la Recherche Scientifique, Paris, 1956– (in progress, 6 vols. in 86 parts in 1969).

National Academy of Sciences, *Catalogue of Data in World Data Center A.,* Washington, D.C., 1961– .

Rice, C. M., *Dictionary of Geological Terms; Exclusive of Stratigraphic Formations and Paleontologic Genera and Species,* Lithoprinted by Edwards, Ann Arbor, Mich., 1940 (reprinted with addenda, 1961).

Royal Geological and Mining Society of the Netherlands, *Geological Nomenclature,* Heineman, New York, 1960 (Dutch, English, French, and German).

Foreign Language Dictionaries

Burgunker, M. E., *Russian-English Dictionary of Earth Sciences,* Telberg, New York, 1961.

Davies, G. M., *French-English Vocabulary in Geology and Physical Geography,* Van Nostrand, Princeton, N. J., 1932.

Huebner, Walther, *Geology and Allied Sciences; A Thesaurus and a Coordination of English and German Specific and General Terms,* Veritas, New York, 1939.

Maps

Birch, T. W., *Maps, Topographical and Statistical,* 2nd ed., Clarendon, Oxford, 1964.

Blyth, F. G. H., *Geological Maps and their Interpretations,* Arnold, London, 1965.

Porter, P. W., *Bibliography of Statistical Cartography,* University of Minnesota, Minneapolis, Minn., 1964.

U. S. Geological Survey, *Index to Geologic Mapping in the United States,* Washington, D.C., 1947– .

U. S. Geological Survey, *Index to Topographic Maps in the United States,* Washington, D.C., 1935– (series of state index maps).

U. S. National Aeronautics and Space Administration, *Earth Photographs from Gemini III, IV and V,* Government Printing Office, Washington, D.C., 1967. (NASA Sp 129).

Watkins, J. B., *Selected Bibliography of Maps in Libraries; Acquisition, Classification, Cataloging, Storage, Uses,* revised ed., Syracuse University Libraries, Syracuse, N.Y., 1967.

Periodicals

Advances in Geology, Vol. 1– , Academic, New York 1965– .

American Association of Petroleum Geologists, *Bulletin,* 1917– .

American Journal of Science, 1818– .

Annals of the International Geophysical Year, 1957– .

Chemical Geology, 1966– .

Earth Science, 1946– .

Earth Science Journal, 1967– .

Earth Science Reviews, 1966– .

Earth Sciences Newsletter, 1967– .

Economic Geology and the Bulletin of the Society of Economic Geologists, 1905– .

Geological Magazine, 1964– .

Geological Society of America, *Bulletin,* 1888– .

Geological Society of America, *Memoirs,* 1934– .

Geological Society of London; *Quarterly Journal,* 1845– ; *Proceedings,* 1826– ; *Transactions,* 1811– .

GeoTimes, 1956– .

International Geology Review, Vol. 1– , American Geological Institute, Washington, D.C., 1959– (translated from *Sovetskaya Geologiya, Izvestiya an SSSR,* Ser. Geol).

Journal of Geology, 1893– .

Mountain Geologist, 1964– .

Review in Engineering Geology, 1962– .

b. GEOCHEMISTRY

Clarke, F. W., *Data of Geochemistry,* 6th ed., U. S. Geological Survey, Washington, D.C., 1960– .

Geochemical Prospecting Abstracts, 1953– , U. S. Geological Survey, Washington, D.C., 1953– (*Bulletins* 1000A, 1000G, 1098B); irregular.

Handbook of Geochemistry, Springer-Verlag, Berlin, 1969.

Mason, B. H., *Principles of Geochemistry,* 3rd ed., Wiley, New York, 1966.

Researches in Geochemistry, Wiley, New York, 1959–1967, 2 vols.

U. S. Geological Survey, *Analytical Methods Used in Geochemical Exploration by the U. S. Geological Survey,* Washington, D.C. 1963 (*Bulletin* 1152).

Geochemistry, 1956– .

Geochemistry International, 1964– .

Geochimica et Cosmochimica, 1950– .

c. GEOMORPHOLOGY

British Geomorphological Research Group, Comp., *Bibliography of British Geomorphology,* K. M. Clayton, Ed., Philip, London, 1964.

Geo Abstracts, Vol. 1– , London School of Economics, London, 1966– ; Section A: *Geomorphological Abstracts* (Continues *Geomorphological Abstracts,* Vols. 1–6, 1960–1965).

Baulig, H., *Vocabulaire Franco-Anglo-Allemand de Géomorphologie,* Belles-Lettres, Paris, 1956.

Chorley, R. J., *et al., History of the Study of Landforms,* Wiley, New York, 1964– .

Chorley, R. J., Ed., *Water, Earth and Man: A Synthesis of Hydrology, Geomorphology and Socio-economic Geography,* Methuen, London, 1969.

Fairbridge, R. W., Ed., *Encyclopedia of Geomorphology,* Reinhold, New York, 1968 (*Encyclopedia of Earth Sciences,* Vol. 3).

U. S. Military Academy, West Point, N. Y., *Atlas of Landforms,* Wiley, New York, 1966.

Zetischrift für Geomorphologie, 1925– .

d. GEOPHYSICS

Abstracts

Bulletin Signaletique, Centre National de la Recherche Scientifique, Paris, 1956– ; Part 2: *Astronomie. Astrophysique. Physique de globe.*

Geophysical Abstracts, no. 1– , U.S. Geological Survey, Washington, D.C., 1929– .

Special Reference Works

American Geophysical Union, *Transactions*, 1919– , Washington, D.C., 1913– .

Annals of the International Geophysical Year, Vol. 1– , Pergamon, London, 1957– .

Geophysical Directory, Vol. 1– , Houston, Tex. (Box 13318), 1946– , annual.

International Dictionary of Geophysics, Pergamon, New York, 1967, 2 vols. and atlas.

International Union of Geodesy and Geophysics, abstracts of papers, Vol. 1– , Pergamon, New York, 1963– .

Physics and Chemistry of the Earth, Vol. 1– , Pergamon, New York, 1957– .

U. S. Air Force, Cambridge Research Laboratories, *Handbook of Geophysics and Space Environments*, McGraw-Hill, New York, 1965.

U. S. Air Force, Geophysics Research Directorate, *Handbook of Geophysics*, revised ed., Macmillan, New York, 1960.

Periodicals

List of Journals Commonly Cited in Geophysical Abstracts, U. S. Geological Survey, Washington, D.C., 1961– .

Advances in Geophysics, Vol. 1– , Academic, New York, 1952– .

Annales de Geophysique, 1945– .

Annali de Geofisica, 1948– .

Geophysical Journal of the Royal Astronomical Society, 1958– .

Geophysics, 1936– .

Geophysics and Space Data Bulletin, 1964– .

Geoscience News, 1967– .

Gerland's Beitrage zur Geophysik, 1887– .

Journal of Geophysical Research, 1896– .

Pure and Applied Geophysics, 1939– (formerly: *Geofisica Pura è Applicata*, 1918–1963).

Referativnyi Zhurnal, Geofizika, 1953– .

Reviews of Geophysics, 1963– .

e. HYDROLOGY

Bibliographies

Bibliography of Hydrology, United States of America, 1935/36–1940, American Geophysical Union, Washington, D.C., 1937–1941 (ceased publication). Continued by: American Geophysical Union, *Annotated Bibliography on Hydrology (1951–1954) and Sedimentation (1950–1954) United States and Canada*, Government Printing Office, Washington, D.C. 1956 (U. S. Inter-Agency Committee on Water Resources. *Joint Hydrology-Sedimentation Bulletin* no. 7).

U. S. Geological Survey, *Annotated Bibliography of Hydrology and Sedimentation, United States and Canada, 1955/1958*, Government Printing Office, Washington, D.C., 1962 (Water supply paper 1546).

U. S. Inter-Agency Committee on Water Resources, *Annotated Bibliography on Hydrology and Sedimentation, 1959–1962 (United States and Canada)*, Washington,

Government Printing Office, Washington, D.C., 1964 (*Joint Hydrology-Sedimentation Bulletin*, no. 8).

U. S. Library of Congress, *Bibliography on Snow, Ice, and Permafrost with Abstracts*, Vol. 1– , Washington, D.C., 1951– .

Abstracts

Desalination Abstracts, Vol. 1– , Center of Scientific & Technological Information, Tel Aviv, Israel, 1965– .

Water Resources Abstracts, Vol. 1– , American Water Resources Association, Urbana, Ill., 1968– .

Special Reference Works

Chow, V. T., Ed., *Handbook of Applied Hydrology; A Compendium of Water Resources Technology*, McGraw-Hill, New York, 1964.

Frey, D. G., Ed., *Limnology in North America*, University of Wisconsin Press, Madison, Wis., 1963.

Surface Water Year-Book of Great Britain; Hydrometric Statistics for British Rivers, Together with Related Rainfalls, H. M. Stationery Office, London, 1965.

Traité de Glaciologie, Masson, Paris, 1964–1965, 2 vols.

U. S. Office of Water Resources Research, *Water Resources Research Catalog*, Government Printing Office, Washington, D.C., 1965– .

U. S. Office of Water Resources Research, *Water Resources Thesaurus*, Government Printing Office, Washington, D.C., 1966.

Periodicals

Advances in Water Pollution Research; Proceedings of the International Conference, Pergamon, New York, 1962– .

California State Water Quality Control Board, *Publications*, 1955– .

Hydrata, 1965– .

Irrigation Age, 1966– .

Water in the News, 1965– .

Zeitschrift fur Wasser -und Abwasserforschung, 1968– .

f. METEOROLOGY

Bibliographies and Abstracts

Kiss, Elemer, *Bibliography on Meteorological Satellites (1952–1962)*, U. S. Weather Bureau, Washington, D.C., 1963.

Meteorological and Geoastrophysical Abstracts, Vol. 1– , American Meteorological Society, Boston, 1950– .

Meteorological and Geoastrophysical Titles, Vol. 1– , American Meteorological Society, Boston, 1961– .

U. S. Weather Bureau, *Selective Guide to Published Climatic Data Sources*, Washington, D.C., 1963.

Special Reference Works

American Meteorological Society, *Compendium of Meteorology*, Boston, 1951.

Annals of the IQSY, Vol. 1– , M. I. T. Press, Cambridge, Mass, 1968– .

Berry, F. A., *et al.*, *Handbook of Meteorology*, McGraw-Hill, New York, 1945.

Clayton, H. H., *World Weather Records*, Smithsonian Institution, Washington, D.C., 1927–1947, 3 vols. (*Smithsonian Miscellaneous Collections*, Vol. 79; Vol. 90; Vol. 105, (Continued by U. S. Weather Bureau, *World Weather Records*)

Conway, H. M., *et al.*, *The Weather Handbook; A Summary of Weather Statistics for Principal Cities throughout the United States and around the World*, Conway, Atlanta, Ga., 1963.

Fairbridge, R. W., Ed., *Encyclopedia of Atmospheric Sciences and Astrogeology*, Reinhold, New York 1967 (*Encyclopedia of Earth Sciences*, Vol. 2).

Glossary of Meteorology, R. E. Huschke, Ed., American Meteorological Society, Boston, 1959.

Great Britain, Meteorological Office, *Meteorological Glossary*, 4th ed., H. M. Stationery Office, London, 1963.

Klimadiagramm-Weltatlas, von Heinrich Walter und Helmuth Lieth, Fischer, Jena, 1960– (loose-leaf).

Smithsonian Institution, *Smithsonian Meteorological Tables*, 6th revised ed., Washington, D.C., 1951 (reprinted 1963).

U. S. Environmental Data Service, *Daily Weather Maps; Weekly Series*, Government Printing Office, Washington, D.C., 1968– (continues: U. S. Weather Bureau, *Daily Weather Map*, 1945–1967).

U. S. Weather Bureau, *Climates of the States*, Government Printing Office, Washington, D.C., 1959– (*Climatology of the United States*, no.60).

U. S. Weather Bureau, *Climatological Data for the United States by Sections*, Vol. 1– Washington, D.C., 1914– .

U. S. Weather Bureau, *Climatological Data; National Summary*, Vol. 1– , Washington, D.C., 1950– monthly and annual.

U. S. Weather Bureau, *World Weather Records*, Vol. 4– , Washington, D.C., 1959– .

Wernstedt, F. L., *World Climatic Data*, Pennsylvania State University, Department of Geography, University Park, Pa., 1959– (loose-leaf).

World Meteorological Organization, *International Cloud Atlas*, Geneva, 1956.

World Meteorological Organization, *International Meteorological Vocabulary*, Geneva, 1966.

Periodicals

American Meteorological Society, *Bulletin*, 1920– .

Annalen der Meteorologie, 1948– .

Archiv für Meteorologie, Geophysik and Bioklimatologie, 1948– ; Series A: *Meteorologie und Geophysik*, Series B: *Allegemeine und Biologische klimatologie*.

Boundary-Layer Meteorology, 1971– .

Journal of Applied Meteorology, 1952– .

Journal of Atmospheric Sciences, 1962– (formerly: *Journal of Meteorology*, 1943–1961).

Meteorologie, 1925– .
Meteorologische Zeitschrift, 1884– .
Weatherwise; A Magazine about Weather, 1948– .
Zeitschrift für Meteorologie, 1946– .

g. MINERALOGY

Bibliographies & Abstracts

Bulletin Signaletique, Centre National de la Recherche Scientifique, Paris, 1956– ; Part 210: *Sciences de la Terre: Mineralogie, Geologie, Extraterrestre, Petrographie.*

Kaplan, S. R., Ed., *Guide to Information Sources in Mining, Minerals, and Geosciences,* Wiley, New York, 1965.

Mineralogical Abstracts; Issued by the Mineralogical Society, Vol. 1– , 1920– , Simpkin, Marshall, London, 1922– .

Zeitschrift für Krystallographie, Vol. 1– , Engelmann, Leipzig, 1877– (contains abstracts).

Zentralblatt für Mineralogie, Vol. 1– , Schweizerbart'sche Verlags, Stuttgart, 1950– .

Special Reference Works

Börner, Rudolf, *Minerals, Rocks and Gemstones,* Oliver and Boyd, Edinburgh, 1966 (a reprint of the 1962 translation of the 1938 German ed. with additional plates and references).

Bradley, J. E. S. and A. C. Barnes, Comps., *Chinese-English Glossary of Mineral Names,* Plenum, New York, 1963.

Bragg, Sir W. L. and G. F. Claringbull, *Crystal Structures of Minerals,* Bell, London, 1965.

Chamber's Mineralogical Dictionary, Chemical Publishing Co., New York, 1948.

Dana, E. S. and C. S. Hurlbut, *Manual of Mineralogy,* 17th ed., Wiley, New York, 1959.

Dana, J. D. and E. S. Dana, *System of Mineralogy,* 7th ed., entirely rewritten and greatly enlarged by Charles Palache, *et al.,* Wiley, New York, 1944–1962, 3 vols.

Deer, W. A., *et al., Rock-Forming Minerals,* Longmans, London, 1962–1963, 5 vols.

Fort-Altaba, M., *World Directory of Mineralogists,* compiled with the help of the representatives of the National Mineralogical Societies, published for the International Mineralogical Association by Editorial Eco, Barcelona, 1962.

Gleason, Sterling, *Ultraviolet Guide to Minerals,* Van Nostrand, Princeton, N. J., 1960.

Hey, M. H., *Index of Mineral Species and Varieties Arranged Chemically, with an Alphabetical Index of Accepted Mineral Names and Synonyms,* printed by order of the Trustees of the British Museum, London, 1950.

Pearl, R. M., *Gems, Minerals, Crystals and Ores; the Collector's Encyclopedia,* Odyssey, New York, 1964 (reprinted by Golden Press, 1967).

Ransom, J. E., *Range Guide to Mines and Minerals; How and Where to Find Valuable Ores and Minerals in the U.S.,* Harper and Row, New York, 1964.

Sinkankas, John, *Van Nostrand's Standard Catalog of Gems,* Van Nostrand, Princeton, N. J., 1968.

Uytenbogaardt, W., *Tables for Microscopic Identification of Ore Minerals*, Princeton University Press, Princeton, N. J., 1951 (reprinted by Hafner, 1968).

Vanders, Iris and P. F. Kerr, *Mineral Recognition*, Wiley, New York, 1967.

Zussman, Joseph, Ed., *Physical Methods in Determinative Mineralogy*, Academic, New York, 1967.

Periodicals

American Mineralogist, 1916– .

Canadian Mineralogist, 1957– .

Fortschritte der Mineralogie, 1911– .

Mineralogical Magazine, 1876– .

Societe Francaise de Mineralogie et de Crustallographie, *Bulletin*, 1878– .

h. OCEANOGRAPHY

Bibliographies & Guides to the Literature

Bibliographia Oceanographica, Vols. 1–29, Venice, 1928–1956.

Current Bibliography for Aquatic Sciences and Fisheries, Taylor and Francis, Winchester, Eng., 1964– .

National Research Council, *Oceanography Information Sources*, Washington, D.C., 1966.

U. S. Defense Documentation Center, Arlington, Va., *Oceanography; A Report Bibliography;* E. E. Thompson, Comp., Arlington, Va., 1963.

U. S. Inter-Agency Committee on Oceanography of the Federal Council for Science and Technology, *Bibliography of Oceanographic Publications*, M. W. Panghorn *et al.*, Comp. Washington, D.C., 1963.

Abstracts

Deep-Sea Research and Oceanographic Abstracts, Vol. 1– , Pergamon, New York, 1953/1954– .

Fogel, L. J., *Composite Index to Marine Science and Technology*, Alfo, San Diego, Calif., 1966.

Oceanic Abstracts, Vol. 1– , Oceanic Library and Information Center, La Jolla, Calif., 1966– , annual.

Oceanic Index, Vol. 1– , Oceanic Research Institute, La Jolla, Calif., 1964– , title varies.

Special Reference Works

American Geographical Society, *Serial Atlas of the Marine Environment*, New York, 1962– , folio.

Emery, K. O., Comp., *International Directory of Oceanographers*, 3rd ed. National Academy of Sciences, National Research Council, Washington, D.C., 1960.

Fairbridge, R. W., *Encyclopedia of Oceanography*, Reinhold, New York, 1966.

Great Britain, Admiralty, Hydrographid Department, *Symbols and Abbreviations Issued by the Hydrographic Department of the Admiralty*, London, various dates.

Handbook of Oceanographic Tables, 1966, Government Printing Office, Washington, D.C., 1967.

Hunt, L. M. and D. G. Groves, Eds., *Glossary of Ocean Sciences and Undersea Technology Terms*, Compass Publications, Arlington, Va., 1965.

Huxley, Anthony, Ed., *Standard Encyclopedia of the World's Oceans and Islands*, Weidenfield & Nicolson, London, 1962.

IGY World Data Center A: oceanography, *Catalogue of Data in the World Data Center A*, Washington, D.C., 1957/1963– ; supplements: 1964– .

International Directory of Oceanographers, R. C. Vetter, Comp., 4th ed., National Academy of Sciences–National Research Council, Washington, D.C., 1964.

Jerlov, N. G., *Optical Oceanography*, Elsevier, New York, 1968.

Riley, J. P. and Geoffrey Skirrow, Eds., *Chemical Oceanography*, Academic, New York, 1965– .

The Sea; Ideas and Observations on Progress in the Study of the Sea, Interscience, New York, 1962–1963, 3 vols.

U. S. Naval Oceanographic Office, *Glossary of Oceanographic Terms*, 2nd ed., Washington, D.C., 1966 (SP35).

Periodicals

Oceanography and Marine Biology; An Annual Review, Vol. 1– , Allen & Unwin, London, 1963– .

Progress in Oceanography, Vol. 1– , Pergamon, New York, 1963– .

Bulletin on Coastal Oceanography, 1962– .

Geomarine Technology, 1964– .

Journal of Hydronautics, 1967– .

Journal of Ocean Technology, 1966– .

National Oceanographic Data Center, *Newsletter*, 1961– .

Ocean Industry, 1966– .

Oceanography Newsletter, 1966– .

Oceanology, 1966– .

i. PALEONTOLOGY

Bibliographies

Bibliography of Vertebrate Paleontology and Related Subjects, 1945/46– , Society of Vertebrate Paleontology, Cambridge, 1947– , annual.

Bulletin Signalétique, Centre National de la Recherche Scientifique, Paris, 1956– , Part 11: *Sciences de la Terre; 2. Physique du globe; Geologie; Paleontologie*.

Camp, C. L. et al., *Bibliography of Fossil Vertebrates*, 1928– , Geographical Society of America, New York, 1940– , quinquennial.

Hay, O. P., *Bibliography and Catalogue of the Fossil Vertebrata of North America*, Vol. 1., U. S. Geological Survey, Washington, D.C., 1902.

Hay, O. P., *Second Bibliography and Catalogue*, Carnegie Institute, Washington, D.C., 1929–1930 (Publ. no.179), 2 vols.

Hiltermann, Heinrich, et al., *Bibliographie Stratigraphisch Wichtiger Mikropalätologischer Publikationen von etwa 1830 bis 1958 mit Kurzreferaten*, Schweizerbart'sche Verlags, Stuttgart, 1961.

Romer, A. S. *et al.*, *Bibliography of Fossil Vertebrates Exclusive of North America*, 1509–1927, Geological Society of America, New York, 1962, 2 vols.

Abstracts

Bulletin Signaletique, Centre National de la Recherche Scientifique, Paris, 1956– ; Part 11: *Sciences de la Terre; 2. Physique du Globe; Geologie; Paleontologie.*

Zentralblatt für Geologie und Palaeontologie; Schweizbart'sche Verlags, Stuttgart, 1807– ; Teil I: *Allgemeine, Angewandte, Regionale und Historische Geologie;* Teil II: *Palaeontologie.*

Special Reference Works

Directory of Paleontologists of the World, International Paleontological Union, Hamilton, Canada, 1968.

Fenton, C. L. and M. A. Fenton, *The Fossil Book; A Record of Prehistoric Life*, Doubleday, Garden City, N. Y., 1958.

Joint Committee on Invertebrate Paleontology, *Treatise on Invertebrate Paleontology*, R. C. Moore *et al.*, Director and Ed., Geological Society of America and University of Kansas Press, New York, 1953– , 13 pts.

Kummel, Bernhard and D. M. Raup, Eds., *Handbook of Paleontological Techniques*, Freeman, San Francisco, Calif., 1965.

Oakley, K. P., *Frameworks for Dating Fossil Man*, Aldine, Chicago, 1965.

Principles of Zoological Micropaleontology, Pergamon, New York, 1963– (translation of German ed. of Pokorný, V., *Zaklady Zoologische Mikropaleontologie*).

Ransom, J. E., *Fossils of America*, Harper and Row, New York, 1964.

Rhodes, F. H. T., *et al.*, *Fossils; A Guide to Prehistoric Life*, Golden Press, New York, 1962.

Seward, A. C., *Fossil Plants, for Students of Botany and Geology*, Cambridge University Press, Cambridge, Mass., 1898–1919, 4 vols. (reprinted by Hafner, 1963).

Termier, Henri and Genevieve Termier, *Atlas de Paleogeographie*, Masson, Paris, 1960.

Traité de Paléontologie, Publie sous la Direction de Jean Piveteau, Vol. 1– , Masson, Paris, 1952– .

Indexes

Andrews, H. N., Jr., *Index of Generic Names of Fossil Plants, 1820–1950*, U. S. Geological Survey, Washington, D.C., 1955 (*U.S.G.S. Bulletin* 1013).

Ellis, B. F. and A. R. Messina, *Catalogue of foraminifera*, American Museum of Natural History, New York, 1940– (Loose-leaf).

Fossilium Catalogus, Vol. 1– , W. Junk, Berlin, 1913– .

Shimer, H. W. and R. R. Shrock, *Index of Fossils of North America*, Wiley, New York, 1944.

Periodicals

Bulletins of American Paleontology, 1895– .

Journal of Paleontology, 1927– .

Journal of Sedimentary Petrology, 1931– .

Micropaleontology, 1955– .

Paleontological Journal, 1959–   (English trans. of *Akademiya nauk SSSR*).

Paleontology, 1957– .

Revue de Micropaleontologie, 1958– .

j. SEISMOLOGY AND VOLCANOLOGY

Bibliography of Seismology, Dominion Observatory, Ottawa, Canada, 1929–1966.

Montessus de Ballore, Fernand, Comte, *Bibliografía General de Temblores y Terremotos,* Publicada por la Sociedad Chilena de Historia y Geografía Chile, Impr. Universitaria, 1915–1919, 7 pts. (Also pub. in *Revista Chilena de historia y geografía,* 1915–1919).

Geophysical Abstracts, Vol. 1– , U. S. Geological Survey, Washington, D.C., 1929.

International Association of Volcanology, *Catalogue of the Active Volcanoes of the World, Including Solfatara Fields,* Part 1– , Naples, 1951– .

U. S. Coast and Geodetic Survey, *Earthquake History of the United States,* Government Printing Office, Washington, D.C., 1958–1961, 2 vols.

U. S. Coast and Geodetic Survey, *United States Earthquakes,* Government Printing Office, Washington, D.C., 1930– , annual.

Earthquake Notes, 1929– .

Seismological Society of America, *Bulletin,* 1911– .

(1) GEOGRAPHY

Bibliographies

American Geographical Society, Library, *Research Catalogue,* Hall, Boston, 1962, 15 vols.

Cox, E. G., *Reference Guide to the Literature of Travel, Including Voyages, Geographical Descriptions, Adventures, Shipwrecks and Expeditions,* University of Washington, Seattle, 1935–1939, 3 vols.

Royal Geographical Society, London, *New Geographical Literature and Maps,* n.s., Vol. 1– , London, 1951– , semiannual.

U. S. Library of Congress, Reference Department, *Soviet Geography; A Bibliography,* Nicholas R. Rodionoff, Ed., Washington, D.C., 1951.

Survey Bibliographies

Bibliographie Geographie Internationale, Vol. 1– , 1891– , Centre National de la Recherche Scientifique, Paris, 1894– , annual.

Geographisches Jahrbuch, Vol. 1– , 1866– , Gotha, Perthes, 1866– , annual; irregular.

Geographisches *Index,* 1866–1925, in vol. 40, pp. ix–xix.

Special Reference Works

British Association for the Advancement of Science, Research Committee, *A Glossary of Geographical Terms,* L. D. Stamp, Ed., Longmans, London; Wiley, New York, 1961.

Fischer, Eric and F. E. Elliott, *A German and English Glossary of Geographical Terms,* American Geographical Society, New York, 1950.

Geographisches Taschenbuch und Jahrweiser für Deutschen Landeskunds, F. Steiner, Wiesbaden, 1949– , biennial, Supplementband, 1960/61, Wiesbaden, 1960.

Gresswell, R. K. and Anthony Huxley, Eds., *Standard Encyclopedia of the World's Rivers and Lakes,* Putnam, New York, 1966.

Grigor'ev, A. A., *Kratkaia Geograficheskaia Entsiklopediia,* Gos. Izd-vo "Sovetskaia Entsiklopediia," Moskva, 1960–1964, 4 vols.

Huxley, Anthony, Ed., *Standard Encyclopedia of the World's Mountains,* Putnam, New York, 1969.

Huxley, Anthony, Ed., *Standard Encyclopedia of the World's Oceans and Islands,* Putnam, New York, 1962.

Mirot, Léon, *Manuel de Géographie Historique de la France,* 2nd ed., Ouvrage posthume revu et publie per Albert Mirot, Picard, Paris, 1947–1950, 2 vols.

Monkhouse, F. V. A., *Dictionary of Geography,* Aldine, Chicago, 1965.

Moore, W. G., *Dictionary of Geography; Definitions and Explanations of Terms Used in Physical Geography,* 3rd ed., Penguin, Harmondsworth, Middlesex, Eng., 1963.

Orbis Geographicus, World Directory of Geography; Adressar Geographique du Monde, Geographiches Weltadressbuch, 1960– , F. Steiner, Wiesbaden, 1960– .

Gazetteers

Chamber's World Gazetteer and Geographical Dictionary, T. C. Collcott and J. O. Thorne, Eds., Chambers, Edinburgh, London, 1954.

Columbia Lippincott Gazetteer of the World, Columbia University Press, New York, 1962.

U.S. Board of Geographic Names, *Gazetteer,* no. 1–85, Government Printing Office, Washington, D.C., 1955–1964.

Webster's Geographical Dictionary; A Dictionary of Names of Places with Geographical and Historical Information and Pronunciations, revised ed., Merriam, Springfield, Mass., 1962.

Geographic Names and Terms

Egli, J. J., *Geschichte der Geographischen Namenkunde,* Brandstetter, Leipzig, 1886. reprinted: Burt Franklin, New York, 1963, 2 vols.

Kane, J. N., *The American Counties,* revised ed., Scarecrow, New York, 1962.

Sealock, R. B. and P. A. Seely, *Bibliography of Place Name Literature; United States and Canada,* 2nd ed., ALA, Chicago, 1967.

U. S. Board on Geographical Names, *Sixth Report, 1890–1932,* Government Printing Office, Washington, D.C., 1933.

U. S. Board on Geographical Names, *Decisions,* 1934/35– , Washington, D.C., 1936– .

Geographic Names and Terms—English

Cameron, Kenneth, *English Place Names,* Batsford, London, 1961.

Ekwall, Eilert, *Concise Oxford Dictionary of English Place-Names,* 4th ed. Clarendon Press, Oxford, 1960.

English Place-Name Society, *English Place-Name Elements,* A. H. Smith, Cambridge University Press, Cambridge, 1956, 2 vols.

Great Britain, Register Office, Census 1951, England and Wales, *index of Place Names,* Statistics Office, London, 1955.

Permanent Committee on Geographical Names for British Official Use, *Glossaries*, Vols. 1–8, London, 1942–1954.

Permanent Committee on Geographical Names for British Official Use, *Lists of Names*, Royal Geographical Society, London, 1921–1929.

Permanent Committee on Geographical Names for British Official Use, *Lists of Names*, new series, London, 1954– .

Atlases

British Museum, Department of Printed Books, Map Room, *Catalogue of Printed Maps, Plans and Charts in the British Museum*, London, 1885, 2 vols. Kept up to date by *Catalog of Maps: Accessions*.

U. S. Library of Congress, Map Division, *A Guide to Historical Cartography; A Selected, Annotated List of References on the History of Maps and Map Making*, 2nd ed. revised, Washington, D.C., 1960.

U. S. Library of Congress *A List of Geographical Atlases in the Library of Congress, with Bibliographical Notes*, Government Printing Office, Washington, D.C., 1909–1963, 6 vols.

University of California, Berkeley, Bancroft Library, *Index to Printed Maps*, Hall, Boston, 1964.

Encyclopaedia Britannica International Atlas, Chicago, 1965.

Encyclopaedia Britannica World Atlas, Chicago, 1964.

Goode's World Atlas, Rand McNally, New York, 1969.

Der Grosse Brockhaus; Erdkunde, Wirtschaft, Geschichte, Brockhaus, Wiesbaden, 1960.

Hammond Incorporated, *International World Atlas*, C. S. Hammond, Maplewood, N. J., 1967.

Hammond Incorporated, *Hammond's Ambassador World Atlas*, new perspective ed., C. S. Hammond, Maplewood, N. J., 1966.

National Geographic Society, Washington, D.C., Cartographic Division, *National Geographic Atlas of the World*, Washington, D.C., 1963.

Rand McNally and Company, *Rand McNally Commercial Atlas and Marketing Guide*, Chicago, 1969.

Rand McNally and Company, *The New Cosmopolitan World Atlas*, Chicago, 1969.

Times Atlas of the World, midcentury ed., Times Publishing Co., London, 1955–1959, 5 vols.

Whyte, F. H., *Whyte's Atlas Guide*, Scarecrow, New York, 1962.

Guidebooks

American Guide Series, compiled by the Federal Writers' Project, Various pubs., 1937–1949.

Avec les "Guides Bleus" à Travers la France et la Monds, Hachette, Paris, 1959 (Bibliothèque des voyages); supplement: 1960–1962.

Encyclopedia of World Travel Nelson Doubleday and C. E. Cooley, Ed., Doubleday, Garden City, N. Y., 1961.

Fielding, T. H., *Fielding's Travel Guide to Europe*, Sloane, New York, 1948– , annual.

Hotel and Motel Red Book, 1886– , American Hotel Association Directory Corp., New York, 1886– , annual.

Kreutz, Barbara and Ellen Fleming, *Introducing America*, Methuen, London, 1963.

Official Airline Guide, 1943–   , American Aviation Pubs., Chicago, 1943–   , monthly.

Official Guide to the Railways and Steam Navigation Lines of the United States, Puerto Rico, Canada, Mexico and Cuba, also time-tables of railroads in Central America, airline schedules, National Railway Pub. Co., New York, 1868, monthly.

Official Steamship Guide; International, Vol. 1–   , Transportation guides, New York, 1932, monthly.

Pan American Airways, Inc., *Pan American's Travel Facts about 109 Countries,* New York, 1964.

Russell's Official National Motor Coach Guide, Russell's Guides, Cedar Rapids, Iowa, 1927–   , monthly.

Periodicals

Harris, C. D., *Annotated World List of Selected Current Geographical Serials in English,* including an appendix of major serials in other languages with regular supplementary or partial basic use of English, 2nd ed. revised and enlarged, University of Chicago, Department of Geography, Chicago, 1964 (Research paper no. 96).

Harris, C. D. and J. D. Fellman, International List of Geographical Serials, University of Chicago, Department of Geography, Chicago, 1960 (Research paper no. 63).

Annales de Géographie et Bulletin de la Societe Geographie, 1891–   .

Association of American Geographers, *Annals,* 1911–   .

Canadian Geographer, 1951–   .

Cartographer, 1964–   .

Geographical Journal, 1893–   .

Geographical Review, 1916–   .

Geography, 1901–   .

Journal of Geography (U. S.), 1902–   .

Professional Geographer, n.s., 1949–   .

Scottish Geographical Magazine, 1885–   .

4. LIFE SCIENCES

a. BIOLOGY

Bibliographies and Guides to the Literature

Altsheler, Brent, *Natural History Index-Guide,* 2nd ed., Wilson, New York, 1940.

Bottle, R. T. and H. V. Wyatt, Eds., *The Use of Biological Literature,* Butterworths, London, 1966; Archon, Hamden, Conn., 1967.

Bulletin Signalétique, Centre Nationale de la Recherche Scientifique, Paris, 1956–   ; Part 12: *Biophysique; Biochimie; Chimie Analytique; Biologie.*

Kerker, A. E. and H. T. Murphy, *Biological and Biomedical Literature,* Purdue University, Lafayette, Ind., 1968.

Special Libraries Association, *Information Sources for the Biological Sciences and Allied Fields,* New York, 1961.

Abstracts and Indexes

Abstracts of Human Development, Vol. 1–   , Excerpta Medica Foundation, Amsterdam, 1961–   .

Berichte über die Gesamte Biologie, Deutsche Pharmakologische Gesellschaft und Deutsche Physiologische Gesellschaft, Berlin, 1920– ; Abt. A: *Berichte über die Wissenschaftliche Biologie,* Vol. 1– , 1926– ; Abt. B: *Berichte über die Gesamte Physiologie und Experimentelle Pharmakologie,* Vol. 1– , 1920– .

Biological Abstracts, 1927– .

Biological and Agricultural Index, 1965– ; supersedes *Agricultural Index,* 1916–1964.

Bioresearch Index, 1965– (formerly *Bioresearch Titles*).

Chemical Abstracts, 1907– .

Index Medicus, 1960– ; *Current List of Medical Literature,* 1941–1959; *Quarterly Cumulative Index Medicus,* 1927–1960.

International Abstracts of Biological Sciences, Vol. 1– , Pergamon, New York, 1954– ; formerly *British Abstracts,* Section AIII.

Referativnyi Zhurnal, Biologiya, 1954– .

Special Reference Works

Abderhalden, Emil, Ed., *Handbuch der Biologischen Arbeitsmethoden,* Urban, Berlin, 1920–1939, 13 pts. in 107 vols.

Altman, P. L. and D. S. Dittmer, Eds., *Biology Data Book,* prepared under the auspices of the Committee on Biological Handbooks, Federation of American Societies for Experimental Biology, Washington, D.C., 1964.

Bittar, E. E. and Neville Bittar, Eds., *The Biological Basis of Medicine,* Vol. 1– , Academic, New York, 1968– .

Jaeger, E. C., *Biologist's Handbook of Pronunciations,* Thomas, Springfield, Ill., 1960.

Jaeger, E. C., *Source Book of Biological Names and Terms,* 3rd ed., Thomas, Springfield, Ill., 1955.

Olivier, H. R., Ed., *Traité de Biologie Appliquée,* Vol. 1– , Maloine, Paris, 1961– .

Oppenheimer, J. M., *Essays in the History of Embryology and Biology,* M.I.T. Press, Cambridge, Mass., 1967.

Physical Techniques in Biological Research, 2nd ed., Academic, New York, 1966– .

Review Serials

L'Annee Biologique, Vol. 1– , Fédération Francaise des Sociétés de Sciences Naturelles, Paris, 1895– .

Ergebnisse der Biologie, Vol. 1– , Berlin, 1926– .

Quarterly Review of Biology, Vol. 1– , Stony Brook Foundation, Stony Brook, N. Y., 1926– .

Survey of Biological Progress, Vol. 1– , Academic, New York, 1949– .

Viewpoints in Biology, Vol. 1– , Butterworth, London, 1962– .

Periodicals

Acta Histochemica, 1954– .

Biochemistry, 1962– .

Biological Bulletin, 1898– .

Biological Reviews, 1923– .

Biophysik, 1963– .

Biorheology, 1962– .

Bioscience, 1951–   (formerly *A.I.B.S. Bulletin).*

Development Biology, 1959– .

Federation of American Societies for Experimental Biology, *Federation Proceedings,* 1942– .

Human Biology, 1929– .

Journal of Experimental Biology, 1923– .

Life Sciences, 1962– .

National Biomedical Instruments Symposium, Biomedical Sciences Instrumentation, *Proceedings,* 1st ed.– , 1963– .

Photochemistry and Photography, 1962– .

Quarterly Review of Biology, 1926– .

Society for Experimental Biology and Medicine, *Proceedings,* 1903– .

Stain Technology, 1925– .

Russian Journals in English Translation

Biophysics, 1957–   (translation of Biofizika).

Bulletin of Experimental Biology and Medicine, 1956– (Translation of *Bulleten' eksperimental' noi Biologii i Meditsiny).*

Journal of Microbiology, Epidemiology, and Immunology, 1957–   (Translation of *Zhurnal Mikrobiologii, Epidemiologii, Immunobiologii).*

b. BIOCHEMISTRY & BIOPHYSICS

Bibliographies and Abstracts

Biochemical Title Index, Vol. 1– , Biological Abstracts, Philadelphia, 1962– .

Excerpta Medica; Section 2: *Biochemistry,* Vol. 18– , 1965– , Excerpta Medica, Amsterdam, 1947– .

Methods and References in Biochemistry and Biophysics, World Publishing Co., Cleveland, Ohio, 1966.

Special Reference Works

Altman, P. L. and D. S. Dittmer, Eds., *Metabolism; Biological Handbook.* Federation of American Societies for Experimental Biology, Washington, D.C., 1968.

Biochemical Preparations, Vol. 1– , Wiley, New York, 1949– .

Biochemical Society, London, *Essays in Biochemistry,* Vol. 1– , Published for the Biochemical Society by Academic Press, London and New York, 1965– .

Biochemical Society, *Symposia,* no. 1– , University Press, Cambridge, 1948– .

Cantarow, Abraham and Max Trumper, *Clinical Biochemistry,* 6th ed. Saunders, Philadelphia, 1962.

Florkin, Marcel & H. S. Mason, Eds., Vol. 1–7, *Comparative biochemistry,* Academic, New York, 1960–1964.

Florkin, Marcel and E. H. Stotz, Eds., *Comprehensive Biochemistry,* Academic, New York, 1960–1964, 7 vols.

Glick, David, Ed., *Methods of Biochemical Analysis,* Interscience, New York, 1954– , Vols. 1–16, published, 1954–1968; Vol. 17 in preparation.

Haldane, J. B. S., *Biochemistry in Genetics*, Humanities, New York, 1954.

Methods of biochemical analysis, Vol. 1– , Interscience, New York, 1954– .

National Research Council, *Specifications and Criteria for Biochemical Compounds;* 2d ed., Washington, D.C., 1967. (NAS-NRC Pub. No. 1344).

Thorpe, W. V., *Biochemistry for Medical Students*, 8th ed., Little, Brown, Boston, 1964.

Williams, R. J. and E. M. Lansford, *Encyclopedia of Biochemistry*, Reinhold, New York, 1967.

Review Serials

Advances in Biological and Medical Physics, Vol. 1– , Academic, New York, 1948– .

Advances in Clinical Chemistry, Vol. 1– , Academic, New York, 1958– .

Advances in Comparative Physiology and Biochemistry, Vol. 1– , Academic, New York, 1962– .

Annual Review of Biochemistry, Vol. 1– , Annual Reviews, Palo Alto, Calif., 1932– .

Progress in Biophysics and Molecular Biology, Vol. 1– , Pergamon, New York, 1950– (former title: *Progress in Biophysics and Biophysical Chemistry*).

Periodicals

Analytical Biochemistry, 1960– .

Applied Biochemistry and Microbiology, 1965– (English trans. of *Prikladnaya Biokhimiya Mikrobiologiya*).

Archives of Biochemistry and Biophysics, 1942– .

Biochemical Journal, 1906– .

Biochemisches Zeitschrift, 1906– .

Biochemistry, Vol. 21, 1956– (English trans. of *Biokhimiya*).

Biochimica et Biophysica Acta, 1947– .

Hoppe-Seyler's Zeitschrift für Physiologische Chemie, 1877– .

Immunochemistry, 1964– .

Journal of Biochemistry, 1905– .

Steroids, 1963– .

c. BOTANY

Bibliographies & Guides to the Literature

Blake, S. F., *Geographical Guide to Floras of the World*, Vol. 1– , Government Printing Office, Washington, D.C., 1942– (Vol. 1, 1942; Vol. 2, 1960).

Ewan, Joseph, *Reference Tools for the Botanist* (in *Stechert-Hafner Book News* **20**: 33–35, 1965).

Huntia; A Yearbook of Botanical and Horticultural Bibliography, Vol. 1– , Hunt Botanical Library, Pittsburgh, 1964– .

Jackson, B. D., *Guide to the Literature of Botany*, Hafner, New York, 1964.

Lawrence, G. H. M., *et al.*, *Botanico-Periodicum-Huntianum*, Hunt Botanical Library, Pittsburgh, 1968.

Pritzel, G. A., *Thesaurus Literature Botanicae Omnium Gentium*, Brockhaus, Leipzig, 1872–1877 (reprinted Görlich, Milan, 1950).

Stafleu, F. A., *Taxonomix Literature; A Selective Guide to Botanical Publications with Dates, Commentaries and Types*, International Bureau for Plant Taxonomy and Nomenclature, Utrecht, 1967.

U. S. National Agriculture Library, *Plant Science Catalog: Botany Subject Index*, Microphotography Co., Boston, 1958.

Abstracts

Abstracts of Mycology, Vol. 1– , Biosciences Information Services of Biological Abstracts, Philadelphia, 1967– .

Biological Abstracts, 1927– .

Bulletin Signalétique, Centre National de la Recherche Scientifique, Paris, 1956– ; Part 370: *Biologie et Physiologie Végétales*.

Excerpta Botanica, Vol. 1– , Fischer, Stuttgart, 1959– .

Torrey Botanical Club, *Index to American Botanical Literature* (in *Torrey Botanical Club Bulletin*, Vol. 13, 1886–); complete index reprinted in book form by G. K. Hall, 1968.

Special Reference Works

Davydov, N. N., Comp., *Botanical Dictionary: Russian-English-German-French-Latin*, 2nd ed., Fitzmatgiz, Moscow, 1962.

DeWit, H. C., *Plants of the World*, Dutton, New York, 1966, 2 vols.

Hagerup, Olaf and Vagn Peterson, *Botanical Atlas*, with translation into English by H. Gilbert-Carter, Munksgaard, Copenhagen, 1959–1960, 2 vols.

Handbuch der Pflanzenphysiologie, Springer, Berlin, 1955–1967, 18 vols.

Horsfall, J. G. and A. E. Dimond, *Plant Pathology; An Advanced Treatise*, Academic, New York, 1959–1960, 3 vols.

Howard, R. A. *et al.*, *International Directory of Botanical Gardens*, International Bureau for Plant Taxonomy and Nomenclature, Utrecht, 1963.

International Plant Index, Vol. 1– , New York Botanical Garden, 1962– .

Jackson, B. D., *Glossary of Botanic Terms with their Derivation and Accent*, 4th revised and enlarged ed., Hafner, New York, 1960.

McLean, R. C. and W. R. I. Cook, *Textbook of Theoretical Botany*, Longmans, New York 1951.

Snell, W. H. and E. A. Dick, *Glossary of Mycology*, Harvard University Press, Cambridge, Mass., 1957.

Stearn, W. T., *Botanical Latin; Grammar, Syntax, Terminology and Vocabulary*, Hafner, New York, 1966.

Steward, F. C., Ed., *Plant Physiology*, Academic, New York, 1959–1969, 6 vols.

Usher, George, *Dictionary of Botany; Including Terms Used in Biochemistry, soil Science, and Statistics*, Van Nostrand, Princeton, N. J., Constable, London, 1966.

Vistas in Botany, Vol. 1– , Oxford, London, Pergamon, New York, 1959– .

Taxonomy

International Code of Botanical Nomenclature, International Bureau for Plant Taxonomy and Nomenclature, Utrecht, 1961.

International Code of Nomenclature for Cultivated Plants, International Bureau for Plant Taxonomy and Nomenclature, Utrecht, 1965.

Lawrence, G. H. M., "Literature of Taxonomix Botany" in *Taxonomy of Vascular Plants,* Macmillan, New York, 1951, pp. 284-331.

Brittonia, 1931- .

Periodicals

Advances in Botanical Research, Vol. 1- , Academic, New York, 1963- .

American Horticultural Magazine, 1922- .

American Journal of Botany, 1914- .

Annals of Botany, 1887- .

Botanical Gazette, 1875- .

Botanical Review, 1935- .

Canadian Journal of Botany, 1929- .

Darwiniana, 1922- .

Doklady Botanical Science, Vol. 154, 1964-   (English translation of *Doklady Akademii Nauk SSSR*).

Economic Botany, 1947- .

FAO Plant Protection Bulletin, 1952- .

Linnean Society, *Biological Journal,* 1838-   (formerly Linnean Society of London, *Proceedings*).

Plant Pathology (Eng.), 1952- .

Plant Pathology (U. S.), 1926- .

d. CYTOLOGY

Special Reference Works

Bittar, E. E., Ed., *Biological Basis of Medicine,* Academic, New York, 1968-1969, 4 vols.

Bourne, G. H., Ed., *Cytology and Cell Physiology,* 3rd ed., Academic, New York, 1964.

Brachet, Jean and A. E. Mirsky, *The Cell; Biochemistry, Physiology, Morphology,* Academic, New York, 1959-1964, 6 vols.

Fawcett, D. W., *The Cell; Its Organelles and Inclusions,* Saunders, Philadelphia, 1966.

Giese, A. C., *Cell Physiology,* 3rd ed., Saunders, Philadelphia, 1968.

Murray, M. R. and G. A. Kopech, *Bibliography in the Research in Tissue Culture, 1884-1950; An Index to the Living Cell Cultivated in Vitro,* Academic, New York, 1953, 2 vols.

Recent Advances in Cytology, Little, Brown, Boston, 1965.

Symposium of Subcellulant Components, London, 1967, *Subcellular Components, Preparation and Fractionation,* Plenum, New York, 1969.

Willmer, E. N., *Cytology and Evolution,* 2nd ed. revised, Academic, New York, 1968.

Wilson, G. B. and J. H. Morrison, *Cytology,* 2nd ed., Van Nostrand, Princeton, N. J., 1966.

Periodicals

Canadian Journal of Genetics and Cytology, 1959– .
Chromosoma, 1939– .
Cytogenetics, 1962– .
Experimental Cell Research, 1950– .
Folio Histochemica et Cytochemica, 1963– .
International Review of Cytology, 1952– .
Journal of Biophysical and Biochemical Cytology, 1951–   (formerly *Journal of Cell Biology*).

e. ECOLOGY

Abstracts

Excerpta Medica; Section 21: *Developmental Biology and Teratology*, Vol. 1– , 1960– , Excerpta Medica, Amsterdam, 1947– .

Special Reference Works

Clarke, G. L., *Elements of Ecology*, 1st ed. revised, Wiley, New York, 1965.

Carpenter, J. R., *An Ecological Glossary*, University of Oklahoma Press, Norman, 1938; Hafner, New York, 1956.

Gleason, H. A. and Arthur Cronquist, *The Natural Geography of Plants*, Columbia University Press, New York, 1964.

Hanson, H. C., *Dictionary of Ecology*, Philosophical Library, New York, 1962.

Odum, E. P. and H. T. Odum, *Fundamentals of Ecology*, 2nd ed., Saunders, Philadelphia, 1959.

Shelford, V. E., *The Ecology of North America*, University of Illinois Press, Urbana, Ill., 1963.

Periodicals

Advances in Ecological Research, Vol. 1– , Academic, New York, 1962– .
Ecology, 1920– .
Journal of Animal Ecology, 1932– .
Journal of Ecology, 1913– .

f. ENTOMOLOGY

Special Reference Works

Index to the Literature of American Economic Entomology, Entomological Society of America, College Park, Md., 1905–1959, 18 vols. Continues *U.S.D.A. Bibliography of the More Important Contributions to American Entymology*, 1889–1905, 18 vols.

Review of Applied Entomology, Vol. 1– , Commonwealth Institute of Entomology, London, 1913– (a monthly abstract journal); Ser. A: *Agricultural* Ser. B: *Medical and Veterinary.*

Chamberlin, W. F., *Entomological Nomenclature and Literature*, 3rd ed. revised and enlarged, W. C. Brown, Dubuque, Iowa, 1952.

Horn, Walther and Sigmund Schenkling, *Index Litteraturae Entomologicae;* Ser. I: *Die Welt-Literatur uber die Gesamte Entomologie Bis Inklusive,* 1863, Dahlem, Berlin, 1928–1929, 4 vols. (Revision of Hagen: *Bibliotheca Entomologica,* 1862–1863, 2 vols.)

Kéler, S. von, *Entomologisches Wörterbuch,* 3rd ed., Akademie Verlag, Berlin, 1963.

Osborn, Herbert, *A Brief History of Entomology,* Spahr and Glenn, Columbus, Ohio, 1952.

Periodicals

Annual Review of Entomology, Vol. 1– , Annual Reviews, Palo Alto, Calif., 1956– .

British Museum (Natural History), *Bulletin, Entomology,* 1949– .

Bulletin of Entomological Research, 1910– .

Canadian Entomologist, 1868– .

Deutsche Entomologische Gesellschaft, Mitteilungen, 1930– .

Deutsche Entomologische Zeitschrift, 1881– .

Entomological News, 1889– .

Entomological Review, 1958– .

Entomological Society of America, *Annuls,* 1908– ; *Bulletin,* 1955– ; *Miscellaneous Publications,* 1959– .

Journal of Economic Entomology, 1908– .

World Review of Pest Control, 1962– .

g. ENZYMOLOGY

Special Reference Works

Barman, T. E., *Enzyme Handbook,* Springer, New York, 1969, 2 vols.

Boyer, P. D. *et al., The Enzymes,* 2nd revised ed., Academic, New York, 1959–1963, 8 vols.

Cohen, S. S., *Virus-Induced Enzymes,* Columbia University Press, New York, 1968.

Colowick, S. P. and N. O. Kaplan, Eds., *Methods in Enzymology,* Academic, New York, 1955–1969, 22 vols.

Dixon, Malcolm and E. C. Webb, *Enzymes,* 2nd ed., Academic, New York, 1964.

Neilands, J. B. and P. K. Stumpf, *Outlines of Enzyme Chemistry,* with a chapter on the synthesis of enzymes by Roger Y. Stainier, 2nd ed. revised and enlarged, Wiley, New York, 1958.

Sumner, J. B. and G. F. Somers, *Chemistry and Methods of Enzymes,* 3rd ed. revised, Academic, New York, 1953.

Periodicals

Advances in Enzyme Regulation, Vol. 1– , Pergamon, New York, 1963– .

Advances in Enzymology, Vol. 1– , Interscience, New York 1941– .

Enzymologia, 1936– .

Enzymologia Biologica et Clinica, 1961– .

Ergebnisse der Enzymforschung, 1932– .

h. GENETICS AND HEREDITY

Abstracts

Excerpta Medica; Section 22: *Human Genetics*, Vol. 1– , 1962– , Excerpta Medica, Amsterdam, 1947– .

Medical Gynaecology and Sociology, 1966– , Pergamon, New York, 1966– (formerly *Fertility Abstracts*).

Special Reference Works

Adelberg, E. A., Ed., *Papers on Bacterial Genetics*, 2nd ed., Little, Brown, Boston, 1966.

Clapper, R. B., *Glossary of Genetics and Other Biological Terms*, Vintage, New York, 1961.

Darlington, C. D., *Genetics and Man*, Macmillan, New York, 1964.

Darlington, C. D. and L. F. La Cour, *Handling of Chromosomes*, 4th ed, Hafner, New York, 1962.

Dunn, L. C., *Short History of Genetics*, McGraw-Hill, New York, 1965.

Gates, R. R., *Human Genetics*, Macmillan, New York 1946, 2 vols.

King, R. C., *Dictionary of Genetics*, Oxford, New York 1968.

Ravin, A. W., *Evolution of Genetics*, Academic, New York, 1965.

Sturtevant, A. H., *History of Genetics*, Harper and Row, New York 1965.

Periodicals

Advances in Genetics, Vol. 1– Academic, New York, 1947– .

Annual Review of Genetics, Vol. 1– Annual Reviews, Palo Alto, Calif., 1967– .

American Journal of Human Genetics, 1949– .

Genetics, 1916– .

Heredity, 1947– .

Journal of Heredity, 1910– .

Journal of Medical Genetics, 1964– .

Mutation Research, 1964– .

i. MICROBIOLOGY

Abstracts

Biological Abstracts, 1927– .

Bulletin Signalétique, Centre National de la Recherche Scientifique, Paris, 1956– Part 14: *Microbiologie, Immunology, Genetique*.

Current Tissue Culture Literature; A Key to the World's Periodicals and Abstract Indexes, M. R. Murray and Gertrude Kopech, Eds. October House, New York, 1966– .

Microbiology Abstracts, Vol. 1– , Information Retrieval Inc., London, 1965– .

Institut Pasteur, Paris, *Bulletin de l'Institut Pasteur*, revues et analyses des travaux de bactériologie et de médicien, biologie générale, physiologie, chimie biologique dans leurs rapports avec la microbiologie, Vol. 1– , Masson, Paris, 1903– .

Special Reference Works

Boyd, W. C., *Fundamentals of Immunology*, 4th ed., Interscience, New York, 1966.

Burnet, F. M. and W. M., Stanley, Eds., *The Viruses*, Academic, New York, 1959, 3 vols.

Davis, B. D., *et al.*, *Microbiology*, Harper and Row, New York, 1967.

Grainger, T. H., *Guide to the History of Bacteriology*, Ronald, New York, 1958.

Gunsalus, I. C. and R. Y. Stanier, Eds., *The Bacteria*, Academic, New York, 1960–1964.

Jacobs, M. B., *et al.,,* *Dictionary of Microbiology*, Van Nostrand, Princeton, N. J., 1957.

Jacobs, M. B. and M. J. Gerstein, *Handbook of Microbiology*, Van Nostrand, Princeton, N. J., 1960.

Lechevalier, H. A. and Morris Solotorosky, *Three Centuries of Microbiology*, McGraw-Hill, New York, 1965.

Society for Applied Bacteriology, *Identification Methods for Microbiologists*, B. M. Gibbs and F. A. Skinner, Eds., Academic, New York, 1966.

Society of American Bacteriologists. *Bergey's Manual of Determinative Bacteriology*, 7th ed., Williams & Wilkins, Baltimore, 1957.

Topley, W. W. C., *Topley and Wilson's Principles of Bacteriology and Immunity*, 5th ed., Williams & Wilkins, Baltimore, 1964, 2 vols.

Review Serials

Advances in Applied Microbiology, Vol. 1– , Academic, New York, 1959– .

Advances in Parasitology, Vol. 1– , Academic, New York 1963– .

Advances in Virus Research, Vol. 1– , Academic, New York 1953– .

Annual Review of Microbiology, Vol. 1– , Annual Reviews, Palo Alto, Calif., 1947– .

Periodicals

Acta Microbiologica, 1953– .

Acta Virologica, 1957– .

Applied Microbiology, 1953– .

Archiv für Mikrobiologie, 1930– .

Bacteriological Reviews, 1937– .

Canadian Journal of Microbiology, 1954– .

Folia Microbiologica, 1956– .

Journal of Applied Bacteriology, 1938– .

Journal of Bacteriology, 1916– .

Journal of General Microbiology, 1947– .

Journal of General Virology, 1967– .

Journal of Medical Microbiology, 1968–   (Supersedes: *Journal of Pathology and Bacteriology*).

Microbiology, 1969–   (English translation of *Mikrobiologiya*).

Zeitschrift fur Allgemeine Mikrobiologie, 1960/1961– .

j. PHYSIOLOGY

Special Reference Works

Excerpta Medica, Excerpta Medica, Amsterdam, 1947– ; Section 2 A: *Physiology,* Vol. 18– , 1965– .

American Physiological Society, *Handbook of Physiology,* Vol. 1– , Williams & Wilkins, Baltimore, 1959– (6 vols. of 15 in 1968).

Best, C. H. and N. B. Taylor, *Physiological Basis of Medical Practice,* 8th ed., Williams and Wilkins, Baltimore, 1966.

Carlson, A. J., *Machinery of the Body,* 5th ed. revised and enlarged. University of Chicago Press, Chicago, 1961.

Hawk, P. B., *Physiological Chemistry,* B. L. Oser, Ed., 14th ed., McGraw-Hill, New York, 1965.

Periodicals

Acta Physiologica Scandinavica, 1940– .

American Journal of Physiology, 1898– .

Annual Review of Physiology, Vol. 1– , Annual Reviews, Palo Alto, Calif., 1939– .

Canadian Journal of Physiology and Pharmacology, 1964– .

Comparative Biochemistry and Physiology, 1960– .

Ergebnisse der Physiologie, Biologischen Chemie und Experimentellen Pharmakologie, 1902– .

Human Development, 1958– .

Journal de Physiologie, 1899– .

Journal of Applied Physiology, 1948– .

Journal of Cellular Physiology, 1932– .

Journal of General Physiology, 1918– .

Journal of Neurophysiology, 1938– .

Journal of Physiology, 1878– .

Physiological Reviews, 1921– .

k. ZOOLOGY

Bibliographies & Guides to the Literature

Harvard University, Museum of Comparative Zoology, *Library Catalogue,* Hall, Boston, 1968, 8 vols.

Index Catalogue of Medical and Veterinary Zoology, Vols. 1–18, Government Printing Office, Washington, D.C., 1932–1952; supplements, 1953– .

McGill University, *Dictionary Catalogue of the Blacker-Wood Library of Zoology and Ornithology,* Hall, Boston, 1967, 9 vols.

Ruch, T. C., *Bibliographia Primatologica; A Classified Bibliography of Primates Other than Man,* Vol. 1– , Thomas, Springfield, Ill., 1941– .

Smith, R. C. and R. H. Painter, *Guide to the Literature of the Zoological Sciences,* 7th ed., Burgess, Minneapolis, 1966.

Wood, C. A., *Introduction to the Literature of Vertebrate Zoology,* Oxford, New York, 1931.

Abstracts

Bulletin Signalétique, Centre National de la Recherche Scientifique, Paris, 1956– ; Part 16: *Biologie et Physiologie Animales.*

U. S. Fish and Wildlife Service, *Wildlife Abstracts; A Bibliography and Index of the Abstracts in Wildlife Review,* no.1/66– , 1935/51– , Washington, D.C., 1954– .

Zoological Record, Vol. 1– , Zoological Society of London, London, 1864– , annual.

Special Reference Works

Blackwelder, R. E., *Directory of Zoological Taxonomists of the World,* Southern Illinois Press, Carbondale, Ill., 1961.

Blackwelder, R. E., *Taxonomy; A Text and Reference Book,* Wiley, New York, 1967.

Blair, W. F., *et al., Vertebrates of the United States,* 2nd ed., McGraw-Hill, New York, 1968.

Florkin, Marcel and B. T. Scheer, Eds., *Chemical Zoology,* Academic, New York, 1967–1968, 2 vols.

Hyman, L. H., *The Invertebrates,* McGraw-Hill, New York, 1940–1959, 5 vols.

International Code of Zoological Nomenclature, International Trust for Zoological Nomenclature, London, 1964.

International Union of Biological Sciences, *Index des Zoologistes,* Paris, Secretariat General de l'U.I.S.B., 1953; supplement, 1959– .

International Zoo Yearbook, Vol. 1– , Zoological Society of London, London, 1959– .

Kaestner, Alfred, *Invertebrate Zoology;* translated from the 2nd German ed. by H. W. & L. R. Levi, Vol. 1– , Wiley, New York, 1967– .

Leftwich, A. W., *Dictionary of Zoology,* Van Nostrand, Princeton, N. J., 1963.

Neave, S. A., *Nomenclator Zoologicus,* a list of the names of genera and subgenera in zoology from the 10th ed. of Linaeus, 1758 to the end of 1945, Zoological Society of London, London, 1939–1950, 5 vols.

Rothschild, N. M. V., *Classification of Living Animals,* 2nd ed., Longmans, New York, 1965.

Traité de Zoologie; Anatomie, Systémique, Biologie, Masson, Paris, 1948–1960, 17 vols.

Birds

Peters, J. L., *Check List of Birds of the World,* Vol. 1– , Museum of Comparative Zoology, Cambridge, Mass., 1931– , in progress.

Strong, R. M., *Bibliography of Birds,* Field Museum of Natural History, Chicago, 1939–1959, 4 vols.

Thomson, A. L., *New Dictionary of Birds,* McGraw-Hill, New York, 1964.

Voous, K. H., *Nelson's Atlas of European Birds,* Nelson, London, 1960.

Fishes

Dean, Bashford, *Bibliography of Fishes,* enlarged and ed. by C. R. Eastmen, American Museum of Natural History, New York, 1916–1923, 3 vols.

Herald, E. S., *Living Fishes of the World,* Doubleday, Garden City, N. Y., 1961.

Hiatt, R. W., *World Directory of Hydrobiological and Fisheries Institutions,* American Institute of Biological Sciences, Washington, D.C., 1963.

Sterba, Gunther, *Freshwater Fishes of the World*, translated and revised by D. W. Tucker, Vista Books, London, 1962.

Walden, H. T., II., *Familiar Freshwater Fishes of America*, Harper and Row, New York, 1964.

Mammals

Burton, Maurice, *Systematic Dictionary of Mammals of the World*, London; Museum Press, Crowell, New York, 1962.

Hall, E. R. and K. R. Kelson, *Mammals of North America*, Ronald, New York, 1959, 2 vols.

Hill, W. C. O., *Primates: Comparative Anatomy and Taxonomy*, Vol. 1– , University Press, Edinburgh, 1953– .

Napier, J. R. and P. H. Napier, *Handbook of Living Primates*, Academic, New York, 1967.

Southern, H. N., Ed., *Handbook of British Mammals*, edited for the Mammalian Society of the British Isles, Blackwell, Oxford, 1964.

Walker, E. P., *et al.*, *Mammals of the World*, 2nd ed., Johns Hopkins Press, Baltimore, 1968, 3 vols.

Reptiles

Ditmars, R. L., *The Reptiles of North America, a Review of the Crocodilians, Lizards, Snakes, Turtles and Tortoises Inhabiting the United States and Northern Mexico*, Doubleday, New York, 1936.

Peters, J. A., *Dictionary of Herpetology*, Hafner, New York, 1964.

Stebbins, R. C., *Field Guide to Western Reptiles and Amphibians; Field Marks of All Species in Western North America*, Houghton, Mifflin, Boston, 1966.

Wright, A. H., *Handbook of Snakes of the United States and Canada*, Comstock, Ithaca, N. Y., 1957, 2 vols.

Periodicals

Acta Zoologica (Sweden), 1920– .

American Zoologist, 1961– .

Archiv für Zoologi, 1950– .

Auk; a Journal of Ornithology, 1884– .

Australian Journal of Zoology, 1953– .

Canadian Journal of Zoology, 1929– .

Folia Primatologica, 1963– .

Journal of Experimental Zoology, 1904– .

Journal of Zoology, 1830– (formerly, *Proceedings of the London Zoological Society*).

Zeitschrift für Angewandte Zoologie, 1912– .

Zoologica (U. S.), 1907– ,

Zoological Society of London, *Transactions*, 1833– .

5. MATHEMATICS

Bibliographies and Guides to the Literature

Forsythe, G. E., *Bibliography of Russian Mathematics Books*, Chelsea, New York, 1956.

Goldman, Sylvia, *Guide to the Literature of Engineering, Mathematics, and the*

Physical Sciences, 2nd ed., Johns Hopkins University Applied Physics Laboratory, Baltimore, 1964.

International Statistical Institute, *Bibliography of Basic Texts and Monographs on Statistical Methods;* 2nd ed., 1945–1960, Heffner, New York, 1963.

Karpinski, L. C., *Bibliography of Mathematical Works Printed in America through 1850,* University of Michigan Press, Ann Arbor, Mich., 1940; Supplements 1–2, in *Scripta Math.* 8:233–236 (1941) and 11:173–177 (1945).

Parke, N. G., *Guide to the Literature of Mathematics and Physics; Including Related Works on Engineering Science,* 2nd revised ed., Dover, New York, 1958.

Pemberton, J. E., *How to Find Out in Mathematics,* Pergamon, New York, 1963.

Referativnyi Zhurnal, Matematika, Akademiia Nauk SSSR, Moscow, 1953– .

Abstracts and Indexes

Jahrbuch über die Fortschritte der Mathematik, Vols. 1–60, DeGruyer, Berlin, 1868–1942.

Mathematical Reviews, Vol. 1– , American Mathematical Society, Providence, R. I., 1940– ; *indexes:* 1940–1959, 1961, 2 vols.

Statistical Theory and Method Abstracts, Vol. 1– , Oliver & Boyd for the International Statistical Institute, Edinburgh, 1959– .

Zentralblatt für Mathematik und ihre Grenzebiete, Vol. 1– , Springer, Berlin, 1931– (suspended November 1944–June 1948.

Special Reference Works

Abramowitz, Milton and I. A. Stegun, *Handbook of Mathematical Functions and Formulas, Graphs, and Mathematical Tables,* Government Printing Office, Washington, D.C., 1964. (U. S. National Bureau of Standards, Applied Mathematics Series 55).

Bauchinger, Julius, and J. Peters, *Logarithmic Trigonometrical Tables to Eight Decimal Places,* 3rd ed., Weinheim/Bergstrasse, Germany, 1958, 2 vols.

Bourbaki, Nicolas, pseud., *Elements de Mathematique,* 3rd ed., Vol. 1– , Hermann, Paris, 1958– (collective pseudanym for a group of French mathematicians).

British Association for the Advancement of Science, *Mathematical Tables,* London, 1931–1952, 10 vols. (Vol. 1, 2nd ed., 1946) (continued as *Royal Society of Mathematical Tables*).

Encyklopädie der Matematischen Wissenschaften mit Einschluss ihrer Anwendungen . . . , Teubner, Leipzig, 1898/1904–1935, 6 vols.; 2 völlig neubearb., vol. 1– , Leipzig, 1939–1958 (in progress).

Owen, D. B., *Handbook of Statistical Tables,* Addison-Wesley, Reading, Mass., 1962.

Royal Society of London, *Royal Society Mathematical Tables,* Vol. 1– , Cambridge University Press, London, 1950– .

U. S. National Bureau of Standards, *Applied Mathematics Series,* No. 1– , Government Printing Office, Washington, D.C., 1948– .

World Directory of Mathematicians, 2nd ed., Tate Institute, Bombay, 1961.

Review Serials

Advances in Mathematics, Vol. 1– , Academic, New York, 1961– .

Annals of Mathematics, Vol. 1– , Princeton University Press, Princeton, N. J., 1884– .

Computers

Bibliographies and Abstracts

Computer Abstracts, Vol. 1– , Technical Information Co., London, 1960– .

Computer Literature Bibliography, Vol. 1– , Government Printing Office, Washington, D.C., 1965– .

Special Reference Works

Auerbach Computer Notebook, Auerbach Info., Inc., Philadelphia, 1968– , monthly.

Computer Graphics: Techniques and Applications, Plenum, New York, 1969.

Condensed Computer Encyclopedia, McGraw-Hill, New York, 1969.

Dictionary of Computer and Control Systems, Abbreviations, Signs, Symbols, Odyssey Press, New York, 1965.

Huskey, H. D., *Computer Handbook*, McGraw-Hill, New York, 1962.

Iverson, K. E., *Automatic Data Processing*, Wiley, New York, 1963 (a review textbook).

Sippl, C. J., *Computer Dictionary*, Sams, Indianapolis, Ind., 1966.

Trollmann, Lilian and Alfred Whittmann, *Dictionary of Data Processing*, Elsevier, New York, 1965.

Serials and Periodicals

Advances in Computers, Vol. 1– , Academic, New York, 1960– .

Advances in Information Systems Science, Vol. 1– , Plenum, New York, 1969– .

Annual Review of Information Science and Technology, Vol. 1– , Interscience, New York, 1966– .

Computing Reviews, Vol. 1– , Association for Computing Machinery, New York, 1960– .

International Journal of Computer Mathematics, Vol. 1– , Gordon and Breach, London, 1964– .

Periodicals

American Mathematical Monthly, 1894– .

American Mathematical Society, Bulletin, 1894– ; *New Publications*, 1961– ; *Notices*, 1953– ; *Proceedings*, 1950– ; *Transactions*, 1900– .

Canadian Mathematical Bulletin, 1958– .

Computer Programs in Biomedicine, 1969– .

Mathematical Gazette, 1894– .

Mathematical Reviews, 1940– .

Mathematische Annalen, 1868– .

Mathematische Zeitschrift, 1918– .

Mathematics of Computation, 1943– .

Mathematics Teacher, 1908– .

Scripta Mathematica, 1933.

6. PHYSICS

Bibliographies and Guides to the Literature

Anthony, L. J., *Sources of Information on Atomic Energy*, Pergamon, New York, 1966.

International Atomic Energy Agency, *List of Bibliographies on Atomic Energy*, Vol. 1– , Vienna, 1960– .

Keenan, S. and P. Atherton, *Journal Literature of Physics: A Comprehensive Study Based on Physics Abstracts,* American Institute of Physics, New York, 1964.

Maizell, R. E. and S. L. Seigel, *Periodical Literature of Physics,* American Institute of Physics, New York, 1961.

Markworth, M. L., *Dissertations in Physics; An Indexed Bibliography to All Doctoral Theses Accepted at American Universities,* 1861–1959, Stanford University Press, Stanford, Calif., 1961.

Parke, N. G., *Guide to the Literature of Mathematics and Physics; Including Related Works on Engineering Science,* 2nd revised ed., Dover, New York, 1958.

U. S. Atomic Energy Commission, *Technical Books and Monographs,* 1st ed., Oak Ridge, Tenn., 1959– .

U. S. Atomic Energy Commission, *What's Available in the Atomic Energy Literature,* Oak Ridge, Tenn., 1966 (11th revision in 1966).

Whitford, R. H., *Physics Literature; A Reference Manual,* 2nd ed., Scarecrow Press, Metuchen, N. J., 1968.

Yates, Bryan, *How to Find Out about Physics,* Pergamon, New York, 1965.

Abstracts and Indexes

Applied Science and Technology Index, 1958– .

Chemical Abstracts, 1907– .

Engineering Index, 1884– .

Physics Abstracts, 1898– (formerly Section A: *Science Abstracts*).

Physics Express, Vol. 1– , International Physics Index, New York, 1958– .

Rheology Abstracts; A Survey of World Literature, Vol. 1– , Pergamon, New York, 1958– .

Solid State Abstracts, Vol. 1– , Cambridge Communications Corp., Cambridge, Mass., 1960– .

Special Reference Works

Burhop, E. H. S., Ed., *High Energy Physics,* Vol. 1– , Academic, New York, 1967– .

Cochran, J. F. and R. R. Haering, Eds., *Solid State Physics,* Gordon and Breach, London, 1968.

Handbuch Der Physik, 2nd ed., Springer, Berlin, 1955– (to be completed in 54 volumes).

Landolt, H. H., *Landolt-Bornstein Zahlenwerte und Funktionen aus Physik, Chemie, Astronomie, Geophysik und Technik,* 6th ed., Springer, Berlin, 1950– (earlier editions published under title: *Physikalisch-Chemische Tabellen*).

Landolt, H. H., *Landolt-Bornstein Zahlenwerte und Funktionen aus Naturwissenschaften und Technik,* neue serie, Springer, Berlin, 1961– .

Methods of Experimental Physics, Vol. 1– , Academic, New York, 1959– .

National Research Council, *International Critical Tables,* McGraw-Hill, New York, 1926–1933, 7 vols. and index.

Nuclear Theory Reference Book, National Research Council, Washington, D.C., 1959 .

Pure and Applied Physics; A Series of Monographs and Textbooks, Pergamon, New York, 1957– .

U. S. National Bureau of Standards National Standard Reference Data Series (NSRDS), No. 1– , Washington, D.C., 1965– .

Review Serials

Advances in Atomic and Molecular Physics, Vol. 1– , Academic, New York, 1965– .

Advances in Chemical Physics, Vol. 1– , Interscience, New York, 1958– .

Advances in Magnetic Resonance, Vol. 1– , Academic, New York, 1965– .

Advances in Mass Spectroscopy, Vol. 1– , Pergamon, New York, 1959– .

Advances in Nuclear Physics, Vol. 1– , Plenum, New York, 1968– .

Advances in Nuclear Science and Technology, Vol. 1– , Academic, New York, 1962– .

Advances in Physics, Vol. 1– , Taylor and Francis, London, 1953– (quarterly supplement to *Philosophical Magazine*).

Advances in Theoretical Physics, Vol. 1– , Academic, New York, 1965– .

Annual Review of NMR Spectroscopy, Vol. 1– , Academic, New York, 1968– .

Annual Review of Nuclear Science, Vol. 1– , Annual Reviews, Stanford, Calif., 1952– .

Progress in Infrared Spectroscopy, Vol. 1– , Plenum, New York, 1962– .

Progress in Physics, Vol. 1– , Physical Society, London, 1934– (formerly *Reports on Progress in Physics*).

Progress in Solid State Chemistry, Vol. 1– , Pergamon, New York, 1964– .

Reviews in Modern Physics, Vol. 1– , American Institute of Physics, New York, 1929– .

Solid State Physics: Advances in Research and Application, Vol. 1– , Academic, New York, 1955– ; supplements, 1958– .

Periodicals

Academy of Sciences of the U.S.S.R.; *Proceedings: Applied Physics Section,* 1957– ; *Bulletin: Physical Series,* 1958– ; *Optics and Spectroscopy,* 1959– ; (in English translation).

American Journal of Physics, 1933– .

Annalen der Physick, 1799– .

Annales de Physique, 1789– .

Annals of Physics, 1957– .

Atomic and Molecular Physics, see (*Journal of Physics,* Section B.)

Beitrage aus der Plasmaphysik, 1961– .

British Journal of Applied Physics, 1950– (see *Journal of Physics:* Section D.)

Canadian Journal of Physics, Vols. 1–46, 1929–1968.

Comments on Nuclear and Particle Physics, 1967– .

Comments on Solid State Physics, 1968– .

Contemporary Physics, 1959– .

Czechslovak Journal of Physics, Section B, 1950– .

Foundations of Physics, 1970– .

Infrared Physics, 1962– .

Journal de Physique, 1872– .

Journal of Applied Physics, 1930– .

Journal of Chemical Physics, 1933– .

Journal of Mass Spectrometry and Ion Physics, 1968– .

Journal of Nuclear Science, Japan, 1964– .

Journal of Physics, 1968– ; *A: General; B: Atomic and Molecular Physics; C: Solid State Physics* and Supplement: *Metal Physics,* 1970– ; *D: British Journal of Applied Physics; E: Journal of Scientific Instruments.*

Journal of Research of the National Bureau of Standards; Section A: *Physics and Chemistry,* 1959– .

Journal of Scientific Instruments, 1923– (see *Journal of Physics,* Section E).

Journal of the Acoustical Society of America, 1929– .

Journal of the Mechanics and Physics of Solids, 1952– .

Journal of the Optical Society of America, 1917– .

Lettere al Nuovo Cimento, 1969– .

Metrologia, 1965– .

Molecular Physics, 1958– .

Nuovo Cimento, 1855– .

Particle Accelerators, 1970– .

Physica Norvegica, 1961– .

Physica Status Solidi, 1961 .

Physica Status Solidi, A: *Applied Research,* 1970– .

Physical Review, Sections A–D, 1893– .

Physical Review Letters, 1958– .

Physics and Chemistry of Liquids, 1968– .

Physics Letters, 1962– .

Physics of Condensed Matter, 1963– . *(Physik der Kondensierten Materie, Physique de la Matière Condensée).*

Physics of Fluids, 1958– .

Physics Teacher, 1963– .

Physics Today, 1948– .

Proceedings of the Physical Society of London, 1874–1967 (title changed to *Journal of Physics*).

Review of Scientific Instruments, 1930– .

Reviews of Modern Physics, 1930– .

Solid State Communications, 1969– (Supplement to the *Journal of Physics and Chemistry of Solids,* Vol. 7).

Solid State Physics, see *Journal of Physics,* Section C.

Sound, 1962– .

Soviet Physics:
    Accoustics, 1955– ;
    Crystallography, 1957– ;
    Doklady, 1956– ;
    JETP, 1956– ;
    JETP Letters, 1965– ;
    Solid State, 1959– ;
    Technical Physics, 1956– ;

Uspekhi, 1959–
(all in English translation).
Surface Science, 1964– .
Ultrasonics, 1963– .
Zhurnal Eksperimental'noi Theoreticheskoi Fiziki, 1931– (see *Soviet Physics: JETP*).

B. Applied Science

1. AGRICULTURE AND FORESTRY

a. AGRICULTURE

Bibliographies

Bibliography of Soil Science, Fertilizers and General Agronomy, 1947– , Commonwealth Agricultural Bureaux, Farnham Royal, Eng., 1951– .

Blanchard, J. R. and Harald Ostvold, *Literature of Agricultural Research,* University of California Press, Berkeley, 1958.

Lauche, Rudolf, *Internationales Handbuch der Bibliographien des Landbaues, World Bibliography of Agricultural Bibliographies . . . ,* Bayerische Landwirtschaftsverlag, Munchen, 1957.

U. S. National Agricultural Library, *Bibliography of Agriculture,* Vol. 1– , Washington, D.C., 1942– .

Abstracts and Indexes

Abstracts of Literature on Milk and Milk Products, 1936– (published monthly in *Journal of Dairy Science*).

Biological and Agricultural Index, 1919– .

Bulletin Signaletique, Centre National de la Recherche Scientifique, Paris, 1956– ; Part 18: *Sciences Agricoles.*

Commonwealth Agricultural Bureaux Publications; Abstracts:
Animal Breeding Abstracts, 1933– ;
Dairy Science Abstracts, 1939– ;
Field Crop Abstracts, 1948– ;
Herbage Abstracts, 1931– ;
Horticultural Abstracts, 1931– ;
Nutrition Abstracts and Reviews, 1931/1932– ;
Plant Breeding Abstracts, 1930– ;
Weed Abstracts, 1952– .

Journal of the Science of Food and Agriculture, 1950– ; contains abstract section.

Pesticides Documentation Bulletin, 1965– ; includes abstracts.

Review of Applied Mycology, 1922– ; includes abstracts and reviews.

Search: Fertilizer Division, Compendium Publishers International Corp., Fort Lee, 1964– .

Soils and Fertilizers; Abstracts of the World Literature, 1938– .

World Agricultural Economics and Rural Sociology Abstracts, Vol. 1– , North Holland Publishing Co., Amsterdam, 1959– .

Special Reference Works

Association of Official Analytical Chemists, *Official Methods of Analysis*, 1st ed.– , Washington, D.C., 1919– .

Dictionary of Agricultural and Applied Terminology, Michigan State University Press, Lansing, Mich., 1962.

Doane Agricultural Service, Inc., *Farm Building Cost Handbook*, St. Louis, 1963, looseleaf.

Farrall, A. W. and C. F. Albrecht, Eds., *Agricultural Engineering; A Dictionary and Handbook*, Interstate, Danville, Ill., 1965.

Finney, D. J., *Introduction to Statistical Science in Agriculture*, 2nd ed., Munksgaard, Copenhagen, 1962.

Haensch, Gunther and Gisela Haberkamp, Comps., *Dictionary of Agriculture: German/ English/French/Spanish*, 2nd ed., Elsevier, New York, 1963.

Richey, C. B. *et al.*, *Agricultural Engineer's Handbook*, McGraw-Hill, New York, 1961.

U. S. Bureau of the Census, *1964 United States Census of Agriculture*, Washington, D.C., 1967–1968, 3 vols.

U. S. Department of Agriculture, *Agricultural Statistics*, Washington, D.C., 1936– (published in *Yearbook of Agriculture*, 1894–1935).

U. S. Department of Agriculture, *Directory of Organizations and Field Activities in the Department of Agriculture*, Vol. 1– , Washington, D.C., 1925– .

U. S. Department of Agriculture, *Handbook of Agricultural Charts*, Government Printing Office, Washington, D.C., 1963– .

U.S. Department of Agriculture, *Summary of Registered Agricultural Pesticide Chemical Uses*, 3rd ed., Government Printing Office, Washington, D.C., 1968– .

U. S. Department of Agriculture, *Yearbook of Agriculture*, 1894– , annual.

U. S. National Agricultural Library, *Agricultural/Biological Vocabulary*, Washington, D.C., 1967, 2 vols., supplement, 1968– .

Usovsky, B. N. *et al.*, *Comprehensive Russian-English Agricultural Dictionary*; 1st English ed., Pergamon, New York, 1967 (based on 1960 Russian ed.).

Westcott, Cynthia, *Plant Diseases Handbook*, 2nd ed., Van Nostrand Reinhold, New York, 1960.

Periodicals

Agricultural and Veterinary Chemicals and Agricultural Engineering, 1960– .

Agricultural Economics, 1949– .

Agricultural Engineering, 1920– .

Agricultural Marketing, 1956– .

Agricultural Research, 1953– .

Agricultural Science, 1963– .

Agronomy Journal, 1907– .

American Dairy Review, 1939– .

Crops and Soils, 1948– .

International Journal of Agrarian Affairs, 1939– .

Journal of Agricultural and Food Chemistry, 1953– .

Journal of Agriculture (Eng.), 1901– .
Journal of Animal Science, 1942– .
Journal of Dairy Research, 1929– .
Journal of Dairy Science, 1917– .
Journal of the Science of Food and Agriculture, 1950– .
Manufactured Milk Products Journal, 1910– .
Pesticides Documentation Bulletin, 1965– .
Review of Applied Mycology, 1922– .
Society of Dairy Technology, *Journal*, 1948– .
Soil Science, 1916– .
Soil Science Society of America, *Proceedings*, 1936– .
Soils and Fertilizers, 1938– .

b. FORESTRY

Bibliographies, Abstracts and Indexes

Commonwealth Forestry Institute, *Basic Library List for Forestry*, 3rd ed., Oxford, 1963.

Shrader, S., *Bibliographien und Bibliographische Sammlungen von Bedeutung für die Forst -und Holzwirtschaft* . . . , Bundesforschungsanwalt für Forst -und Holzwirtschaft, Reinbek, 1963.

Yale University, School of Forestry Library, *Dictionary Catalogue of the Henry S. Graves Memorial Library*, Hall, Boston, 1962, 2 vols.

Biological and Agricultural Index, 1919– .

Forestry Abstracts, Vol. 1– , Commonwealth Agricultural Bureaux, Farnham Royal, Eng., 1939– .

Special Reference Works

Davis, K. P., *Forest Management: Regulation and Valuation*, 2nd ed., McGraw-Hill, New York, 1966.

Elsevier's Wood Dictionary in Seven Languages: American, French, Spanish, Italian, Swedish, Dutch and German, Elsevier, New York, 1964– .

Food and Agriculture Organization, Forestry Research, *A World Directory of Forest and Forest Products Research Institutions*, F.A.O., Rome, 1963.

Forbes, R., Ed., *Forestry Handbook*, edited for the Society of American Foresters, Ronald, New York, 1955.

Hough, R. B., *Hough's Encyclopedia of American Woods*, Speller, New York, 1957, 16 vols.

International Review of Forestry Research, Vol. 1– , Academic, New York, 1964– .

Little, E. L., *Checklist of Native and Naturalized Trees of the U. S.*, Washington, D.C., 1953 (*U.S.D.A. Agricultural Handbook*, No. 41).

Sargent, C. S., *Manual of the Trees of North America*, 2nd ed., P. Smith, Gloucester, Mass., 1962.

Society of American Foresters, *Forestry Terminology; A Glossary of Technical Terms Used in Forestry*, 3rd ed., Washington, D.C., 1958.

U. S. Department of Agriculture, Forest Service, *Silvics of Forest Trees of the U. S.,* Washington, D.C., 1965.

Weck, Johannes *et al., Dictionary of Forestry, in Five Languages,* American Elsevier, New York, 1966.

Weltforstatlas, (published by the Bundesanstalt für Forst -und Holzwirtschaft, Reinbek, in collaboration with F.A.O.). Haller, Berlin-Grunewald, 1951– .

Lumber

Bolza, E., *German-English Glossary of Forest Products Terms,* C.S.I.R.O., Division of Forest Products, South Malbourne, 1959; supplement, 1962.

Evans, H. T., *Woodworkers Book of Facts,* Technical Press, Ltd., London, 1962.

Konig, E., *Holz-lexikon: Nachschlagewerk für die Holzwerkschaftliche Praxis,* Berlin, Verlags-GmbH, 1962.

Panshin, A. J. *et al., Textbook of Wood Technology,* 2nd ed., McGraw-Hill, New York, 1964.

Titmuss, F. H., *Commercial Timbers of the World,* 3rd ed., enlarged of *A Concise Encyclopedia of World Timbers,* Technical Press, Ltd., London, 1965.

Food and Agriculture Organization, Yearbook of Forest Products Statistics, Vol. 1– , F.A.O., Rome, 1947– .

Periodicals

Food and Agriculture Organization, *World List of Periodicals and Serials of Interest to Forestry,* F.A.O., Rome, 1960.

Allgemeine Forst -und Jagdzeitung, n.s., 1838– .

American Forests, 1895– .

Carribean Forester, 1939– .

Empire Forestry Review, 1922– .

Forest Science, 1955– .

Forestry, 1927– .

Journal of Forestry, 1902– .

Pennsylvania Forests, 1886– .

Quarterly Journal of Forestry, 1907– .

Schweizerische Zeitschrift für Fortwesen, 1850– .

Unasylva, 1947– . ·

Zeitschrift für Weltforstwirtschaft, 1933– .

British Columbia Lumberman, 1917– .

Canadian Forest Industries, 1964– (absorbed *Lumberman* and *Timbers of Canada*).

Forest Products Journal, 1947– .

Revue du Bois et ses Applications, 1946– .

Southern Lumberman, 1881– (incorporated *Southern Lumber Journal* and *Building Material Dealer*).

Timberman, 1963– (absorbed *Lumberman,* 1889–1962).

Wood and Wood Products, 1896– .

Wood Construction and Building Materials, 1914– .

2. *ENGINEERING SCIENCES*

a. GENERAL

Bibliographies, Indexes, and so on

Engineering Societies Library, *Classed Subject Catalog*, Hall, Boston, 1964, 13 vols.; supplements: 1964– .

Sternberg, V. A., *How to Locate Technical Information*, Prentice-Hall, Englewood Cliffs, N. J., 1964.

Applied Science and Technology Index, 1958– .

British Technology Index, vol. 1– , Library Association, London, 1962– .

Bulletin Signaletique, Centre National de la Recherche Scientifique, Paris, 1956– ; Part 9: *Sciences de l'Ingenieur.*

Engineering Index, 1884– .

Special Reference Works

Eilon, Samuel, *Industrial Engineering Tables*, Van Nostrand Reinhold, New York, 1962.

Eshbach, O. W., Ed., *Handbook of Engineering Fundamentals*, prepared by a staff of specialists, 2nd ed., Wiley, New York, 1952 (Wiley Engineering Handbook Series).

Hvistendahl, H. S., *Engineering Units and Physical Quantities*, Macmillan, London, 1964.

Kempe's Engineer's Year-Book, Morgan, London, 1894– , revised annually.

Lueger, O., *Lexicon der Technik;* Vol. 1– , Hrsg. von Alfred Ehrhardt und Hermann Franke, 4 Vollst. neuarb. und erw. Auf 1. Deutsche Verlags-Anstalt, Stuttgart, 1960– , 17 vols, projected.

Maynard, H. B., Ed., *Industrial Engineering Handbook*, 2nd ed., McGraw-Hill, New York, 1963.

Newnes' Engineer's Reference Book, F. J. Camm, Ed., 9th ed., Newnes, London, 1965.

Periodicals

Advances in Information Systems Science, 1969– .

Engineering Journal, 1918– .

Engineering Journal News, 1961– .

Engineering News-Record, 1874– .

Engineer's Journal, 1940– .

Industrial and Engineering Chemistry, 1923– .

Ingenieur, 1915– .

International Journal of Engineering Science, 1963– .

Magazine of Standards, 1930– .

Russian Engineering Journal, 1959–   (English translation of *Vestnik Mashinostroeniya*).

Science and Technology, 1964– .

Soviet Engineering Journal, 1965–   (English translation of *Inzhenernyy Zhurnal*).

Tech Engineering News, 1919– .

b. AEROSPACE ENGINEERING

Bibliographies and Guides to the Literature

Air University Library, *Index to Military Periodicals*, Vol. 1– , Air University Library, Maxwell Air Force Base, Ala., 1949– .

Benton, M. C., *The Literature of Space Science and Exploration*, U. S. Naval Research Laboratory, Washington, D.C., 1958.

Fry, B. M. and F. E. Mohrhardt, *Guide to Information Sources in Space Science and Technology*, Interscience, New York, 1963.

Ordway, F. I., *Annotated Bibliography of Space Science and Technology*, with an astronomical supplement; a history of astronautical book literature, 1931–1961, 3rd ed., ARFOR Publ., Astronautics Education Division, Washington, D.C., 1962.

U. S. Library of Congress, Science and Technology Division, *Aeronautical and Space Serial Publications; A World List*, Washington, D.C., 1962.

Abstracts and Indexes

Engineering Index, 1884– .

International Aerospace Abstracts, Vol. 1– , AIAA Service, New York, 1961– .

NASA, *Scientific and Technical Aerospace Reports; A Semimonthly Abstract Journal with Indexes* (STAR), Vol. 1– , Washington, D.C., 1963– ; supplement: *Guide to the Subject Indexes for Scientific and Technical Aerospace Reports*, No. 1– , April 1964– .

Research Abstracts and Technical Reviews, NASA, Washington, D.C., 1961– .

Special Reference Works

Above and Beyond; The Encyclopedia of Aviation and Space Science, New Horizons, Chicago, 1968, 14 vols.

Aerospace Year Book: Official Publication of the Aerospace Industries Association of America, Inc., Vol. 1– , American Aviation Publication, Washington, D.C., 1919– .

Barr, James and W. E. Howard, *Spacecraft and Missiles of the World*, Harcourt, New York, 1962.

Jane's All the World Aircraft, Vol. 1– , McGraw-Hill, New York, 1909– , annual.

McGraw-Hill Encyclopedia of Space, McGraw-Hill, New York, 1968.

NASA, *Aeronautics and Astronautics; an American Chronology of Science and Technology in the Exploration of Space, 1915–1960*, E. M. Emme, Washington, D.C., 1961; supplement: *Astronautical and Aeronautical Events*, 1961– .

North Atlantic Treaty Organization, *AGARD Aeronautical Multilingual Dictionary*, Macmillan, New York, 1960; supplements: 1963– .

Webb, Paul, Ed., *Bioastronautics Data Book*, Government Printing Office, Washington, D.C., 1964.

Who's who in World Aviation and Astronautics, Vol. 1– , American Aviation Publications, Washington, D.C., 1955–1958, 2 vols.

World Aviation Directory, Vol. 1– , American Aviation Publications, Washington, D.C., 1940– , semi-annual.

World Space Directory Listing U. S. and Foreign Missile/Space Companies, Officials and Government Agencies, Vol. 1– , American Aviation Publications, Washington, D.C., 1962– .

Review Serials

Advances in Space Science and Technology, Vol. 1– , Academic, New York, 1959– .

Progress in Astronautics and Aeronautics, Vol. 1– , Academic, New York, 1960.

Periodicals

Pacific Aerospace Library Uniterm Index to Periodicals, Pacific Aerospace Library, American Institute of Aeronautics and Astronautics, Los Angeles, Calif., 1944– , annual volume, 1955– .

Aero/Space Engineering, 1942– (formerly *Aeronaut*).

Aeronautical Quarterly, 1949– .

AIAA Journal, 1963– (combines *ARS Journal* and *Journal of Aerospace Sciences*).

American Aviation, 1937– .

Applied Mechanics Reviews, 1947– .

Astronautics and Aeronautics, 1957– .

Aviation Week and Space Technology, 1916– .

Flight International, 1909– (incorporated Aeroplane, 1911–1968).

International Journal of Heat and Mass Transfer, 1960– .

Journal of the British Interplanetary Society, 1934– .

Planetary and Space Science, 1959– .

Royal Aeronautical Society, *Journal,* 1897– .

SAE Journal, 1917– .

Space Science Reviews, 1962– .

5. CHEMICAL ENGINEERING; RESINS, RUBBER, PLASTICS, AND SO ON

Guide to the Literature

Yescombe, E. R., *Sources of Information on the Rubber, Plastics and Allied Industries,* Pergamon, New York, 1968 (International Series of Monographs in Library and Information Science, Vol. 7).

Abstracts and Indexes

Applied Science and Technology Index, 1958– .

Chemical Abstracts, 1907– .

Gas Abstracts, Vol. 1– , Institute of Gas Technology, Chicago, 1945– .

British Plastics Federation Abstracts, 1945–1964, London, 1945–1964, continued as *RAPRA abstracts,* 1965– .

Plastics Abstracts, Vol. 1– , Plastics Investigations, Welwyn, Herts, Eng., 1959– .

RAPRA Abstracts, 1965– , Rubber and Plastic Research Association of Great Britain, Shawbury, Shrewsbury, Shropshire, Eng., 1965– .

Resins, Rubbers, Plastics Yearbook, Vol. 1– , Information for Industry, Inc., New York, 1948– , annual, contains abstracts.

Rubber Abstracts, 1923–1964, Rubber and Plastics Research Association of Great Britain, Shawbury, Shropshire, Eng., 1923–1964, continued as *RAPRA Abstracts,* 1965– .

Search: Plastics and Resins Division, Compendium Publishers International Corp., Fort Lee, Va., 1964– .

Search: Rubber Division, Compendium Publishers International Corp., Fort Lee, Va., 1964– .

Theoretical Chemical Engineering Abstracts, Vol. 1– , Technical Information Co., London, 1964– .

Special Reference Works

American Gas Association, *Gas Engineers Handbook; Fuel, Gas Engineering Practices,* Industrial Press, New York, 1965.

Considine, D. M. and S. D. Ross, *Handbook of Applied Instrumentation,* McGraw-Hill, New York, 1964.

Cremer, H. W. and Trefor Davis, *Chemical Engineering Practice,* Butterworth, London, 1956–1965, 12 vols.

Dictionary of Chemical Engineering, Elsevier, New York, 1969, 2 vols.

Elsevier's Dictionary of the Gas Industry in Seven Languages . . . , Elsevier, Amsterdam, 1961.

Encyclopedia of Chemical Technology, 2nd ed., Interscience, New York, 1963– .

Graham, A. K. and H. L. Pinkerton, *Electroplating Engineering Handbook,* 2nd ed., Reinhold, New York, 1962.

Hampel, C. A., *Encyclopedia of Electrochemistry,* Reinhold, New York, Chapman and Hall, London, 1964.

Industrial and Engineering Chemistry, Modern Chemical Processes, Reinhold, New York, 1962–1963, 7 vols.

Mead, W. J., Ed., *Encyclopedia of Chemical Process Equipment,* Reinhold, New York, 1964.

Modern Chemical Engineering, Reinhold, New York, 1963– (monograph series).

Naunton, W. J. S., Ed., *Applied Science of Rubber,* E. Arnold, London, 1961.

Rubber Red Book; Directory of the Rubber Industry, Rubber Age, New York, biennial.

Society of the Plastics Industry, Inc., *SPI Plastics Engineering Handbook,* 3rd ed., Reinhold, New York, 1963.

Shreve, R.N., *Chemical Process Industries,* 3rd ed., McGraw-Hill, New York, (1969).

Wittfoht, Annemarie, *Plastics Technical Dictionary; Nomenclature Used in Processing, in Testing and Mold Construction,* Interscience, New York, 1961.

Review Serials

Advances in Chemical Engineering, Vol. 1– , Academic, New York, 1948– .

Advances in Cryogenic Engineering, Vol. 1– , Plenum, New York, 1960– .

Advances in Polymer Science, Vol. 1– , Springer, New York, 1958– .

Periodicals

A.I.Ch.E. Journal, 1955– .

British Chemical Engineering, 1956– .

Canadian Journal of Chemical Engineering, 1929– .
Chemical Age, 1887– .
Chemical and Engineering News, 1923– .
Chemical Engineering, 1902– .
Chemical Engineering Progress, 1947– .
Journal of Chemical Engineering Data, 1956– .

Plastics

Applied Plastics, 1958– .
British Plastics, 1929– .
Canadian Plastics, 1943– .
Engineering Plastics Monthly, Vol. 5– , Society of Plastics Engineers, New York, 1969– ; supersedes *Engineering Index: Plastics Section*, Vols. 1–4, 1965–1968.
Journal of Applied Polymer Science, 1959– .
Journal of Cellular Plastics, 1965– .
Journal of Teflon, 1960– .
Kunstoff-Rundschau, 1954– .
Kunstoffe, 1900– .
Kunstoffe-Plastics, 1954– .
Materie Plastiche, 1934– .
Modern Packaging, 1927– .
Modern Plastics, 1925– .
Plastics, 1937– .
Plastics and Polymers, 1932– .
Plastics and Rubber Weekly, 1884– .
Plastics Technology, 1955– .
Plastics World, 1943– .
Reinforced Plastics, 1956– .

Resins

Resin News, 1961– , incorporated *Adhesives and Resins*, 1953–1960.
Resin Review, 1951– .

Rubber

Chemical Industry Report, 1954– , formerly *Chemical and Rubber Industry Report*.
I.R.I. Journal, 1924– , formerly *Institution of the Rubber Industry; Transactions and Proceedings*.
Kautschuk und gummi Kuntstoffe, 1948– .
Rubber Age, 1917– .
Rubber and Plastics Age, 1920– .
Rubber Chemistry and Technology, 1928– .
Rubber Journal, 1884– .
Rubber Statistical Bulletin, 1946– .

Rubber Trends (Quarterly).
Rubber World, 1889– .

d. CIVIL ENGINEERING—AIR POLLUTION, TRANSPORTATION, HIGHWAYS, AND SO ON

Special Reference Works

American Institute of Steel Construction, *Manual of Steel Construction,* 6th ed. New York, 1963.

Comrie, James, *Civil Engineering Reference Book,* 2nd ed., Plenum, New York, 1961, 4 vols.

Gaylord, E. H., Jr., and C. N. Gaylord, *Structural Engineering Handbook,* McGraw-Hill, New York, 1968.

King, H. W. and E. F. Brater, *Handbook of Hydraulics for the Solution of Hydrostatic and Fluid Flow Problems,* 5th ed., McGraw-Hill, New York, 1963.

Kolupaila, Steponas, *Bibliography of Hydrometry,* University of Notre Dame Press, Notre Dame, Ind., 1961.

Merritt, F. S., Ed., *Standard Handbook for Civil Engineers,* McGraw-Hill, New York, 1968.

Air Pollution

Air Pollution Bibliography, Government Printing Office, Washington, D.C., 1957–1959, 2 vols., includes abstracts.

Air Pollution Abstracts, 1968– , Warren Spring Laboratory, Ministry of Technology, Stevenage, Herts, Eng., 1968– .

Air Pollution Titles, 1965– , Pennsylvania State University, University Park, Pa., 1965– .

APCA Abstracts, Vol. 1– , published by the Air Pollution Control Association in cooperation with the United States Public Health Service and the Library of Congress, Air Pollution Control Association, Pittsburgh, 1955– .

Davenport, S. J. and G. C. Morgis, *Air Pollution; A Bibliography.* Government Printing Office, Washington, D.C., 1954 (U. S. Bureau of Mines, *Bulletin,* No. 537).

Stern, A. C., *Air Pollution,* Academic, New York, 1962, 2 vols.

Transportation, Highways

Blaisdell, R. F., *et al., Sources of Information in Transportation,* Northwestern University, Evanston, Ill., 1964.

Current Literature in Traffic and Transportation, Vol. 1– , Northwestern University, Evanston, Ill., 1960– .

Highway Research Abstracts, Nos. 1–142, Vol. 17, No. 7– , Highway Research Board, National Research Council, National Academy of Sciences, Washington, D.C., 1931– ; *Index,* 1931–1961, 1963; *Annual Subject Index,* 1962– .

Road Abstracts, Vol. 1– , Statistical Office, London, 1934/1935– .

U. S. Bureau of Public Roads, *Highway Statistics; Summary to 1945,* Government Printing Office, Washington, D.C., 1947.

U. S. Bureau of Public Roads, No. 1– , 1945– , Government Printing Office, Washington, D.C., 1947– , annual.

Wood, K. B. *et al.*, *Highway Engineering Handbook*, 1st ed., McGraw-Hill, New York, 1960.

Periodicals

APCD Report, 1955– .

APWA Reporter, 1934– .

Air Pollution Control Association, *Journal*, 1951– .

American Highways, 1922– .

American Road Builder, 1923– .

American Society of Civil Engineers, *Proceedings*, 1873– .

Civil Engineering, 1930– .

Civil Engineering and Public Works Review, 1905– .

Environmental Science and Technology, 1967– .

Environmental Technology and Economics, 1967– .

Highway and Municipal Construction, 1910– .

Highway Research News, 1963– .

Municipal Engineers Journal, 1903– .

Traffic Safety, 1927– .

Transportation Research, 1967– .

e. ELECTRICAL AND ELECTRONIC ENGINEERING

Bibliographies and Abstracts

Codlin, E. M., Comp., *Handlist of Basic Reference Material for Librarians and Information Officers in Electrical and Electronic Engineering*, 3rd ed., Aslib, Electronics Group, London, 1964.

Moore, C. K. and K. J. Spencer, *Electronics: A Bibliographical Guide*, MacDonald, London; Plenum, New York, 1961– , Vol. 1—1961; Vol. 2—1966.

Bulletin Signalétique, Center National de la Recherche Scientifique, Paris, 1956– ; Part 4: *Physique*; II: *Electricité*.

Computer and Control Abstracts (CCE), Institute of Electrical and Electronic Engineers, New York, Institution of Electrical Engineers, London, 1969– .

Electrical and Electronics Abstracts; 1898– (formerly Section B, *Science Abstracts*).

Electronics and Communications Abstracts, Vol. 1– , Multiscience Pub., Brentwood, Eng., 1961– .

Referativnyi Zhurnal, Elektrotekhnika i energetika, 1956– .

Special Reference Works

Crowhurst, N. H., *Electronics Reference Databook*, G/L Tab Books, Blue Ridge Summit, Pa., 1969.

Graf, R. F., *Modern Dictionary of Electronics*, 3rd ed., Sams, Indianapolis, 1968.

Illuminating Engineering Society. *IES Lighting Handbook; The Standard Lighting Guide*, 4th ed., New York, 1966.

Sams, H. W. and Company, *Handbook of Electronic Tables and Formulas,* Donald Herrington and Stanley Meacham, Comps. and Eds., 2nd ed., Sams, Indianapolis, 1962.

Sarbacher, R. I., *Encyclopedic Dictionary of Electronics and Nuclear Engineering,* Prentice-Hall, Englewood Cliffs, N. J., 1959.

Simonyi, Károly, *Foundations of Electrical Engineering,* Macmillan, New York, 1963.

Stetka, Frank, *NFPA Handbook of the National Electrical Code,* 2nd ed., McGraw-Hill, New York, 1969.

Susskind, Charles, *Encyclopedia of Electronics,* Reinhold, New York, 1962.

Periodicals

Electrical Construction and Maintenance, 1901– .

Electrical Construction Design, 1966– .

Electrical Engineer, 1924– .

Electrical Equipment, 1941– .

Electrical Equipment News, 1956– .

Electronics, 1930– .

Electronics Illustrated, 1958– .

Electronics World, 1919– .

IEEE Proceedings, 1913– .

Popular Electronics, 1954– .

Qualified Contractor, 1939– .

Solid State Electronics, 1960– .

Telemetry Digest, 1964– .

Telemetry Journal, 1966– .

f. MECHANICAL ENGINEERING—AUTOMOTIVE AND REFRIGERATION ENGINEERING

AUTOMOTIVE ENGINEERING

Abstracts and Indexes

Applied Mechanics Review, 1948– (abstracts).

Applied Science and Technology Index, 1958– .

Automobile Abstracts, Vol. 1– , Motor Research Association, Warwickshire, Eng., 1955– .

Business Periodicals Index, 1958– .

Engineering Index, 1884– .

Special Reference Works

Camm, F. J., *Newnes Engineer's Reference Book,* revised by A. T. Collins, 9th ed. Newnes, London, 1960.

Flugge, Wilhelm, *Handbook of Engineering Mechanics,* 1st ed., McGraw-Hill, New York, 1962.

Machinery's Handbook, 18th ed., Industrial Press, New York, 1968.

Georgano, G. N., Ed., *Complete Encyclopedia of Motorcars, 1885–1968*, Dutton, New York, 1968.

Internal Combustion Engine; A Glossary of Technical Terms in English/American, French, Dutch, German, Spanish, Italian, Portuguese, Russian, Elsevier, Amsterdam, 1961.

Muller, Wolfgang, *Technical Dictionary of Automotive Engineering . . .* , Macmillan, New York, 1964.

Review Serials

Advances in Applied Mechanics, Vol. 1– , Academic, New York, 1948– .

Advances in Automobile Engineering, Vol. 1– , Pergamon, New York, 1966– .

Periodicals

Applied Mechanics Review, 1848– .

ATZ (Automobil Technische Zeitschrift), 1898– .

Automobile Engineer, 1910– .

Automotive Industries, 1899– .

Automotive News, 1925– .

Automotive Service, 1962– .

Corrosion, 1945– .

Design News, 1946– .

Deutsche Kraftfahrtforschung, 1938– .

Diesel and Gas Turbine Progress, 1935– .

Engineer (England), 1856– .

Engineer (U. S.), 1960– .

Engineering, 1866– .

Industrial Design, 1954– .

Ingenueurs de l'Automobile, 1927– .

Institute of Fuel, Journal, 1926– .

Institute of Petroleum, Journal, 1914– .

Lubrication, 1911– .

Lubrication Engineering, 1945– .

MTZ (Motortechnische Zeitschrift), 1938– .

Machine Design, 1929– .

Materials Engineering, 1929– (formerly *Materials in Design Engineering*).

Mechanical Engineering, 1925– .

Moteurs, n.s., 1957– .

Motor (England), 1903– .

Motor (U. S.), 1903– .

Motor Italia, 1926– .

Motor Revue, 1952– .

Motor Rundschau, 1923– .

NPN Bulletin, 1961– (formerly *National Petroleum News*).

Noise Control, 1955– .

Product Engineering, 1930– .

Scientific Lubrication, 1948– .

Society of Automotive Engineers, *Journal*, 1917– .

Society of Automotive Engineers, *Transactions*, 1926– .

VDIZ für die Gesamte Ingenieure, 1858– .

REFRIGERATION ENGINEERING

Abstracts

International Institute of Refrigeration, *Bulletin*, 1920– , abstracts.

Thermal Abstracts, Vol. 1– , 1966– (formerly Heating and Ventilating Research Association, *Library Bulletin*).

Special Reference Works

ASHRAE Guide and Data Book, American Society of Heating, Refrigerating, and Air-conditioning Engineers, New York, 1963–1964, 2 vols.

Codlin, E. M., *Cryogenics and Refrigeration; A Bibliographical Guide*, Plenum, New York, 1968.

International Institute of Refrigeration, *International Dictionary of Refrigeration; English-French-German-Russian-Spanish-Italian*, Paris, 1961(?).

Strock, Clifford and R. R. Koral, Eds., *Handbook of Air Conditioning, Heating and Ventilating*, 2nd ed., Industrial Press, New York, 1965.

Periodicals

Air Conditioning, Heating and Refrigeration News, 1926– .

Air Conditioning, Heating and Ventilating, 1904– .

Electric Heat and Air Conditioning, 1955– .

Heating and Air Conditioning Contractor, 1874– .

Heating, Piping and Air Conditioning, 1929– .

Heating, Plumbing and Air Conditioning Age, 1923– (incorporated *Canadian Refrigeration and Air Conditioning*.

Industrial Refrigeration, 1891– (formerly *Ice and Refrigeration*).

Institution of Heating and Ventilating Engineers, *Journal*, 1933– .

Kaelte, 1947– .

Modern Refrigeration and Air Conditioning, 1898– .

Refrigeration Journal, 1947– .

World Refrigeration and Air Conditioning, 1950– .

g. MINING AND METALLURGICAL ENGINEERING

MINING ENGINEERING

Bibliographies and Abstracts

U. S. Bureau of Mines, *List of Journal Articles by Bureau of Mines Authors Published July 1, 1910 to January 1, 1960*, Government Printing Office, Washington, D.C., 1960, subject Index, M. W. Hardison and O. V. Weaver, Comps.

U. S. Bureau of Mines, *List of publications issued by the Bureau of Mines from July*

1, 1910 to January 1, 1960 with subject and author index by H. J. Stratton, Government Printing Office, Washington, D.C., 1960. Supplements.

Mineralogical Abstracts, issued by the Mineralogical Society, Vol. 1– , 1920– , Simpkin, Marshall, London, 1922– .

Special Reference Works

Johnstone, S. J. and M. G. Johnstone, *Minerals for the Chemical and Allied Industries,* 2nd ed., Chapman & Hall, London, 1961.

Nelson, Archibald, *Dictionary of Mining,* Philosophical Library, New York, 1965.

Pryor, E. J., *Dictionary of Mineral Technology, Mining,* London, 1963.

U. S. Bureau of Mines, *Mineral Facts and Problems,* Bulletin 630; Government Printing Office, Washington, D.C., 1965.

U. S. Bureau of Mines, *Minerals Yearbook, 1932/33–* , Government Printing Office, Washington, D.C., 1933– , annual.

Review Serials

Mines Register, Vol. 1– , Mines Register, New York, 1900– .

Mining Year Book, Vol. 1– , Skinner, London, 1887– .

Periodicals

Annales des Mines, 1795– .

Annales des Mines de Belgique, 1896– .

British Museum (Natural history), *Bulletin, Mineralogy,* 1962– .

Canadian Mining and Metallurgical Bulletin, 1898– .

Canadian Mining Journal, 1879– .

Coal Age, 1911– .

Coal Mining and Processing, 1964– .

Colorado School of Mines, *Mineral Industries Bulletin,* 1958– .

Jernkontorets Annaler, 1817– .

Mining Engineering, 1949– .

Mining Journal, 1835– .

Mining Magazine, 1909– .

METALLURGY

Guides to the Literature

Gibson, E. B. and E. W. Tapia, Eds., *Guide to Metallurgical Information,* 2nd ed., SLA, New York, 1965 (SLA Bibliography Series, No. 3).

Milek, J. T., *Guide to Foreign Sources of Metallurgical Literature,* Richard Rimbach Associates, Pittsburgh, 1951.

Abstracts

BCIRA Abstracts of Foundry Literature, Council of the British Cast Iron Research Association, Birmingham, Eng., 1960 (formerly *B.C.I.R.A. Journal*).

Bulletin Signalétique, Centre National de la Recherche Scientifique, Paris, 1956– ; **Part** 8: *Chimie;* II: *Chimie Appliquée, Métallurgie.*

Metallurgical Abstracts (General and Non-Ferrous), n.s., Vol. 1– , Institute of Metals, London, 1934–1967.

Metals Abstracts, Vol. 1– , American Society for Metals, Metals Park, Ohio, 1968– , merger of *Review of Metal Literature*, 1944–1967, and *Metallurgical Abstracts*, 1909–1967.

Search: Metals Division, Compendium Publishers International Corp., Fort Lee, N. J., 1964– .

Special Reference Works

American Society for Metals, *Metals Handbook*, 8th ed., Metals Park, Ohio, 1961.

Birchon, Donald, *Dictionary of Metallurgy*, Newnes, London, Philosophical Library, New York, 1965.

Directory of Iron and Steel Plants, 1916– , Steel Publications, Pittsburgh, 1916– .

Elsevier's Dictionary of Metallurgy in Six Languages . . . , Elsevier, New York, 1967.

Hampel, C. A., Ed., *Rare Metals Handbook*, 2nd cd., Van Nostrand Reinhold, New York, 1961.

Merriam, A. D., *Concise Encyclopedia of Metallurgy*, Elsevier, New York, 1965.

Metal Statistics, Vol. 1– , American Metal Mart, New York, 1908– .

Osborne, A. K., *Encyclopedia of the Iron and Steel Industry*, 2nd ed, Heineman, New York, 1957.

Parker, E. R., *Materials Data Book*, McGraw-Hill, New York, 1967.

Simons, E. N., *Dictionary of Alloys*, Muller, London, 1969.

Simons, E. N., *Guide to Uncommon Metals*, Hart, New York, 1967.

Sittig, Marshall, Ed, *Inorganic Chemical and Metallurgical Process Encyclopedia*, Noyes, New York, 1968.

Smithells, C. J., Ed., *Metals Reference Book*, 4th ed., Plenum, New York, 1967, 3 vols.

Trinks, Willibald, *Industrial Furnaces*, Wiley, New York, 1961–1967, 2 vols. Vol. 1, 5th ed., 1961; Vol. 2, 4th ed., 1967.

Watkins' Cyclopedia of the Steel Industry, Steel Publications, Pittsburgh, annual.

Woldman, N. E., *Engineering Alloys: Names, Properties, Uses*, 4th ed., Van Nostrand Reinhold, New York, 1962.

Periodicals

Progress in Materials Science, 1961– , Pergamon, New York, 1961– (formerly *Progress in Metal Physics*).

Acier/Stahl/Steel, 1932– .

American Institute of Mining and Metallurgical Engineers, *Transactions*, 1871– .

American Metal Market, 1882– .

American Society for Metals Transactions Quarterly, 1961–1969 (continued as *Metallurgical Transactions*, 1970–).

Archiv für das Eisenhuettwesen, 1927– .

Blast Furnace and Steel Plant, 1913– .

British Steel, 1968– (supersedes *Steel Review*, 1956–1967).

British Steelmaker, 1935– .

Canadian Metalworking/Machine Production, 1938– .

Eastern Metals Review, 1948– .

Industry Week, 1967– .

Institute of Metals, *Journal*, 1908– .

International Journal of Powder Metallurgy, 1965– .

Iron Age, 1855– .

Iron and Steel, 1927– .

Iron and Steel Engineer, 1924– .

Iron and Steel Institute, *Journal*, 1869– .

Journal of Metals, 1949– .

Metal Bulletin, 1913– .

Metal Progress, 1930– .

Metallurgia, 1929– .

Metallurgical Transactions, 1970– (continues *American Society for Metals Transactions Quarterly*, 1961–1969).

Metallurgist, 1959– (English translation of *Metallurg*).

Metallography, 1968– (includes *Metallurgical Reviews*).

Metals and Materials, 1967– .

Physics of Metals and Metallography, 1957– (English translation of *Fizika Metallov i Metallovedenie*).

Revue de Métallurgie, 1904– .

Stahl und Eisen, 1881– (contains abstracts).

Steel, 1882–1967.

Steel in the U.S.S.R., 1971– (Replaces *Stal in English*, 1959–1969).

Zeitschrift für Metallkunde, 1911– .

h. NUCLEAR ENGINEERING

Bibliographies, Abstracts

International Atomic Energy Agency, *List of Bibliographies on Nuclear Energy*, Vol. 1– , Vienna, 1960– .

International Atomic Energy Agency, *List of References on Nuclear Energy*, Vol. 1– , Vienna, 1959– .

U. S. Atomic Energy Commission, *Bibliographies of Interest to the Atomic Energy Program*, J. M. Jacobs et al. Comps., rev. 2, U. S. Atomic Energy Commission, Division of Technical Information, Oak Ridge, Tenn., 1962.

Bulletin Signalétique, Centre National de la Recherche Scientifique, Paris, 1956– , Part 5: *Physique Nucléaire*.

Nuclear Engineering Abstracts, Vol. 1– , Silver End Documentary Publication, Ltd., London, 1961– .

U. S. Atomic Energy Commission, *Nuclear Science Abstracts*, Vol. 1– , Government Printing Office, Washington, D.C. 1948– .

Special Reference Books

Dzhelepov, B. S. and L. K. Perker, *Decay Schemes and Radioactive Nuclei*, translation, D. L. Allen Ed., Pergamon, New York, 1960.

Frisch, O. R., *The Nuclear Handbook* . . . , Newnes, London, 1958.

Glassner, Alvin, *Introduction to Nuclear Science,* Van Nostrand Reinhold, New York, 1961.

National Research Council Conference on Glossary of Terms in Nuclear Science and Technology, *A Glossary of Terms in Nuclear Science and Technology,* American Society of Mechanical Engineers, New York, 1957.

Nuclear Data Sheets, Academic, New York, 1966– .

Plutonium Handbook; A Guide to the Technology, Gordon & Breach, London, 1967.

Preston, M. A., *Physics of the Nucleus,* Addison Wesley, Reading, Mass., 1962.

Reactor Handbook, prepared under contract with the United States Atomic Energy Commission, 2nd ed., revised and enlarged, Interscience, New York, 1960–1964, 4 vols.

Ritson, D. M., *Techniques of High Energy Physics,* Interscience, New York, 1961.

Schultz, M. A., *Control of Nuclear Reactors and Power Plants,* 2nd ed., McGraw-Hill, New York, 1961.

United Nations, Terminology Section, *Atomic Energy; Glossary of Technical Terms,* 4th ed., New York, 1958.

Weinstein, R. M. *et al., Nuclear Engineering Fundamentals,* McGraw-Hill, New York, 1964, 5 vols.

Review Serials

Annual Review of Nuclear Science, Vol. 1– , Annual Reviews, Palo Alto, Calif., 1952– .

Progress in Nuclear Physics, Vol. 1– , Pergamon, New York, 1950– .

Periodicals

Atomkernenergie, 1956– .

Atompraxis, 1955– .

Bulletin of the Atomic Scientists, 1945– .

International Journal of Applied Radiation and Isotopes, 1956– .

Journal of Nuclear Energy, 1959–   (Early vols. contained a section of English translations of *Atomnaya Energiya*).

Nuclear Applications and Technology, 1965– .

Nuclear Canada/Canada Nucleaire, 1963– .

Nuclear Data, 1965– .

Nuclear Energy, 1959– .

Nuclear Engineering and Design, 1964– (formerly *Nuclear Structural Engineering*).

Nuclear Engineering International, 1956– .

Nuclear Industry, 1954– .

Nuclear Instruments and Methods, 1956– .

Nuclear Physics, 1956– .

Nuclear Power Newsletter, 1955– .

Nuclear Safety, 1959– .

Nuclear Science and Engineering, 1956– .

Nukleonik, 1958– .

Plasma Physics, 1959– (formerly *Journal of nuclear energy;* Part C: *Plasma physics.*) (contains a section of English translations of *Atomnaya energiya*).

Radioisotopes, 1952– .

Reactor and Fuel, Processing Technology, 1958– (formerly *Power Reactor Technology*).

Reactor Materials, 1958– .

Soviet Atomic Energy, 1956– (English translation of *Atomonaya Energiya*).

i. PETROLEUM ENGINEERING

Bibliographies

DeGolyer, E. L. and Harold Vance, *Bibliography on the Petroleum Industry,* College Station, Tex., 1944 (School of Engineering, Texas Engineering Experiment Station, Bulletin No. 83).

Muckleroy, J. A., *Bibliography on Hydrocarbons, 1946–1960,* Natural Gas Producers Association, Tulsa, Okla., 1962.

Swanson, E. B., *A Century of Oil and Gas in Books; A Descriptive Bibliography,* Appleton, New York, 1960.

Abstracts and Indexes

American Petroleum Institute Abstracts of Petroleum Substitutes Literature and Patents, American Petroleum Institute, New York, 1969– , available on cards.

Applied Science and Technology Index, 1958– .

Chemical Abstracts, 1907– .

Engineering Index, 1884– .

Journal of the Institute of Petroleum, Vol. 7– , London, 1921– (abstract section) (published as *Journal, Institution of Petroleum Technologists,* Vols. 1–24, 1914–1938).

Petroleum Abstracts, Vol. 1– , University of Tulsa, Tulsa, Okla., Petroleum Abstracts Committee, 1961– .

Petroleum Literature Index, Vol. 1– , National Petroleum Bibliography, Amarillo, Tex., 1956– , annual.

Search: Petroleum Division, Compendium Publishers International Corp., Fort Lee, N. J., 1964– .

Special Reference Works

American Chemical Society, Division of Chemical Literature, *Literature of the Combustion of Petroleum,* Washington, D.C., 1958.

American Petroleum Institute, *Glossary of Terms Used in Petroleum Refinery,* 2nd ed., New York, 1962.

American Petroleum Institute, *Petroleum Facts and Figures,* New York, 1928– , annual.

Frick, T. C. and R. W. Taylor, *Petroleum Production Handbook,* McGraw-Hill, New York, 1962.

Gruse, W. A. and D. R. Stevens, *Chemical Technology of Petroleum,* 3rd ed., McGraw-Hill, New York, 1960.

Guthrie, V. B., *Petroleum Products Handbook,* 1st ed., McGraw-Hill, New York, 1960.

Institute of Petroleum, *Modern Petroleum Technology*, 3rd ed., London, 1962.

Matheson Company, Inc., *Matheson Gas Data Book*, 3rd ed., East Rutherford, N. J., 1961.

Moody, G. B., *Petroleum Exploration Handbook*, 1st ed., McGraw-Hill, New York, 1961.

Oil and Petroleum Yearbook, Vol. 1– , Skinner, London, 1910– .

Petroleum Data Book, Petroleum Engineer Publishing Co., Dallas, Tex., annual.

Petroleum Processing Handbook, McGraw-Hill, New York, 1967.

Rocq, M. M., Comp., *Sources of Petroleum and Natural Gas Statistics*, SLA, New York, 1961 (SLA Petroleum Section, Committee on U. S. sources of petroleum and natural gas) (updates *Osborne's Index to American Petroleum Statistics*, 1943).

The Science of Petroleum; A Comprehensive Treatise of the Principles and Practice of the Production, Refining, Transport and Distribution of Mineral Oil, Vol. 1– , Oxford University Press, London, 1938– .

Waddams, A. L., *Chemicals from Petroleum*, Noyes, Pearl River, N. Y., 1962.

Periodicals

Advances in Petroleum Chemistry and Refining, Vol. 1– , Interscience, New York, 1958– .

American Association of Petroleum Geologists, *Bulletin*, 1917– .

American Gas Association Monthly, 1912– .

American Gas Journal, 1854– .

American Petroleum Institute, Department of Statistics, *Weekly Statistical Bulletin*, 1965– .

Bulletin of Canadian Petroleum Geology, Vol. 12, 1664– .

Butane-Propane News, 1939– .

Canadian Petroleum, 1956– .

Gas, 1925– .

Gas Industries, 1956– .

Gas Journal, 1829– .

Hydrocarbon Processing-Petroleum Refiner, 1922– .

Institute of Petroleum, *Journal*, 1914– .

Journal of Petroleum Technology, 1948– .

Lubrication Engineering, 1945– .

National Petroleum News, 1909– .

Oil and Gas Journal, 1902– .

Petroleum Chemistry, 1962– (English translation of *Neftekhimiya*).

Petroleum Engineer, 1929– .

Petroleum Times, 1899– .

Petroleum Today, 1959– .

World Oil, 1916– .

World Petroleum, 1930– .

3. *MEDICAL SCIENCES*

Bibliographies

Blake, J. B. and Charles Roos, Eds., *Medical Reference Works: 1679–1966,* a selected bibliography, Medical Library Association, Chicago, 1967.

British Medical Book List, Vol. 1– , British Council, Medical Department, London, 1950– .

Kelly, E. C., *Encyclopedia of Medical Sources,* Williams & Wilkins, Baltimore, 1948.

U. S. National Institutes of Health, Office of Research Information, *National Institutes of Health Scientific Directory 1965 and Annual Bibliography 1964,* Bethesda, Md., 1965.

U. S. National Library of Medicine, *Bibliography of Medical Translations,* Washington, D.C., 1959–1966.

U. S. Public Health Service, *Public Health Service Numbered Publications; A Catalog,* 1950–1962, Washington, D.C., 1964 (Public Health Service, Publication No. 1112; Bibliography Series No. 55); supplement, No. 1, 1963–1964.

Abstracts and Indexes

Abstracts of World Medicine; A Monthly Critical Survey of Periodicals in Medicine, Vol. 1– , British Medical Association, London, 1947– .

Biological Abstracts, 1927– .

British Medical Abstracts, 1961– , Haymarket Press, London, 1961– .

Bulletin Signalétique, Centre National de la Recherche Scientifique, Paris, 1940– ; Part 15: *Pathologie Générale et Expérimentele.*

Chemical Abstracts, 1907– .

Excerpta Medica, Sections 1–24, Excerpta Medica Foundation, Amsterdam, 1947– .

Index Medicus, Vol. 1– , U. S. National Library of Medicine, Washington, D.C., 1960– .

Indexes Superseded by Other Publications

Index-Catalogue of the Library of the Surgeon General's Office, 1880–1950, Series I–IV.

Current List of Medical Literature, Vols. 1–36, U. S. National Library of Medicine, Washington, D.C., 1941–1959.

Quarterly Cumulative Index Medicus, Vols. 1–60, American Medical Association, Chicago, 1927–1956.

Special Reference Works

American Medical Association, Division of Scientific Publications, *Style Book and Editorial Manual,* Chicago, 1965.

Black's Medical Dictionary, 25th ed., Black, London, 1963.

Blakiston's New Gould Medical Dictionary, 2nd ed., McGraw-Hill, New York, 1956.

British Encyclopedia of Medical Practice, 2nd ed., Butterworth, London, 1950–1953, 12 vols, annual cumulative supplement.

Brown, J. A. C., *Pears Medical Encyclopedia,* revised ed., Arco, New York, 1963.

Butterworths Medical Dictionary, Butterworth, London, 1965.

Cyclopedia of Medicine, Surgery and Specialties, 3rd ed., F. A. Davis, Philadelphia, 1950– , 14 vols. and index, loose-leaf, annual revision service, 1950– .

MacNalty, Sir A. S., *British Medical Dictionary,* revised ed., Lippincott, Philadelphia, 1963.

Mettler, F. A., *Medical Sourcebook; A Reference Handbook for Legal, Legislative, and Administrative Personnel,* 1st ed., Little, Brown, Boston, 1960.

National Conference on Medical Nomenclature, *Standard Nomenclature of Diseases and Operations,* 5th ed., Philadelphia, 1961.

Parr, J. A., *Parr's Concise Medical Encyclopedia,* Elsevier, Amsterdam, 1965.

Root, K. B. and E. E. Byers, *The Medical Secretary . . . ,* McGraw-Hill, New York, 1960.

Directories

American Dental Directory, 1st ed., American Dental Association, Chicago, 1947– .

American Medical Directory; A Register of Legally Qualified Physicians, 1st ed., American Medical Association, Chicago, 1906– (rev. irregularly).

American Men of Medicine, Vol. 1– , Institute for Research in Biography, Farmingdale, N. Y., 1945– .

Canadian Medical Directory, 1955– , Seccombe House, Toronto, 1955– , annual.

Directory of Medical Specialists Holding Certification by American Specialty Boards, Vol. 1– Advisory Board of Medical Specialties, Chicago, 1939– .

Medical Directory, Vol. 1– , Churchill, London, 1845– , annual.

World Directory of Dental Schools, 1st ed., World Health Organization, Geneva, 1961– .

World Directory of Medical Schools, 1st ed., World Health Organization, Geneva, 1953– .

World Medical Association, U. S. Committee, *International Medical Directory,* Vol. 1– , New York, 1965– .

Terminology

American Medical Association, *Current Medical Terminology,* 3rd ed., Chicago, 1966.

Flood, W. E., *Scientific Words; Their Structure and Meaning,* Duell, Sloan and Pearce, New York, 1960.

Frenay, Sister M. A. C., *Understanding Medical Terminology,* 3rd ed., Catholic Hospital Association, St. Louis, 1964.

Harned, J. M., *Medical Terminology Made Easy,* 2nd ed., Physicians Record Co., Chicago, 1968.

Roberts, Ffrangcon, *Medical Terms; Their Origin and Construction,* 4th ed., Heinemann, London, 1966.

Strand, H. R., *An Illustrated Guide to Medical Terminology,* Williams and Wilkins, Baltimore, 1968.

Review Serials

Advances in Biomedical Engineering and Medical Physics, Vol. 1– , Wiley, New York, 1968– .

Advances in Internal Medicine, Vol. 1– , Year Book Medical Publishers, Chicago, 1942– , biennial.

Annual Review of Medicine, Vol. 1– , Annual Reviews, Palo Alto, Calif., 1950– .

Medical Progress: A Review of Medical Advances, Vol. 1– , New York, 1952– .

Progress in Medicinal Chemistry, Vol. 1– , Butterworth, London; Plenum, New York, 1961– .

Recent Advances in Medicine, 14th ed., Churchill, London, 1964– .

Recent Progress in Hormone Research, Vol. 1– , Academic, New York, 1947– .

Scientific Basis of Medicine, Annual Reviews, British Postgraduate Medical Federation, London, 1951/1952– .

Year Book of Medicine, Year Book Medical Publishers, Chicago, 1901– .

Periodicals

World Medical Periodicals, 3rd ed., World Medical Association, New York, 1961.

Acta Medica Scandinavica, 1869– .

Akademiya Meditzinskikh Nauk SSSR, Vestnik, 1946– .

American Journal of Medicine, 1946– .

American Journal of Public Health and the Nation's Health, 1911– .

American Journal of the Medical Sciences, 1820– .

American Medical Association, *Journal,* 1848– .

American Medical Women's Association, *Journal,* 1915– .

Angiology, 1950– .

Annales Medicinae Experimentalis et Biologiae Fenniae, 1919– .

Annals of Internal Medicine, 1922– .

Antibiotica et Chemotherapia, 1954– .

Applied Therapeutics, 1960– .

Archives of Internal Medicine, 1908– (the American Medical Association publishes a series of "archives" in various fields).

British Journal of Clinical Practice, 1947– .

British Medical Bulletin, 1943– .

British Medical Journal, 1832– .

Canadian Medical Association, *Journal,* 1911– .

Helvetica Medica Acta, 1934– .

Journal of the History of Medicine and Allied Sciences, 1946– .

Lancet, 1823– .

New England Journal of Medicine, 1812– .

Perspectives in Biology and Medicine, 1957– .

Zeitschrift für Klinische Chemie und Klinische Biochemie, 1963– .

a. PHARMACY AND PHARMACOLOGY

Bibliographies and Abstracts

Evans, A. J. and David Train, *Bibliography of the Tabletting of Medicinal Substances,* Pharmaceutical Press, London, 1963, supplement 1, 1964.

U. S. National Library of Medicine, *Drug Literature* . . . , Government Printing Office, Washington, D.C., 1963.

Bulletin Signalétique, Centre National de la Recherche Scientifique, Paris, 1956– , Part 13: *Sciences Pharmacologiques, Toxicologie.*

International Pharmaceutical Abstracts, Vol. 1, No. 1– , American Society of Hospital Pharmacists, Washington, D.C., 1964– .

Pharmaceutical Abstracts, 1957– , University of Texas, College of Pharmacy, Austin, Tex., 1957– .

RINGDOC, Derwent Pooled Pharmaceutical Literature Documentation, Abstracts Journal, Vol. 1– , London, 1964– .

Search: Drugs Division, Compendium Publishers International Corp., Fort Lee, N. J., 1964– .

Pharmacopoeias, Dispensatories, and so on

American Drug Index, 1956– , Lippincott, Philadelphia, 1956– .

American Medical Association, *New Drugs,* Vol. 1– , Chicago, 1965– , annual.

American Pharmaceutical Association, *The National Formulary,* 12th ed. Lippincott, Philadelphia, 1965.

Drug Digests from Foreign Language Literature, Vol. 1– , published for the National Library of Medicine and the National Science Foundation by the Israel Program for Scientific Translations, Jerusalem, 1965– .

Drug Information Sources, SLA, Pharmaceutical Division, New York, published in *American Journal of Pharmacy,* November/December 1964.

Modern Drug Encyclopedia and Therapeutic Index, 10th ed., Donnelly, New York, 1965, supplement: *Modern Drugs.*

Pharmacopoeia of the United States of America (USPXVII), 17th ed., Mack Printing Co., Easton, Pa., 1965, supplement: 1966– .

U. S. Dispensatory and Physician's Pharmacology, 26th ed., Lippincott, Philadelphia, 1967, 2 vols, title varies.

U. S. National Library of Medicine, *Russian Drug Index,* 2nd ed., Washington, D.C., 1967.

Unlisted Drugs, Vol. 1– , Pharmaco-Medical Documentation, Chatham, N. J., 1948– .

Unlisted Drugs on Cards, Pharmaco-Medical Documentation, Chatham, N. J., 1966– .

Special Reference Works

Accepted Dental Remedies . . . , American Dental Association, Chicago, annual.

American Druggist Blue Book, American Druggist, New York, annual.

American Pharmaceutical Association, *Proprietary Names of Official Drugs,* Washington, D.C., 1960 (*APhA Manual* 102).

Best, C. H. and N. B. Taylor, *Physiological Basis of Medical Practice,* 8th ed., Williams and Wilkins, Baltimore, 1966.

Chatten, L. G., Ed., *Pharmaceutical Chemistry,* Dekker, New York, 1966, 2 vols.

Chute, A. H. and E. J. Hall, *Pharmacist in Retail Distribution,* 3rd ed., Hemhill, Austin, Tex., 1960.

Dreisbach, R. H., *Handbook of Poisoning; Diagnosis and Treatment,* 5th ed., Lange Medical Pubs., Los Altos, Calif., 1966.

Drill, V. A., *Pharmacology in Medicine,* 3rd ed., McGraw-Hill, New York, 1965.

Drug Topics Red Book, Topics Publishing Co., New York, annual.

Gehe's Codex . . . , 9th ed., Wissenschaftliche Verlagsgesellschaft, Stuttgart, 1960.

Goodman, L. S. and A. Z. Gilman, *Pharmacological Basis of Therapeutics,* 3rd ed., Macmillan, New York, 1965.

Grollman, Arthur, *Pharmacology and Therapeutics,* 6th ed., Lea and Febiger, Philadelphia, 1965.

Hocking, G. M., *A Dictionary of Terms in Pharmacognasy and Other Divisions of Economic Botany,* Thomas, Springfield, Ill., 1955.

Kremers, Edward and George Urdang, *History of Pharmacy,* 3rd ed., Lippincott, Philadelphia, 1963.

Marler, E. E. J., *Pharmacological and Chemical Synonyms, a Collection of More than 13,000 Names of Drugs and Other Compounds Drawn from the Medical Literature of the World,* 3rd ed., Excerpta Medica, Amsterdam, 1961.

Martindale, William, *Extra Pharmacopoeia,* 25th ed., Pharmaceutical Press, London, 1967.

Merck Index of Chemicals and Drugs, 8th ed., Merck and Co., Rahway, N.J., 1968.

Merck Manual of Diagnosis and Therapy, 11th ed., Merck and Co., Rahway, N. J., 1966.

Meyler, L. and A. Herxheimer, *Side Effects of Drugs,* Williams and Wilkins, Baltimore, 1969.

Modell, Walter, *Drugs of Choice, 1970–1971,* Mosby, St. Louis, 1970.

Negwer, Martin, *Organisch-chemische Arzneimittel und ihre Synonyma; eine tabellarische Übersicht,* 3rd ed., Akademie Verlag, Berlin, 1966.

Pettit, William, *Manual of Pharmaceutical Law,* 3rd ed., Macmillan, New York, 1962.

Pharmaceutical Society of Great Britain, *British Pharmaceutical Codex,* Pharmaceutical Press, London, 1959.

Physicians Desk Reference to Pharmaceutical Specialties and Biologicals (PDR), Medical Economics, Rutherford, N. J., 1947– , annual with supplements.

Plunkett, E. R., *Handbook of Industrial Toxicology,* Chemical Publishing Co., New York, 1966.

Remington, J. P., *Practice of Pharmacy* . . . , 12th ed., Lippincott, Philadelphia, 1961.

Robson, J. M. and R. S. Stacey, *Recent Advances in Pharmacology,* 3rd ed., Little, Brown, Boston, 1969.

Rote Liste, herausgegeben von Bundesverband der Pharmazeutischen Industrie, Württemberg, Germany, 1961.

Saunders, L. and R. Fleming, *Mathematics and Statistics for Use in Pharmacy, Biology and Chemistry,* revised ed., Pharmaceutical Press, London, 1966.

Sollman, T. H., *Manual of Pharmacology,* 8th ed., Saunders, Philadelphia, 1957.

Spector, W. S., ed., *Handbook of Toxicology,* Saunders, Philadelphia, 1956–1959, 5 vols.

Steinbichler, Eveline, *Steinbichler's Lexikon für Die Apothekenpraxis in Sieben Sprachen,* Govi-Verlag G.M.B.H.-Pharmazeutischer Verlag, Frankfurt/Main, 1963.

Vidal, L., *Dictionaire des Spécialités Pharmaceutiques,* Office de Vulgarisation Pharmaceutiques, Paris, 1961.

Review Serials

Advances in Chemotherapy, Vol. 1– , Academic, New York, 1964– .

Advances in Drug Research, Vol. 1– , Academic, New York, 1964– .

Advances in Pharmaceutical Sciences, Vol. 1– , Academic, New York, 1964– .

Advances in Pharmacology and Chemotherapy, Vol. 7– , Academic, New York, 1969– ; combines *Advances in Chemotherapy,* Vols. 1–3, 1964–1968 with *Advances in Pharmacology,* Vols. 1–6, 1952–1968.

Annual Review of Pharmacology, Vol. 1– , Annual Reviews, Palo Alto, Calif., 1961– .

Progress in Chemical Toxicology, Vol. 1– , Academic, New York, 1963– .

Progress in Drug Research/Fortschritte der arzneimittelforschung/Progres des recherches pharmaceutiques, Vol. 1– , Birkhaeuser Verlag, Basel, 1959– .

Progress in Medicinal Chemistry, Vol. 1– , Plenum, New York, 1961– .

Year Book of Drug Therapy, Year Book Medical Publishers, Chicago, 1949– .

Periodicals

Andrews, Theodora, *World List of Pharmacy Periodicals,* American Society of Hospital Pharmacists, Washington, D.C., 1963.

American Druggist, 1871– .

American Journal of Pharmacy and the Science of Supporting Public Health, 1825– .

American Pharmaceutical Association, *Journal,* 1912– (absorbed *Practical Pharmacy Edition,* 1940–1960).

American Professional Pharmacist, 1935– .

Annales Pharmaceutiques Francaises, 1943– .

Archiv der Pharmazie und Berichte der Deutschen Pharmazeutschen Gesellschaft, 1822– .

Canadian Pharmaceutical Journal, 1868– .

Chain Store Age, 1925– .

Chemist and Druggist, 1859– .

Drug and Cosmetic Industry, 1914– .

Drug Research Reports: Blue Sheet, 1957– .

Drug Topics, 1857– .

Drug Trade News, 1925– .

F-D-C Reports: Pink Sheet, 1939– .

Food, Drug, Cosmetic Law Journal, 1946– .

Journal of Pharmaceutical Sciences, Vol. 50– , 1961– (combined with *Drug Standards,* 1951–1960).

Journal of Pharmacy and Pharmacology, 1949– .

Oil, Paint and Drug Reporter, 1871– .

Pharmaceutica acta Helvetiae, 1926– (supplement to *Schweizerische Apotheker-Zeitung*).

Pharmaceutical Journal, 1841– .

Die Pharmazie, 1946– .

Pharmacological Reviews, 1949– .

Produits et Problemes Pharmaceutiques, 1946– .
Toxicology and Applied Pharmacology, 1959– .
Unlisted Drugs, 1948– .
Unlisted Drugs on Cards, 1966– .
Weekly Pharmacy Reports: Green Sheet, 1951– .

b. VETERINARY MEDICINE

Abstracts and Indexes

Accumulative Veterinary Index, a Selective List of Publications from the American Literature, Vol. 1– , Index Incorporated, Arvada, Colo., 1960/1963– .

Index-Catalogue of Medical and Veterinary Zoology, Government Printing Office, Washington, D.C., 1932–1952, 18 vols, supplement no. 1– , 1953– .

Animal Breeding Abstracts, 1933– , Commonwealth Agricultural Bureaux, Farnham Royal, Eng., 1933– .

Biological Abstracts, 1927– .

Index Veterinarius, Vol. 1– , Commonwealth Agricultural Bureaux, Farnham Royal, Eng., 1933– .

Veterinary Bulletin, Vol. 1– , Commonwealth Bureau of Animal Health, Weybridge, Eng., 1931– .

Special Reference Works

American Veterinary Medical Association, *Directory,* 1st ed., Chicago, 1924– , biennial.

Barnes, C. D. and L. G. Etherington, *Drug Dosage in Laboratory Animals; A Handbook,* University of California Press, Berkeley, 1964.

Blood, D. C. and J. A. Henderson, *Veterinary Medicine,* 3rd ed., Williams and Wilkins, Baltimore, 1968.

Daykin, P. W., *Veterinary Applied Pharmacology and Therapeutics,* Balliere, Tindall and Cox, London, 1960.

Jones, L. M. *et al., Veterinary Pharmacology and Therapeutics,* 3rd ed., Iowa State University Press, Iowa, 1965.

Merck Veterinary Manual, 2nd ed., Merck and Co., Rahway, N. J., 1961.

Merino-Rodriguez, Manuel, *Elsevier's Lexicon of Parasites and Diseases in Livestock,* Elsevier, New York, 1964.

Miller, W. C. and G. P. West, *Encyclopedia of Animal Care,* 8th ed., Williams and Wilkins, Baltimore, 1967 (formerly *Black's Veterinary Dictionary*).

Pharmaceutical Society of Great Britain, *British Veterinary Codex,* 1953, London, 1953; supplement, 1959, 1960.

Register of Veterinary Surgeons, and the Supplementary Veterinary Register, Royal College of Veterinary Surgeons, London, 1884– , annual.

Schulz, H. E., Ed., *Vocabularium Veterinarium Polyglotte,* Deutsches Archiv für Veterinarmedizinische Nomenklatur, Halle, 1962.

Seiden, Rudolph, *Livestock Health Encyclopedia,* W. J. Gough, Ed., 3rd ed., Springer, N. Y., 1968.

Seiden, Rudolph, *Veterinary Drugs in Current Use,* 2nd ed., Springer, New York, 1969.

U. S. National Agricultural Library, *Veterinary Medical Periodicals Currently Received*, Washington, D.C., 1963.

U. S. National Cancer Institute, *Standard Nomenclature of Veterinary Diseases and Operations*, 1st ed. revised, Bethesda, Md., 1966 (Public Health Service. Publication No. 1466).

Veterinarian's Blue Book, 1st ed., Donnelly, New York, 1953– (formerly *Veterinary Drug Encyclopedia and Therapeutic Index*, 1953–1966).

World Directory of Veterinary Schools, 1st ed., F.A.O., Rome, 1963– .

Review Serials

Advances in Veterinary Science, Vol. 1– , Academic, New York, 1953– .

Animal Health Yearbook, 1963– , F.A.O., Rome, 1964– .

Veterinary Annual, Vol. 1– , Wright, Bristol, 1959– .

Year Book of Veterinary Medicine, Vol. 1– , Year Book Medical Publishers, Chicago, 1963– .

Periodicals

Academie Veterinaire de France, *Bulletin*, 1928– .

American Journal of Veterinary Research, 1940– .

American Veterinary Medical Association, *Journal*, 1869– .

Archiv für Experimentelle Veterinaermedizin, 1950– .

British Veterinary Journal, 1880– .

Canadian Veterinary Journal/Revue Veterinaire Canadienne, 1960– .

Journal of Animal Science, 1942– .

Journal of Dairy Science, 1917– .

Modern Veterinary Practice, 1920– .

Monatshefte für Veterinaermedizin, 1946– .

National Institute of Animal Health Quarterly, 1961– .

Pathologia Veterinaria, 1964– .

Poultry Science, 1908– .

Research in Veterinary Science, 1960– .

Veterinary Medicine; Small Animal Clinician, 1905– .

Veterinary Record, 1888– .

4. MISCELLANEOUS

a. CERAMICS

Abstracts

American Ceramic Society, *Bulletin*, Columbus, Ohio, 1918– .

American Ceramic Society, *Journal* (Ceramic abstracts), Columbus, Ohio, 1918– .

Applied Science and Technology Index, 1958– .

British Ceramic Abstracts, 1906– , British Research Association, Shelton, Stoke-on-Trent, Eng., 1906– .

Chemical Abstracts, 1907– .

Special Reference Works

British Ceramic Society, *Transactions*, Shelton, Stoke-on-Trent, Eng., 1901– .

Campbell, I. E. and E. M. Sherwood, *High Temperature Materials and Technology*, 2nd ed., Wiley, New York, 1967.

Ceramic Data Book, Industrial Publications, Chicago, annual.

Dodd, A. E., *Dictionary of Ceramics* . . . , Newnes, London, 1964.

Kingery, W. D., *Introduction to Ceramics*, Wiley, New York, 1960.

Levin, E. M. *et al.*, *Phase Diagrams for Ceramists*, 2nd ed., American Ceramic Society, Columbus, Ohio, 1964.

National Research Council, *Data on Chemicals for Ceramic Use*, revised ed., Government Printing Office, Washington, D.C., 1949 (Bulletin 118).

Norton, F. H., *Elements of Ceramics*, Addison-Wesley, Cambridge, Mass., 1952.

Norton, F. H., *Refractories*, 4th ed., McGraw-Hill, New York, 1968.

Parmelee, C. W., *Ceramic Glazes*, Cahners, Chicago, 1968.

Salmang, Herman, *Ceramics: Physical and Chemical Fundamentals*, Plenum, New York, 1961.

Searle, A. B., *Encyclopedia of the Ceramic Industries*, Benn, London, 1929–1930, 3 vols.

Singer, Felix and Sonja Singer, *Industrial Ceramics*, Chemical Publishing Co., New York, 1965.

Review Serials

Progress in Ceramic Science, Vol. 1– , Pergamon, London, 1961– .
Science of Ceramics, Vol. 1– , Academic, New York, 1962– .

Periodicals

Berichte der Deutschen Keramischen Gesellschaft, 1920– .
Brick and Clay Record, 1892– .
British Ceramic Society, Journal, 1963– .
Bulletin de la Société Francais de Ceramique, 1948– .
Ceramic Age, 1921– .
Ceramic Forum, 1934– .
Ceramic Industry, 1923– .
Ceramica, 1951– .
Ceramics, 1949– .
Clay Products News and Ceramics Record, 1928– .
Glass and Ceramics, Vol. 13 in 1956– (English translation of *Stekle i Kerimika*).
Interceram, 1951– .
Keramische Zeitschrift, 1949– .
Sprechsaal für Keramik, Glas, Email, Silikate, 1868– .

b. CHEMICAL TECHNOLOGY

Abstracts and Indexes

Chemical Abstracts, 1907– .
Chemical Market Abstracts, 1950– , Snell, New York, 1950– .

Chemisches Zentralblatt, Vols. 1–140, 1830–1969.

Engineering Index, 1884– .

Journal of Applied Chemistry, abstracts, 1951– , Society of Chemical Industry, London, 1951– .

Search: Chemical Materials and Production Division, Compendium Publishers International Corp., Fort Lee, N. J., 1964– .

Theoretical Chemical Engineering Abstracts, 1964– , Chemical Engineering Abstracts, Liverpool, 1964– .

Special Reference Works

American Chemical Society, *Patents for Chemical Inventions*, Washington, D.C., 1965. (Advances in Chemistry Series, No. 46).

American Chemical Society, *Reagent Chemicals*, 4th ed., Washington, D.C., 1968.

Bennett, Harry, Ed., *Chemical Formulary*, Chemical Publishing Co., New York, 1933– ; Cumulative index, Vols. 1–10, 1933–1957. 1958.

Bourton, K., *Chemical and Process Engineering: Unit Operations; A Bibliographical Guide*, IFI/Plenum, New York, 1968.

Buyers' Guide of Chemicals, Chemical Plant and Laboratory Equipment, Society of Chemical Industry, London, annual.

Chem Sources, Vol. 1– , Directories Publishing Co., Flemington, N. Y., 1958, annual.

Chemical Engineering Catalog, 1916– , Reinhold, New York, 1916– ; Suppl. 1: *The Flow Sheet*, 1931– ; Suppl. 2: *Process Engineering*, 1946– .

Chemical Industry Directory and Who's Who, Benn, London, 1923– , annual.

Chemical Materials Catalog and Directory of Producers, Reinhold, New York, 1949/1950– .

Dorian, A. F., Comp., *Elsevier's Dictionary of Industrial Chemistry, in Six Languages*, American Elsevier, New York, 1964, 2 vols.

International Chemistry Directory, W. A. Benjamin, New York, 1969– .

Kent, J. A., *Riegel's Industrial Chemistry*, J. A. Kent, Ed., 6th ed., Van Nostrand Reinhold, New York, 1962.

Manufacturing Chemists' Association, *Chemical Industry Fact Book*, Washington, D.C., 1953– .

Modern Chemical Processes, edited by the editors of *Industrial and Engineering Chemistry*, Reinhold, New York, 1950– , 7 vols. in 1963.

Noyes Development Corporation, *Chemical Guide to Europe*, Pearl River, N. Y., 1963– .

Noyes Development Corporation, *Chemical Guide to the United States*, Pearl River, N. Y., 1962– .

Shreve, R.N., *Chemical Process Industries*, 3rd ed., McGraw-Hill, New York, 1969.

Ullmann, Fritz, *Ullmann's Encyklopädie der Technischen Chemie*, 3 völlig neu gestattete Aufl. hrsg. von Wilhelm Foerst, Urban und Schwarzenberg, Berlin, 1951– .

Review Serials

Advances in Chemical Engineering, Vol. 1– , Academic, New York, 1948– .

Reports on the Progress of Applied Chemistry, Vol. 1– , Society of Chemical Industry, London, 1916– , annual.

Periodicals

A.I.Ch.E. Journal, 1955– .

Academy of Sciences of the U.S.S.R., Chemical Technology Section, *Proceedings,* 1956–
(English translation of *Doklady Akademiia Nauk S.S.S.R.*).

Angewandte Chemie, 1888– (International edition in English, 1962–).

British Chemical Engineering, 1956– .

Canadian Chemical Processing, 1917– .

Canadian Journal of Chemical Engineering, 1929– .

Carbon, 1963– .

Chemical and Engineering News, 1923– .

Chemical Engineering, 1902– .

Chemical Engineering Progress, 1947– .

Chemical Engineering Science, 1951– .

Chemical Processing, 1938– .

Chemical Week, 1914– .

Chemie-Ingenieur-Technik, 1928– .

Chemische Industrie International, 1954– .

Chemistry and Industry, 1881– .

Combustion Science and Technology, 1969– (absorbed *Pyrodynamics*).

Cost Engineering, 1951– (absorbed *Chemical Engineering Costs Quarterly* in 1957).

Cryogenics, 1960– .

Industrial and Engineering Chemistry, 1909– .

Industrial and Engineering Chemistry Fundamentals, 1962– .

Industrial and Engineering Chemistry Process Design and Development, 1962– .

Industrial and Engineering Chemistry Product Research and Development, 1962– .

Journal of Applied Chemistry, 1951– .

Journal of Applied Chemistry U.S.S.R., 1950– (English translation of *Zhurnal Priklad-noi Khimii*).

Journal of Chemical and Engineering Data, 1959– .

Oil, Paint and Drug Reporter, 1871– .

Revue Internationale des Hautes Temperatures et des Refractaires, 1964– .

c. COSMETICS

Abstracts and Indexes

Applied Science and Technology Index, 1958– .

Chemical Abstracts, 1907– .

Search: Essential Oils, Soaps and Toiletries Division, Compendium Publishers International Corp., Fort Lee, N. J., 1964– .

Special Reference Works

Carriére, Gerardus, *Lexicon of Detergents, Cosmetics and Toiletries,* American Elsevier, New York, 1966.

Conference on the Evaluation of Safety of Cosmetics, Washington, D.C., 1968. *Evaluation of Safety of Cosmetics (Papers)*, Academic, New York, 1969.

DeNavarre, M. G., *Chemistry and Manufacture of Cosmetics*, Van Nostrand Reinhold, New York, 1962.

Drug and Cosmetic Catalog, Drug and Cosmetic Industry, New York, annual.

Gattefossé, R. M., *Formulary of Perfumes and Cosmetics*, Chemical Publishing Co., New York, 1959.

Harry, R. G., *Principles and Practice of Modern Cosmetics*, Chemical Publishing Co., New York, 1962, 2 vols.

Hibbott, H. W., *Handbook of Cosmetic Science*, Pergamon, New York, 1964.

Poucher, W. A., *Perfumes, Cosmetics and Soaps, with Special Reference to Synthetics*, 6th–7th ed., Chapman and Hall, London, 1959– , 3 vols.

Sagarin, Edward, Ed., *Cosmetics; Science and Technology*, Wiley, New York, 1957.

Soap, Perfumery and Cosmetics Year Book and Buyers' Guide, 1967–1968, United Trade Press, London, 1967–1968, 2 vols.

Wells, F. V. and I. I. Lubowe, *Cosmetics and the Skin*, Van Nostrand Reinhold, New York, 1964.

Periodicals

American Perfumer and Cosmetics, 1906– .

Cosmetics Fair, 1967– .

Detergents and Specialties, 1964– .

Drug and Cosmetic Industry, 1914– .

International Perfumer, 1950– .

Manufacturing Chemist and Aerosol News, 1929– .

Perfumery and Essential Oil Record, 1910– .

Seifen-Ole-Fette-Wachse met Kosmetik un Chem-Tech, Industrie, 1874– .

Soap and Chemical Specialties, 1925– .

Soap, Perfumery and Cosmetics, 1928– (incorporated *Trade Review*).

Society of Cosmetic Chemists, *Journal*, 1947– .

d. EXPLOSIVES

Abstracts and Indexes

Applied Science and Technology Index, 1958– .

Chemical Abstracts, 1907– .

Chemisches Zentralblatt, Vols. 1–140, 1830–1969.

Journal of Applied Chemistry; Abstracts, 1951– .

Special Reference Works

Cook, M. A., *Science of High Explosives*, Van Nostrand Reinhold, New York, 1958 (ACS Monograph No. 139).

E. I. duPont de Nemours & Co., Inc., *Blaster's Handbook*, 15th ed., Wilmington, Del., 1966.

Encyclopedia of Chemical Technology, Vol. 1– , 2nd ed., Interscience, New York, 1963– .

Federoff, B. T. *et al.*, *Encyclopedia of Explosives and Related Items*, Office of Technical Services, Washington, D.C., 1960 (PB 171603).

Gilman, Henry, *Organic Chemistry*, Wiley, New York, 1953, 4 vols., see Vol. 4, pp. 951–1000).

Kit, Boris and D. S. Evered, *Rocket Propellant Handbook*, Macmillan, New York, 1960.

Morgan, B. S., *Explosions and Explosives*, Macmillan, London, 1967.

Taylor, Wilfrid, *Modern Explosives*, Royal Institute of Chemistry, London, 1959.

Teller, Edward *et al.*, *Constructive Uses of Nuclear Explosives*, McGraw-Hill, New York, 1968.

Thorpe's Dictionary of Applied Chemistry, 4th ed., Longmans, New York, 1937–1956, 12 vols., see Vol. 4, pp. 453–562.

Urbanski, T., *Chemistry and Technology of Explosives*, 4th ed. (authorized translation by Irena Jeczlikowa & Sylvia Laverton), Pergamon, New York, 1964, 3 vols.

Periodicals

Explosifs, 1948– .

Explosives and Pyrotechnics, 1968– .

Explosivstoffe, 1952– .

Industrial Explosive Society, Japan, *Journal/Kogyo Kayaku*, 1938– .

Mémorial de l'Artillerie Francaise, 1862– .

Mémorial des Poudres, 1882– .

e. GLASS

Bibliographies, Abstracts, Indexes

Duncan, G. S., Comp., *Bibliography of Glass (from the Earliest Records to 1940)*, Violet Dimbleby, Ed., Dawsons of Pall Mall, for the Society of Glass Technology, Sheffield, London, 1960.

Applied Science and Technology Index, 1958– .

Chemical Abstracts, 1907– .

Glass Technology, 1960– , abstracts; Section A of the *Journal of the Society of Glass Technology*.

Physics and Chemistry of Glasses, 1960, abstracts; Section B of the *Journal of the Society of Glass Technology*.

Special Reference Works

Advances in Glass Technology; Technical Papers of the VI International Congress on Glass, Plenum, Washington, D.C., 1962–1963, 2 vols.

Brandt, J., *et al.*, *Emails, Enamels, Emaux, Smalti . . .*, a *Dictionary in Four Languages*, Farbenfabriken Bayer Atkiengesellschaft, Leverkusen, 1960.

British Standards Institution, *Glossary of Terms Used in the Glass Industry*, London, 1962.

British Standards Institution, *Classification of Glass for Glazing and Terminology for Work on Glass*, London, 1964.

Davis, Pearce, *Development of the American Glass Industry*, Harvard University, Cambridge, Mass., 1949; reprinted 1969 by Russell and Russell, New York.

Eitel, Wilhelm, *Physical Chemistry of the Silicates,* University of Chicago Press, Chicago, 1954.

Elmer, T. H., *German-English Dictionary of Glass, Ceramics and Allied Sciences,* Interscience-Wiley, New York, 1963.

Glass and Glass Manufacture, Encyclopaedia Britannica, Chicago, 1970, 23 vols and Index, see Vol. 10, pp. 456–476.

Hoffman, E., *Fachworterbuch für du Glasindustrie, (Dictionary for the Glass Industry . . . deutsch–englisch, englisch–deutsch)* Springer-Verlag, Berlin, 1963.

International Commission on Glass, Sub-Committee A-1, *Dictionary of Glass Making,* Charleroi, Belgium, 1965.

MacKenzie, J. D., *Modern Aspects of the Vitreous State,* Plenum, New York, 1964, 3 vols.

Phillips, C. J., *Glass; the Miracle Maker; Its History, Technology and Applications,* 2nd ed., Pitman, London, 1948.

Phillips, C. J., *Glass: Its Industrial Applications,* Reinhold, New York, 1960.

Shand, E. B., *Glass Engineering Handbook,* 2nd ed., McGraw-Hill, New York, 1958.

Stevels, J. M., "The Electrical Properties of Glass," in *Handbuch der Physik,* Vol. 20: *Electrical Conductivity II,* Springer, Berlin, 1957.

Weyl, W. A. and E. C. Marboe, *The Constitution of Glasses,* Wiley, New York, 1962–1967, 2 vols.

Wheeler, E. L., *Scientific Glassblowing,* Wiley, New York, 1958.

Periodicals

American Glass Review, 1882– .

Glass, 1923– .

Glass and Ceramics, Vol. 13 in 1956– .

Glass Digest, 1922– .

Glass Industry, 1920– .

Glastechnische Berichte, 1922–1943, 1948– .

Jenaer Rundschau/Jena Review, 1956– .

Silikat Technik, 1950– .

Silikaty, 1957– .

Society of Glass Technology, *Journal,* 1917–1959.

Sprechsaal für Keramik, Glas, Email, Silikate, 1868– .

Verres et Refractaires, 1946– .

f. NUTRITION AND FOOD TECHNOLOGY

Bibliographies

Baker, E. A. and D. J. Foskett, *Bibliography of Food: A Select International Bibliography of Nutrition, Food and Beverage Technology and Distribution, 1936–1956,* Academic, New York, 1958.

Commonwealth Agricultural Bureaux, *Evaluation of the World Food Literature; Results of an International Survey,* Farnham Royal, Eng., 1967.

Abstracts and Indexes

Applied Science and Technology Index, 1958– .

Biological Abstracts, 1927– .

Biological and Agricultural Abstracts, 1919– .

Bulletin Signalétique, Centre National de la Recherche Scientifique, Paris, 1956– ; Part 18: *Science Agricoles* . . . .

Chemical Abstracts, 1907– .

Dairy Science Abstracts, Vol. 1– , Commonwealth Agricultural Bureaux, Farnham Royal, Eng., 1939– .

Food Processing Abstracts, 1963– , Lowry-Cocroft Abstracts, Evanston, Ill., 1963– .

Food Science Abstracts, 1967– , New Brunswick Research and Productivity Council, Fredericton, N. B., Canada, 1967– .

Food Science and Technology Abstracts, 1969– , Commonwealth Agricultural Bureaux, Farnham Royal, Eng., 1969– .

Journal of the Science of Food and Agriculture, 1950– ; abstract section covers chemistry of agriculture, food, and sanitation.

Nutrition Abstracts and Reviews, Vol. 1– , Commonwealth Bureau of Animal Nutrition, Aberdeen, 1931– .

Search: Foodstuffs Division, Compendium Publishers International Corp., Fort Lee, N. J., 1964.

Vitamin Abstracts, 1946– , Association of Vitamin Chemists, Chicago, 1946– .

Special Reference Works

Alexander, Peter and R. J. Block, Eds., *Laboratory Manual of Analytical Methods of Protein Chemistry,* Pergamon, New York, 1960–1965, 4 vols.

Almanac of the Canning, Freezing, Preserving Industry, Vol. 1– , E. E. Judge, Westminster, Md., 1916– , annual.

Association of Official Analytical Chemists, *Official Methods of Analysis,* 1st ed.– , Washington, D.C., 1919– .

Bender, A. E., *Dictionary of Nutrition and Food Technology,* 3rd ed., Butterworths, London, 1968.

Bender, A. E., *Dietetic Foods,* Chemical Publishing Co., New York, 1968.

Borgstrom, Georg, *Principles of Food Science,* Macmillan, New York, 1968, 2 vols.

Comar, C. L. and Felix Bronner, Eds., *Mineral Metabolism; An Advanced Treatise,* Academic, New York, 1960–1963, 2 vols. in 4 pts.

Cox, H. E. and D. Pearson, *Chemical Analysis of Foods,* Chemical Publishing Co., New York, 1962.

Desrosier, N. W., *Radiation Technology in Food, Agriculture and Biology,* Avi Publishing Co., Westport, Conn., 1960.

Desrosier, N. W., *Technology of Food Preservation,* 2nd ed., Avi Publishing Co., Westport, Conn., 1966.

Deuel, H. J., Jr., *The Lipids; Their Chemistry and Biochemistry,* Wiley, New York, 1951–1957, 3 vols.

Field, H. E., *Foods in Health and Disease: A Practical Guide,* Macmillan, New York, 1964.

Food Chemical News, guide to the current status of food additives and color additives, L. Rothchild, Washington, D.C., 1967.

Goldblith, S. A., *Exploration in Future Food-Processing Techniques,* M.I.T. Press, Cambridge, Mass., 1963.

Goldblith, S. A. *et al.,* Introduction to Thermal Processing of Foods, Avi Publishing Co., Westport, Conn., 1961.

Goldblith, S. A. and M. A. Joslyn, *Milestones in Nutrition,* Avi Publishing Co., Westport, Conn., 1964.

Goodhart, R. S. and M. G. Wohl, *Manual of Clinical Nutrition,* Lea & Febiger, Philadelphia, 1964.

Greenberg, D. M., Ed., *Metabolic Pathways,* 3rd ed., Academic, New York, 1967–1969.

Greenstein, J. P. and Milton Winitz, *Chemistry of the Amino Acids,* Wiley, New York, 1961, 3 vols.

Gunderson, F. L. *et al., Food Standards and Definitions in the United States; A Guidebook,* Academic, New York, 1963.

Handbook of Food Additives, Chemical Rubber Co., Cleveland, 1968.

IFI-Plenum Data Corporation, *Directory,* 1965–1968, New York, 1968, loose-leaf; annual revision service.

IFI-Plenum Data Corporation, *Food and Color Additives,* index, New York, 1968.

Laboratory Handbook of Methods of Food Analysis, Chemical Rubber Co., Cleveland, 1968.

Lamb, C. A., *et al,* Eds., *Trace Elements,* Academic, New York, 1958.

Long, Cyril, *Biochemists' Handbook,* Van Nostrand Reinhold, New York, 1961.

Matz, S. A., *Bakery Technology and Engineering,* Avi Publishing Co., Westport, Conn., 1960.

Matz, S. A., *Cereal Science,* Avi Publishing Co., Westport, Conn., 1969.

National Academy of Sciences-National Research Council, *Recommended Dietary Allowances,* 6th ed., Washington, D.C., 1964.

Sebrell, W. H. and R. S. Harris, Eds., *The Vitamins: Chemistry, Physiology, Pathology, Methods,* Vols. 1–2, 6–7, Wiley, New York, 1967–1968, Vols. 3–5 in preparation.

Unilever, Ltd., *Chemistry and Technology of Edible Oils and Fats . . . ,* Pergamon, New York, 1961.

U. S. Department of Agriculture, *Composition of Foods: Raw, Processed, Prepared,* Washington, D.C., 1963 *(Agricultural Handbook,* No. 8).

U. S. Panel on the World Food Supply, *The World Food Problem; A Report,* Government Printing Office, Washington, D.C., 1967, 6 vols.

Wohl, M. G. and R. S. Goodhart, *Modern Nutrition in Health and Disease; Dietotherapy,* 3rd ed., Lea & Febiger, Philadelphia, 1964.

Review Serials

Advances in Carbohydrate Chemistry, Vol. 1– , Academic, New York, 1945– .

Advances in Food Research, Vol. 1– , Academic, New York, 1948– .

Advances in Protein Chemistry, Vol. 1– , Academic, New York, 1944– .

Recent Advances in Food Science, Vol. 1– , Butterworths, London, 1962– .

Vitamins and Hormones, Vol. 1– , Academic, New York, 1943– .

World Review of Nutrition and Dietetics, Vol. 1– , Hafner, New York, 1959– .

Periodicals

American Dietetic Association, *Journal,* 1925– .

American Journal of Clinical Nutrition, 1952– .

American Oil Chemists' Society, *Journal,* 1917– .

Applied Microbiology, 1953– .

Archives of Biochemistry and Biophysics, 1942– .

Association of Food and Drug Officials of the United States, *Quarterly Bulletin,* 1937– .

Association of Official Analytical Chemists, *Journal,* 1915– (formerly Association of Official Agricultural Chemists, *Journal*).

Bakers' Digest, 1926– .

Baking Industry, 1887– .

Biochemical Journal, 1906– .

Canner/Packer, 1895– .

Cereal Chemistry, 1924– .

Food Engineering, 1928– .

Food in Canada, 1941– (incorporates *Canadian Baker*).

Food Manufacture, 1927– .

Food Processing and Marketing, 1931– .

Food Technology, 1947– .

Journal of Applied Nutrition, Vol. 21, 1969– .

Journal of Biological Chemistry, 1905– .

Journal of Food Science, 1936– .

Journal of Home Economics, 1909– .

Journal of Lipid Research, 1959– .

Journal of Milk and Food Technology, 1937– .

Journal of Nutrition, 1928– .

Manufacturing Confectioner, 1921– .

National Provisioner, 1891– .

Nutrition Reviews, 1942– .

Nutrition Society, *Proceedings,* 1944– .

Poultry Science, 1921– .

Quick Frozen Foods, 1938– .

Wallerstein Laboratories Communications, 1937– (contains abstracts).

Zeitschrift für Lebensmittel-Untersuchung und -Forschung, 1890– .

g. OILS, FATS, SOAPS, AND WAXES

Bibliographies and Abstracts

"Annual Review of the Literature on Fats, Oils, and Detergents," in *Journal of the American Oil Chemists' Society,* annual.

Applied Science and Technology Index, 1958– .

Chemical Abstracts, 1907– .

Commonwealth Economic Committee, *Vegetable Oils and Oilseeds, a Review of Production, Trade, Utilization and Prices Relating to Groundnuts, Cottonseed, Linseed, Soya Beans, Coconut and Oil Palm Products, Olive Oil and Other Oil Seeds and Oils,* H. M. Stationery Office, London, 1932– , annual.

Glycerine News, 1957– , United Kingdom Producers Association, London, 1957– .

Search: Essential Oils, Soaps and Toiletries Division, Compendium Publishers International Corp., Fort Lee, N. J., 1964– .

Search: Oils, Fats and Waxes Division, Compendium Publishers International Corp., Fort Lee, N. J., 1964– .

Special Reference Works

American Oil Chemists' Society, *Official and Tentative Methods of the American Oil Chemists' Society,* annual additions and revisions, Chicago.

American Society for Testing Materials, *ASTM Standards on Soaps and Other Detergents,* Philadelphia, revised annually.

Bennett, Harry *et al.,* Eds., *Practical Emulsions,* Chemical Publishing Co., New York, 1967–1968, 2 vols., Vol. 2 in 2nd ed.

Cotton Gin and Oil Mill Press, *International Green Book of Cottonseed and Other Vegetable Products,* Dallas, Tex., annual.

Eckey, E. W., *Vegetable Fats and Oils* . . . , with a chapter by L. P. Miller, Reinhold, New York, 1954 (ACS Monograph Series, No. 123).

Guenther, Ernest and Darrell Althausen, *The Essential Oils,* Van Nostrand Reinhold, New York, 1948–1952, 6 vols.

Gunstone, F. D., *Introduction to the Chemistry and Biochemistry of Fatty Acids and Their Glycerides,* 2nd ed., Barnes and Noble, New York, 1968.

Schwartz, A. M. and J. W. Perry, *Surface Active Agents and Detergents,* Wiley, New York, 1958, 2 vols.

Soap and Chemical Specialties, *Blue Book and Catalog, Annual Buyers' Guide for Manufacturers, Converters, and Repackers of Soaps, Detergents, and Chemical Specialties,* MacNair-Dorland, New York, annual.

Review Serial

Progress in the Chemistry of Fats and Other Lipids, Vol. 1– , Pergamon, New York, 1952– .

Periodicals

American Oil Chemists' Society, *Journal,* 1917– .

American Perfumer and Cosmetics, 1906– .

Cotton Gin and Oil Mill Press, 1889– .

Detergent Digest, 1967– .

Fats and Oils in Canada, 1965– .

Fats and Oils Situation, 1937– .

Fette-Seifen-Anstrichmittel, 1894– (combined with *Ernaehrungindustrie*).

Lipids, 1966– .

National Provisioner, 1891– .

Oil Mill Gazetteer, 1895– .

Oil, Paint and Drug Reporter, 1871– .

Oils and Oilseeds Journal, 1949– .

Oleagineux, 1946– .

Perfumery and Essential Oil Record, 1910– .

Seifen-Ole-Pette-Wachse mit Kosmetik und Chem.-Tech. Industrie, 1874– .

Soap and Chemical Specialties, 1925– .

Soap, Perfumery and Cosmetics, 1928–   (incorporated *Trade Review*).

h. PAPER TECHNOLOGY

Bibliographies

Hunter, Dard, *Handmade Paper and Its Water Marks; A Bibliography,* Burt Franklin, New York, 1968 (Bibliography and Reference Series, No. 218).

Hunter, Dard, *Literature of Papermaking: Thirteen Ninety to Eighteen Hundred,* Burt Franklin, New York, 1969 (Bibliography and Reference Series, No. 203).

Technical Association of the Pulp and Paper Industry, *Basic Bibliography of Papermaking and U. S. Patents,* 1900– , New York, 1900– .

Abstracts

Chemical Abstracts, 1907– .

Institute of Paper Chemistry, *Abstract Bulletin,* Vol. 1– , Appleton, Wisc., 1930– .

Institute of Paper Chemistry, *Bibliographic Series,* No. 1– , Appleton, Wisc., 1936.

Paper and Board, 1965– , Pira, Kenley, Surrey, Eng., 1965–   (formerly *Kenley Abstracts*).

Paper and Board Abstracts, 1968– , Pira, Leatherhead, Surrey, Eng., 1968– .

Search: Pulp and Paper Division, Compendium Publishers International Corp., Fort Lee, N. J., 1964– .

Special Reference Works

American Pulp and Paper Association, *Dictionary of Paper; Including Pulp, Paper Board, Paper Properties and Related Papermaking Terms,* 3rd ed., New York, 1965.

Casey, J. P., *Pulp and Paper,* Wiley, New York, 1960, 3 vols. (Vol. 1 in 2nd ed.).

General Dyestuff Corporation, *Dyestuffs for Paper; Better Coloring,* n.d, New York (GDC-329).

Hunter, Dard, *Papermaking; The History and Technique of an Ancient Craft,* 2nd ed., revised and enlarged, Knopf, New York, 1947.

Lockwood's Directory of the Paper and Allied Trades, Lockwood Publishing Co., New York, annual.

Paper Makers' and Merchants Directory of All Nations, 77th ed., Admark Directories, Ltd., London, 1970.

Phillips' Paper Trade Directory of the World, S. C. Phillips & Co., Ltd., London, annual.

Posts . . . Pulp and Paper Directory, Miller Freeman Publications. Research and Directory Dept, San Francisco, Calif., annual.

Pulp and Paper Directory of Canada, National Business Publications Ltd., Gardenvale, Que., Canada, annual, published 1907–1965 as the *National Directory of the Canadian Pulp and Paper Directory*.

Pulp and Paper Manual of Canada, National Business Publications Ltd., Gardenvale, Que., Canada, annual.

Stephenson, J. N., Ed., *Pulp and Paper Manufacture*, McGraw-Hill, New York, 1950–1955, 4 vols.

Technical Association of the Pulp and Paper Industry, *TAPPI Standards and Suggested Methods: Tentative and Official . . .* , New York, 1954– , loose-leaf.

Technical Association of the Pulp and Paper Industry, *Technical Information Sheets*, New York, 1968, loose-leaf.

Walden's ABC Guide and Paper Production Yearbook: The Complete Paper Directory, Walden-Mott Corp., New York, annual.

Periodicals

Allgemeine Papier-Rundschau, 1949– .

American Paper Industry, 1919– .

Bumazhnaya Promyshlennost, 1922– .

Canadian Pulp and Paper Industry, 1948– .

Chemical Twenty-Six, 1965– .

Finnish Paper and Timber, 1950– .

Forest Products Journal, 1947– .

Holzforschung, 1947– .

Indian Pulp and Paper, 1946– .

Norskskogindustrie, 1913– .

Paper Age, 1884– .

Paper-Maker, 1891– (formerly *Paper-Maker and British Paper Trade Journal*).

Paper Technology, 1960– .

Paper Trade Journal, 1872– .

Paperi Ja Puu/Papper Och Tra/ Paper and Timber, 1921– .

Papeterie, 1878– .

Papier, 1947– .

Pulp and Paper, 1927– (combined with *Paper Mill News*).

Pulp and Paper International, 1959– .

Southern Pulp and Paper Manufacturer, 1938– .

Svensk Papperstidning, 1898– .

Tappi, 1949– .

Trend, 1963– .

Wochenblatt für Papierfabrikation, 1870– .

World's Paper Trade Review, 1879–   .
Zellstoff und Papier, 1952–   .

i. TEXTILES

Bibliographies

Aslib Textile Group, *Union List of Holdings of Textile Periodicals,* 3rd ed., London, 1962.

Cotton Board Library, *Catalogue of Periodicals,* 1962, Manchester, Eng., 1962.

Freedland, V. D., *Textile Information: How and Where to Find It,* (in *Aslib. Proceedings,* Vol. 8, No. 3, 1956, pp. 177–194).

The Shirley Institute, *Summary of Current Literature,* Cotton, Silk and Manmade Fibres Research Association, Manchester, Eng., 1964.

Abstracts

Chemical Abstracts, 1907–   .

Natural and Synthetic Fibers Abstract Service, Interscience-Wiley, New York, 1944–1959, bound annual volume: *Natural and Synthetic Fibers Yearbook.*

Search: Dyes, Pigments and Coating Division, Compendium Publishers International Corp., Fort Lee, N. J., 1964–   .

Search: Textiles Division, Compendium Publishers International Corp., Fort Lee, N. J., 1964–   .

Textile Institute Journal Abstracts, Manchester, Eng., 1910–January 1964, Abstracts consist of 4 parts:
   (a) Shirley Institute, *Summary of Current Literature;* (b) *Wool Abstracts;* (c) *Abstracts of Hosiery;* (d) *Abstracts of Jute.*

Textile Technology Digest, 1944–   , Institute of Textile Technology, Charlottsville, Va., 1944–   .

Wool Abstracts, Wool Industries Research Association, Torridon, Leeds, Eng., 1964–   .

World Textile Abstracts, Vol. 1–   , Shirley Institute, Didsbury, Eng., 1969–   .

Special Reference Works

Cook, J. C., *Handbook of Textile Fibres,* 3rd ed., Merrow Publishing Co., Watford, 1964.

DeVries, Louis, *Worterbuch der Textilindustrie,* Brandstetter GmbH, Wiesbaden, 1959.

Encyclopedia of Textiles, 2nd ed., Prentice-Hall, New York, 1966.

Fabierkiewicz, Waclaw, *Handy Textile Dictionary in Five Languages,* English title, Interscience, New York, 1960.

Fairchild's Dictionary of Textiles, 2nd ed., Fairchild Publishers, New York, 1967.

Hamby, D. S., Ed., *American Cotton Handbook,* 3rd ed., Interscience, New York, 1965, 2 vols.

International Cotton Advisory Committee, *Cotton—World Statistics,* Vol. 1–   , No. 1–   , Washington, D.C., 1947–   .

International Cotton Advisory Committee, *Multilingual Glossary of Cotton Terms . . . ,* Washington, D.C., 1964.

Kaswell, E. R., *Handbook of Industrial Textiles*, Wellington Sears, Ed., Textile Book Service, Metuechen, N. J., 1969.

Klapper, Marvin, *Fabric Almanac*, Fairchild Publishers, New York, 1966– .

Kopycinski, J. V., Ed., *Textile Industry Information Sources*, Gale, Detroit, 1964.

Linton, G. E., *Modern Textile Dictionary*, Duell, New York, 1963.

Linton, G. E., *Natural and Manmade Textile Fibers; Raw Material to Finished Product*, Duell, New York, 1966.

Mark, H. F., *et al.*, *Chemistry and Technology of Man-Made Fibres*, Interscience, New York, 1967–1968, 3 vols.

Mark, H. F., *et al.*, *Encyclopedia of Polymer Science and Technology*, Interscience-Wiley, New York, 1964–1969, 9 vols.

Moncrieff, R. W., *Man-Made Fibers*, 4th ed., Wiley, New York, 1963.

Polanyi, Michael, *Technical Trade Dictionary of Textile Terms: German–American/American/English–German*, 2nd ed., Pergamon, New York, 1967.

Press, J. J., Ed., *Man-Made Textile Encyclopedia*, Wiley, New York, 1959.

Skinner's Cotton and Man-Made Fibres Directory of the World, Skinner, London, 1923– , annual.

Skinner's Wool Trade Directory of the World, Skinner, London, 1926– , annual.

Textile Institute and Society of Dyers and Colourists, *Textile Terms and Definitions*, 5th ed., Manchester, Eng., 1963.

Textile Institute and Society of Dyers and Colourists, *Yearbook*, Manchester, Eng., 1948/1949– .

Von Bergen, Werner, *Wool Handbook*, 3rd enlarged ed., Wiley, New York, 1963, 3 vols.

Review Serials

Advances in Textile Processing, Vol. 1– , Interscience, New York, 1961– .

Textile Institute and Society of Dyers and Colourists, *Review of Textile Progress*, Plenum, New York, 1949– , 17 vols. in 1968.

Periodicals

American Dyestuff Reporter, 1917– .

American Fabrics, 1946– .

America's Textile Reporter, 1887– .

Canadian Textile Journal, 1883– .

Ciba Review, 1937– .

Cordage, Canvas and Jute World, 1919– .

Deutsche Textiltechnik, 1951– .

Fibre and Fabric, 1885– .

Fibre Science and Technology, 1968– .

Institut Textile de France, *Bulletin*, 1947– .

International Dyer, Textile Printer, Bleacher and Finisher, 1879– .

JTI/Journal of the Textile Institute, 1910– .

Modern Textile Magazine, 1925– .

Revue Textile, 1901– .

Textil-Praxis, 1946– .

Textile Bulletin, 1911– .

Textile Chemist and Colorist, 1969– .

Textile Industries, 1899– .

Textile Month, 1968–   (incorporates *Skinner's Record of Manmade Fibres Industry* and *Manmade Textiles and Textile Recorder*).

Textile Research Journal, 1930– .

Textile World, 1868– .

Author Index

Subject Index